PENNY WHIMSY

PENNY WHIMSY

A Revision of

EARLY AMERICAN CENTS

1793-1814

An Exercise in Descriptive Classification with
TABLES OF RARITY AND VALUE

by

WILLIAM H. SHELDON, M.D.

With the collaboration of
DOROTHY I. PASCHAL
and
WALTER BREEN

DURST PUBLICATIONS LTD.
New York, N.Y.

Copyright
©
1958
William H. Sheldon

Reprinted with the kind permission
of the
Early American Coppers Club, Inc.

New Material
©
1990
Durst Publications Ltd.
29-28 41st Avenue
Long Island City, NY 11101

Phone 718-706-0303
FAX: 718-706-0891

ISBN No. 0-942666-62-3
Library of Congress No. 90-091500

This is a reprint of the last (1965) printing of *Penny Whimsy*. The text is exactly as printed in 1958 except for corrections of proofreaders' errors. During the intervening years of continuing inflation there has been a particularly dramatic advance in the auction prices of early copper cents, which remains the most beloved of American coins. For current evaluation of particular coins, it is suggested that you seek the guidance of a professional numismatist or dealer well versed in Large Cents and read various numismatic journals.

Special thanks is extended to Dennis Loring for preparation of the new Introduction and Appendices in this volume.

The numbering system employed in this book, together with the rarity scale and listing of basal values, may be reprinted by a periodical or by a coin dealer in an advertisement, circular, price list or auction catalog, issued for free distribution, if acknowledgment is made to Dr. Sheldon as compiler of the numbering system, rarity scale and basal value listing. Should the use of the numbering system, rarity scale and basal value listing, however, be incorporated in a pamphlet, catalog or book offered for sale, written permission in advance of publication must be obtained from the author, or his successors in interest.

The material in this book may not be reproduced in any form or manner or stored in any computer or information retrievel system.

Contents

List of Tables	vii
Glossary of Abbreviations	viii
Preface	ix
Preface to the Revised Edition	xi
Introduction to the 1990 Edition	xiii

PART ONE. *The Story of Cents*

Introducing the Big Cents
The Charm of the Old Copper Cents	3
Kitchen Table Science on Friday Nights	4

Birth and Childhood of the Big Cents
The Mint: First Beginnings	8
Hardships and Difficulties	10
Under the Thumb of an Unfriendly Congress	12
Beginnings of Inflation	15
Prosperity Comes to the Mint	16

Review of the Principal Cent Literature
Six Major Contributions	17
The Story of the 1794's	17
Crosby and the 1793's	19
Two Comprehensive Monographs on Cents: Frossard and Proskey-Doughty	20
The Later-Date Cents: Andrews and Newcomb	21
Gilbert-Elder on the 1796's	22
The Newcomb Monograph on 1801-1802-1803	23
The Clapp Monographs on 1798-99 and 1804-1814	24
Clapp-Newcomb on 1795-1796-1797 and 1800	24

Bibliography   26

Toward a Science of Cent Values
The Job that Remains	28
The First Step: Quantitative Grading of Condition	29

[v]

CONTENTS

A Testing Ground for the Condition-Value Relationship—The 1794's	31
The Basal Value: A First Point on a Scale for Condition and Value	33
Definitions of Other Points on the Scale	34
Poor and Proof	38
From Definitions to a Point Scale Applicable to Both Value and Condition	39
A Scale for Rarity	42
Value as Related to Care and Treatment	44
Collectibles and Noncollectibles	49
The Condition Census	51
Estimation of Value	52

PART TWO. *The Early Cents. 1793-1814*

1793	61	*1804*	312
1794	83	*1805*	314
1795	143	*1806*	316
1796	152	*1807*	317
1797	184	*1808*	321
1798	207	*1809*	324
1799	244	*1810*	325
1800	248	*1811*	328
1801	270	*1812*	329
1802	281	*1813*	331
1803	296	*1814*	333

Epilogue	
On Collecting Early Cents	335
Old Cent Whist	336
Appendix—Die Break Discoveries	339
Plates *Following page*	340

List of Tables

Table 1	A Quantitative Scale for Condition	41
Table 2	The Scale for Rarity	44
Table 3	Rarity and Value: 1793 Cents	82
Table 4	Comparative Populations of the Different Rarity Groups Among One Thousand 1794 Cents	135
Table 5	Key to the 1794 Cents	136
Table 6	Rarity and Value: 1794 Cents	140
Table 7	Finding List for the Hays Numbers	142
Table 8	Rarity and Value: 1795 Cents	151
Table 9	Key to the 1796 Cents	180
Table 10	Rarity and Value: 1796 Cents	181
Table 11	Gilbert-Elder Numbers, Duplicates or Unknown	183
Table 12	Key to the 1797 Cents	204
Table 13	Rarity and Value: 1797 Cents	206
Table 14	Key to the 1798 Cents	240
Table 15	Rarity and Value: 1798 Cents	242
Table 16	Key to the 1800 Cents	267
Table 17	Rarity and Value: 1800 Cents	269
Table 18	Key to the 1801 Cents	279
Table 19	Rarity and Value: 1801 Cents	280
Table 20	Key to the 1802 Cents	294
Table 21	Rarity and Value: 1802 Cents	295
Table 22	Key to the 1803 Cents	310
Table 23	Rarity and Value: 1803 Cents	311

Glossary of Abbreviations

ANA. American Numismatic Association
ANS. American Numismatic Society
Basal. Basal Value, or value in Condition 1
Condition, Abbreviations for: G Good
    VG Very Good
    F Fine
    VF Very Fine
    EF Extremely Fine
    AU About Uncirculated
    MS Mint State
    Poor, Fair and Very Fair not abbreviated

EAC. Early American Cents
HWH. Highest wave of hair
JHF. Junction of the hair with the forehead
NC. Noncollectible. Less than 3 specimens known to be in collectors' hands
NC. When italicized, read Now-Collectible
PC. The point of the curl at the top of the head
PFL. Point of the fifth leaf
PHL. Point of the highest leaf
PLF. Point of the leaf under F
PLLL. Point of lowest leaf on the left
PLLR. Point of the lowest leaf on the right
PLO. Point of the outer leaf in the cluster under O in OF
PSL. Point of the seventh leaf
R. Rarity. For Scale of Rarity, see p. 44
VD. Variation of the die. Used on the plates usually to indicate die break variations

Preface

GENERATIONS OF AMERICANS HAVE MAINTAINED A CURIOUS affection for the "old pennies" of the early years of the country. This affection for the early coppers has not as a rule been particularly associated with any general interest in numismatics, or with hobbies, or with the disease of collecting things.

It seems to be, rather, that the old pennies are intimately associated with family traditions and with the memories of grandparents and the like. Throughout the nineteenth century an American home without a box or bag of the old coppers, secreted somewhere about the house, was something of a rarity. More recently, there have been many famous collections of these pieces and much interest in the relative rarities of the different varieties. Separate monographs have been written on most of the dates before 1800. The fascination of the pennies, far from dying out, seems to be increasing.

Traditionally the cents from 1793 to 1814 are called the *early* cents. Some 327 different varieties of them are now known. The present book for the first time describes and illustrates them all, in a single volume, and also offers information on the rarity and on the established value of each variety.

It may seem a risky thing to quote values at a time when money itself is of uncertain and unstable value. As we come up to the midpoint of the century our culture appears to be far along in the economic decadence of an inflationary spiral. So I should make it clear that my object in recording values is neither to predict nor to try to influence future prices, but simply to round out the story and to record history. Values are assigned in accordance with what the cents have brought, as an average, during the second quarter of the century. These values may serve as an interesting baseline for comparison a century hence.

I have written this book because ever since childhood I have wanted to read it and it wasn't there. It was virtually necessary to write it in order to get at the truth concerning the cents—

PREFACE

their identification, their rarity, their price history. It was not that dealers and "experts" in this fascinating field of early Americana were more dishonest than in other such fields—they *couldn't* be—but rather that the temptation was greater, for the dependence of the layman on their tender solicitude was almost absolute. Although there were books, there was no *book*.

There is some degree of indebtedness to virtually every advanced student or collector of the early cents who has been active during the past four decades, and to most of the dealers. To name many without naming all would be unfair. The heaviest indebtedness is to the Chapman brothers of Philadelphia, to Carl Würtzbach and J. G. Macallister, and to George H. Clapp. No one could do research on early cents, in this generation, without realizing his debt to Henry C. Hines and Howard R. Newcomb. Clapp, Newcomb and Hines are rightly known as the Big Three of the Big Cents, for the first half of the twentieth century. Just before them it was the Chapmans, David Proskey, Dr. George P. French, Ebenezer Gilbert and many more. These are the men who wrote the present book. I have been the recording secretary.

Of my collaborators, Mr. Downing has helped in the preparation and ordering of the plates and also in the final checking, revising, and proofreading of the manuscript. M. H. Sheldon participated in much of the original research on which the book is based. Mr. William L. Clark of the American Numismatic Society took many of the photographs from which the plates are made. The Society and Mr. Clapp are to be thanked for permitting the use of photographs of many of the cents in the Society's collection—formerly Mr. Clapp's collection. Mr. Ernest Henderson, Mr. Robert Moore and Mr. Harold Whiteneck, all of Boston, helped with business arrangements which facilitated the actual writing of the book. Two present-day collectors, Mr. T. James Clarke and Mr. Thomas L. Gaskill, have been generous allies in the undertaking. Horatio and Hazard Sheldon assisted with spirit.

W. H. S.

New York
April 1948

Preface to the 1958 Edition

THE BOOK *Early American Cents* WAS WRITTEN, A DECADE OR SO ago, in a spirit of pleasant nostalgia not only for the old pennies themselves but also for the associations and the way of life for which they are reminiscent. Meanwhile the writer, together with his present collaborators and some other good friends, has kept up a set of systematic notes with an eye to revising the basic data of the original book. The task has been a lighthearted one —almost a whimsy—and in certain quarters the project has come to be known as "the penny whimsy."

At first the intention was simply to publish a supplemental new list of rarities and basal values, with new condition censuses and a few notes on such discoveries as have turned up. Two considerations, however, induced a decision to revise and republish the book as a whole. First, the supply of the original edition having become exhausted, there has been a strong demand for a reprinting. But it would scarcely make sense to reprint the old book without bringing it up to date. We have therefore revised it, adding all of the available new data and retaining as much of the old book as has not been superseded by new information.

The second consideration was the fact that the old pennies have fulfilled the most sanguine expectations with respect to both abundance and elusiveness—that quality of elusive mystery that adheres to them like a fragrance. So there is a great deal of new information to report, although only four new varieties and one sub-variety have been unearthed during this intervening decade.

The present revision undertakes to provide as complete a report as is now possible on each variety of early cent, and on the half dozen finest coins extant for each variety. We have revised the condition census for a variety whenever a previously unknown coin proved fine enough to win a place among the recognized top six. There are about nineteen hundred of the condition census coins. On these a notebook has been kept for some one hundred and twenty months, starting from the first condition census estimates made by WHS in 1947 for the earlier book. Necessary changes have averaged something like five per month as late as 1956 and it is apparent that the assignment, far from being finished, is perhaps hardly more than well begun. Many of the "best ones" are undoubtedly still at large. During the ten-year period we have probably made as many as six hundred changes in the condition census lists, and this is to say that about a third of the best cents were either unknown to us or incorrectly known when the book was written. Old cents are elusive. They have a way of hiding out, sometimes for half a century or more. Yet in the end they usually outlive their ever-so-secretive hosts, and then they return, perhaps as sleepers in some sale.

It is evident that the present revision by no means exhausts the subject of the early cents or closes the condition census lists. Possibly someone among us will find time to write another revision in another decade. But to present all the rarities and the condition censuses with full confidence (not to mention the assignment of basal values in a shifting economy) will require a very long lifetime. Some of the new finds that have recently come to light had been in hiding for more than fifty years. What proportion of them all have we now seen, and what number are still in hiding? We cannot know, and it is fortunate, for that is what whets the whimsy.

In preparing this revision we have become more or less indebted to almost every active cent watcher in the country, and to many of the dealers. It would be unfair to list our friends without mentioning all. However, Kenneth Bressett's skillful photography has improved the appearance of many of the varieties on the plates, Douglas Smith has been virtually another collaborator and T. J. Clarke, before his lamented death, was both able friend and generous benefactor. There is an even greater debt to Eugene Exman, of Harper & Brothers, for without his generous co-operation *Early American Cents* would never have been a beautiful book, and *Penny Whimsy* would not have been published at all.

New York, April, 1957   W. H. S.

INTRODUCTION

Dr. Sheldon's seminal work on the early coppers, *Early American Cents*, was published by Harper in 1949. The book was revised and updated as *Penny Whimsy* in 1958, reissued with trivial corrections in 1965, and reprinted by Quarterman in 1976.

It's now 1990. The book in your hands is a verbatim reprinting of the 1965 edition of *Penny Whimsy*, plus this introduction and two Appendices. Except for these, it would look comfortably familiar to the collector of 1965. The actual cent hobby, though, would be unrecognizable. For example:

NEW VARIETIES. No fewer than *twelve* new varieties have been discovered since 1965. Brief descriptions of these varieties are given in the Appendix. In addition, two new subvarieties (1795 NC-1a and 1797 S-121a) are now recognized, and numerous new die states have appeared.

RARITY. Many rarity ratings have dropped, some precipitously. In 1958, Sheldon rated 30 of the numbered varieties as R-7; most of these were still R-7 in 1965. Today, *none* of these varieties are still R-7, and at least five are now R-5!

CONDITION CENSUS. Well over a thousand new CC-level cents have come to light in the past 25 years. For more than a few varieties, the finest known specimen list in *PW* wouldn't even make the top six today.

PRICES. The cent collector of 1965, transported to 1990, wouldn't be able to decide if he were in fantasyland or a nightmare. Dream on...

Century sale, Paramount 4/65	Matthews sale, Superior 5/89
1798 S-178 AG-3, $85	another AG-3, $797.50
1803 S-264 G-5, $180	another G-5, $6710
1807 S-272 AG-3, $67.50	*the same* AG-3, $1155

THE PASSING OF THE TORCH. Sheldon, Paschal, Blaisdell, Exman, Kissner, Starr. Their cents have been dispersed, publicly and privately, to bring pleasure to a new generation of enthusiasts. These grand old collectors may have passed on — as did Newcomb, Clapp and Downing before them — but the hobby thrives as never before.

How has cent collecting changed so? Why is the world of 1990 so different from that of 1965? Or does it just seem that way, as it did in 1965 looking back at 1940, or 1940 reminiscing about 1915? In this collector's opinion, the world of early cents *is* qualitatively and irrevocably different from 1965. I offer three reasons for this difference:

1. Fellowship — the Early American Coppers Club.
2. Scholarship — the dissemination of information.
3. A guide to spending money — Copper Quotes by Robinson.

The Early American Coppers Club. EAC was founded by Herb Silberman in 1966. Today, it has well over 1500 members around the world. Its bimonthly journal, *Penny-Wise,* is often considered to be the finest numismatic publication, of *any* sort, in existence today. More information on the early cents has appeared in its pages than had been published in the entire prior history of numismatic periodicals.

Through *Penny-Wise,* national and regional meetings of *EAC,* and innumerable private gatherings, early copper collectors have discovered and nurtured a fellowship without peer in numismatics. It is inconceivable that the cent hobby could have evolved to its present state were it not for the dominating presence of *EAC.*

In particular, *EAC* plays a central role in the second major force that has shaped the large cent world of 1990:

The dissemination of information. Simply put, far more is known about the early cents, and far more people know it. While *Penny-Wise* is the primary wellspring, numerous books, monographs, and articles in various publications are constantly enlarging the body of cent knowledge in the public domain. What secrets have been shared in private collector correspondence and tete-a-tetes we can only guess!

One particular source of information deserves special mention: the auction catalog. Beginning with the Robinson S. Brown, Jr. collection, Superior Stamp and Coin set a whole new standard in the art and science of cataloging. You need only compare the two catalogs mentioned earlier — the 1965 Century sale and the 1989 Matthews sale — to understand why auction catalogs now form an indespensible part of the body of early cent literature.

No matter how much information it may offer, the primary function of an auction catalog is to sell coins. And, for most collectors, the central purpose of their activity is to build their collections, which usually means buying coins. Scholarship and fellowship are wonderful, but let's face it: the hobby would be hollow if collectors couldn't collect.

We have seen examples of rarity downgradings, CC changes, and the astonishing escalation of prices in the last 25 years. In this environment, how can a collector keep up? In particular, how can he hope to spend his money intelligently? Sheldon's Basal Value system is hopelessly obsolete, this R-7 is now only R-6- but ten times as many people want one... so what's the darn thing worth?

Fortunately, the cent collector of 1990 has help. He has a cream-colored, pocket-sized friend that, to me, is the third pillar of today's cent hobby:

Copper Quotes by Robinson. Jack Robinson started *CQR* in 1983 as a few stapled pages of "MY OPINIONS of the values of Large Cents..." Now in its ninth edition, *CQR* lists the rarity, CC, and current price estimates for *every* variety of early cents (late dates and half cents, too), in 13 or 14 numerical grades and three different qualitative conditions. It also offers analysis of recent auction results, and incisive commentary on the current state of the market. *CQR* has become *the* pricing guide for early copper, accessible to both uninformed dealer (sigh) and sophisticated collector. For many of us, it is the reliable lifeboat in the sometimes calm, sometimes rolling sea that is the large cent market of today.

And yet, despite rarities, plummeting, prices skyrocketing, EAC, *Penny-Wise*, and *CQR*, the epicenter of the world of early cents remains unchanged: Dr. Sheldon's *Penny Whimsy*. We are pleased to present the 1990 edition of this numismatic classic, and echo Dr. Sheldon's hope that it will "... help a younger generation... to 'make out the big cents.' "

Denis W. Loring
July, 1990

PART ONE

The Story of Cents

Introducing the Big Cents

IN THE NEW ENGLAND VILLAGE WHERE I WAS BORN, QUITE A FEW years ago, the long winter evenings about the open fire—or in colder weather around the kitchen stove—were filled with a number of pleasant occupations.

First there was the general care and upkeep of guns, fishing tackle, and associated equipment. Chores done, there were chestnuts, apples, and sweet potatoes for roasting, popping corn and parching corn, checkerberries, walnuts and butternuts, cider. All these were part of the regular harvest of the countryside and so were taken for granted, like the logs in the fireplace and one's parents. There was one thing, however, which retained at all times such a halo of mystery and enchantment that it never came to be taken for granted.

This was the cigar box of old copper cents which my father kept locked up in the grandfather sea chest along with certain papers, some old spoons and jewelry, and other trinkets. On evenings when he was feeling especially well disposed, the kitchen lamp would be meticulously trimmed, the red kitchen tablecloth would be cleared of debris and brushed, then out would come the magnifying glass, four or five well-thumbed coin books, and the cigar box with the big cents.

There were about a hundred of these old coppers, along with a handful or two of other numismatic miscellanies, mostly early American gold and silver pieces. The latter would always be looked at in passing—they had their interest—but the real objective was to "study and try to make out" the big cents. We wanted to learn about those cents, but encountered difficulties which at that time were insuperable. We knew each individual coin fairly well, recognized it readily, knew its date (if that could be made out), its color and external physical characteristics, and could in most instances describe from memory the various insults and injuries, the nicks, bruises, cuts, dents, scratches, file marks, acid burns, and corrosion pits that it bore.

Also we had tried, by poring through the few cent books that could be found and by diligent comparative study of the cents themselves, to determine the die variety of each of them. The books revealed that in 1793 for instance, which was the first year in which cents were coined, three main types and some twenty varieties were struck. For *that* year, 1793, we had an excellent book (Crosby), and also for 1794 (Frossard-Hays), but it soon became clear that dependable information on the old cents, beyond the first two years, was not to be had. There seemed to be no way in which we, by our own effort, could discover the die variety, the rarity, and the value of such cents as were to be found in that old cigar box.

Possibly the fascination of the task lay to no small extent in the difficulties encountered. At any rate, now that I have achieved a neighborly acquaintanceship with old age, and meantime have written other, less soul-satisfying books, I am no longer able to summon up a good reason for *not* requisitioning the necessary time and materials to write a book aimed at helping a younger generation of kitchen-table-scientists-on-Friday-nights to "make out the big cents."

The Charm of the Old Copper Cents

One of the remarkable features of American life has been the sustained and almost universal affection shown for the humble copper cent. When the Mint started operations in 1793, cents were the first United States coins struck for circulation. This was at the Old Mint building on Seventh Street in Philadelphia, and cents have been issued every year ever since, except during 1815 when an acute scarcity of copper resulted from the second war with England. No other coin was issued with comparable regularity during the early years of the nation, but it is necessary to look beyond mere occurrence of dates to account for the traditional vogue and charm of the "old coppers."

At least three other factors must have contributed: *First,* a relatively great number of cents found their way into circulation. Almost everybody could afford to keep a few, especially bright, new ones. Being too big to swallow, they were safe as well as frugal gifts for infants and young children, and so they have been among the first familiar memories of childhood. Hundreds of thousands of them have been hidden away and forgotten, to be rediscovered and resurrected by rummaging offspring or descendants. Even now, occasional new discoveries of early cents enter the arteries of numismatic distribution. Viewed as a numismatic commodity, cents of early date are sufficiently numerous to have prevented any individual or group from being able to corner the market and control prices. Early coppers have long been looked upon by coin dealers as the bellwethers of the market, and for a century and a half now they have been the backbone of American numismatics. They are less influenced by depressions and booms than are other coins, are less subject to speculative buying, and in the lower grades of condition, at least, can be obtained in decent numbers by people of slender means. For generations American schoolboys bought, sold, swapped, or swiped old coppers. Some of these boys, especially in old age, have returned to the early enchantment, there to forget or condone the singular incompatibility between human dreams and fulfillments.

Second, the early coppers are rich in die varieties, cracked dies, imperfect and unusual planchets, misstruck coins, and other minor variations. If one possesses even a rudimentary flair for classification, these coins present a challenge which easily becomes a fascination. Among the cents from 1793 through 1803, the first eleven years of the series, 301 different true varieties are known. That is to say, coins of these dates are in existence which were struck from 301 different pairs or combinations of obverse and reverse dies. Dates mean but little to the advanced student of cents. It is the die variety that largely determines the rarity and value of the coin.

In the early days at the Mint the dies were all cut by hand, and a good deal of the personality of the die cutter was likely to find its way into the new die. Moreover the method for hardening steel then in use was ineffective. The new die soon cracked, sometimes in many places, and the resulting coins showed these cracks as ridges, irregular lines, and extra masses of metal on their surfaces. Often coins are found with cracks on both obverse and reverse—both dies were cracked. Die crack variations are not counted as different die varieties, but they are of great interest to collectors, who sometimes are able by means of them to trace the history of a die from the first few coins struck by it, through the whole progression of increasingly severe breaks, until at last it shattered and broke down altogether. Specialists on early cents have a keen eye for die breaks and have made great use of them in establishing, among other things, the probable order of issue of the known varieties of a date. Thus what the lovers of old coins like to call a *science* of numismatics is gradually built up.

Third, old copper, like beauty, appears to possess a certain intrinsic quality or charm which for many people is irresistible. An experienced dealer in American numismatic materials recently wrote as follows: "Sooner or later, if a collector stays at the business long enough, it is three to one his interest in all the other series will flag and he will focus his attention on the early cents." Gold, silver, and even bronze appear to be very much the same wherever you see them. Coins made of these metals become "old money" and "interesting," like the stuff seen in museums, but copper seems to possess an almost living warmth and a personality not encountered in any other metal. The big cent is something more than old money. Look at a handful of the cents dated before 1815, when they contained relatively pure copper. You see rich shades of green, red, brown, yellow, and even deep ebony; together with blendings of these not elsewhere matched in nature save perhaps in autumn leaves. If the light is good (direct sunlight is preferable) you will possibly observe that no two of the coins are of quite the same color.

Copper oxidizes differently in different atmospheres, and the way it colors and weathers depends also upon the impurities and traces of other metals which it may contain. The copper that went into the early cents must have been of highly variable assay, recruited as it was from almost every possible source.

Some came from Sweden, some from England, some was obtained by melting up copper nails, spikes, and copper finishings from wrecked ships (including both British and American men-of-war). Some of it came from kitchen and other household utensils donated or sold to the Mint in response to urgent appeals. George Washington is said to have donated "an excellent copper tea-kettle as well as two pairs of tongs" early in 1793 for the first cents. It is not surprising, therefore, that to some extent the different early die varieties are recognizable by characteristic color and surface texture, as well as by die breaks, peculiarities of the planchets, and so on. Every early cent has a character of its own.

These three factors—plentifulness of the coins, nearly inexhaustible variation both in number and in condition of the dies, and the intrinsic beauty and variability of old copper—account in part at least for the unique regard in which early copper cents have been held.

Birth and Childhood of the Big Cents

THERE ARE A NUMBER OF FRAGMENTARY RECORDS OF EARLY beginnings at the U.S. Mint, and at least two systematic histories have been written (*History of the U.S. Mint*, by George G. Evans, 1893, and *History of the First United States Mint—Its People and Its Operations*, by Frank H. Stewart, 1924).

Scattered through the files of the numismatic journals are frequent references to contemporary documents bearing on the early struggle to produce a U.S. coinage. Crosby devotes about a third of his famous monograph (8) on the cents and half cents of 1793 to an introduction describing the "action taken by the authorities towards the establishment of a mint, and the proceedings following that action, as well as some which preceded it." For the main facts, briefly touched upon, perhaps no better reference can be given than this short introduction by Crosby. For the whole story, up to the time of abandoning the Old Mint in 1833, Stewart's book is the most valuable source, and the brief background sketch which follows is indebted particularly to Stewart.

At least three separate efforts to establish a Mint were made before success was achieved. Robert Morris, often called The Financier of the Revolution, and Superintendent of Finance from 1781 to 1784, while he was in office presented a plan to Congress for setting up a Mint. His diary, now in the Library of Congress, describes various hunts for a location in the "City of Government" (then Philadelphia).

For a while the Dutch Reformed Methodist Church was con-

BIRTH AND CHILDHOOD OF THE BIG CENTS

sidered as a home for the Mint. Later, the Masons' Lodge appears to have been offered and considered. Various tools and machinery were made for the proposed venture, some of this at Morris' expense. Copper was shipped from Boston after quite a lively job of collecting or begging it from influential citizens. And several sample coins were made at Congressional expense by one Benjamin Dudley, an English die sinker with whom Morris became acquainted in Boston. These are the historic *Nova Constellatio* silver patterns of 1783, illustrating Morris's extremely ingenious plan for a coinage reconciling all the diverse moneys of account in the colonies. Dudley was intermittently employed by Morris for about four years, but his other dies, if any, are not identified. Morris is traditionally supposed to have been the "gentleman from New York" at whose instance Thomas Wyon struck the well known *Nova Constellatio* coppers of 1783-85 (of design copied after Dudley's silver patterns) in Birmingham, England, then the leading copper coinage center of the world.

In the end the enthusiasm of Morris failed to surmount the opposition of Thomas Jefferson; the Morris plan was discarded, and Dudley's position went with it. He next turned up in New Jersey where he seems to have done work for both the Rahway and Morristown Mints (1787). Thereafter he disappears from American history. He is said to have returned to England where it is thought that he became responsible for some of the flood of copper tokens, store cards, Washington pieces and the like which in the late seventeen eighties and early nineties poured over to this country in "most annoying volume." Perhaps Dudley enjoyed his revenge.

On October 16, 1786, the Continental Congress passed an ordinance that a Mint be established for the coinage of gold, silver, and copper money. However, when the detailed task of carrying out the ordinance was considered, singular differences of opinion as to procedure soon came to light, and after long debate, Congress did no more; but on April 21, 1787, the legislative body, stimulated by a few well-placed bribes, awarded one James Jarvis a franchise for copper coins (the familiar *Fugio* cents). Jarvis was to coin 300 tons of these, plus 45 tons extra to be paid to the government. The total coinage, according to research by Damon G. Douglas, seems to have been a small fraction of this amount, and Jarvis did not fulfill his obligations to the government. He minted the coins at New Haven, Connecticut. (Many are known today in Mint State because of a keg full of them found in the vaults of the Bank of New York in 1860.) This enterprise ended with the copper panic of 1789 when all copper coins fell to their bullion value.

The third attempt was successful, final establishment of the Mint, by Congressional Act of April 2, 1792, being due in large measure to the efforts of Alexander Hamilton and Thomas Jefferson. The decimal system of money was at this time legally adopted, and the weight of a cent—the one-hundredth part of a dollar—was fixed at eleven pennyweights, or about 264 grains, of pure copper. The confusion resulting from the introduction of the new decimal system may be imagined. During this period, nearly every registry, directory, and almanac contained tables showing the comparative values of the different currencies in circulation.

In May, 1792, President Washington provided for the purchase of an L-shaped plot of ground on Seventh Street, Philadelphia, near Market Street, together with three small buildings of different size and shape. Here the Mint of the United States was established, and remained for forty-one years, with an extensive remodeling in 1816.

Hardships and Difficulties

There is no precise record of just what went on at the Mint during its first years. Only fragmentary notes and later "recollections" are available. However, the general conditions under which work was carried on, and some of the difficulties peculiar to the undertaking are known. All employees worked eleven hours a day, 66 hours a week, beginning at five in the morning during the summer and at seven during the winter. Average pay for the coin press operators was $1.25 per day. The presses used for cents during the first eight or nine years—we do not know exactly when they were replaced—were imported from England and are believed to have been two in number.

All power, prior to 1816, was furnished by horses and human

muscle, a small steam engine being installed in the above-mentioned year. Horses were used only for what proved to be the most difficult and unsatisfactory part of the operation, namely that of rolling out the copper into sheets prior to cutting it into strips from which the planchets or coin blanks were to be punched. Power was transmitted from a turntable to the rollers by means of copper gears, since iron gears were for some reason not available. The copper gears wore down rapidly and in many other respects the rolling machinery fell short of expectations.

For a decade or more there was a chronic, and often an acute, shortage of copper, as well as great variability in the assay and consequently in the color and hardness of that metal which did find its way to the Mint.

We have only begun the list of hardships and difficulties. During 1793-4-5-6 the struggle to manufacture copper planchets was apparently heroic. The available metal, as it came to the Mint, was often in the form of copper nails, old sheet copper shipped from England, Sweden, and elsewhere, copper kettles and similar articles brought by individuals to the Mint or to collecting stations in Boston and other coastal cities (whence it could be shipped by water), and copper scrap from all sources. The recovery of copper from wrecked ships was at that time considered a patriotic (as well as profitable) duty. Great difficulty was encountered in melting some of this metal, as well as in processing it into sheets and planchets. There were a few shipments of manufactured planchets from England, but these generally varied in quality and finish, as well as in size and weight.

We begin to understand why some of the early cents are found on imperfect or clipped planchets, why certain dates and dies take on characteristic color or show a peculiar grain in the surface of the metal, or oxidize rapidly, and why many of the varieties can be recognized from the "texture" of their metal alone.

During these years Philadelphia was subject to an annual epidemic of yellow fever. Those who could afford it went elsewhere for the summer months, and thousands moved out from the heart of the city to live in rural districts, especially along

BIRTH AND CHILDHOOD OF THE BIG CENTS

the Schuylkill River where tent colonies were set up each summer—not an ideal place to escape mosquitoes. Between 1793 and 1797 at least four men from the Mint died of yellow fever, and the ravages of the disease were "particularly severe" in 1796. The Director of the Mint finally secured permission from Congress to close down for several months in 1797, for the three months of the summer in 1798, and probably for a longer period in 1799. The Mint was also closed for a time because of yellow fever in 1802, 1803, and 1804.

Early perplexities at the Mint were not confined to the handling of copper. Thomas Pinckney, Minister to England in 1792, succeeded in persuading Albion Cox to come to this country to accept the position of Assayer of the new Mint. The job of Chief Coiner was given temporarily to Henry Voight, while Pinckney, Jefferson, and others sought to induce one J. P. Drost (or Droz—both spellings recur) to move from Paris to Philadelphia to take over that position. Drost was a Swiss engraver who had settled in Paris. It was he who ordered and sent over our first coin presses, and he is supposed to have made the dies for the first cents (Chain Cents of 1793), but in the end he resisted our blandishments.

Meanwhile Cox and Voight, under a new law passed by Congress, were required to furnish security to the amount of $10,000 each before being permitted to coin gold and silver. Since neither was able to meet this requirement, no gold or silver was coined in 1793, and none that was intended for general circulation in 1794. For a time it seemed doubtful that Congress would permit even the coinage of copper, for the same reason, but to this metal the restriction was not finally applied. In 1794 Jefferson persuaded Congress to lessen the required securities for gold and silver (Act of March 3, 1794), and a few silver pieces were coined late in that year. No gold was coined until 1795.

Under the Thumb of an Unfriendly Congress

The list of hardships continues. Popular opinion at the turn of the century was far from unanimously favorable to the operation of a Mint in this country. Congress seems to have

BIRTH AND CHILDHOOD OF THE BIG CENTS

been well seeded with unkind critics. The eagle on the reverse of the silver and gold coins was "a sick turkey cock"; the head of Liberty, on all obverses, was a "wild squaw with the heebie jeebies." The 1793 Chain Cent was a particular target for invective. This was the "Liberty in chains" cent. The Mint was referred to as an extravagant, foolish waste of public money, a place where men tinkered away the life blood of the nation and produced "caricatures in copper."

In March, 1800, a committee of the U.S. Senate recommended abolishing the Mint on the ground that the expense of coinage was altogether disproportionate to the advantages derived from (the very limited) circulation of its coins. This committee branded the Mint experiment a failure, and suggested that another arrangement should be made (with some private concern) for providing the nation with coins.

A second bill for abolishing the Mint was introduced in Congress in April, 1802, and only after most vigorous debate was pigeonholed nearly a year later. During these years all employees at the Mint were reminded frequently that the tenure of their jobs was uncertain, that reductions in pay were probable, and that to keep a weather eye open for a safer job would be a good idea. In the light of this general state of affairs, such cents as the "three errors" variety of 1801, the recurrent denominational fraction $\frac{1}{000}$, the "LIHERTY" cent of 1796, misstruck, overstruck, understruck, and badly centered coins, the use of defective planchets and of shattered dies, the occurrence of freak coins and of oddly individualistic experiments like the so-called Jefferson cent of 1795—all these symptoms of uncertainty and poor discipline take on sympathetic significance. Those fellows had been doing their best with a tough assignment and were getting about the encouragement of a soldier in peacetime. Something was being "expressed" in the early cents.

In 1802, when it looked very much as if the Mint would be abandoned, Elias Boudinot, then Director (there were at least five changes of Director of the Mint during the first ten years), was asked by the Secretary of the Treasury to submit a complete invoice of the property of the Mint. This invoice, given by Stewart in full (page 65), is repeated here in part as constituting a more revealing picture of the Mint in the days of the early cents than could be encompassed in many pages of narrative.

THE INVOICE:

Two lots on Seventh Street, between Market and Arch Streets, 20 feet on Seventh and extending back about 100 feet, with a dwelling house on the North lot, and a shell of a house on the South lot, which last lot widens on the rear to about 60 feet, on which the stable stands. These lots pay a ground rent of $27.50 per annum.

A lot on Sugar Alley, at the rear of the above, 20 ft. front on the alley and about 100 ft. deep.

A frame building improved for a large furnace, in the common at the North end of Sixth Street, of little value, the ground being merely loaned to us.

As to personal estate, this consists wholly of—

The copper planchets on hand, amounting to about 22 tons.
Three horses, good for little but the use of the Mint.
The machinery of the Mint, of no value but for the use of the mint.
Five striking presses with machinery.
Three cutting presses.
One milling machine.
Five pairs of rollers, great and small.
One drawing machine.
Three pairs of smith's bellows.
A set of blacksmith's tools. . . .

Following the invoice is Mr. Boudinot's answer, evidently, to the really pertinent part of the Secretary's inquiry: "I am perfectly satisfied that no modification of the Mint could be contrived to lessen (expense) below 17 or 18,000 dollars per annum. . . . In the above estimate of expenses, it should be remembered that the copper cents may produce a profit of $5,000 per annum, that ought to be credited against the expenditure of the Mint in future, which reduces the amount considerably."

The item "Five striking presses with machinery" conceals an interesting story. Two of these had arrived from England on September 21, 1792, supposedly sent from the Boulton & Watt Mint at Soho near Birmingham, where Droz was employed. Adam Eckfeldt had in the meantime constructed a third. The Mint purchased the fourth for $47.44 on June 3, 1794, from Mrs. Hannah Ogden, widow of Matthias Ogden, Revolutionary

War hero and New Jersey coiner. This press had been in use first at the Rahway Mint in 1786-88, and later at the Elizabethtown Mint (1789) where Ogden made overstrikes of Jersey cent dies upon all kinds of worn coppers, as Jersey coppers then passed at a higher rate than the rest. On March 25, 1795, the Mint bought the fifth press from Samuel Howell, Jr., & Co., for $134.07 including porterage. Howell is known to have signed notes issued by the State of Pennsylvania in 1775.

Beginnings of Inflation

Here a paragraph of digression may perhaps be forgiven. It will be recalled that for more than a century prior to the Revolutionary War one of the major complaints against the mother country was that it did not always provide "honest money," or coin in which the weight of contained metal represented the full face value of the piece. In particular, the colonies had bitterly attacked the copper coinage, which then comprised a large proportion of the circulating metallic money. We had attempted to refuse ha'penny pieces on the ground that too much profit was being made on them, or too little copper was being put into them.

Later, during the early congressional arguments over the establishment of a Mint, the point was frequently brought up that by cheating the public a little on the relatively voluminous copper coinage—that is, by inflating copper money more or less—enough profit could be garnered to defray the expenses of a Mint. This "legalized robbery" plan was scornfully assailed both in Congress and in the public press, yet its proponents were able to effect a degree of compromise and we find that on January 14, 1793, the legal weight of the cent was changed from 264 grains to a "reasonable profit" weight of 208 grains.

Such a compromise with inflation elicited a bitter storm which even yet has never entirely abated, but the storm was not of sufficient intensity to prevent Congress from directing the President, in December of 1795, to *again* reduce the weight of the cent. This time the official weight was fixed at 168 grains, and there it remained until in 1857 the old copper cent was replaced by a smaller, frankly token coin.

The Mint's profit on its cents was one of the scandals of the time, but the profit may have been what saved the Mint in the congressional battle of 1802. After this crisis matters appear to have progressed more smoothly. The first decade of the Mint had been completed. The nation was becoming accustomed to its existence, and in the end was to contemplate with equanimity an outlay of ten to fifteen thousand dollars a year.

Prosperity Comes to the Mint

Because of the high price of copper, coinage of copper coins in 1804 was confined to the output of a single press. In 1806 the press for cents was out of repair "during a large part of the time," sharply reducing the output for that year. In 1815 no cents were coined because of the scarcity of copper which grew out of the War of 1812.

But in 1816 prosperity came to the Mint in the form of a "substantial brick building" replacing the old wooden one, together with a large shipment of new machinery and apparatus. In this year a new mechanical method of die cutting was introduced, and also a new method for hardening the dies. The cents from 1816 on (now called *Coronet* cents) are of an entirely different, more stereotyped, and, I believe, less artistic design. Also they are of harder metal. In 1820 we find the production of copper coins suspended for six months because, for the first time in American history, the demand was oversupplied. Modern efficiency methods had won out.

The era of the Old Mint ends with the year 1833, when the New Mint was opened at Juniper and Chestnut Streets, with machinery of such a nature that both the preparation of dies and the operation of the presses became almost wholly mechanical. Collectors of old American coins generally find that their interest wanes after this date is reached.

Review of the Principal Cent Literature

THERE ARE ROUGHLY HALF A DOZEN CONTRIBUTIONS OR GROUPS of contributions to the literature on the large cents that may be considered essential to a working knowledge of the subject. Presented in the order of their appearance, or rather in the order of their first beginnings, these include: (1) a famous series of studies on the cents of 1794 (14; 12; 2); (2) Crosby's classic work on the 1793's (8); (3) the Andrews (1) and the Newcomb (19) monographs on the later cents, 1816-1857; (4) Newcomb on the cents of 1801-1802-1803 (18); (5) Clapp on 1798-1799 (3) and on 1804-1814 (4); (6) the Clapp-Newcomb collaboration on the remaining four dates (1795, 1796, 1797, and 1800) (5).

Other supplementary material is needed to appreciate the whole story of the early cents, but the essentials will be found in the six hunting grounds indicated. The present generation has seen the completion of the last four of these works, and it has now become possible, for the first time, to write a comprehensive book dealing with the whole series of the early large cents.

The Story of the 1794's

In 1869 Dr. Edward Maris, of Philadelphia, published a little 17-page brochure or bound pamphlet on *The Cents of 1794*, describing and naming 39 varieties. In the following year he issued a revision which added four more varieties, making 43 in all. Nine years later (1879), in a letter to Edward Frossard which was subsequently published, Maris mentions

REVIEW OF THE PRINCIPAL CENT LITERATURE

that during the interim he had become acquainted with nine *further* varieties of 1794, so that the list then stood at 52.

The Maris numbers have been superseded by other and more complete lists, but several of the Maris names survive and in the older collections envelopes are still seen bearing such designations as *Double Chin Variety, Young Head, The Coquette, Tilted 4, The Ornate, Egeria, Venus Marina, Diana, Patagonian, Amiable Face, The Roman Plica,* and so on.

In 1893 Edward Frossard again described—and this time illustrated—the 1794 cents, now presenting 56 varieties and assigning to each a new designative number. A dealer himself, Frossard collaborated with W. W. Hays in this work, and in the preface he wrote, "It is but just to my collaborator, Mr. Hays, the man through whose patience and perseverance a complete set of the 1794 cents was collected, that the varieties in this new classification should bear his name." They have borne the name of Hays, for the most part, to the present day. The old *Double Chin* variety of Maris became Hays 2; *The Coquette,* Hays 9; *The Roman Plica,* Hays 54, and so on.

In 1910 Thomas Elder, another dealer, published a second edition of the Frossard-Hays work, repeating the descriptive text but adding three more varieties (Nos. 57, 58, and 59). Meanwhile it had been discovered that the varieties called Hays 38 and Hays 53 were but worn or altered specimens of other dies. Elder illustrated the new edition from the collection of Mr. Ebenezer Gilbert, of New York, and it is generally known as the Gilbert-Elder edition. There were now 57 known varieties of the 1794 cents.

The last monograph on 1794's was published in 1923 by S. H. Chapman, one of two brothers who, as Philadelphia coin dealers, played a great part in American numismatics for several decades. Chapman added two more 1794 varieties which had been discovered during the interim, thus raising the number to 59. He also rearranged the listing of the varieties, substituting new numbers for the Hays numbers. The Chapman monograph is illustrated by excellent plates, and it is perhaps the most generally adequate presentation of the subject. However, the older Hays numbers seem to have taken deep root in the affections of cent collectors, and it now appears likely that

[18]

the name Hays will long be associated with this the most extensive one-date series of American coins.

Crosby and the 1793's

For the April, 1869, number of the *American Journal of Numismatics*, Sylvester S. Crosby with the collaboration of J. N. T. Levick, prepared an illustrated treatise on *The United States Cents of 1793*, and this remained the standard reference on the subject until Crosby himself, in 1897, published a more extensive monograph entitled *The United States Coinage of 1793—Cents and Half Cents*. Crosby's book was so accurate and complete that in the half century since its publication no further varieties of 1793 have been found.

The 1793 cents have for several decades been almost unanimously known by their Crosby numeral-letter designations. This method of attribution possesses the inherent advantage of indicating in the very *name* of the coin just what obverse (heads) and what reverse (tails) die was used. Crosby assigned numerals to the obverses and letters to the reverses, in (so far as he could tell) the most probable order of issue of the various die combinations from the Mint. Thus the cent 1-A is what seemed to be the first cent coined—the first obverse combined with the first reverse. The 9-G is the ninth obverse in the Crosby series, combined with the seventh reverse. The 9-H is the same obverse, a comparatively tough die which outlasted its first reverse partner, combined with the eighth reverse, and so on. The marriage of obverse and reverse dies was like human marriages, sometimes terminating in the untimely breakdown of one partner or the other, sometimes ending in arbitrary divorce by the chief coiner's whim.

Crosby described 14 different 1793 obverses and 12 reverses, appearing in 22 different combinations. One of the reverses (B) was later shown to be a tooled or mutilated specimen of reverse C. There is no such variety, therefore, as the Crosby 3-B (which was really a 3-C), and but 21 different die combinations of 1793 are in fact known.

REVIEW OF THE PRINCIPAL CENT LITERATURE

Two Comprehensive Monographs on Cents:
FROSSARD AND PROSKEY-DOUGHTY

In 1879 Frossard published a small treatise entitled *Monograph of United States Cents and Half Cents, 1793-1857*. This was the first attempt at a comprehensive treatment of the whole series of large cents, and it stands today as one of the most readable contributions to the field. Frossard wrote English in a compact, precise style, and his descriptions of the general types of die used during the 64 years in which big cents were issued have never been surpassed. This book added nothing of a scientific or classificational nature. Frossard merely followed the early monographs of Maris and Crosby for the first two dates, and indicated the well-known varieties of the other dates only in the most general terms. But his book is worth owning for the descriptions of the "seven general classes" of large cents.

These are: *Chain* or *Link* Cents (1793 first type); *Wreath* Cents (1793 second type); *Liberty Cap* Cents (1793 third type through 1796 first type); *Draped Bust* Cents (1796 second type through 1807); *Turban Head Cents* (1808 through 1814); *Coronet* Cents (1816 through 1839 first type: no cents struck in 1815); and *Braided Hair Coronet* Cents (1839 final type through 1857). The descriptions to be found in Part II of the present book follow Frossard closely, in some cases verbatim.

David Proskey, a younger contemporary of Frossard and a fellow coin dealer, was not only a close student of cents but was also a man of classificational bent. During 1879 and 1880 he contributed to the *Coin Collector's Journal* a series of articles which for the first time attempted detailed descriptions of all the *varieties* of cents from 1795 through 1814. Proskey revised some of these studies in 1887 for the same Journal, having worked on the material intermittently for a decade or more. Considering his work as a whole, he achieved one of the pioneering tasks in American numismatics. It was he who established the designations by which the various dies from 1795 through 1814 (except 1796) were almost universally known to collectors for four decades, or from 1890 until the modern work of Newcomb and Clapp became generally known.

But Proskey never finished his job. For some reason he tired of it—there have been various explanations of this—and he seems to have turned over all his material, including a mass of unfinished notes, to Francis Doughty, another dealer. Doughty, not particularly interested in cents himself, republished under his own name the whole series of Proskey articles (1890), including unfinished notes without revision, and called the resulting book *The Cents of the United States*. The Proskey designations thus became Doughty designations, although it has been said that Doughty scarcely knew one date from another.

Despite its incompleteness this work was an advance in numismatics, and the large cents, through 1814, soon were known by their "Doughty numbers." Proskey was the first to try to bring descriptive order to the study of early cents as a whole, although he failed to provide either a good method of classification or a defensible nomenclature, and he missed about a third of the available varieties.

The Later-Date Cents:
ANDREWS AND NEWCOMB

Most cent collectors have fixed their attention on the early dates, finding that interest flagged after the disappearance of the Draped Bust coins in 1807, or stopped entirely with the end of the Turban Head series in 1814. The later dates are less attractive in many respects. In the words of one prominent collector, they are "only machine made tokens." However, some collectors have become interested in these later, more stereotyped dies, and among them are found two great numismatic names—Andrews and Newcomb.

Frank Andrews is said to have worked quietly on the later dates for twenty years before publishing, in 1881 (second edition 1883), his remarkably thorough little monograph, *The United States Copper Cents, 1816-1857*. This publication, listing somewhat more than four hundred varieties by "Andrews numbers," became the accepted standard and remained so until Howard R. Newcomb, in 1944, brought out another monograph under the same title. Newcomb's book doubtless achieves the highest pinnacle for numismatic completeness, adding as it does many new varieties to the old Andrews list. Yet in fairness to Andrews it should be pointed out that the great bulk of Newcomb's additions are in the very late dates—the 1840's and 1850's—and that a large number of these depend upon a kind of numismatic hairsplitting which requires the combination of a perfect Mint State coin and a magnifying glass. Newcomb made new varieties of what in some cases were only slight retouchings, redressings, or even irregular strikings of previously recognized varieties.

Gilbert-Elder on the 1796's

During the last quarter of the nineteenth century Ebenezer Gilbert was one of the most active collectors of early date cents, and being of a scientific turn of mind he made extensive notes on die variations of the different dates, especially 1794 and 1796, although apparently never with intent to publish his material. We noted (p. 18) that Elder illustrated the Gilbert-Elder (1910) publication on 1794 cents from Gilbert's collection.

In 1909 Elder brought out a brochure called *United States Cents of 1796,* also illustrated from Gilbert's collection, and in this instance the descriptive matter was taken almost entirely from a sheaf of Gilbert's loose notes. (Gilbert afterwards protested goodnaturedly that he never intended that material to be published, since he knew it to be both incomplete and in some respects inaccurate.) During the succeeding several years Elder issued a number of brief supplements to this monograph, adding new varieties until 14 Liberty Cap and 40 Draped Bust die combinations were described.

This publication on the "Gilbert" varieties of 1796 has been, on the whole, the most vexing and misleading of all the literature available to cent collectors. Elder, a brilliant and popular merchandiser but never himself a student in the field, seems to have turned over to the printers a mass of essentially unedited or undigested notes. The principal resulting difficulty lay in a confused duplication of varieties. Three of the Gilbert-Elder Liberty Cap varieties (Nos. J, M, and N) and 11 of the Draped Bust varieties (Nos. 8, 21, 22, 26, 27, 28, 31, 32, 37, 39, and 40) are either unknown or duplicates of other numbers (see Table 11, p. 183).*

Gilbert himself must have observed 1796 cents with remarkable thoroughness, since Newcomb and Clapp, and the rest of us, have found only four varieties not included in the original monograph and its supplements. Gilbert had the material for a first-rate monograph. It was either not ready or not intended for publication and was badly edited.

The Newcomb Monograph on 1801-1802-1803

During the first quarter of the twentieth century and until his death in 1945, Howard R. Newcomb was so closely identified with the big cents that to mention cents was to mention Newcomb. For several decades he turned his major attention to collecting and classifying cents, and produced two principal publications: the book mentioned on page 21, and *The United States Cents of the Years 1801-1802-1803,* published in 1925.

This latter monograph marks a milestone in the cent literature. Approaching a field which had been left almost in chaos by the Doughty book, Newcomb assembled a vast quantity of numismatic material, ordered and reordered it, finally set up a new classificational system and a list which seemed adequate; and after testing the new list for upwards of a decade, published. The verdict of time on this work has been favorable. Twenty-three years after publication, only two minor reverse variations for 1801 and one new 1803 reverse have turned up. For these three additions Newcomb issued supplements shortly after the publication of the book, leaving the list of known 1801 cents at 14, the 1802's at 20, and the 1803's at 24. Meanwhile it may be said that nearly every close student of the dates under discussion has used the Newcomb designations.

* Certain collectors and dealers, in describing Draped Bust 1796 cents, have used "Gilbert numbers" higher than 40—such as 41, 42, 43, and even numbers in the fifties and sixties. This was never authorized by Elder, however, and the practice should perhaps be attributed to overenthusiasm or to salesmanship. All such specimens examined by Clapp, the present writer, and other cent students have turned out to be known varieties of less astronomical designation.

REVIEW OF THE PRINCIPAL CENT LITERATURE

The Clapp Monographs on 1798-99 and 1804-14

Only Clapp's work and his studies in collaboration with Newcomb are now lacking to complete our survey of the cent literature. Following his retirement from business life, Mr. Clapp had devoted much of his time to the study of the early cents. In 1931 he published *The United States Cents of the Years 1798-1799*. Parsimonious of language and accurate of detail, Clapp lists and illustrates 47 varieties of 1798 cents, as compared with the 27 varieties which had been in many instances confusingly described by Proskey. The adequacy of the work is attested by the fact that during the thirty years since its publication not even a new minor variation of a 1798 die has turned up.

In 1934 Clapp wrote a small brochure for the *Coin Collector's Journal* (4), clearing up the question of die varieties of cents from 1804 through 1814, correcting the Proskey-Doughty omissions and errors of description, as well as one error of inclusion: the 1813 cent listed as Doughty 223 was a fraud.

Clapp-Newcomb on 1795-1796-1797 and 1800

But four dates now remained to fulfill the one-time Newcomb dream of a complete descriptive literature on the large cents. These were 1795 (an easy one with only eight known die combinations); 1797; and the two difficult dates 1796 and 1800, the last an especially hard one because of the minute differences between some of the reverse dies. Clapp and Newcomb set to work to collaborate on these dates, and the job was just about finished at the time of Newcomb's death early in 1945. As the present book is being written, this Clapp-Newcomb collaboration has not yet come off the press, but through Mr. Clapp's kindness I have had the advantage of reading his manuscript and of adapting my own descriptions to his.

In summary, the *essential* contributions to the literature of the large cents, listed in the order of their beginnings, are: (1) The Maris-Frossard-Hays-Gilbert-Chapman work on the 1794's; (2) Crosby on the 1793's; (3) The Andrews-Newcomb monographs on 1816-1857; (4) Newcomb on 1801-1802-1803;

(5) Clapp on 1798-99 and on 1804-14; and (6) Clapp-Newcomb on 1795-1796-1797 and 1800.

The Proskey-Doughty work on the series as a whole and the Gilbert-Elder publication on the 1796's may now be considered of historical value only, although if a history of large cent activity during the first half of the twentieth century were to be written these two references would bulk large. Whoever has collected cents during the period mentioned will continue to keep his well-thumbed Doughty and his Gilbert-Elder at hand, and will for a long time catch himself lapsing into such terminology as the "Gilbert F variety," and the "Doughty 66."

Bibliography

1) Andrews, F. D. *An Arrangement of United States Copper Cents, 1816–1857*. 2d edition. Vineland, N. J., 1883.
1a) Breen, Walter H. "The United States Patterns of 1792." *Coin Collector's Journal*, Vol. 21, No. 2 (March–April, 1954), New York.
1b) Breen, Walter H. "The United States Minor Coinages, 1793–1916." *Coin Collector's Journal*, Vol. 21, No. 3 (May–June, 1954), New York.
2) Chapman, S. H. *The United States Cents of the Year 1794*. Philadelphia, 1923. 2d edition, 1926.
3) Clapp, George H. *The United States Cents of the Years 1798–9*. Sewickley, Pa., 1931.
4) Clapp, George H. "The United States Cents, 1804–1814." *Coin Collector's Journal*, Vol. I, No. 9 (December 1934).
5) Clapp, George H. and Newcomb, Howard R. *The United States Cents of the Years 1795–1796–1797–1800*. Published by the American Numismatic Society. New York, 1947.
6) Crosby, S. S. and Levick, J. N. T. "The United States Cents of 1793." *American Journal of Numismatics*, Vol. III, No. 12 (April 1869).
7) Crosby, S. S. *The Early Coins of America*. Boston, 1875.
8) Crosby, S. S. *The United States Coinage of 1793—Cents and Half Cents*. Boston, 1897.
9) Doughty, F. W. *The Cents of the United States*. New York, 1890.
10) Evans, George G. *Illustrated History of the United States Mint*. Philadelphia, 1893.
11) Frossard, Ed. *Monograph of United States Cents and Half Cents*. Irvington, N. Y., 1879.
12) Frossard, Ed. and Hays, W. W. *Varieties of United States Cents of the Year 1794*. New York, 1893. Reprinted by Gilbert-Elder, New York, 1910.
13) Gilbert, E. and Elder, T. L. *The Varieties of the United States Cents of 1796*. New York, 1909.
14) Maris, Edward. *Varieties of the Copper Issues of the United States Mint in the Year 1794*. 2d edition. Philadelphia, 1870.

BIBLIOGRAPHY

15) McGirk, C. E. "United States Cents and Die Varieties, 1793–1857." *The Numismatist,* April 1913–December 1914.
16) Mehl, B. Max. *Catalogue of the Dr. French Collection of Large U. S. Cents.* Fort Worth, Texas, 1929.
17) Morgenthau, J. C. and Co. *Auction Catalogue of the Howard R. Newcomb Collection.* New York, 7 February 1945.
18) Newcomb, Howard R. *The United States Cents of the Years 1801–1802–1803.* Detroit, 1925.
19) Newcomb, Howard R. *United States Copper Cents, 1816–1857.* New York, 1944.
20) Numismatic Gallery, N. Y. *Catalogue of the Oscar J. Pearl Collection.* New York, 1944.
21) Proskey, David. Series of articles in *The Coin Collector's Journal,* 1879–1881 and 1887–1888.
22) Stewart, F. H. *History of the First United States Mint.* Camden, N. J., 1924.
23) Venn, T. J. *Large United States Cents* (Monograph). Chicago, 1915.
24) Watson, D. K. *History of American Coinage.* Putnam, N. Y., 1899.

Toward a Science of Cent Values

WITH A LITERATURE AVAILABLE WHICH NOW COVERS THE whole field of the large cents, the question might reasonably be asked, What then is still needed? What is lacking to such a degree as to call for another book? The answer is multiple, but some of it, at least, can be expressed as follows:

1. Most of the literature mentioned in the preceding section is not actually available, or at any rate not available to the average beginner who may find himself interested in cents. Some of the books will turn up in auctions within a period of five or ten years, but the prices have become prohibitive, and it is not always feasible to wait five years. For a long time the need of a single book on the early cents has been felt—a book available at reasonable cost, and carrying the information necessary for identification of *all* the varieties. *The first need, then, is a comprehensive book systematically presenting the whole series of the early cents.*

2. There has been a good deal of confusion as to nomenclature and designation of the different varieties of cents. Some of this is natural, or healthfully transitional. It is the collectors themselves who must in the long run determine by what symbol a particular cent is to be known. Practice or usage must be the final arbiter. But a book presenting *all* the various nomenclatures that are in use, and *systematically ordering them* so that a beginner can find his way from one to another, may help clarify the problem of nomenclature. *The second need is clarification of nomenclature.*

3. When a cent is identified and correctly attributed, the next

question is, What is its value? To answer, even approximately, it is necessary to know three things: (1) The *condition* of the coin (how worn or how perfect it is); (2) Its *rarity*; (3) The history of the numismatic market with reference to the variety, in comparable condition. A professional numismatist devotes his life mainly to becoming expert at these three matters— recognition of condition, knowledge of rarity, and knowledge of what prices particular coins have brought and will bring in various quarters. We cannot expect a book to provide expert training in all of this overnight, but I think we *can* expect a book to provide even a beginner with enough armament and documentation on condition, rarity, and value to help him climb out of the sucker class—almost overnight.

Numismatics, especially cent numismatics, has always had its shady fringe of unscrupulous dealers—men who exaggerate condition, rarity, and value when they sell, and understate some or all of these when they buy. These men depend on a large turnover in the collector population, with a resulting continuous supply of suckers. Now I am not sure that the world would be any better without suckers in it, or even without shady coin dealers, but one object in writing this book is to try to give the former a little better run for their money and to provide better bait for the latter. In short, to give the amateur cent lover "a chance," so that he may trade a bit in cents and perhaps own a few of the rarities without thereby losing his shirt. *The third need, then is the rudiments of a science of cent values.*

In the chapters which follow, we shall attempt to progress toward a science of cent values.

The First Step:
QUANTITATIVE GRADING OF CONDITION

Study of the photographs in the text with an ordinary reading lens will reveal that "condition" can be made to take on a degree of objective meaning. There will remain a certain difference between the appearance of a coin in a photograph and its appearance "in the copper," but the difference is not as great as one might fear, and with a large number of photographs to examine, a workable idea can be formed as to how the various shades of condition from a poor coin to a perfect one can be scaled or graded. This progression is of course a continuum, not a series of discrete steps, and for those who think quantitatively rather than adjectivally it is more accurate to grade coins on a *numeral scale* than to try to fit them into a series of adjectival pigeonholes.

Years ago, when as a high-school boy I used to appraise cents from my section of the country for one of the coin dealers of that day (Chapman), I standardized a numeral scale which progresses from 1 to 70. On this scale, 1 means that the coin is identifiable and not mutilated—no more than that.

A 70-coin is one in flawless Mint State, exactly as it left the dies, with perfect mint color and without a blemish or nick. With these two extremes on the scale defined, for anchorage, it is not difficult to establish fairly clear criteria for a 4-coin, a 20-coin, a 40-coin, and so on.

So much for what a numeral scale of condition is. In actual practice, dealers and collectors take arbitrary points on such a scale, assign conventional adjectives to the selected points, and try to describe coins in terms of these adjectives. The most widely used adjectives are *Fair, Good, Very Good, Fine, Very Fine, Extremely Fine,* and *Mint State.* Some years ago it occurred to me that with thousands of collectors and scores of dealers using these terms and with hundreds of thousands of cents in more or less continuous numismatic circulation, there must be some underlying matrix of meaning—some rhyme and reason—beneath the adjectival concepts which had become established. The terms *Good* and *Fine,* for instance, might be translated into points on a quantitative scale of condition, *and these points, if rarity were also known or held constant, ought then to represent with some accuracy the long-run value (sales history)* of a coin. To the extent that condition could be made quantitative, value might become objective.

To make a beginning toward a science of values, then, it was necessary first to find out what relationship existed, if any, between values and (a quantitative scale of) condition. This could be done only by watching, and to some extent participating in, cent transactions through a long period of years, while keeping quantitative records of both price and condition. Condition, that is to say, on a quantitative scale; and by price I did not mean announced auction prices or catalogue prices. Many of these I knew to be dishonest and inflated. Frequently the coins did not actually change hands, and in some instances they never existed. By price I meant what people *actually paid* for coins and particularly what experienced collectors *were ready to pay*.

A Testing Ground for the Condition-Value Relationship—The 1794's

The most famous and popular date for the big cents has always been 1794. In the course of time it has been possible to observe transactions involving quite a few thousands of 1794 cents, some of the individual coins reappearing many times over. If for the present we disregard the rare ones of that date and consider only the common dies, certain generalizations can be admitted.

For example, the common 1794 cent in condition 1 (identifiable and unmutilated), during the second quarter of the twentieth century, has usually been regarded as worth about a dollar. Sometimes, in lots, it has sold as low as fifty cents, and sometimes when carefully attributed and described it has brought a dollar and a half. These same coins in *Fair* condition (condition 2) have consistently brought just about twice what the condition 1 coins commanded. During the past quarter century Fair 1794 cents of common die have averaged not far from two dollars.

In the condition rated *Good* (see p. 41), which is condition 4, these cents have rather uniformly brought about twice the price of the *Fair* examples. Four dollars can be put down as pretty close to the average selling price of the *Good* 1794 cent during the period under consideration. Before 1925 that price would have been considered too high.

For at least three grades of condition, then, there appears to be some relationship between value and conventional descriptions of condition. Value about doubles with each of the first two conventional progressions of condition. The *Good*

1794 of a common die is worth about four times what condition 1 is worth. Moreover, I found the same thing to be true of most of the *uncommon* dies of that year. That is to say, the ratio remains the same, although the *basal value*—a term to which we shall return presently—is in some cases much higher. Some of the extremely rare 1794's are so few in number that no more than one or two are known in any condition, so our generalization will not apply to them.

It may be as well to add at this point, however, that the generalization does hold, for the most part, for all the early dates. My observations began with the 1794's. That was the date I liked best and watched most closely, but in this instance the rule holds nearly as well for 1793's, 1795's, or 1796's as for 1794's. In the case of the prohibitively rare dies, of any date, there are frequently too few records for generalization.

The grade *Fine* is usually defined as that condition in which *all the detail of the coin is sharp and stands out boldly*, although some wear may be present on the highest relief (see p. 41). My early expectation was that *Fine* 1794's would generally bring about twice the price of *Good* ones, but it did not turn out so. The *Fine* coins, taken as an average through two decades, have sold for about three times as much as the *Good* coins or about twelve times the value of condition 1. *Fine* 1794 cents, when honestly graded, have averaged just about 12 dollars each during the second quarter of the century. Around 1932 they could be bought for 8 or 9 dollars. During 1944 and 1945, a period of rising inflation, this grade averaged possibly 15 dollars. In 1947 these values had fallen back a little. The Fine 1794 cent seems to be affected relatively little by the ebb and flow of economic tides, although it does of course reflect the trend. It is a deep-water anchor for the numismatic ship.

During this quarter century top grade 1794 cents of common die have held pretty well to a recognized value of around 50 dollars. The late Dr. French, in looking at 1794's, would pick up a common one in 50 condition (About Uncirculated), would hold it off to look at it, and exclaim, "Now that's what I call a 50-dollar cent!" Henry Chapman, who generally marked up his coins 50 per cent above purchase price, was always ready to pay 35 dollars for an AU-50 (see p. 41) common 1794; and usually would sell it for about 50 dollars. At auction, common 1794's in AU-50 condition averaged about 45 dollars in the nineteen twenties, and about the same in the nineteen thirties. In the nineteen forties they have been higher, but *not much* higher. This particular numismatic commodity is so well known, and its value is so well established that it resists the swings of the market.

In the Newcomb sale of February 7, 1945, there were fourteen common or near common 1794 cents in approximately AU-50 condition. Their average selling price was within a few cents of 55 dollars, and probably there will never be a better test of the cent market than the Newcomb sale—one of the most famous collections catalogued by perhaps the most respected cent dealer of the generation (Macallister).

We now have before us a few data bearing on the relationship between value and condition—not enough yet to frame a hypothesis, but enough to point the hope that a science of cent values may not be impossible. Paralleling the conventional graduation of condition, some sort of structure seems to exist which possibly can be developed into a usable scale of value. At any rate *Fair, Good, Fine,* and *About Uncirculated* 1794 cents show a history of reasonably constant respective values, and for these grades we find that *if the condition is known, the approximate value of the coin can in most cases be arrived at by multiplying a basal or unit value by a quantitative measure of condition.*

The Basal Value:
A FIRST POINT ON A SCALE FOR CONDITION AND VALUE

By the *basal value* of a given die is meant that value which during the second quarter of the present century has come to be attached to the coin in condition 1. When the basal value is a well-established one, a coin of the die can be appraised with tolerable accuracy by rating the condition on a quantitative 70-point scale and then multiplying the basal value by this quantitative rating.

The *Constant* in this formula is the basal value, and the

variable is the condition of the coin, expressed quantitatively. A tolerably accurate scale of value can be arrived at, then, if basal value and condition are known, and the basal value can be determined if a fairly good number of records of sales of the variety are available. In the text of Part II I have ventured to assign a basal value to every known collectible variety of the early cents.

The principal problem in setting up a science of cent values, aside from the need for experience and a degree of bookkeeping, resided in the difficulty of finding out just what different collectors and dealers have meant by the adjectives with which they have been accustomed to grade the condition of coins. One of the "tricks of the trade," of course, has always been to grade coins *up* when selling, and *down* when buying. Assume that a scale of values, as I have begun here to outline it, is now well established. There will still be opportunity for rich profit through chicanery of grading. Let us suppose a coin is at about condition 4. You buy it as *Very Fair* (condition 3), and you sell it as *About Fine* (condition 10, let us say).

There you have a nice profit of several hundred per cent, and the sucker gets the experience at no extra charge. But if the basal value of the coin had been known, and if the coin had been graded quantitatively, the fishing would have been more difficult, and therefore more fun. My object in writing this book, then, is not to *prevent* fishing but to make it more sporting.

Definition of Other Points on the Scale

Returning to the Scale of Condition, we need next to consider where the condition called *Very Good* (p. 41) falls in practice. This grade is used widely, and is usually defined as between *Good* and *Fine*. I used to assume that that meant *halfway* between, but such is not quite the case. Prices for *Very Good* cents fall nearer to *Good* than to *Fine,* and they can be pegged, on the average, at about seven times the basal value. Therefore we may define *Very Good* as that condition which falls at a point about three eighths of the distance along a scale between *Good* (the 4-coin) and *Fine* (the 12-coin). The *Very Good* coin, in my experience, is usually a 7-coin.

Very Fine, Extremely Fine, and *Mint State* have to be considered in relation to one another. The term *Very Fine* was first used, apparently, to refer to a coin just short of the perfect *Mint State*. But it was soon found that "just short of" can cover an astonishingly wide stretch of territory, and then the term *Extremely Fine* was introduced to describe a coin "really" just short of *Mint State*.

In practice, *Very Fine* and *Extremely Fine* have been used to refer to coins falling along a stretch of territory extending all the way from the 12-coin (*Fine*) to the perfect 70-coin. No wonder, then, that confusion has attached to these terms. In general, the early meaning of both grades was a distinctly higher one than it is now. These grades have "deteriorated" within the memory of the older generation of collectors. Reasons for this are doubtless complex, but certainly one factor has been that too much was asked of a couple of adjectives.

I have bought coins listed as EF which turned out to be very close indeed to MS (Mint State). As I write I have on my desk a 1795 cent, bought from Chapman a long time ago as VF, and it is just about a 60-coin. Beside it is another 1795 cent, recently bid in at auction, where it was listed as EF, and this is a 15-coin—barely better than the conventional *Fine*.

When the original Hays-Phelps collection of 1794 cents was catalogued for auction in March 1907 (by Lyman H. Low), each of the 57 pieces was graded according to the standards then prevailing. I now have 11 of these in my possession, all of which have been purchased within the past ten years, and *all* of which were offered as EF or better. Yet in 1907 only two of the 11 were called better than VF.

Despite such an inflationary shift in grading, the two terms in question seem recently to have settled at more stable respective levels. If we consider average prices paid for 1794 cents labeled VF during the second quarter of the century, the prices fall mostly at a point about 20 times the basal value. And during this same period the prices for EF have been just about twice that figure, or 40 times basal value. Common 1794 cents at the VF grade have brought 20 dollars on the average, and at the EF grade, 40 dollars. The conventional VF, then, is approximately a 20-coin, and the conventional EF may be called a 40-coin.

There remains a wide gap to account for between the EF-40 and the MS-70. In practice, much of the slack is taken up by various modifications, qualifications, stretchings, and constrictions of the term "Uncirculated." This is an unfortunate word in numismatic description, because it does not refer to *condition*, but describes behavior, or what the coin has (not) done. To state that a coin has not circulated tells nothing in particular about its condition, and that is doubtless one reason for the confusion arising from use of the term. A soft copper cent which has never been in circulation may be corroded, scratched, dented, discolored, even mutilated. Sometimes the term "cabinet friction" seems to cover all these misadventures, and more too. "About Uncirculated" has in practice been applied to anything from a 40-, or even a 30-, to a 65-coin. It might be better, at these higher levels of condition, if cataloguers could agree to drop the term "uncirculated" entirely, substituting quantitative designations which would indicate the degree of departure from Mint State.

The 40-coin, EF, is now a numismatic entity fairly well standardized by current usage. If you bid on such a coin at auction, you visualize a nearly perfect surface, with only the lightest touch of wear on the highest relief. You do not expect perfect mint color, but you do expect to be told what the color is. If there are any dents, scratches, or blemishes, you expect to be told exactly what they are, and where. Under a hand lens the EF surface may show, near or at the high points, some minute "hairline" scratches, but if the field or milling, or edge of the coin has any blemish whatever, you expect to be told about it. All this constitutes about the average standard for EF.

The conventional VF standard falls between EF and Fine, and somewhat nearer to the latter. On VF coins the little flat spot of wear "at the highest part of the hair" is expected to be present and perceptible to the unaided eye. The fine detail constituting the veins of the leaves on the reverse may be partly lost, although if this detail is *entirely* gone, the coin is probably not VF. If the leaves themselves are not sharply and boldly defined, the coin is not Fine but of a lower grade. In describing VF coins, the cataloguer is expected to list *all* dents, flaws, blemishes, and discolorations, as in the case of EF, although of course more of these are to be tolerated.

To help cover the territory between EF-40 and the perfect MS-70, I have found it convenient to designate three intermediate points on the Scale: AU-50, MS-60, and MS-65.

The MS-65 is a coin which would be a perfect MS-70 except for some small minor blemish. It may lack full mint luster, or some microscopic or almost negligible blemish may be demonstrable. There may be a spot of discoloration, a fingermark, or a single barely discernible nick.

The MS-60 is a Mint State or Strictly Uncirculated coin which nevertheless is not quite a "lustrous gem." It *must not* show wear, and its color will usually be the even light brown of a well-cared-for Mint State early copper cent. It may exhibit a slightly more conspicuous blemish of the sort just mentioned in connection with the MS-65. This coin is still *Mint State,* although not quite *perfect* Mint State.

The grades from MS-60 to MS-70 will in general include those coins over which cataloguers enthuse, calling them "brilliant uncirculated," "gem of the first water," "glittering cameo-like jewel," and so on. These are the *truly* top-grade coins, although when carefully examined they show minute differences, and sometimes the highest prices depend upon precisely such minute differences. As an average there is little price difference between MS-60 and MS-65; but once in a while, especially when two such coins are in the same sale, the latter will bring a price greatly disproportionate to the real difference that exists.

The grades MS-60, AU-50, and EF-40 represent hypothetically equal increments of wear or loss of perfection, as the coin descends from gem condition toward the lower categories. AU-50 is the grade to which cataloguers refer by the term About Uncirculated (AU). Such coins usually will show a faint trace of wear or "cabinet friction," or may have departed quite a little way from their original color. Tons of paper and barrels of ink have been used to tell prospective buyers just how beautiful and desirable these almost perfect coins are. The cataloguers get all tangled up in their descriptions and the collector must know his cataloguer well to make out whether the coin is a 40 or a 60. Yet from the point of view of value, the difference between 40 and 60 is quite as important as that between 0 and 20. To sell a 40-coin as a 60-coin should be a misdemeanor of the same magnitude as stealing a 20-coin.

Exact designation of the steps between EF-40 and MS-70 is verbally difficult but in practice is no more difficult than learning to throw or shoot accurately at targets of varying distance. For my own part, I have just about as clear a mental picture of AU-50 as I have of VF-20 or VG-7, but in the present book we need not further labor the question of verbalizing these arbitrary points on the scale. The idea I want to emphasize is that a whole continent of numismatic distance does exist between EF and Mint State. It probably can be mapped as accurately as the distance between Fair and EF has been mapped, and this may constitute one of the pleasant exercises in numismatics.

Poor and Proof

A word needs to be said concerning two numismatic conditions which I have hitherto avoided bringing into the discussion, namely *Poor* and *Proof*. Poor is a difficult term to define, because it often means too much. Frossard, Proskey, Chapman, and others used it for many years about as I have used the term Condition 1. Many of Chapman's *Poors* were in fact *Fair* or *Very Fair*—really attractive, evenly worn, aesthetically desirable pieces. I have several of them in my collection today, as the best obtainable examples of rare dies. The older dealers had still another category below *Poor*; called "junk," and including holed, mutilated, badly damaged, or unidentifiable coins—worth face value only, if that. Present-day cataloguers often apply the term *Poor* only to "junk," but a few of them adhere to the older meaning of "identifiable and not mutilated." As an average, it might be practicable to value *Poor* cents at about half the basal value, but anyone bidding on cents listed as *Poor* in present-day auction catalogues should be prepared for a shock.

Proof coins were never struck for circulation and therefore, strictly speaking, should not be regarded as coins at all. They belong rather in the class with medallic and ornamental pieces, which are struck on highly polished and specially prepared planchets. Proofs were first used as presentation pieces, principally for politicians, members of Congress, and the like. They were regarded as "polished up portraits" of the coinage. Now I for one prefer the honest and humble coinage itself. I find something artificially glittering about proofs—something suggestive of "pretense and prosperity." Proof cents do not appear until 1817, the year in which the Old Mint building was replaced by a new brick one and many new pieces of equipment were added, presumably including that for the special polishing of planchets.

For some time it has been the custom of certain dealers and cataloguers, in their ecstasy upon encountering an unusually attractive early cent, to indicate that it "might be called a proof," or "is almost a proof," or "has a proof surface," or "was struck as a proof." This is to be charged to enthusiasm, to lack of real knowledge of cents, and possibly to limitation of vocabulary.

Although there are no proofs before 1817, some of the early cents have a singularly lovely surface, as if the coiner had perhaps rubbed the planchet a little on his leather apron before dropping it into the press. As Mr. Proskey used to put it, "I can imagine that once in a while the press operator may have inadvertently rubbed a planchet back and forth on his apron as he finished a yarn." The early cents are to my way of thinking more attractive than proofs. Their surfaces always possess a personality of their own, some evidence of grain, granulation, or irregularity of relief. This is removed by the machining and polishing processes that are applied to proof dies and planchets.

From Definitions to a Point Scale Applicable to Both Value and Condition

Concerning the merits of a quantitative scale over the adjectival method of grading, I think we can afford to be almost dogmatic. Had standard quantitative gradings been in use for a few decades, the problem of establishing cent values accurately would now be a comparatively easy one. For what was a 12-coin in 1895 would still have been a 12-coin in 1945, and the question of value would have been simply the historical one of determining what the 12-coins of a particular variety have brought. But the term *Fine* had a different meaning in 1945 from what it had in 1895, or in 1915, and therefore old records of "prices brought" sometimes only confuse the picture. Standardization of a quantitative scale has long been an imperative need in numismatics.

TOWARD A SCIENCE OF CENT VALUES

TABLE 1. A QUANTITATIVE SCALE FOR CONDITION

Condition

1	BASAL STATE	*Identifiable* and *unmutilated*, but so badly worn that only a portion of the legend or inscription is legible. Enough must remain for positive identification of the variety, although for some varieties this need not necessarily include a readable date.
2	FAIR	The *date* and *more than half* of the inscription and detail can be made out, although perhaps faintly.
3	VERY FAIR	The *date will be clear* and *practically all* of the detail of the coin can be made out, although faint areas are to be expected, and the coin as a whole may be worn nearly smooth.
4 5 6	GOOD	The *date* together with *all of the detail* must be *very clear*. The general relief of the coin may be well worn down.
7 8 10	VERY GOOD	*Everything* is *boldly clear*, but the sharpness of the coin may be largely gone. Signs of wear are seen uniformly over the whole coin, not merely on the high surfaces.
12 15	FINE	*All of the design* and *all of the inscriptions* are *sharp*. Wear is appreciable only on the high surfaces. If the coin is examined with a glass, the *microscopic* detail is gone.
20 30	VERY FINE	*All the detail is in sharp relief*, and *only the highest surfaces show wear*, even when the glass is applied. The microscopic detail is largely intact except on the high points. These high surfaces will show a little rubbing, or flattening, even to the unaided eye.
40	EXTREMELY FINE	Only the *slightest trace* of *wear*, or of rubbing, is to be seen on the *high points*.
50	ABOUT UN-CIRCULATED	Close attention or the use of a glass should be necessary to make out that the coin is *not* in perfect Mint State. Typically, the AU-50 coin retains its full sharpness but is darkened or is a little off-color.

60	MINT STATE	*Free from any trace of wear*, and the color should be that of a copper coin which has been kept with great care. The color will vary from mint red to light brown or light olive, according to the chemical content and moisture of the prevailing atmosphere in which the coin has been kept. The light brown and light olive colors indicate the first beginnings of a protective patina, or surface "set." When these colors are attractively blended and permanently set on a Mint State early cent, the coin is as highly prized by discerning collectors as is one of brighter color. For condition 60 a minor blemish, perhaps some microscopic injury, or light trace of discoloration may be tolerated. For condition 70, the coin must be exactly as it left the dies, except for a slight mellowing of the color. Condition 60 means Mint State. Condition 70 means *perfect* Mint State.
65		
70		

NOTE. These descriptions are based on the supposition that no mutilations are present. Many cents have injuries, scratches, or bruises which of course detract from numismatic value and modify condition. Since there is no way of standardizing just how much a particular mutilation damages a coin, it is probably best to grade the coin *as if without* the injury, and then to list or describe the injury separately. This procedure is usually followed by cataloguers when the coin is of any importance or has any particular value. It should be noted that a number of the early varieties are always found with certain portions of the coin weak—a result of injured or bent dies. Such coins, even when in Mint State, will lack some of their detail. The cataloguer or student of coins must acquaint himself with these varieties and must learn to judge the condition of a particular cent according to the amount of actual wear after it left the dies. In this ability lies much of the skill and art of cent numismatics. The early cents present so many peculiarities and variations in the dies, as well as differences in striking and in later coloration of the copper, that even the keenest of observers could scarcely master them all in a lifetime of study.

A Scale for Rarity

One of the most neglected questions in the literature on cents is that of rarity. Competent students in the field have always been hesitant to express an opinion on the rarity of a die because they were aware of how easy it is to be mistaken. No one can ever know *for certain* just how many examples of a particular variety exist, since there is no way of canvassing the entire supply of cents in one lifetime. Also, there is always the possibility of a new "find," in which a whole kegful of a particular variety may turn up. This has happened. There is another good reason for caution. Some of the die varieties of which few examples are known resemble common varieties so closely that the difference is for years passed over without detection, and then when somebody "puts his neck out" that only three or four of the rare ones are believed to exist, along comes a nice old lady with half a dozen.

Crosby commented on the differential rarities of the 1793's only in the most general way, and nobody since Crosby's time has dealt systematically with rarity for this date. In consequence, when 1793's of any variety are offered, the collector is generally assured that the variety under consideration is "the rarest," or at least excessively rare. Chapman did pretty well on the rarities of the 1794's, although naturally he made mistakes. On the rest of the early dates, virtually no reliable data on rarity have been available. The Doughty ratings on rarity are entirely unreliable, while Clapp and Newcomb have been uncommunicative on the subject, merely pointing out that a few varieties *are* rare.

Rarity, then, will remain to some extent a matter of opinion, subject to revision in the light of further experience, and ratings on rarity should be accepted in charity for what they are, namely, an author's best guess on the subject. In that spirit I have attached rarity ratings to each of the known varieties of the early cents, and will let the ratings stand without further apology. No student of cents ever says that such-and-such a number of a variety "are known." He states simply that such-and-such a number have been reported or are known *to him*. The reader should realize, of course, that most of the errors arise from overrating, not from underrating rarity. If a coin is called rare, it may be common, but if it is called common, it almost certainly is not rare. If Jones was seen, he probably was there. If he wasn't seen, he still may have been there.

The Scale for Rarity which I use is a simple 8-point one with the various steps in the progression defined as in the following table. Note that the five highest degrees of rarity are quantitative, not merely adjectival.

TABLE 2. A SCALE FOR RARITY

R-1 COMMON
R-2 NOT SO COMMON
R-3 SCARCE
R-4 VERY SCARCE (Population estimated at 76-200)
R-5 RARE (31-75)
R-6 VERY RARE (13-30)
R-7 EXTREMELY RARE (4-12)
R-8 UNIQUE OR NEARLY UNIQUE (1, 2 or 3)*

* In this book R-8 will indicate that not more than three examples have been reported or are known outside of, or in addition to, the permanently impounded collection in the museum of the American Numismatic Society.

Value as Related to Care and Treatment

Since value is dependent on condition, it is important to protect copper cents against depreciation of condition. This can be done easily enough if two simple facts about copper will be borne in mind. First, it is a soft metal, easily dented, scratched, or bruised. Cents of fine condition should therefore never be jostled against one another, and they should never be handled over pavement or hard floors. They possess a genius for jumping out of people's hands under such circumstances, and the resulting dent is generally on the obverse edge in the most conspicuous spot, perhaps changing a 40-coin to a 20-coin. Always handle cents by their edges, and *over something soft*. It is best to keep them either in pasteboard display boxes made for the purpose or in individual coin envelopes.

Second, copper oxidizes or corrodes easily in certain atmospheres or in the presence of moisture, but it will not do so if kept clean and dry. If a copper cent is left by itself for some six months or a year, it will gradually accumulate on its surface a thin film of dirt, grease, and other impurities from the atmosphere. This will happen to some extent even in an envelope unless the coin is wrapped in tissue paper (jeweller's tissue is safest). If the film is left undisturbed on the copper surface for a sufficient length of time—depending on the chemical composition of this film and on the amount of moisture in the atmosphere—a chemical reaction with the copper will begin, color will change (darken), and eventually corrosion will appear. Once this has happened, nothing can be done about it except stop it from progressing by keeping the coin dry and clean.

Discoloration and corrosion cannot be undone, but they can be effectively prevented by either of two methods: (1) Wrapping the clean, dry coin in tissue paper and leaving it there. The surface will then remain unchanged as long as the tissue paper lasts—certainly for a century or two under ordinary conditions. (2) Thoroughly brushing the coin, or dusting it off lightly with a silk cloth, two or three times a year.

Jewelers have a brush which looks like a somewhat enlarged toothbrush and is made of No. 4 goat hair. This makes an ideal coin brush. Collectors who are fond of their cents and dislike to put them away in tissue paper will find that this second method of protection is fully as effective as the first. As a third alternative, if a man has some valuable cents and doesn't think enough of them to want to get them out to be brushed up a little and admired two or three times a year, he should sell them to a more appreciative owner.

At the moment there is quite a fad for coin holders with transparent celluloid slides, and for transparent (acetate) envelopes. This equipment is doubtless excellent for other kinds of coins, but it is not to be recommended for copper cents. The transparent envelopes in particular should be avoided. Assuming that the chemical composition of the material used is harmless to copper (not a perfectly safe assumption), the danger lies in the impermeability of such envelopes to moisture. They really are moisture traps. Moisture gets in but cannot readily get out. I have seen copper cents taken out of these envelopes, after a spell of rainy weather, in *wet* condition. In a few months they would have begun to corrode.

Many a cent has been ruined by an attempt to improve it. Amateurs, and some who are not so amateur, are forever trying to improve the condition or appearance of an old cent. Two methods are employed—tooling and coloring. In either case the result is usually disastrous. There are two circumstances which perhaps justify an effort to improve a cent artificially. One of these arises when you come into possession of one which has been transformed into a brassy nightmare by some well intended effort to "clean" it, perhaps with acid, or an eraser; or even with a buffing wheel (it has been done!). When this tragedy has happened the coin may be numismatically worthless unless it can be recolored and can again be made, to some extent, to look like old copper.

I say *to some extent*, for despite what you may be told there is no known way of perfectly simulating the natural color which results from slow aging of copper. The student of cents can invariably recognize a "tampered" coin, and he almost invariably will avoid buying it if he can get another, unspoiled, one of the variety. In the course of many years, however, a recolored coin sometimes tends to return gradually to a natural coppery appearance, and as it does so, its numismatic value returns also. Therefore if you have a rare cent which has been cleaned, perhaps the best thing to do will be first to experiment with some cheap or modern copper coins, and then try to recolor it. If it is of excessive rarity, send it to a professional cent recolorer, of whom there are four or five about the country.

There are a dozen or more everyday or "home" methods of trying to recolor cents, and none will be found very satisfactory. However, for what they are worth, here are a few of them:

(1) Make a mixture of one part fuller's earth with about ten parts ordinary sifted earth, add water, and knead into a sort of doughy biscuit. Insert the cent into this biscuit and bake it slowly in an oven for several hours or leave it on the back of the stove for a week. After the biscuit has slowly cooled, break it open, take out the cent, brush it lightly, and leave it in sunlight for several days. It will then *sometimes* take on a rather attractive, somewhat natural coppery color, usually with a faint and undesirable irridescence.

(2) Place aqueous ammonia in a small open vessel on a plate. Over the open vessel, but on the plate, invert an ordinary drinking glass or larger utensil. Within the inverted utensil you will then have an atmosphere of concentrated ammonia vapor. The cent should be held on some sort of makeshift rack within this vapor, for possibly an hour. The result will be an unattractive brownish color, which if allowed to deepen (by leaving the cent longer in the vapor) will take on a decidedly

unattractive reddish tinge. This method has been widely used for "improving" cents, and has spoiled more than its share of good specimens.

(3) Essentially the same method as the last can be employed, substituting powdered sulfur for the ammonia, but in this instance a degree of heat will be needed. The sulfur can be put into a perforated cardboard box, or ordinary salt shaker, and the whole apparatus then left on or near the radiator for a day or so. If the process is carried a little too far, the result will be a sort of dirty black color, but if watched closely, a kind of "dark irridescence" may be achieved which will take on a glossy polish when lightly brushed.

(4) A variation of the sulfur treatment is simply to rub the clean, dry coin lightly with a cotton pledget which has been dipped in powdered sulfur. This method has the advantage of extreme simplicity, and also one can watch the coin closely so as to observe exactly what is going on.

(5) A further variation of the sulfur method, particularly useful for "touching up" fresh scratches and similar minor injuries to color, is this: Place the coin between two pieces of old inner tube, under a weight of some sort, and leave in a warm place or over a radiator for a day or so. The rubber contains a small amount of sulfur. This is the slowest of the sulfur methods, and is likely to yield the most even result. But remember that the effect of sulfur, in the final analysis, is simply that of blackening copper.

(6) A method employed by several collectors (and dealers) of the older generation was that of wrapping up the coin in a small piece of flannel and, after attaching it to a sort of string belt, wearing it around the waist next to the skin for a matter of a few weeks. Dr. French used to say that this method was more efficacious in winter than in summer—winter underclothing holds the sweat better. The underclothing should of course under no circumstances be removed or changed until a satisfactory color has been achieved.

(7) Another method is simply to wrap the coin lightly in porous tissue paper and bury it in a flower pot filled with sifted earth. Water the earth from time to time. This experiment will generally require several weeks for good results, but will

yield perhaps the nearest obtainable approach to natural aging of copper. A somewhat similar procedure is that of simply exposing the coin to the sun and the weather for a few weeks.

The second circumstance in which an effort to improve a cent may occasionally be justified is that where some edge injury has left a jagged, projecting surface. I have seen cents considerably improved by having the roughened distortion tooled away, but this is to be recommended only for very rare pieces which cannot be duplicated, for the result will be by no means a perfect coin. There are two or three engravers in the country who have become skilful at such an art, but unfortunately these men are more often asked to attempt a kind of re-engraving of coins which is hopeless and ruinous. The most fatal mistake of all is to try to re-engrave the hair, or some other worn part. After a tragedy like that, the coin can be sold only as a mutilated specimen.

Another unfortunate mistake is that of trying to remove corrosion spots. The result is nearly always a spot of a more damaging nature (showing tool marks), or perhaps mutilation of a wide area of the surface of the coin, followed by disastrous polishing down or buffing and recoloring. So many such attempts have been made, through the past century, that there is quite a large population of mutilated and buffed cents in numismatic circulation. Dealers who know cents, if they are honest, sell these only as what they are—mutilated coins. Collectors who find that they have purchased such a coin at auction or elsewhere, without it being so specified, should return the coin promptly, for it is almost as much of a crime to *encourage* the mutilation of a coin as to take part in it.

For removing dirt from the surface of a cent Xylol is effective and harmless. If none is at hand, use warm water and soap, with a soft hand brush or old tooth brush. If this method fails boil the cent, for not more than a few seconds, in a dish of water to which a teaspoonful of ordinary baking soda has been added. This treatment will remove all ordinary dirt, and some waxes, but if continued for long it will change the color of the cent, *particularly* if the cent has been artificially colored. (One of the old standard tests for true patina on ancient bronze coins is that of boiling the coin in soda. If the coin has been artificially colored—and is therefore presumably a fake—the alleged patina will ordinarily disappear quickly, but a true ancient patina is said to stand such treatment for hours.)

Concerning the value of old cents, a good maxim to remember is that in general value can be improved rarely and with great difficulty; but it can be lessened with no trouble at all.

In summary, although a literature now exists which includes identification of the known varieties of the early cents, it is a difficult literature to get at, and at least the minimal essentials for identification of every known variety will therefore be included in the sections which follow. The alternative nomenclatures in current use are presented, with emphasis placed on the Crosby numeral-and-letter method of designation. An effort is made here to impart the rudiments of a science of cent values through the use of standardized scales both for condition and for rarity. In the text I have made bold to hazard a guess as to the *basal value* of each variety discussed. The basal value is not intended to represent the highest or peak price for which a coin may have sold; but rather a *fair value* for the present day, based on what the market for the coin has been, on the average, during the second quarter of the century.

Collectibles and Noncollectibles

Of the Early Cents 331 true varieties or obverse-reverse combinations are now known and are herein described. However, not all of the 331 are collectible in the sense of being available to collectors, or in the sense that a collector would have a reasonable chance of being offered one in the course of his lifetime. Fourteen of the varieties are unique in that each is known by only a single example, and eight of these fourteen unique coins are now in the museum of the American Numismatic Society; they are permanently off the market. Five other varieties are known by but two examples each, and seven varieties are represented by three examples each, with only two of the three specimens in collectors' hands.

Such practically unobtainable varieties need to be set apart and listed separately. In EAC they were given the designation

NC for Noncollectible. A watchful collector will now and then encounter an opportunity to acquire one of these NC's and there lies one of the rarest thrills of cent hunting, but by and large the NC's will remain uncollectible and the cent hunter will be happier in the long run to leave them off his want list.

In EAC the term NC was standardized to mean precisely this: That the writer and his collaborators did not know of the existence of as many as three examples of the variety in numismatic circulation, i.e. in collectors' hands. A noncollectible variety was one of which no more than two examples were available to collectors. In EAC we listed 32 NC varieties. We hoped that the continuing hunt for cents would presently render some of these no longer noncollectible, and indeed it has. Enough new specimens of nine of the 32 varieties have been found to remove these nine from the list of Noncollectibles (the details will be given in the text as each variety is discussed). The question soon arose, how best to designate the varieties which, formerly on the list of Noncollectibles, had later achieved their necessary quorum of at least three examples in collectors' hands and therefore were now to be regarded as Collectibles. The problem was how to make such a designational change without breaking into the already established straight-through list of the collectible varieties.

An acceptable solution was readily at hand. When it became known that three specimens of an NC variety were now in collectors' hands, we simply italicized the NC, and this *NC* we read as Now Collectible instead of Noncollectible. Thus when you encounter the listing *NC*-1 of 1796 you know immediately that the variety was originally designated a Noncollectible, but that now three or more of its coins are known to be in collectors' hands. So it is a Now Collectible.

Nine of the original 32 NC's have become Now Collectibles. One more, NC-6 of 1796, has turned out to be a hoax or fraudulent coin. That leaves 22 of the original NC's. To these, five new NC's have been added: two new 1794 varieties and one sub-variety, a new 1797 variety, and a new 1801 variety. So in addition to the original collector's list of 295 varieties and six sub-varieties, there are now nine *NC*'s and 27 NC's.

The great advantage in listing the NC's separately for each

year is that when a new variety is discovered, the new discovery takes its place in the NC list for that date without disrupting or in any way affecting the straight-through list of established Collectibles. Thus for 1794, when EAC was written, there were 56 Collectibles and three NC's. The Collectibles were given permanent serial numbers, from No. 17 through No. 72. Meanwhile a new variety and a new sub-variety of 1794 have been found. These are presently listed as NC-4 and NC-5.

The Condition Census

In the text of Part Two the known varieties of Early Cents are presented in their serial order. The first line of each descriptive sketch includes the serial number (or the NC number), the obverse-reverse designation, and usually some characteristic feature of both obverse and reverse by which the variety can be quickly recognized. The obverse is then described in full; and the reverse; and the principal obverse and reverse die break variations that have been noted for the variety. The final paragraph of the sketch gives the rarity rating (R), the basal value (Basal), the condition census, and perhaps some brief comment on the variety or on some of its famous examples. To follow our reasoning in trying to objectify the numismatic value of a coin, it is necessary first to understand what is meant by the term condition census.

For an example, take No. 66 of 1794 (p. 126). The condition census is 35-15 (35-30-20-15-12-10). This is simply a mnemonic summary of the following information: (1) The finest example of the variety known to the writer or to his collaborators is now believed to merit a condition grading of VF-35. (2) The *average* condition of the *next five* finest coins of this variety, to the best of our present knowledge, is about F-15. (3) In detail, the six finest coins of Variety 66, listed in descending order of condition, are VF-35, VF-30, VF-20, F-15, F-12, and VG-10. It cannot be too often repeated that research in such a field as this will never be perfectly complete. We will never be quite *certain* that the six coins listed are actually the six finest of the variety. It is in fact this element of uncertainty that lends much of the charm to the study of Early Cents. The goal is not to become certain, but to try to get the condition census a little more nearly correct as time goes on.

Consider another example. The condition census for No. 71 is 55-45 (55-50-50-50-45-40). It will be recognized at a glance that here is a variety with at least a half dozen excellent coins available but without a known representative in full Mint State; that is to say, without a coin between MS-60 and MS-70. The finest known to us is graded AU-55 but there are at least three more that challenge this one closely and one would correctly suppose that when it comes to assigning values to the best coins of the variety there will be no very sharp differential among the first half dozen.

The variety following No. 71 is NC-3 of 1794. Here the condition census reads 8-0, meaning that the coin is unique and in condition VG-8. NC-1 of the same year has the condition census 3-3 (3-3-3), meaning that only three examples are known and all of them are at condition 3, or Very Fair. Turning to the variety now listed as *NC*-1 of 1796 (p. 160), we find the condition census 30-12 (30-15-12-12-6). Since only five are listed in the condition census, this means that only five are known, but the italicized *NC* (Now Collectible) indicates that some of these five must have come to light since EAC was written.

The condition census offers to a scientifically inclined student a basis for objective calculation of a coin's true numismatic value. It tells him just how rare the coin is in its upper range of condition, and gives him a measuring device for comparison with the known top level coins of the variety. With rarity, condition census and basal value known, a student of cents has only to be certain of the correct condition grading of a coin in order to assign it a numismatic value, or price, which should then be objective within the limits of human error, and should not vary much from one individual to another.

Estimation of Value

In EAC the calculation of value for a coin was presented as simply a matter of multiplying the basal value by the condition, numerically expressed. Thus a 50-coin, which is a coin of about AU-50 condition, might have a basal value of $1. It would then possess a value rating, or book rating, of $50. Even in the earlier book we noted that there were circumstances which would give some coins a higher book rating, and these special circumstances were referred to under the general heading of Pedigree Premium, or excess value beyond the simple formula, *Condition × Basal Value.* We then conceived of Pedigree Premium as deriving largely from the known history and fame of a particular coin; or in some instances from the fame of a particular variety, such as one of the 1799's. It was noted that certain famous coins, and especially some of the finest known examples of famous varieties, sold regularly at prices well in excess of their simple book rating as calculated by the formula just given.

EAC was written during the middle nineteen forties. By 1950 it was evident that an inflationary tide was affecting the price of Early Cents and that the coins of highest condition were being affected more markedly than those of the middle and lower condition ratings. In the calculation of value we began to make special allowances, first to Mint State coins, and later to other coins of high condition even when not Mint State. It was by now apparent that the finest coins of all varieties were bringing prices in excess of their book ratings. Gradually it became necessary to raise basal values a little, too, on nearly the whole list of Early Cents. The original basal values had been calculated from prices prevailing during the second quarter of the century. That period, taken as a whole, was also a period of inflation, but that was an inflation sharply interrupted by the retrenchment of the early thirties, and inflation of Early Cent values was not very manifest until the late nineteen forties, after EAC was written.

It has been difficult to stay abreast of the tide and to keep basal values currently revised during the more recent period of "managed inflation" or progressive economic degradation of our culture. When EAC was written, most of the collectors felt that the basal values were a little high. Mr. George Clapp, who at that time owned the largest collection of Early Cents, was good enough to read the manuscript of that book. He said, "The basal value is an excellent concept without any doubt, but you have got the values 25 per cent too high." Those values were in fact about 10 per cent in excess of prices realized at the Newcomb sale in 1945. However, we were just then entering a stage of violent acceleration of the inflationary spiral, and by 1952 the now explosive economic malignancy had fully caught up with the EAC basal values. The book ratings for the Downing collection, in 1952, totaled almost exactly $20,000. The coins realized $20,200.

Meanwhile, during the half decade since Downing's sale, there is no doubt that the inflationary disease has further flourished. We are in a far-advanced stage of an economic illness which is of course also a social and a political illness. The illness carries with it a prevailing social philosophy of self-perpetuation; that is to say, perpetuation of the illness and thereby postponement of an ultimate crisis, or reckoning, for as long as the toboggan ride can be made to last—at any rate "for our time" at all costs.

In brief, the prevailing philosophy throughout the country today is that of Dionysian inflation. Dancing to Bacchanalian music, this population progresses along an inflationary spiral whose end point can hardly be other than a jumping-off point. In the face of the tidal surging of so vast a human population, itself now caught also in a biological inflation of numbers, in the face of this current human circumstance there would be little point in merely republishing the basal values which seemed correct a decade ago. The aim of the present book is not to attempt to halt the inflation by thus ignoring it, but to reflect its progress in the field of cents as accurately and faithfully as we can.

In 1954, for the purpose of cataloguing the "Dupont" collection for a New York dealer, WHS worked out a new trial set of basal values which were calculated to reflect the progress of the inflation at that time. For that sale, coins known to belong in the Condition Census—the first half dozen—for a variety were given an extra premium. The premium was derived simply by multiplying the book rating by $1\frac{1}{2}$. This plan worked out quite well except that in those few instances where we were dealing with a coin near the *top* of the condition census list, that is to say, with one of the two or three finest known of a variety, there was a tendency for the bidding to stampede to even higher levels. In the cases where that collection offered what was actually the finest known coin of a variety, the selling point seemed usually to be reached at just about three times the uncorrected book rating (*Condition*×*Basal Value*). In those two or three cases where the coin offered was not only finest known but also Mint State, the selling level was about four times the uncorrected book rating. It was found, too, that *all* Mint State coins were in stronger demand than the uncorrected book rating would indicate, and the selling level for these Mint State coins, apart from any condition census state, turned out to lie usually at about twice the uncorrected book rating.

These clues led to some hypotheses, and the hypotheses led to a very careful re-examination of the records of cent transactions and auctions during the past several decades. To shorten the story, out of this has emerged a set of rules which appear to meet nearly all of the contingencies likely to be encountered in trying to affix to an Old Cent an accurate prediction of present market value. These rules are dependent only upon an accurate knowledge of the condition census of the variety in question, upon the use of a basal value which truly reflects the current market, and of course on accurate grading of condition. The book has done its best toward standardizing the criteria for grading condition; the condition censuses given here are accurate so far as our present knowledge reaches; the basal values appear to be about right for the year 1958. We are ready, then, to write down some rules for calculating the numismatic value of a cent:

1. If the cent is not one of the first half dozen of its variety, and is not MS-60 or better, Value equals Condition times Basal Value.
2. If finest reported of the variety, but not full MS, Value equals Condition times Basal Value times 3.
3. If known to be No. 2 of the variety, and not full MS, Value equals Condition times Basal Value times 2½.
4. If known to be No. 3 of the variety, and not full MS, Value equals Condition times Basal Value times 2.
5. If known to be in the first half dozen but not among the first three, and not full MS, Value equals Condition times Basal Value times 1½.
6. If known to stand alone as the finest reported of the variety, and full MS, Value equals Condition times Basal Value times 4.

7. If known to be No. 2 of the variety, and full MS, Value equals Condition times Basal Value times 3.
8. If known to be No. 3 of the variety, and full MS, Value equals Condition times Basal Value times $2\frac{1}{2}$.
9. If full MS-60 or better, but not known to be among the first three, Value equals Condition times Basal Value times 2.
10. If tied for honors with one or more other coins, simply calculate what the total value of these coins would be when placed in descending order of rank as if there were no tie, and divide by the number of tied coins.

With these ten rules it is possible to make an accurate book rating on the value of any coin if the basal value is at hand, and basal values are now included in the text for all varieties of which at least two examples are known to be in collectors' hands. Thus even the NC varieties have now been given basal values, except those that are unique or unique in collectors' hands.

For illustrative examples in the calculation of book ratings, consider the six coins in the condition census for variety No. 12 of 1793. The condition census is 50-12-10-8-6-5. This is an easy one, with no ties. By our rules the 50-coin has a book rating of $50 \times \$20 \times 3$, \$3,000; the 12-coin $12 \times \$20 \times 2\frac{1}{2}$, \$600; the 10-coin $10 \times \$20 \times 2$, \$400; the 8-coin $8 \times \$20 \times 1\frac{1}{2}$, \$240; the 6-coin $6 \times \$20 \times 1\frac{1}{2}$, \$180; the 5-coin $5 \times \$20 \times 1\frac{1}{2}$, \$150.

Now do the same for No. 13, whose condition census is 55-55-50-45-45-45. The two 55-coins have similar ratings of $55 \times \$12.50 \times 2\frac{3}{4}$, \$1890.63; the 50-coin, $50 \times \$12.50 \times 2$, \$1250; each of the three 45-coins, $45 \times \$12.50 \times 1\frac{1}{2}$, \$843.75.

Lastly, turn to No. 78, with its condition census of 70-70-65-65-65-65. Here the condition census correction, for the two 70-coins, would be $3\frac{1}{2}$ (rules 6 and 7), and the book listing would be $70 \times \$1 \times 3\frac{1}{2}$, \$245; for the four 65-coins the condition census correction would be $2\frac{1}{8}$ (rules 8 and 9). In this last instance the book rating for each coin would be $65 \times \$1 \times 2\frac{1}{8}$, \$138.13. No doubt the reader will by now have noticed that ordinarily it is a little easier first to multiply the basal value by the correction, and then to multiply this product by Condition, than to go about it the other way around.

These rules have emerged from a best effort to reflect the Early Cent market for 1958—not this market as the writer would like it or wishes it to be but the market as it actually is at just the present point in time. It is an inflation market and therefore one which before long will destroy itself. For it lives and progresses by debasement of its own substance, the money unit. In the final collapse one of the items to deflate most precipitantly will be precisely such a commodity as old coins, with copper coins perhaps leading the return parade to earth. The rules just presented are not therefore particularly recommended as safe buying guides. They represent only an attempt to define a situation. Perhaps an eleventh rule should be added: Do not invest more in any luxury, such as an old penny, than you feel you can good-humoredly afford to lose. And just one more kindly thought. When a prospective seller uses a magic term like "finest known," or "third finest" or something of the sort, and puts an estimate of a thousand dollars on a coin, make sure that the man's personal integrity is worth your thousand before you part with it.

PART TWO

The Early Cents, 1793-1814

1793

THE THREE GENERAL CLASSES OF CENTS ISSUED DURING 1793 ARE known as *Chain, Wreath,* and *Liberty Cap* cents. The obverse-reverse nomenclature of the varieties for this date will here follow Crosby exactly, and no designations other than Crosby's are now being used to any appreciable extent.

THE CHAIN CENTS

General Description
Obverse: Head of Liberty facing right. Outline of the face delicate, with faint relief for the entire obverse. Forehead low and markedly receding. Hair dishevelled "as though facing a gale." Bust short, ending in a point. Above the head, the legend LIBERTY. Below, the date. **Reverse:** The words $\substack{\text{ONE}\\\text{CENT}}$ and the fraction $\frac{1}{100}$ within an endless chain of fifteen links, the whole encircled by the legend UNITED STATES OF AMERICA (or UNITED STATES OF AMERI.). The entire reverse is nearly always more strongly struck than the obverse. The edge bears in four unequal alternate sections bars and a slender vine with leaves. The planchets are thick; size varying from 25 to 28 mm. Obverse and reverse rims are plain and usually are a little raised.

1	1·A	Wide Date
		AMERI.

Obverse 1. The *Wide Date* obverse. *Widest date among the Chain cents.* Width of date at bottom, just over 9 mm. Widest spacing between 7 and 9.

1 7 9 3

Reverse A. *The word* AMERICA *in the legend is abbreviated to* AMERI. Fraction bar equally distant from the numerator and from the ciphers of the denominator. The AMERI. (Am er eye) reverse.

Die break variations. *Reverse:* Found perfect and with crack over TATE. Two or three examples known with heavy rim break over TAT. One of these is now in the ANS collection. On many specimens there is a slight bulge or mound under 1 of date, and over U of UNITED.

R-4. Basal $10. 60-50 (60-50-50-50-45-45). Still one of the most prized American coins, and common enough that any seriously enamoured collector can count on acquiring one. Probably in the lower or middle range of R-4, which would mean that the known population for the variety is well over 100 but perhaps less than 200. The Mickley-Hall-Brand-Pearl coin remains unquestionably the finest presently known. On being properly brushed it was revealed as a full MS-60. The former grading on this piece (AU-50), was made from an imperfect photograph. Among the other coins in the finest half dozen seen—the condition census half dozen—there does not appear to be a really good claimant for second honors. At least three can be called 50-coins but we have not seen a 55.

2	1·C	Wide Date
		AMERICA

Obverse 1.

Reverse C. *The word* AMERICA *in the legend is spelled out in full.* The fraction bar is high and relatively distant from the denominator, while the figures of the fraction are smaller than those of Reverse A. The *Perfect* reverse.

Die break variations. None seen.

R-4. Basal $8.50. 60-50 (60-55-55-55-50-45). Slightly rarer than the 1-A but more often seen in the better condition states. Certainly less rare than the 1-A as a VF coin, possibly because the obverses are more boldly struck. The Beckwith-French example remains the only 60-coin seen but at least three more are in 55 condition and the half dozen best of this variety are a little finer and sharper, as a group, than the corresponding half dozen 1-A's.

[62]

1 7 9 3

NC·1   2·C   Wide LIBERTY

Obverse 2. Width of LIBERTY at the top, 17 mm. LIBERTY *more widely spaced than on any other 1793 cent*, and lower than on any other Chain cent. The B is less than 0.5 mm. from the hair. *A lock of hair almost touches 1 of the date*—a feature easily distinguishing this obverse from obverse 3, which it somewhat resembles.

Reverse C.

Die break variations. *Obverse:* On the only specimen seen, there is a small crack from the border, across the figure 1 to the rim.

R-8. Unique. 50-0. The only example positively known was discovered in England in 1889 and was sold to Dr. Hall. Thence to the Brand collection, and to Clapp for ANS in 1942. There have been recurrent rumors of a second one, Poor or Fair, and such a coin was catalogued in a Chapman sale in 1906, but to date all trails have led only to well-worn examples of one of the other Chain cents.

3·B

The coin described in Crosby as a 3-B was altered from a 3-C by tooling away the last two letters of AMERICA and adding a crude period. This coin is now in the ANS collection, along with a "1-B," similarly altered from a 1-C.

3   *3·C*   The Leaning R
                AMERICA

Obverse 3. Width of LIBERTY at the top, just over 16 mm. *Letters of LIBERTY irregular in both size and position. The R is large, high, and leans to the right.* The seven lower locks are relatively long, and the nearest one is almost 2 mm. from the 1 of the date. The date, which measures 7 mm. at the bottom, is nearer to the point of the bust than to the hair.

Reverse C.

Die break variations. None seen. Incused outlines of links of the chain from the reverse are often seen in front of the mouth and throat and under the neck. These have sometimes been called "suction marks." Their probable cause is injury to the

1 7 9 3

dies resulting from the obverse and reverse dies meeting with no planchet between them—an accident of apparently frequent occurrence.

R-3. Basal $7. 65-50 (65-55-55-50-50-50). Commonest Chain cent and probably half of the Chains are of this variety. However, there are not as many of them at the highest levels of condition as seemed to be the case ten years ago. The Cleneay-Jackman-Ryder coin, MS-65, still holds top honors, but re-examination of all the other "good ones" available has failed to confirm the existence of even one other full MS example.

4   4·C   **Periods Variety**
                                  AMERICA

Obverse 4. *Both* LIBERTY *and the date are followed by a period,* and both are closely spaced. L and B are low; LI very close.

Reverse C.

Die break variations. *Obverse:* Found perfect and with a break behind and below the lower locks, growing progressively heavier.

R-4. Basal $9. 65-50 (65-60-55-45-45-40). Certainly the second most sought after of the Chain cents, and second rarest of the collectibles. Probably the Hall-Hines piece, MS-65 and in almost full mint brilliance, holds top honors. This is the coin pictured on the Crosby plate. It has a very close second in the Brand-Pearl-Clarke coin, MS-60 and of full mint sharpness although of darker color. The Lyman-Würtzbach-ANS piece is about AU-55.

The Chain cents, now among the most beloved of American numismatic treasures, were a target for much abuse in their day. Crosby quotes the following from a letter which was published in a Philadelphia paper on March 18, 1793: "The American cents do not answer our expectations. The chain on the reverse is but a bad omen for liberty, and liberty herself appears to be in a fright. May she not justly cry out in the words of the Apostle, 'Alexander the coppersmith hath done [Crosby changes it to *did*] me much evil: the Lord reward him according to his works!' " And Stewart (p. 106) adds another

1 7 9 3

gem, this one an excerpt from a letter written by a Mr. Carlisle Pollack to General Williams: "Nothing can be more wretched. . . . A plow and a sheaf would be better than an idiot's head with flowing hair which was meant to denote liberty, but which the world will suppose was intended to designate the head of an Indian squaw." Present day cent collectors would scarcely concur.

THE WREATH CENTS

General description

Obverse: Head of Liberty to the right. The head has stronger, better defined outlines than are seen on the Chain cents. Point of bust long, slender, and curving downward. Hair in heavy, detached masses terminating in pointed locks. Above, the legend LIBERTY. Below, the date. Between the bust and the date is a sprig of three leaves on a stem. **Reverse:** Within a wreath formed by two curving branches of laurel, ornamented with sprays of berries and trefoils, and tied together at the bottom with a ribbon, are the words $\frac{ONE}{CENT}$. In the exterior angle formed by the ribbon ends, the fraction. Around the wreath, the legend UNITED STATES OF AMERICA.

Around the extreme border of both obverse and reverse is a continuous circle of small pellets or beads. The edge device is the same as that on the Chain cents, except that some examples of one variety (11-J) show on the edge, in place of the vine and bars, the inscription ONE HUNDRED FOR A DOLLAR.

NC·2   5·D $\frac{\text{Strawberry Leaf Variety}}{\text{ONE CENT CENTRAL}}$

Obverse 5. Instead of a sprig of three pointed, ovate leaves between the bust and the date, such as appear on all of the other obverses of this class, there is a spray of three trefoil leaves, resembling strawberry or possibly clover leaves, and a blossom or (as Crosby believes) a boll of cotton. This is the *Strawberry Leaf* obverse.

Reverse D. $\frac{ONE}{CENT}$ is central in the wreath, C of Cent low, and T rather high. The ribbon is heavy and forked at its ends.

1 7 9 3

The fraction is high and central in the space between the ribbon ends.

Die break variations. None seen.

R-8. Unique. 1-0. Still known by only a single example, condition 1. This coin was in the Hall collection, was afterward owned by Brand, and later by a succession of collectors. It was last sold with the Williams collection in 1950. The unique Strawberry Leaf cent.

NC·3   5·E   Strawberry Leaf Variety
                ONE CENT HIGH

Obverse 5.

Reverse E. ONE/CENT is high in the wreath, and the letters NT of CENT are rather low. The bow is higher, narrower, and more heart shaped than that of the D reverse. The ribbon is much lighter, with its ends shorter and less forked. The fraction is low, and a little to the right.

Die break variations. None seen.

R-8. Basal $35. 7-3 (7-3-3). Second Strawberry Leaf. Now assigned a basal value, since at least two are known to be in collectors' hands, and this basal of $35 is exceeded only by that of the more famous Liberty Cap 14-K. Only the three previously reported examples of 5-E have been seen by any of us. Rumors of one or two more float about but to date these have led only to the examination of electrotypes. Probably the finest of the variety is the one sometimes called the Parmelee-Staples piece, about VG-7. The Crosby-Hall coin, condition 3, was given to ANS by J. S. Saltus in 1916. The Rabin example, found in Philadelphia by Mr. Rabin, is rough and blackened but perhaps can be rated condition 3 also. If another 5-E turns up, this will become a collectible variety and the basal value will doubtless fall.

Speculation over these strawberry leaf, or clover leaf, or cotton leaf coins has been extensive. Crosby apparently regarded them as true "cents," since he included them with the regular series, and most of the present generation of collectors have followed Crosby. Dr. Hall regarded them as patterns,

1 7 9 3

presumably as discarded patterns for the wreath cents, and he placed "little value" on the pair which he owned. S. H. Chapman thought they should be classed as patterns, and should therefore be omitted from the cent series. They may have been struck from trial or experimental dies made *after* the first Wreath cents were coined, but there seems to me to be no good reason for supposing that these pieces were ever issued from the Mint for circulation as cents. There is no indication of failure or breaking of the dies, hence little likelihood of their having been discarded *because of use*. In 1944, J. G. Macallister expressed himself as "highly sceptical" about the strawberry leaf coins, but thought it would be a fine idea to get all of them together and examine them at one time. He seemed to feel that they might be counterfeit since too little of any one of them can be seen for us to be quite certain that they are *not* counterfeit.

For what one guess is worth, I suggest that these coins might have been struck from experimental dies which for some reason were not accepted. If such a view is correct, the coins are not, strictly speaking, cent collectors' items. At any rate, they should not be looked upon by the variety collector as something he "ought to have" to complete his series.

5   6·F   The Large Date
                      SMALL HEAVY BOW

Obverse 6. The letters of LIBERTY are large, nearly filling the space between head and border. All of the other obverses of the wreath cents have LIBERTY in small letters. Width of LIBERTY at the top, a little over 15 mm. Date also large, and nearer to the point of the bust than to the hair. *It is the only large date and the only large* LIBERTY *among the Wreath cents.* The stem of the sprig is almost in a straight line with the upright of the 7.

Reverse F. ONE/CENT rather high in the wreath, with the center dot at the exact center of the word CENT. *The bow is smaller and heavier than on any other reverse among the big cents.* The ribbon is broad and heavy. The left stem lies very close to the ribbon throughout its length. The clear space within the bow measures about 1.5 mm. by 0.5 mm. The fraction is low and central, with a long bar. The legend is very close to the border, and this is the *only reverse having three trefoils on each branch.*

Die break variations. *Obverse:* Found perfect and with die broken over BER and LI, the perfect die being slightly the more scarce.

R-4. Basal $8. 65-60 (65-65-65-60-60-55). Probably in the lower range of R-4. Sometimes called the most beautiful Wreath cent. At least five are known in full Mint State, MS-60 or 65, but among them there is no one coin which stands out, or stands alone for first honors. Certainly three of the 6-F's can be called MS-65—these are the Winsor-Bement-ANS coin, the Hall-Brand-Pearl coin, and the Hall-Sisson-Hines coin. At least four that are MS-60 or better are in collectors' hands. This is true, we believe, of no other 1793 variety except the common 9-H.

6   7·F   **The Sprung Die**
<u>SMALL HEAVY BOW</u>

Obverse 7. The head closely resembles No. 6, but the hair is more massive, and in heavier tresses. LIBERTY and the date are small. Width of LIBERTY at the top, 11.5 mm. The date is about 1 mm. from the hair, and far from the point of the bust. I of LIBERTY is high and leans to the left. The R is large, and Y is about over the junction between hair and forehead. The 7 of the date is small and lightly cut. The left leaf of the sprig almost touches the double curl at the back of the neck, and also nearly touches the lowest strand of hair.

Reverse F.

Die break variations. *Obverse: There is always a bulge or convexity on the obverse, running from back of the hair to the rim,* and this is so prominent a hallmark of the 7-F that the variety can be recognized at a glance. It is supposed that the die was a little "sprung," or "caved," and the 7-F has long been known as the *Sprung Die* variety. On some specimens the convexity is very prominent, appearing also in the right field as a slight line or ridge from the mouth to the border. *Reverse:* On some specimens there is a short break through TE of UNITED.

1 7 9 3

R-3. Basal $7.50. 70-55 (70-65-60-55-55-50). Probably not quite R-4 but in the upper range of R-3. The Hall-Beckwith-French coin, one of the two most perfect Wreath cents known, is considered MS-70. The Bement-ANS coin is MS-65, and a third mint state example, MS-60, turned up in a remnant of the Brand collection that was marketed in 1951. At least three more between MS-60 and AU-50 are in collectors' hands.

7 8·F The Faint Curl
<u>SMALL HEAVY BOW</u>

Obverse 8. The double curl in the angle between the lower locks and the neckline of the bust is *very faint* and can scarcely be seen at all unless the coin is Fine. *The lowermost part of this curl joins with the tip of the left leaf of the sprig.* On all other varieties the curl is conspicuous, and in no other instance does the lower part of the curl touch the leaf. The stem of the sprig starts about a full millimeter above and to the left of the 9 and curves enough to point nearly at the upper right corner of the 7. *The left leaf of the sprig is wider than the center leaf, while the right leaf, smaller and narrower than either, is of scarcely half the width of the left one.* This obverse could be confused only with obverse 10, on which all three of the leaves are narrow (and the left very long).

Reverse F.

Die break variations. *Obverse:* On all examples known the die has sunk a little at the date, leaving a swell, or raised area, which tends to weaken the last three figures. By this characteristic the coin can be readily recognized. *Reverse:* Usually seen with a light break through TE of UNITED.

R-6. Basal $15. 50-20 (50-40-20-20-20-12). There has been a shower of new "finds" in this variety. Ten years ago we knew of eight examples. Now six more have turned up, making a total of 14, thus automatically dropping the rarity from R-7 to R-6. But the basal value has been held at $15 despite the drop in rarity. It was felt that the general advance in prices might about offset the loss in rarity. The Winsor-Hall coin, far the finest of the 8-F's, turned out to be AU-50. The Macallister-ANS piece is EF-40. The Proskey-Hines coin is now rated VF-

1 7 9 3

20 and two of the newly discovered ones are also VF-20.

8   9·G   The Horizontal Stem
<u>HIGH TRIANGULAR BOW</u>

Obverse 9. On this obverse the *stem of the sprig, which is slightly curved, parallels the top of the date,* and since the stem points downward on all of the other Wreath cent obverses, this single characteristic is sufficient for identification. The 7 of the date is taller than the other figures.

Reverse G. *The upper trefoil on the outside of the left branch of the wreath is under the first* T *of* STATES (no trefoil seen here on any other reverse). *The bow is heavy, high, and almost triangular,* in contrast with the lighter, more rounded bow of reverse H. The very long fraction bar, which is also curved, almost touches both ribbon ends. This reverse has been called the *Triangular Bow* reverse.

Die break variations. *Obverse:* A faint crack is usually seen from the point of the bust to the border. Sometimes a short crack runs from the left top of Y to the border, another from the left top of R, and still another from the top of B to the border. When this obverse is combined with the G reverse, the 9 and 3 of the date are poorly formed or partially broken down, there are heavy "suction marks," and several other small imperfections may be noted. *Reverse:* Always found with a rather delicate break, and sometimes with a sort of bulge, extending almost straight across the coin, from the first T of STATES to the last A of AMERICA, and running through the center dot.

The 9-G variety was clearly the result of a second marriage for the obverse, and the 9-G and 9-H should have been presented in the reverse order (as Crosby himself realized after writing the text).

R-3. Basal $7. 65-55 (65-60-60-55-55-50). Of just about the same rarity as the 7-F but never quite so highly prized, perhaps because of its association with the commoner 9-H. The most perfect 9-G appears to be the Crosby-Hall-French cent, MS-65. The Hall-Brand cent and the Frossard-Hines piece are both about MS-60. At least three more fall between the 60 level and the 50 level.

1 7 9 3

9   9·H   Horizontal Stem
                      ―――――――――――
                      LARGE ROUND BOW

Obverse 9.

Reverse H. There are two trefoils on each branch of the wreath, and *all four of the trefoils are directly in line with the word* CENT. The fraction bar, straight and heavy, rests solidly on the entire denominator, which is closely spaced. *The bow is wide and rounded,* in contrast with that of Reverse G. Sometimes called the *Round Bow* reverse.

Die break variations. *Reverse:* Found perfect and also with several progressions of short breaks. One break starts at the top of C in AMERICA, crosses A and the ribbon ends. Another runs from R *of* AMERICA to the lower leaves on the right. A light crack is sometimes found running through UNITED.

R-2. Basal $5.50. 65-65 (65-65-65-65-60-60). Commonest 1793 cent. There are at least a half dozen in full Mint State but among them there is no outstanding candidate for first honors. Probably the Dr. French, the Crosby-Hall, the Bement-ANS, and the Jackman-Newcomb coins should be regarded as sharing this distinction, and it is possible that one or two more ought also to be included at the top.

NC·4   9·I   Horizontal Stem
                      ―――――――――――
                      PERIOD AFTER LEGEND

Obverse 9.

Reverse I. Closely resembles reverse H. The four trefoils are nearly in line with the word CENT, but on each side, *the outer trefoil is higher than the inner one* (on reverse H the four are at practically the same level). The left stem is much shorter than the right, and ends within 0.5 mm. of U in UNITED. The bow is shaped similarly to that of reverse H, but smaller. *There is a period after the legend,* placed a full millimeter to the right of the last A in AMERICA. The period is seen on only one other reverse (J), where it is about 0.5 mm. from the A. In the fraction, the space between 1 and 00 is wide.

Die break variations. *Obverse:* Perfect die. *Reverse:* Rim break and injury as on later examples of No. 10.

R-8. Basal $25. 12-4 (12-8-3-3). Four now known, three of them in collectors' hands. Two have turned up since publica-

[71]

tion of EAC and oddly enough both are better coins than the two previously known examples. A West Coast collector found a Fine one, F-12, about 1950. This is the finest reported. Another appeared at the 1955 ANA Convention sale, VG-8. Of the remaining two, one is in the ANS collection, about condition 3. The other, also a 3-coin, was sold with the Williams collection in 1950. Since there are three of these in collectors' hands the variety is now by definition "collectible" and the designation *NC,* italicized, may be read Now Collectible (instead of Non-collectible).

Extreme rarities like this one, where both the obverse and reverse dies are comparatively common in other marriages, have been called *freak mules* by some collectors. Such coins may have been struck in an idle hour, as the result of a coiner's whim. The variety to follow is also a freak mule, and another good example will be NC-1 of 1794 Hays 30.

NC·5   10·F   Injured Rim / SMALL HEAVY BOW

Obverse 10. *The left leaf of the sprig is very long, seems to have no stem, and is set almost at right angles with the middle leaf.* The stem of the sprig has a heavy end, as if retaining a small piece broken from the branch on which it grew, and it points nearly downward, half way between the 7 and the 9. The date, well formed and well spaced, is about 2 mm. from the lowest lock of hair and nearly 3 mm. from the point of the bust. *Near and in the beading at the rim, opposite the nose and mouth, there is always a depression or small sunken area where the die was defective.* It is by this latter characteristic that in practice the die is readily recognized.

Reverse F.

Die break variations. On the single example of this combination that is known, the short die break through TE of STATES is more advanced than it appears to be on any of the other F reverses I have seen. Therefore the brief marriage between obverse 10 and reverse F, or the indiscretion—whichever it was—presumably occurred late in the life of the latter.

R-8. Unique. 50-0. No more have been reported. ANS has the only example known.

1 7 9 3

10   *10·I*   Injured Rim
                     <u>PERIOD AFTER LEGEND</u>

Obverse 10.·
Reverse I.

Die break variations. *Obverse:* None, but the die failure at the rim in front of the nose is always present in varying degree. In some of the later struck coins the flaw has become so advanced that the beading is entirely gone for three or four millimeters. Frequently called the *Injured Rim* variety. *Reverse:* Some examples have a rim break over NITE. Sometimes seen with an injury involving the beading over S OF.

R.-5. Basal $8.50. 65-45 (65-60-50-45-40-40). Formerly rated R-4, now believed to be in the lower range of R-5. The Beckwith-French-ANS coin, MS-65, and the Crosby-Hall coin, MS-60, are the top examples of the variety. The Brand hoard remnant which was sold in 1951 yielded a previously unlisted AU-50.

1 1

11a   *11·J*   Vertical Left Leaf   VINE AND
                     <u>BEADS FAR FROM LEGEND</u>   BARS EDGE

Obverse 11. The upper part of the double curl nearly touches the point of the left leaf of the sprig. The sprig is small, has a very short stem which starts from a point 0.5 mm. directly above the 9, and *the left leaf points straight upward, or toward the* E *of* LIBERTY. On all other obverses this leaf points to the left. All of the leaves are small. The middle one points to the end of the chin, and the right one almost toward the point of the bust. The 1 is 1 mm. from the hair, and the 3 about 4 mm. from the point of the bust. This is considered one of the more handsome obverses of the series.

Reverse J. The conspicuous characteristic is the relatively *great distance (1.5 mm. as an average) between the legend and the border of beads.* This distance increases progressively from the F reverse, where it is almost nil, to the J reverse. Another feature, equally pronounced, is the position of the *fraction at the extreme right of the space between the ribbons.* The fraction bar is very faint, curved, and almost touches the right ribbon. The numerator is nearly 1 mm. above the bar. The left ribbon is markedly shorter than the right, and less

1 7 9 3

forked. The legend is followed by a period, as on reverse I, but this period is at the end of a spray of berries, and there has been a question as to whether it may not be a berry. The bow is of medium size and almost flat at the top.

Die break variations. *Obverse:* Traces of the wreath usually seen incused below the chin. *Reverse:* A faint crack is often seen, crossing the left ribbon and stem, the bottom of the numerator, the fraction bar, and reaching the end of the right ribbon.

This obverse and reverse die were presumably the last ones for the Wreath series, and they seem to have "gone out" together, after producing a large number of offspring. During their lifetime much experimenting was going on with different sizes and thicknesses of planchets, and a new edge device—the lettered edge—was introduced. Some of the 11-J coins are only 25 mm. in diameter but above average in thickness. Others are broad and thinner. I have seen one which measured 29.5 mm., but that was one of the Lettered Edge variety.

Many defective planchets were used for the 11-J cents, particularly for those with the Vine and Bars edge. The defects often look like die breaks, and it is common to hear of 11-J cents with various die breaks, but all such "breaks" that I have seen have turned out to be planchet defects.

R-6. Basal $9. 70-45 (70-60-55-45-35-30). Formerly called R-5, now clearly R-6. However, an MS-70 example turned up in that Brand hoard remnant which has played so prominent a part in the recent history of the 1793's, and this coin is apparently one of the two finest Wreath cents known (along with the Hall-Beckwith 7-F).

11b	11·J	Vertical Left Leaf	LETTERED EDGE,
		BEADS FAR FROM LEGEND	DOUBLE LEAF

Same as No. 11a except that a new edge device has been substituted for the Vine and Bars. The edge is plain, with the incused inscription, ONE HUNDRED FOR A DOLLAR, followed by two leaves which are arranged end to end. In all probability the double leaf coins were struck before the single leaf coins (subvariety 11c), since the double leaf does not appear again on the big cents, and it is reasonable to suppose that it was abandoned in favor of the single leaf.

1 7 9 3

A description of this two leaved variation was published by W. W. Neil in the *Numismatist* for March, 1928, but Crosby had long before commented on it in his original article on the 1793 cents in 1869.

R-5. Basal $8. 60-30 (60-35-35-30-25-20). Only a single example reported in Mint State. This is an MS-60 from the Ellsworth and Hines collections. Now R-5, the 11b variety is sufficiently scarce in the finer condition grades to permit a VF-20 to be included in the first half dozen.

11c	11·J	Vertical Left Leaf	LETTERED EDGE,
		BEADS FAR FROM LEGEND	SINGLE LEAF

Same as 11b except that only a single leaf is seen after the word DOLLAR.

R-3. Basal $6.50. 55-50 (55-55-50-50-45-45). Review of the best-known examples of 11c fails to sustain our earlier impression that a 60-coin is extant. The T. J. Clarke piece, probably finest, is an AU-55, as is the ANS coin. There are at least four more that hover near the grade AU-50, or fall between 50 and 45.

It should be emphasized that Nos. 11a, 11b, and 11c make up a single *die variety*. The edge device was imprinted on the planchets independently of and prior to the striking of the coins, and consequently edge variations do not enter into the definition of die varieties. Occasionally an 11-J cent is seen with a plain edge—doubtless the result of a careless error of omission. Plain edges also turn up once in a while among the 1794 cents and I have seen two plain-edged 1793 Liberty Caps. Since the Lettered Edge coins are many times more numerous than the Vine and Bars variation, it is probable that the change of edge device was introduced early in the 11-J marriage.

1 7 9 3

THE LIBERTY CAP CENTS

General description

Obverse: Head of Liberty to the right. Head well poised. Forehead high. Bust longer. Hair confined around the head by a narrow ribbon and falling in graceful curls behind the shoulder. Cap on staff over the left shoulder. Above, the legend LIBERTY. Below, the date. The hair is shorter now, flows less freely, and falls in a "more kempt mass" behind the neck. The profile is finer, endowed with a suggestion of Roman sternness, and it has been referred to as a *gynandroid* profile, a term indicating the presence of both masculine and feminine characteristics. *Reverse:* The wreath enclosing the words $\frac{\text{ONE}}{\text{CENT}}$ is formed of two slender olive branches bearing their fruit singly on axillary stems. The stems of the branches below the knot are straight and slender and are tied with a ribbon which forms a double bow within the wreath. The ribbon ends are long, falling well below the stems, and in the space between them is the fraction. The legend UNITED STATES OF AMERICA, almost encircles the wreath, and just outside the legend is a circle of beads which forms the border.

The edge bears the inscription, ONE HUNDRED FOR A DOLLAR, in letters which vary somewhat in size and also vary in the direction of reading. The planchets are usually 29 mm. in diameter, and are thinner than those of the Chain and Wreath cents, but thicker than the plain-edge planchets of 1795 and later. Occasionally a 1793 Liberty Cap is found with a diameter as great as 30 mm., and I have seen one which measured only 27.5 mm.

12	12·K	Two Beads Over I
		HIGH CENTER REVERSE

Obverse 12. A full millimeter of the staff shows clearly between hair and cap. The lower end of the staff is heavy, bold, and rounded at the tip, tapering toward the throat, and less than its own diameter from the bust. Two beads are directly or centrally over the I of LIBERTY (Ï). The letters of the legend are very close to the border, the L in particular almost touching the beads.

1 7 9 3

Reverse K. This reverse can be recognized at a glance, as the central part is raised or elevated, so that $_{CENT}^{ONE}$, a considerable part of the left wreath, and some of the inner leaves of the right wreath are always weak. If the coin is a little worn, these parts are in many instances entirely gone. *A leaf terminates 0.5 mm. from the right foot of* M, *and points directly at the center of the bottom of that letter.* On the L reverse this leaf is distant from the M, is almost parallel to that letter, and points to the bottom of the adjacent A. The two lower leaves on the left of the knot are broad and single, the lower one arising directly from the ribbon without a stem. Under o in OF there is a single leaf. The border has eighty-five beads.

Die break variations. No breaks, although the reverse die must have been considerably bent, or convexed, to have produced so marked a blotting out of the center of the coin. Reverse K is rare, not over two dozen impressions of it being known to me all told, and among these I can recall only four instances in which $_{CENT}^{ONE}$ could fairly be called legible. In all other cases the center is so obliterated that you can read the words only by knowing that they are there. The defect in the die possibly accounts for the shortness of its life, or the paucity of its use. A number of electrotypes are in existence.

R-6. Basal $20. 50-8 (50-12-10-8-6-5). No new ones have been reported. Probably just about twenty examples of this aristocrat of cents are known. We know of only a single 12-K that can truthfully be graded better than F-12. This is the Crosby-French-Clapp coin now incarcerated permanently in ANS. Such a coin would almost surely now bring its current book rating at auction (50×$20×3, or $3000).

13	12·L	Two Beads Over I
		LEAF UNDER ME PARALLEL

Obverse 12.

Reverse L. Readily distinguished from the K reverse by the position of the leaf under ME of AMERICA. *The leaf runs almost parallel to the bottoms of the two letters, and points at the bottom of the adjacent* A. The two lower leaves on either side of the knot are narrow and double, or attached by a single stem. *Under the* o *in* OF *there is a triple leaf.* The border has ninety-

[77]

1 7 9 3

one beads. This reverse is almost always evenly struck and evenly worn, in contrast with the raised center of the K reverse.

Die break variations. None seen.

R-4. Basal $12.50. 55-50 (55-55-50-45-45-45). Probably the two finest are the Ellsworth-Hines piece and the Cleneay-Bement-Eliasberg coin. Neither is quite Mint State but both can be graded AU-55. The Beckwith-Dupont coin is a full AU-50 and at least three more fall between 50 and 40. Probably every one of the top half dozen of this variety has been sold as "finest known" within the memory of collectors now living.

14   13·L   The Bisecting Crack

Obverse 13. The *Cracked Die* Liberty Cap. *A straight, heavy crack, running from the border above* E *to the border just to the right of the 3, divides this obverse into two almost equal parts.* No examples are known without the crack, so this variety can be identified at long range. About 0.5 mm. of the staff shows faintly between the cap and the head but this part of the staff is rarely seen except on fine specimens. The lower end of the staff is faint, more than its own diameter from the bust, and so weakly cut at the tip that even on fine coins it is difficult to make out just where the tip is. Cap, date, and legend are more distant from the border than on obverse 12. The I and the R in LIBERTY are high, the E low. There is a bead over the right half of the ï, while another would almost miss the extreme left extension of that letter.

Reverse L.

Die break variations. None seen except the identifying obverse break noted. Since this variety has not been reported without the break it is quite possible that the break occurred before any coins were struck, perhaps during the process of hardening the die.

R-5. Basal $15. 55-20 (55-25-20-20-20-15). The Winsor-French-ANS coin is an AU-55, rather than MS-60 as formerly graded. But this is probably the finest known Liberty Cap 1793, having better color and a more even surface than either of the two leading 12-L's. The Miller-Hines 13-L, second finest seen, is a VF-25.

1 7 9 3

15	*14·K*	The Dotted I
		HIGH CENTER REVERSE

Obverse 14. On this die, *a bead perfectly dots the* I *of* LIBERTY (İ) *and this is the best distinguishing characteristic.* Less than 0.5 mm. of the staff, or pole, is visible between the head and the cap, and on anything short of a very fine specimen the staff is not seen at this point at all. The end of the staff is long, points directly at a bead, and is distant from the bust a little more than its own thickness. *The lowest lock of hair has a short, heavy hook at the end,* as contrasted with its delicate termination on the other two obverses. A faint crack is nearly always seen, from a bead at the border, across the right top of Y to the forehead, and sometimes (faintly) from the lower lock of hair to the border. The border contains ninety-seven beads, as compared with ninety-five on the other two obverses.

Reverse K.

Die break variations. None except as noted. It is probable that this obverse die was cracked in the same manner as that of obverse 13, although far less conspicuously, and on some of the well-worn 14's the crack can scarcely be made out.

R-8. Basal $50. 20-7 (20-15-7-4-4). The aristocrat of the Liberty Cap cents, and therefore an aristocrat of aristocrats among the Large Cents. Finest known is the VF-20 Gies-Clapp piece, now in the ANS museum. Next is the Wilharm-Hines coin, F-15. Third finest is the Dr. French piece, VG-7, now in a Philadelphia collection. A 14-K in condition 4 was sold in an Eastern auction in 1953, and ANS has a second example of the variety, also condition 4. This last is the original Levick-Crosby coin. Rumors of another 14-K circulate perennially. These lead usually to an examination of electrotypes or of badly worn 12-K's (of which there are three or four so far gone as to be almost unattributable). Perhaps it is dangerous to assign so high a basal value as $50 to a cent. If a 60-coin should turn up it would have a book rating, by our current rules, of $60 \times 50 \times 4$, or $12,000. Suppose a keg of them should turn up! The answer, of course, is that as more of a variety appear the basal value falls automatically.

1 5

1 7 9 3

16   *14·L*   The Dotted I
LEAF UNDER ME PARALLEL

Obverse 14.
Reverse L.

Die break variations. *Obverse:* **An example is known with a heavy break, or failure of the die, between the chin and the border, measuring about 4×5 mm. A number of electrotypes are in existence.**

R-7. Basal $22.50. 12-8 (12-10-8-8-7-6). Eleven of these now accounted for. The variety remains R-7, although barely so. If two more appear it will become R-6. The Steigerwalt-Hall-Brand-ANS piece is F-12 and finest seen. Second is the Brand-Hines example with the heavily broken obverse die, VG-10. Third and fourth, presumably, are the French and Newcomb coins, both about VG-8.

There are three of the 14-L's, and about half a dozen of the 12-K's, that never seem to find an appreciative home, but appear in the sales over and over again. One 14-L, to my knowledge, has been sold at least five times since 1930. I have bought it three times. One can see how after a while these rarities and the collectors get to be old friends. When the bug bites *hard*, you bid on a 14-L listed as "about Fine" in the hope that it will be strictly Good. It turns out to be Very Fair, so when the bug rests you sell it. Then the bug returns to normal again, and you go after *another* 14-L, this one "Very Fine for coin." And it is the same 14-L. But this is all in good fun, and for those who don't like exercise and are too old for romance, it is not a bad game. Furthermore it is one of the very few games in which the professionals—the dealers, or fishermen—have almost as exciting a time as the amateurs, or "fish." For unless it is a well-worn cent itself, there is nothing in the world harder to "make out" than a cent collector.

The total return of cents in 1793, given by Stewart as 110,-512, included 36,103 Chain cents, all struck in the period March 1 to 12; 63,353 Wreaths, coined between April 9 and July 17; and 11,056 Liberty Caps, delivered September 18.

It is generally thought that the dies for the three classes of

1 7 9 3

1793 cents were cut by three different engravers. Crosby attributed the Chain cents to Jean Pierre Droz, the Swiss die sinker mentioned on page 12, whom we failed to induce to come to this country as resident engraver. This attribution now seems unlikely in view of some correspondence on the subject between R. H. Williamson and C. H. V. Sutherland, author of *Art in Coinage*. We have recently examined some British patterns made by Droz and the style is highly classical and sophisticated in feeling. It is therefore more likely that some native American engraver made the dies for the Chain cents, and in the absence of contrary evidence we attribute them to Robert Birch, who was responsible for the large copper cents of 1792. The Wreath cents are with good reason credited to the modeler, painter, portrait engraver and die sinker Joseph Wright, who died in the summer of 1793 during one of Philadelphia's frequent yellow fever epidemics. Most writers have attributed the Liberty Cap dies to Robert Scot, but since he was not appointed Engraver of the Mint until November 23, 1793, the attribution is presumably in error. An alternative legend indicates that these 1793's, together with the first four varieties of 1794 (which are from the same hub as the 1793 Liberty Caps) "were struck from dies made abroad, presumably by Droz, and perhaps as retribution for the wretched quality of the first dies he sent us." This quotation is from a lecture on the early cents given in Providence, many years ago, by the late Foster Lardner. And it is a fact that these coins—with perhaps the best designs in the series—were long known as the "French heads." C. H. V. Sutherland is inclined, on stylistic grounds, to think that Droz probably did make the hub which was used for the heads on these six obverses.

1793

TABLE 3. RARITY AND VALUE: 1793 CENTS

No.	Crosby No.	Rarity	Basal Value (Dollars)
1	1-A	4	10.
2	1-C	4	8.50
NC-1	2-C	8	—
3	3-C	3	7.
4	4-C	4	9.
NC-2	5-D	8	—
NC-3	5-E	8	35.
5	6-F	4	8.
6	7-F	3	7.50
7	8-F	6	15.
8	9-G	3	7.
9	9-H	2	5.50
NC-4	9-I	8	25.
NC-5	10-F	8	—
10	10-I	5	8.50
11a	11-J Vine and Bars	6	9.
11b	L.E., 2 leaves	5	8.
11c	L.E., 1 leaf	3	6.50
12	12-K	6	20.
13	12-L	4	12.50
14	13-L	5	15.
15	14-K	8	50.
16	14-L	7	22.50

1794

THERE ARE SO MANY ADVANTAGES IN CROSBY'S OBVERSE-REVERSE method of designation that collectors frequently ask why the method has not been applied to all of the early date cents. As a matter of fact, Clapp and Newcomb *have* now applied it to all the remaining early dates except 1794. Meanwhile I have for some time used an obverse-reverse designation for 1794's and have found it of great assistance in keeping track of the numerous varieties, but have hesitated to publish it because of a certain affection for the Hays numbers.

In this book, however, since all of the other dates are presented with obverse-reverse designations, the 1794's will be similarly listed, and I think that perhaps this can be done without jeopardizing the popularity of the Hays numbers.

Chapman renumbered the 1794 cents, and there are a few collectors who have learned and prefer the Chapman numbers. These will also be included here for completeness, but it is my belief that Hays, rather than Chapman, is the man to be remembered for the 1794's. Chapman was not either a particular fancier or a great master of 1794 cents. He never knew or especially loved the thick lettered edge cents of this date as Hays did, and never made a collection of them. To Hays they were magic talismans to the nostalgic past and to a wistful future. By owning one you established a fraternal bond with both past and future owners. To Chapman they were merchandise and profit.

Clapp and Newcomb always maintained that the cent known as Hays 4 is most likely to have been the first in the series of 1794. This obverse closely resembles the last obverse (obverse 14) of 1793, but there is also a better reason for supposing the coin to have been the first of its date. On all 1794's except Hays 4, the leaf following the edge inscription is found on its back; that is, with the end of the leaf and the stem pointing upward. The regular 1794 edge lettering is different from and larger than the 1793 edge lettering. But the Hays 4 has the 1793 edge lettering, and always has the leaf pointing downward, as on the 1793's. The Hays 3 and Hays 2 coins are found with both types of edge device, probably indicating that they came after the Hays 4, and are in a sense transitional between that and later varieties.

The Hays 4, then, will be our 1-A of the 1794's, and the rest of the series will follow an order which seems to be indicated by the various marriages and similarities of the dies. Chapman's division of the whole series into six general classes is of help in studying the probable relationships of the dies, as will be seen from the text to follow. In certain cases (only two, I think) it has been necessary, in order to maintain both the obverse and reverse progressions unbroken, to present a later marriage of a die (as indicated by die breaks) ahead of a presumed earlier marriage. There probably was not quite a "true order of progression" of these dies at the Mint, and presumably there was at times a certain whimsicality in the die marriages, but a *general* order of progression does seem to be manifest, and an attempt has been made to follow it.

The material on identification is of course not written to "stand alone," but to accompany the photographs and to point out, rather minimally, salient features by which cent students can learn quickly to identify the dies.

| 17a | 1·A | Head of '93, Wide Straight Date | EDGE DEVICE OF '93 | HAYS 4 CHAPMAN 4 |

Obverse 1. Obverses 1 and 3 are distinctive in that the *dates are almost perfectly horizontal, with the bottoms of the figures on a straight line.* The date of obverse 1 is much more widely spaced, and is comparatively distant from the bust. On both of these obverses the 4 seems to tilt a little to the right, since

1 7 9 4

we are accustomed to seeing it in a curve which tilts it to the left. Maris called obverse 1 the *Tilted 4*. A more descriptive name might be the *Wide Straight Date*.

The lowest lock of hair is thicker than on any other variety, with a heavy, hooklike point like that of obverse 14 of 1793, which this very closely resembles. The pole is heavy, flattened at the end, and not much more than a hair's breadth from the bust. The pole shows between the head and cap. On the first three 1794 obverses, the relief over the face and head is so high and rounded that the coins will not stack perfectly, and the same is true of the Liberty Caps of 1793.

Reverse A. There are eight berries on the left branch, seven on the right. *Both ribbons miss the ribbon knot entirely,* and this is diagnostic. The knot is placed at the crossing of the wreath stems instead of at the meeting of the ribbons, and is almost centered in the angle where the ribbon ends diverge. The stem of the lowest pair of leaves on the left is remarkably thick and *arises from the bottom of the ribbon bow instead of from the wreath stem*. All of the berries are small, poorly formed, dried up in appearance. The two at the top on the left are almost microscopic, and the corresponding two on the right are stemless. The T of CENT leans to the left. Fraction bar faint, rather long, and slightly curved. On all specimens seen there is a slight crack from the bottom of F to the nearest leaf.

Die break variations. *Obverse:* On somewhat more than half of the coins seen, there is a swell or bulge, and sometimes a faint crack, extending from the border through the bottom of L to the head, and running nearly parallel to the edge of the cap. On coins showing this bulge clearly there is usually a short crack from the tip of the pole to the border. *Reverse:* The die has been injured, and faint traces of an obverse are sometimes seen under STATES and in the lower part of the wreath.

R-6. Basal $9. 40-15 (40-30-12-12-12-10). Edge device of 1793. The ANS coin, EF-40, was found by an American dealer in England in the 1890's. In 1950 another turned up, also in England, this one VF-30 and now far the finest in collectors' hands. The Hines coin, the original Hays coin, and the Macallister coin can all be graded F-12, the last being a new discovery or rediscovery

1 7 9 4

since publication of EAC. But despite two important new additions a 10-coin is still included in the first half dozen. This is the 1-A of 1794, with the same head as the rare Obverse 14 of 1793. Together with Nos. 18, 19 and 20 it merits distinction, along with the Liberty Cap cents of '93, as among the aristocrats of the Large Cent series.

		Head of '93, Wide Straight Date	EDGE DEVICE OF '94	HAYS 4 CHAPMAN 4
NC·4	*1·A*			

R-8. Unique. 4-0. Same as No. 17a but with the edge device of 1794—so-called because it appears on the subsequent varieties of this date. The stem and point of leaf after DOLLAR point up, as on 18b, 19b and all later varieties. The only one so far reported was identified as a new sub-variety in 1950 by Douglas Smith. This coin, condition G-4, had lain unrecognized in the Borcky and Garrabrant collections before Smith "took a good look at it." If more of these appear, and NC-4 becomes collectible, the sub-variety should be known as 17b, thus maintaining the progression with 18b and 19b.

		Head of '93, Double Chin	EDGE DEVICE OF '93	HAYS 3 CHAPMAN 3
18a	*2·A*			

Obverse 2. The *Double Chin*. Almost an exact replica of obverse 12 of 1793, *but has a pronounced double chin*. Legend and date are nearer to the milling than to the bust. The date is rather compact and curved, with the 9 leaning a little to the left. Pole shows distinctly between head and cap. The end of the pole is well struck up and is about its own width from the bust. *The head is in rounded, high relief.*

Reverse A.

Die break variations. *Obverse:* A minute crack or projection usually present on the twelfth denticle to the left of the 1. *Reverse:* On nearly half of the specimens known to me there is a pronounced bulge, or swelling, caused by sinking of the die and extending from the letters TED through the left branch of the wreath. This *die* variety is found with *both the 1793 and the 1794 styles of edge device*. No. 18a, with the 1793 edge, has the stem and point of the leaf pointing *down*.

1794

R-7. Basal $7.50. 25-8 (25-15-10-8-6-4). Only six or seven of these presently reported, the same ones that were known when EAC was written. One of them, however, then described to one of us as a 20-coin, turned out to be a 6-coin. The finest seen is the Proskey-Hines piece, VF-25. The ANS coin, F-15, is equally sharp but injured.

| 18b | 2·A | Head of '93, Double Chin | EDGE DEVICE OF '94 | HAYS 3 CHAPMAN 3 |

Same as No. 18a, but with the 1794 edge device. The stem and point of the leaf point *up*.

R-4. Basal $3.50. 55-55 (55-55-55-55-55-50). Oddly, there are at least a half dozen examples of this beautiful cent in near-MS condition, although no one of them stands out for top honors and none of them can be graded quite MS-60. Probably all of these best ones have been sold at one time or another as finest known—and in this instance almost with justice. Some of the famous ones are the French-Clarke, the Cleneay-ANS, the Beckwith-Würtzbach, the Hall-Brand, and the Hays-Phelps coins. This is the only variety among the head-of-'93 Liberty Caps within which several top grade coins are available to collectors.

| 19a | 2·B | Head of '93, Double Chin | EDGE DEVICE OF '93 | HAYS 2 CHAPMAN 2 |

Obverse 2. The *Double Chin*.

Reverse B. In this marriage of dies the denticles are long and heavy, with sharp points. Maris used to call this the "ugly tooth" reverse. There are eight berries to the left branch, the two upper ones very small and close to the stem, and eight to the right. The berry under the left foot of M has a second berry, just outside it, "weak and feebly defined." Frossard includes this in his count of eight, but Chapman omits it and sees only seven on that branch. The berry opposite this one, on the other side of the wreath stem, seems to be almost a mere stem without any berry at all. *Legend so close to the border that several of the letters almost touch.*

1 7 9 4

Die break variations. *Obverse:* On all specimens that I have seen fine enough to show it, the small crack on the twelfth denticle to the left of 1 is present. The *die* variety is *found with both the 1793 and 1794 edge device.* No. 19a, with the 1793 edge, has the stem and point of the leaf pointing *down.*

R-7. Basal $7.50. 45-12 (45-20-15-12-8-6). Still only about eight accounted for, and apparently the same eight that were known when EAC was written. The H. P. Smith-Hines piece stands alone at EF-45 (formerly graded AU-50). Second finest seen is the Würtzbach-Dupont coin, VF-20. ANS has a 15-coin. At least seven, all told, are in collectors' hands, with all but two of them on the condition census list.

20	19b	2·B	Head of '93, Double Chin	EDGE DEVICE OF '94	HAYS 2 CHAPMAN 2

Same as No. 19a, but with the 1794 edge device. The stem and point of the leaf, following the word DOLLAR, point *up.*

R-5. Basal $5. 45-20 (45-45-20-20-15-12). Rarity underestimated in EAC. In fine condition H-2 is a great numismatic prize. The two top examples, from the Chapman-French and Hays-Newcomb-ANS collections, were graded AU-50 in EAC but are here regraded EF-45. After these two the best H-2 we know is VF-20, and an F-12 is a condition census coin. Chapman used to say, "Whoever owns a nice Hays 2 has the foundation for a good collection."

20	3·B	Head of '93, Close Straight Date	HAYS 1 CHAPMAN 1

Obverse 3. Called by Maris *The Exact Head of 1793,* and like obverse 2 it is a close replica of obverse 12 of 1793. *The date is straight, as on obverse 1, but is more closely spaced* (measuring 7 mm. at the bottom) *and is much closer to the bust.* No trace of the pole shows between cap and head. There is no loop on the bust under the shoulder, in contrast with the heavy loop on obverse 1. The 9 is only 0.5 mm. from the bust,

1 7 9 4

and on no other 1794 except No. 63 (obverse 31) is it nearly so close. Might be called the *Close Straight Date*.

Reverse B.

Die break variations. None seen.

R-5. Basal $6.50. 50-30 (50-40-40-35-20-15). The last of the Head-of-'93 cents, and to many of our predecessors one of the most desired pieces in American numismatics. George Clapp once remarked that he valued his Hays 1 above anything else he owned—and he owned enough to make multimillion dollar gifts. Clapp had paid $600 for his H-1, AU-50, in 1926. This coin was found in England in the eighteen nineties. The two 40-coins of the variety are the Hall-Brand piece, pictured on the Hays plate; and the Chapman-Beckwith coin, pictured on the Chapman plate. The 35 is the Gilbert-Newcomb-Downing coin, pictured on the Gilbert-Elder plate.

2 1

| 21 | 4·B | The Flat Pole | HAYS 5
CHAPMAN 5 |

Obverse 4. Maris called this the *Sans Milling*, because the milling is rarely (if ever) seen complete on the obverse, but collectors often call it the *Flat pole variety*. *The pole at its tip is flattened to a full millimeter in width, although at the point where it joins the neck it is not more than a quarter of that width.* This obverse departs from the 1793 style and ushers in what Chapman calls Style II. The bust is in lower relief, the hair is combed out in eight neat curls or locks, and there is an excellent aesthetic balancing to the whole coin, which is considered one of the most beautiful cents. LIBERTY widely spaced, especially R-T-Y, with the nearest point of the L about 1 mm. from the cap. The date, curved to follow the circumference of the border, as on all subsequent obverses except obverse 31, is slightly closer to the bust than to the hair (1 mm. from the hair, and less than 1 mm. from the bust).

Reverse B. In this marriage the border is not struck so deeply as on the Hays 2, and the denticles are not so pronounced.

Die break variations. *Obverse:* On nearly all specimens seen there is a faint crack from the border to the top of the cap, touching the upper left corner of B. A crack is frequently seen from the cap through LIB to the forelock, to the base of T. Fine cracks sometimes seen from the top of the cap into the left field, and from the border to the left edge of the cap. *Reverse:* In this combination reverse B usually shows a short crack extending into the field from the second denticle to the right of the last s of STATES, and a similar one from the first denticle to the left of the E of AMERICA. This coin often seen with the planchet large (29 mm.).

R-3. Basal $2. 60-55 (60-55-55-55-50-50). A much-favored variety sometimes classed with the Head-of-'93 cents although the only justification for this is the fact that it shares its reverse with Nos. 19 and 20. The scarcity of H-5 was underestimated in EAC. Several collectors have complained of the difficulty in finding a nice one. On objective scrutiny only the Proskey-Hines piece seems to stand up to the rather rigorous criteria of MS-60. But there are at least a half dozen of AU-50 grade or better and only one of these is impounded in ANS.

| 22 | 5·C | The Bent Lock
MOUNDS ON REVERSE
(Usually) | HAYS 43
CHAPMAN 6 |

Obverse 5. The *Bent Hair Lock*. Very similar to the last in general appearance, but the pole is not flattened at the end, and is usually not visible between head and cap. LIBERTY closely and evenly spaced. Usually, but not always, seen on a large planchet (29 mm.) and called by Maris the *Large Planchet* variety. Conspicuous loop at the lower left corner of the bust. Nine locks of hair, *with the tip of the sixth one* (*numbering from the bottom*) *bent sharply downward* (diagnostic).

Reverse C. The *Mounded Reverse*. This reverse is usually, although not always, seen with the die badly sunken so as to produce mounds or swellings on the coin embracing the upper part of the right wreath, and a considerable portion of the lower half of the wreath on both sides. There are eight berries on the left, and seven on the right branch. *The left ribbon seems to be severed from the knot, while the right ribbon leaves the knot crazily, somewhat more than a millimeter above*

1 7 9 4

the crossing of the stems. The numerator almost rests on the fraction bar, and the last 0 of the denominator is high.

Die break variations. *Obverse:* A faint break is sometimes present from the end of the pole to the nearest denticle. Traces of the reverse are frequently seen from below the nose to the bust. Examples of this die are common on which the metal has flowed unevenly, and minute centrifugal radiations have resulted. *Reverse:* As noted. The perfect die reverse (without the mounds) is often called rare. It is scarce, not rare. I have seen twenty or thirty. Mr. Carl Würtzbach has a collection of Hays 43's showing six different progressions in the development of the die sinking which produced the bulges.

R-1. Basal $1. 60-55 (60-60-55-55-50-50). Although second commonest of the 1794's the Bent Lock variety is not so common in Mint State as we formerly supposed. In the present review only two 60-coins have been accounted for. These are the Proskey-Hines and ANS pieces.

2 3

| 23 | 6·D | Shattered Obverse
RIGHT RIBBON HIGH | HAYS 18
CHAPMAN 7 |

Obverse 6. *Usually seen with shattered dies,* a crack running from the border along the the top of the cap, across the head and downward along the jaw, to the end of the pole and to the border. From this main crack another branches off at the angle of the jaw, runs across the face, to the right of Y and to the border. The (extremely rare) perfect die of this obverse resembles obverse 5 closely, but the pole is more slender, tapers a little toward the neck, and is at least twice its own width from the bust. Also the date is more closely spaced, and there are seven locks of hair instead of eight. Called by Maris the *Standless 4.* The stand of this figure is usually weak, but so it is on obverse 5, and on two or three others.

Reverse D. *The right ribbon* seems to come off from the bow above the knot, and *is much higher than the left ribbon,* as on reverse C. There are six berries on the left, and seven on the right branch. *Numerator of the fraction very tall and touches the fraction bar,* which is heavy and extends well to the right of the second 0 of the denominator. The die was

[91]

1 7 9 4

sunken a little and the center of the coin is raised, so that ONE CENT is generally obliterated if the coin is a little worn.

Die break variations. *Obverse:* The perfect die is seldom seen —I can recall only two examples of it and both are now out of circulation forever; but various stages in the progression of the break are seen. Usually found on a rather large planchet.

R-5. Basal $4. 60-40 (60-50-40-35-35-30). The Mougey-Chapman-ANS coin remains the only mint state example known or reported. A new EF-40 coin turned up in England in 1949 and was sold with the Downing collection in 1952. The 50-coin is a discovery of recent months. The ANS coin and the 40-coin have perfect die obverses. All of the other fine ones known to us show advanced obverse die breaks. The Newcomb coin and the Proskey-Hines piece are both about VF-35. Below the first half dozen of this variety condition drops off steeply so that the rather high condition census is misleading. There probably are not more than nine or ten Hays 18's that can be graded Fine or better.

| 24 | 7·D | Scarred Head, Full Cheeks | HAYS 17 CHAPMAN 8 |

Obverse 7. Named by Maris the *Scarred Head*. There is an approximately ear-shaped depression ("scar") in the hair below the ear at the back of the neck, some 2×5 mm. in extent. The lower curl ends with a long, sharp hook. Date wide, with the 1 and 4 close to hair and bust. *The face has exceptionally rounded, full cheeks*—a characteristic by which collectors recognize it easily. My father used to call it the *Apple Cheek* variety. Seven points to the hair, and all but the lowest delicate. The second point is severed from its lock. The hair above and behind the ear is in very high relief.

Reverse D.

Die break variations. *Obverse:* Found perfect, and with a faint crack which curves slightly downward across the coin from L, through the hair, neck, and bust to the border just to the right of the 4. The die nearly always seems delicately roughened or "rusted" on the lower part of the neck and between date and bust.

1 7 9 4

R-2. Basal $1.50. 65-55 (65-65-60-55-55-50). The Proskey-Hines piece and the Würtzbach-Mathewson coin are both MS-65—numismatic gems in almost full mint brilliance. The Newcomb coin is an MS-60. After these there are perhaps half a dozen fairly legitimate claimants for the other three positions in the condition census, and in the grades between 50 and 40 it may be that a dozen Hays 17's are known. However, it is apparent that in EAC we overestimated the frequency with which this beautiful coin is to be encountered "close to Mint State."

		The Wide 7-9; Severed Hair Strands	
25	8·E		HAYS 22 CHAPMAN 17

Obverse 8. Called by Maris the *Separated Date*. The date is wide, with *especially great distance between* 7 *and* 9. The 4 slants markedly to the left and is less than 0.5 mm. from the bust. The pole is a little more than its own width from the bust. Hair terminates in seven points, the upper six of which are singularly slender and of nearly the same length. *Below the highest point are two severed strands of hair, faintly seen.* LIBERTY is high, the nearest letter being about 2 mm. from the top of the hair.

Reverse E. *The center dot is seen as a thickening or protuberance on the left stand of* N *of* CENT. There are eight berries on the left and seven on the right. Two berries under the left ribbon bow, and *two dotlike berries touch the stem of the upper leaf on the left.* Very short fraction bar, failing to extend over the 1 or over the last 0 of the denominator.

Die break variations. *Reverse:* Faint traces of an obverse are usually seen in the upper part of the reverse, and a short break is sometimes seen through D to the leaves. This variety is nearly always struck a little weak on the upper right obverse and the lower right reverse.

R-4. Basal $3. 65-45 (65-55-55-45-30-30). The Proskey-Hines piece is MS-65, with the Newcomb and Brand coins in near proximity to it at AU-55. Rarity of the variety underestimated in EAC. This is one of the difficult ones in fine condition, despite the high condition census.

1 7 9 4

| 26 | 8·F | The Wide 7-9;
Severed Hair Strands
BREAK THROUGH E | HAYS 21
CHAPMAN 18 |

Obverse 8. The die has now been ground down a little, taking off the ends of some of the curls at the back of the neck, and detaching others so that they appear like little islands.

Reverse F. This coin is recognized easily by its reverse die breaks. *The o in OF has a short, curved projection from its left side,* which is always present. Nearly all specimens have a *break through E of STATES* to the point of the upper left leaf. Most specimens, certainly two thirds, have a heavy break from the first s of STATES to the c of CENT. Many "suction marks," or traces of injury to the die are present. There are five berries on the left and six on the right branch. The fraction bar is long, and pointed at both ends.

27   **Die break variations.** No obverse breaks seen. Reverses showing only the break at o in OF are known.

R-2. Basal $1.50. 70-55 (70-60-55-50-50-50). Far less rare than the Hays 22, and almost common in the lower or intermediate condition states, but the EAC estimate of condition census (70-60) was too high. The French-Hines coin is the showpiece of the variety.

| 27 | 9·G | Buckled Obverse | HAYS 25
CHAPMAN 19 |

Obverse 9. Called by some collectors the *Buckled Die* variety. There is always a *slight bulge or ridge, running from the left border to the fifth hair lock from the bottom,* across the hair to about the angle of the jaw, where it turns a little, runs along the jaw and from the point of the chin to the right border. On some specimens the bulge becomes a visible break, but it is present to some degree on all of them, and the variety resembles the 1793 7-F in that respect. Hair terminates in seven very distinct points, the lowest one pointing directly to the top of 1, and the uppermost one projecting beyond all the others. LIBERTY high. Date well spaced. The 1 is 2 mm. distant from the tip of the curl, and the 4 about 0.5 mm. from the bust. Maris named this obverse *Egeria,* after the elusive and

secretive wife of legendary King Numa of Rome—perhaps because it was hard to find in good condition.

Reverse G. Six berries on each branch, but the *upper one on the left is so small that a glass is required to make it out.* It sits close atop the stem of the highest leaf. I of UNITED low. Numerator of fraction short and rather distant from the slender fraction bar, *which curves upward a little* and almost perfectly covers the denominator. A very slight break, or line, is always seen *extending from the upper portion of* D about 2 mm. toward the border.

Die break variations. Several "perfect die" obverses have been reported, but these have always turned out to be worn coins which when held at the proper angle with the light reveal the characteristic bulging of the die.

R-6. Basal $5. 50-20 (50-45-20-15-10-10). The Proskey-Hines coin, AU-50, and the ANS coin, EF-45, stand in rather lonely relief at the head of the condition list. However, a VF-20 came to light in an Eastern collection in 1949, increasing the list of Fine-or-better examples to four. Above VG, the Egeria remains a rare and elusive lady.

28   10·G   LIBERTY High; Locks End in Vertical Line   HAYS 23   CHAPMAN 20

Obverse 10. Maris' *Ornate* variety, and deserving of the name. The hair is, as Chapman says, the most simply treated of all the dies. The locks terminate in eight distinct points of "excellently proportioned length." *A line drawn through the 3rd, 4th, 5th, 6th and 8th points would be a straight perpendicular in the field.* LIBERTY very high, with the R 1.5 mm. above the top of the hair. L distant from cap. Date widely and evenly spaced, with the 4 distant from the bust. The cheek is full, exuberant-looking.

Reverse G.

Die break variations. *Obverse:* A faint crack is frequently seen on perfect specimens, running into the field from the fifth denticle to the right of the pole. There is a minute chip out of the die, opposite the end of the fourth hair lock from the bottom. Faint crack from border to top of cap through the base of L to I; from lower edge of cap to the lowest hair lock, crossing the 2nd and 3rd; from nose to a denticle at border. The crack from cap to hair lock is, in the very latest stage, joined by another from the border, at a point about 1 mm. below the cap. All of these cracks are faint, and visible only on Fine coins. This variety is often seen with a weak lower obverse and upper reverse. *Reverse:* OF is nearly always weaker than the rest of the legend. Two or three delicate, hairline cracks, and some faint injury marks are seen on perfect specimens in and near the left branch.

R-2. Basal $1.50. 65-55 (65-60-60-50-50-50). Ten years ago we would have guessed that at least four or five MS coins could be turned up for this famous Ornate variety. The present review has revealed only three, but there are probably half a dozen between 60 and 50, and certainly we have seen more than a dozen between 50 and 40.

29	10·H	LIBERTY High; Locks End in Vertical Line THE TAILED RIGHT RIBBON	HAYS 24 CHAPMAN 21

Obverse 10. All of the cracks listed for the preceding variety can now be seen more plainly, but they are still delicate.

Reverse H. The *Tailed Reverse. The right ribbon end and the* R *of* AMERICA *have long tails,* and this is one of the most easily recognized reverses of the series. The long ribbon occurs only in this one instance, and the long-tailed R on only two other reverses (W and FF). Reverse H is also characterized by a *heavy border with coarse denticles* which extend rather close to the legend (like reverse B). Ten berries on the left branch and eight on the right, the lower outside berry on the left having an abnormally long, curved stem. A double berry under the left foot of M. The legend is unevenly spaced, with extra distance between N and I, also between M and E.

Die break variations. *Reverse:* Crack seen frequently from the border through R to the wreath.

R-3. Basal $2. 65-55 (65-65-55-50-50-45). The Ornate with the Tailed reverse. The Proskey-Hines and the Hays-Newcomb examples are full MS-65, and these two are supported by at least three more that will score AU-50. The Hays 24 is another

1794

source of embarrassment to us because of failure to document the earlier impression that more of them are available in Mint State.

30   *11·H*   The Marred Field   HAYS 37
TAILED REVERSE   CHAPMAN 22

Obverse 11. Head of Liberty low in the field, crowding the space for the date. The 1 just touches the lowest lock of hair, and the 4 is close to the bust. *The lowest lock is heavy and double,* a characteristic which almost identifies the coin, since obverse 12 is the only other die to show it, and the differential diagnosis between these two is easy. *There is a small break in the die, or chip out of the die,* in the field about one millimeter from the points of the fifth and sixth hair locks, and just the suggestion of another farther out in the field, near the border. The hair is luxuriant, and the cheeks are full, like those of obverse 10. Miss Liberty seems to smile. Maris called her *Amiable Face,* and the die has also been called the first *Marred Field.*

Reverse H. The die break from the rim through R to the wreath is now heavier, and always present. The central and upper parts of the wreath are always more or less weakly struck in this variety, because of the increased amount of metal taken up on the obverse by the relatively heavy mass of hair.

Die break variations. None seen. The obverse die was injured early, and parts of the wreath are seen between hair and cap, in front of the forehead, and sometimes under the cap. The reverse die also has been injured, and there are faint traces of an obverse near the upper leaves of the wreath. This variety is seen frequently on a large planchet.

R-1. Basal $1. 70-55 (70-60-60-55-55-50). Dr. Maris called this lady the Amiable Face. He thought she seemed to smile, and he once owned the coin which we have here graded MS-70. At least two more stand up to MS-60, including one of the ANS pieces. Yet even in this common variety we have found it necessary to include an AU-50 in order to fill out the condition census half dozen.

30

3 0

[97]

1794

31	12·1	Marred Field	HAYS 39
		LONG FRACTION BAR	CHAPMAN 23

Obverse 12. *Second Marred Field.* Resembles the preceding variety closely, but the under part of the double lower lock is cut much more lightly, and *the 1, instead of touching the lock is clear of it by 0.5 mm.* The tip of the lowest lock points well above the foot of the 1 (on obverse 11 it points slightly below the 1). *The tip of the fourth lock projects far beyond the third.* This obverse shows nearly the same *little breaks in the field, or chips out of the die,* as the preceding one, but now they are larger or more developed. The peculiar similarity of these injuries remains a source of numismatic mystery. Maris, Frossard, Hays, and Chapman thought that the two obverses came from totally different dies, but others have considered that obverse 12 is from the same *hub die* as obverse 11, although the many minor differences indicate that there must have been a great amount of retouching and retooling before obverse 12 was considered ready for use. I am inclined to this latter view. Possibly the engraver was disturbed over the manner in which obverse 11 seemed to blur out its reverse mate, and he may have approached the task of "dressing down" this obverse with considerable energy. Maris called obverse 12 the *Marred Field.*

Reverse I. This is the *long fraction bar* reverse. The fraction bar is heavy, extends well beyond the denominator at both ends, and is *the longest found in the 1794 series.* Six berries on each side, the fourth on the left merging with the top of a leaf. The ribbon knot is very heavy and prominent. Between the leaf under T in CENT and adjacent berries the tip of a leaf without its body appears. Another such tip appears to the left of O, and a third above E in ONE.

Die break variations. None seen. This variety is usually found on a large planchet, about 29 mm.

R-2. Basal $1.50. 65-60 (65-65-65-60-55-55). Here for the first time in the current listing we can present a 1794 variety with at least four full MS coins positively known. The showpiece of the lot is probably the Ryder coin, MS-65.

1 7 9 4

32   13·J   Off Center to the Right, Up-turned Locks   HAYS 26
CHAPMAN 11

Obverse 13. Hair terminates in eight long locks, of which the fifth from the bottom is double. *The points immediately above and below the double lock turn upward,* and this characteristic is not seen on any other 1794 die. Maris named this the *Venus Marina* die. Some others have called it the *Upturned Locks.* Date wide, close to the milling, and rather distant from both hair and bust. The lowest curl points directly at the top of the 1. LIBERTY also high and distant from both cap and hair.

Reverse J. This reverse is easily confused with reverse F, since the two have an almost identical heavy die break from the border through the first s, through the wreath, and terminating in the general vicinity of the o in ONE. The F reverse is scarce without this break, and the J is rare without it. The differential diagnosis, however, is easy. The F reverse also has a break down through the E of STATES, and a long fraction bar which is pointed at both ends and extends well beyond the 1 of the denominator. *The J reverse has a short fraction bar which does not cover the* 1. In addition to the break noted, the die has been injured by (apparently several) contacts with other obverse dies, and the result is a complex mass of "suction marks" mostly on the left and upper parts of the wreath. Six berries on each branch of the wreath, but in the common broken die condition of the coin, only five of these can be seen on the left branch—quite an important consideration in attempting to attribute coins "by the berries." All berries small, except the first outside one on the right.

Die break variations. *Obverse:* Found perfect and with a short rim break over LI. *Reverse:* Found perfect (rarely) and with breaks as noted. *This coin is always struck a little off center to the right, so that the right obverse milling is weak or absent,* and frequently the whole right sides of the obverse and reverse are weak.

R-1. Basal $1. 55-45 (55-55-50-45-45-40). The Venus Marina variety remains a collector's enigma, for although common (R-1) there does not seem to be an available example at MS-60.

1 7 9 4

The best we can offer are three in the 50's and a comparative abundance of nice examples at the F and VF levels.

33	13·K	Rim Break Over LI	HAYS 27
		REVERSE WEAK IN THE CENTER, SIX "WHEEL SPOKE" BREAKS	CHAPMAN 12

Obverse 13. In this marriage obverse 13 *always* has the short rim break over LI, and some specimens show also a faint break from the top of L to a point on the top of the cap about 3 mm. from the border.

Reverse K. The die is raised at the center so that $\frac{ONE}{CENT}$ is usually not legible, and six short breaks are seen at the periphery of the coin, radiating from the border almost like spokes. These occur near the end of the left ribbon, through I of UNITED, between D and S, between A and T, through the first A of AMERICA, and from the right ribbon end. Two specimens are known on which only four of the breaks are visible, and I have seen one worn example on which no breaks can be made out. The breaks are in this instance almost diagnostic for the variety. Six berries on each branch. First berry on the left touches the loop, and the second nearly touches.

Die break variations. As noted. This has been known as the *Hays* variety, since it was discovered and reported by Mr. Hays in 1888.

R-7. Basal $15. 20-10 (20-12-12-10-10-10). Nine examples of this famous rarity are now known to us but unfortunately three of them are impounded in ANS, and two of the remaining six are injured or burnished coins. This leaves the collector a small field of choice and accounts for the high basal value. The 20-coin is a new discovery, turned up by a West Coast collector in 1950. Of the others, one of the 12's and two of the 10's are in ANS.

34	13·L	Rim Break Over LI	HAYS 28
		SINGLE BERRY LEFT OF BOW	CHAPMAN 13

Obverse 13. The break over LI now has an extension across the top of the cap and curves back to the border at the fourth denticle beyond.

[100]

1 7 9 4

Reverse L. First single berry reverse. Easily recognized by the fact that *there is but a single berry adjacent to the left side of the bow*. On all other 1794 reverses but one (the next following) there are two berries in this position. Five berries left and six right. The meeting of the loops of the ribbon bow "misses" the knot, and is misplaced well to the left of it. This, then, is the "misplaced bow with the single berry" reverse. On the end of the left stem is a die scratch 1 mm. in length. The die has been slightly injured by contact with an obverse die, and many faint traces of the injury can be seen on Fine coins.

Die break variations. None seen.

R-7. Basal $12.50. 35-15 (35-35-12-10-10-10). Ten now known to us, eight of them in collectors' hands. One of the 35-coins and about a 5-coin are in ANS. Four examples new to the present writer have appeared since EAC was written. Still a great rarity, most fervently desired by collectors who are dangerously sick with the cent disease. The original Hays coin and the Dr. French coin, both now called VF-35, were graded EF-40 in EAC.

35

35   14·L   Delicate Lower Lock   HAYS 29
              SINGLE BERRY LEFT OF BOW   CHAPMAN 28

Obverse 14. Shattered die and slender locks. Hair shorter, less massive, and terminating in *seven slender, well-separated locks, the lowest of which is more delicate than on any other 1794 obverse*. LIBERTY close to the border, and the R, which is double cut at the top, just touches one of the denticles. *This obverse usually seen shattered* (see below), and when the break between E and R is present, RTY seems to be higher than LIBE. The cheek is rounded and full. The date is very close to the border, the bottom of the 9 merging with a denticle, and the lower part of the 4 usually missing.

Reverse L.

Die break variations. *Obverse:* A few examples are known with perfect die, but most of the coins show a heavy break starting at the border between E and R, extending down across the head and bust to the border just left of the 4; another, from the border across the lower part of the cap to the hair; and sometimes a slighter crack across the hair midway between the

1 7 9 4

two mentioned. Coins are known showing various stages in the progression of these breaks. Traces of the wreath are sometimes seen back of the hair and under the cap, and traces of the obverse die are visible on the reverse. The two dies "met" at some point in their careers.

R-6. Basal $6. 50-20 (50-30-30-15-15-12). The AU-50 and one of the VF-30's are in ANS, leaving available to collectors only four above the grade Fine. At least a dozen of this variety are known in the very low condition grades, between 6 and 1. It is an especially desired collector's item because of the dramatic obverse die breaks.

NC-1   15·L   Low Head / SINGLE BERRY LEFT OF BOW   HAYS 30 / CHAPMAN 15

Obverse 15. Head of Liberty low, crowding the date, which is very close to the border. *The bust seems virtually to rest on the 4, which in turn rests on the border.* Point of the lowest curl distant a good 2 mm. from the 1. Fourth lock from the bottom much shorter than the one above or below it. Seven locks to the hair. LIBERTY very high, close to the border, distant from the hair, and widely spaced, particularly between R and T. Called by Maris the *Crowded Date*.

Reverse L.

Die break variations. None seen.

R-8. 3-3 (3-3-3). No new ones. Only the three are known that were reported in EAC. However, all three are now graded Very Fair, or condition 3, instead of condition 2. Perhaps this is inflation. Just one of these is in collectors' hands. Two of them were given to ANS. If another should appear, a basal value would have to be assigned to the variety.

36   15·M   Low Head, / Single Berry Left of Bow / LOWEST RIGHT LEAF POINTS TO C   HAYS 31 / CHAPMAN 14

Obverse 15.

Reverse M. Second single berry reverse. *Only a single berry adjacent to the left side of the bow.* Six berries left and seven right. The lowest leaf on the right points to C (on reverse L

[102]

1 7 9 4

the lowest leaf points to and nearly reaches the left foot of A). The fraction bar does not quite cover either the 1 or the last 0 of the fraction.

Die break variations. None seen.

R-6. Basal $6. 55-30 (55-55-45-25-15-12). Upper range of R-6, not far from R-7. This variety was considered R-7 before the two finest examples now known were brought in from England in 1934. One of these went to ANS. Another new one, VF-25, was found in an Eastern collection in 1949, and now at least five are known in collectors' hands above the level of Fine. However, it is still a very rare variety.

| 37 | 16·M | The Distant 1 SINGLE BERRY LEFT OF BOW | HAYS 59 CHAPMAN 16 |

Obverse 16. Distant 1 with small 7. The date is wide, with the 1 *and* 7 *far apart* and the 9 leaning a little to the left. The figures are small, as on all the obverses so far presented. (Beginning with obverse 19 a new set of figures, with a 7 which seems particularly larger, will be seen.) Eight distinct ends to the hair locks. The second one from the bottom is longer than usual and bends sharply down over the lowest lock. Called by some the *Distant 1 variety.* Also called *Steigerwalt variety,* after its discoverer.

3 8

Reverse M.

Die break variations. None seen.

R-7. Basal $15. 50-10 (50-15-15-7-6-4). No new ones. We can account for seven of these, two of them (the best and the worst) in ANS. In the present review the Sargent coin and the Hills-Clapp coin are called F-15. Both were graded F-12 in EAC. The Sargent coin was graded VF by Macallister in the Newcomb collection. The Hills-Clapp coin, handled by Chapman in 1932, was then graded "VF but lightly eroded."

| 38 | 17·M | Marred Field SINGLE BERRY LEFT OF BOW | HAYS 41 CHAPMAN 24 |

Obverse 17. *Third Marred Field.* Close general resemblance to obverses 11 and 12, and believed by some to have come

1 7 9 4

from the same hub die as these two. The same small breaks or defects are present in the field back of the hair. The full cheeks and smiling expression (*Amiable Face*) are about the same, as is treatment of the hair, spacing of LIBERTY and the date, and the low position of the head of Liberty. However, the double lower lock is now replaced by a single one and this obverse can be recognized easily by the *single lower lock, together with the little pear-shaped breaks behind the hair.*

From its appearance, I think that it could well be from the same hub die that produced obverse 11, but now for the second time radically retouched and tooled. The relief of the hair on obverse 12 is flatter than that on obverse 11, and on obverse 17 it is still more flat, as if the die had been ground down a little and retooled on each occasion.

Reverse M.

Die break variations. None seen, except with respect to the two small chiplike breaks back of the hair, which vary somewhat in size on different specimens. On some the smaller break, nearest the border, is scarcely visible. This variation may be a result of the way the coin happened to be struck.

R-6. Basal $5. 55-20 (55-30-25-20-20-15). Only one is known near MS. This is the Winsor-Newcomb-ANS piece, called MS-60 in EAC but graded AU-55 in the present review. The Gilbert-Hines coin, second finest we have seen, is on later examination a VF-30 rather than EF-40. No important new examples of H-41 have appeared. The rarity is in the lower range of R-6 but the condition census is lower than the earlier estimate.

39	17·N	Marred Field	HAYS 40
		SPRAWLED RIBBON ENDS	CHAPMAN 25

Obverse 17. The breaks back of the hair are usually a little more prominent than on the preceding variety.

Reverse N. Sprawled ribbon ends. Broad border with the coarsest or *largest denticles seen on any 1794 cent.* ONE CENT high in the wreath, with the center dot just to the left of the left upright of N in CENT. The ribbon ends sprawl widely (distance between them at the bottom, 7 mm.). The two lower leaves on the right are very close to C, and from the upper one

1 7 9 4

a fine line extends for 1 mm. under the base of c. Seven berries left, six right. The fraction bar is short, barely reaching the 1 of the denominator and failing to cover the center of the last 0.

Die break variations. *Reverse:* A crack extends from the rim near 1 of the denominator, across the left ribbon, under UN and into I. This crack is faintly present on all but one of the specimens I have seen.

R-7. Basal $12.50. 55-30 (55-50-35-35-30-7). The Granberg-Hines coin, AU-55, and the Hall-Brand coin, AU-50, stand alone in the uncirculated class. The second mentioned is now in ANS. In EAC it was stated that six of the nine known examples were in VF to AU condition. The "sixth" one proved to be a fiction. The collector reporting it had a Hays 40 all right, but in condition 2. The coin on which he had reported was a Hays 39—a very typical and familiar incident for cent hunters.

40 17·O Marred Field / SPRUNG REVERSE DIE   HAYS 42   CHAPMAN 26

Obverse 17. The breaks back of the hair are now still further developed, the larger one extending from the fourth lock to slightly above the sixth.

Reverse O. The bow is small and high above the knot. Distance between the ribbon ends is 5.5 mm. *The right ribbon terminates in a line about 1 mm. in length* (engraver's slip). Seven berries on each branch. The fraction bar is rather long, extending beyond the 1 of the denominator. The ribbon ends are much nearer to the fraction than to the adjacent letters (on reverse N, the converse).

Die break variations. The reverse is seen perfect, and with two short cracks: from the border between U and N to the nearest leaf; and from the border to the bottom of the upright of D. *This die was "sprung" a little, so that the center of the reverse of the coin is higher than the periphery.* On worn specimens $\frac{ONE}{CENT}$ is likely to be faint or obliterated. There is a faint line, apparently a diecutter's scratch, extending from the leaf above C in CENT to the left ribbon, and another short one branching from the first into the right side of the bow.

R-6. Basal $5. 55-25 (55-45-30-25-20-15). The Hays-Gilbert-

1 7 9 4

Granberg coin, AU-55, and the Hall-Brand-ANS piece, EF-45, are the only occupants of the upper condition bracket so far as we know. Second finest seen in collectors' hands is a VF-30. The variety appears to fall in the middle range of R-6 but we know of no more than a half dozen fine ones.

NC-2	17·P	Marred Field	HAYS 61
		FATAL BREAK VARIETY	CHAPMAN 27

Obverse 17. The small breaks behind the hair are of about the same prominence as on the preceding variety.

Reverse P. Very similar to reverse N. Sprawled ribbon ends (distance between them, 8 mm.). These two reverses, N and P, have *the most widely spreading ribbon ends seen on the 1794 cents.* Seven berries left and six right. The left ribbon terminates in a short thin line (engraver's scratch). On the only example known, *the die is badly broken from the border above* E *in* UNITED, through D, along the bottom of ST and upwards over the top of A. This whole area is raised above the surface of the coin, and certainly no more were struck from the die after this one. So far as anybody now knows, this may indeed have been the only one struck. The die may have broken at its first use. The *Fatal Break* variety.

Die break variations. None seen.

R-8. Unique. 60-0. Phelps-Sargent-Newcomb-ANS coin. Full Mint State sharpness and surface but without the brilliancy necessary for MS-65. No more of them reported.

41	18·Q	Truncated Hair Locks	HAYS 19
		MINUTE BERRIES	CHAPMAN 9

Obverse 18. *Between the cap and the head, two short locks terminate abruptly, one above the pole and one below it.* Only this die presents the characteristic, which therefore is diagnostic. Called by Maris the *Abrupt Hair* variety. The next lock below the truncated ones is separated from the hair, while the six remaining are long and wavy. LIBERTY and the date are very close to the border, the former distant from cap and head, and in the date the 1 and the 4 are relatively distant from the central figures.

[106]

1 7 9 4

Reverse Q. *Heavy border with short, rounded denticles.* Three minute and four medium sized berries on the left, *seven minute berries on the right.* Beautifully spaced reverse, with the letters and fraction lightly punched in, lending an impression of delicacy to the coin. Fraction low, well centered in the continuation of the circle formed by the legend. Center dot touches the left perpendicular of N. Short wreath stems pointing at right foot of A and at bottom of U. Fraction closely spaced, with short fraction bar.

Die break variations. *Obverse:* Usually perfect, but seen with crack from the border between 7 and 9.   *Reverse:* Seen perfect, but usually cracked: From border through D along the top of CE to N, thence curving into N of ONE; from the border between A and T, and thence curving into O of ONE. Various stages of these breaks are seen.

R-4. Basal $3. 60-30 (60-40-35-30-30-25). The Cleneay-Earle-ANS coin remains the only Mint State one reported and no new fine ones have appeared. The variety is in the upper range of R-4 but probably is not quite R-5.

42	18·R	Truncated Hair Locks WEAK OF	HAYS 20 CHAPMAN 10

Obverse 18. In this marriage, the obverse die is always seen perfect, so far as I know. Therefore it presumably was an earlier marriage than 18-Q, and we here knowingly violate the probable order of issue. Reason: the next variety, 19-R, follows naturally after 18-R, according to the evidence of the *reverse* die breaks, and one or the other of the two "natural" sequences had to be violated. The cause of such a dilemma probably lies in some whimsicality at the Mint, whereby a marriage of dies was interrupted and later resumed.

Reverse R. Six large berries on each branch. Fraction rather widely spaced with long fraction bar. The left stem has a thin line, 1 mm. long (engraver's scratch) at its tip. The center dot is merged in the top of N, to left of upright. This reverse is *always struck a little weak in the right upper portion.* OF *is weak* and the top of the O is scarcely visible, even on Extremely Fine coins. The *Weak* OF reverse.

1 7 9 4

Die break variations. None seen.

R-5. Basal $4. 50-30 (50-40-35-30-25-20). A previously unreported AU-50 came to light in one of the remnant lots from the Brand hoard sold in 1951. The variety remains R-5, rather than R-6, but in the upper range of R-5.

43	19·R	Short Bust	HAYS 34
		WEAK OF; BREAK OVER A	CHAPMAN 35

Obverse 19. Named by Maris the *Short Bust* variety. *The bust is very short in back,* and like obverses 2, 3, 4, 7, 21, 22, and 23, it lacks the loop at the bottom where the bust joins the lower lock. The hair is thick and in wavy lines, with the *locks decidedly shorter than on previously listed obverses.* Hair terminates in seven fine locks of about equal thickness. The date is tall, closely spaced, with the 4 touching the bust, and the 1 almost touching the hair.

Here for the first time in the series we see a *new set of figures,* with longer and larger 7, tall, pointed 4, taller, more pointed 1, and a slightly taller 9. This is the beginning of Chapman's Style 3, and in this group (obverses 19 through 23) the busts are a little smaller and narrower, with the *hair in rolled locks over the ear, and the lowest curl only about the same thickness as those above it.* The hair is treated in more minute detail, as if to try to delineate the separate hairs. The faces have *full, plump cheeks.*

Reverse R. In this marriage the die is *always* broken over A in STATES.

Die break variations. *Obverse:* Found perfect and with crack from border downward along back of cap and extending briefly into the field; another from the border through the lower part of 7 and upper part of 1 to the lowest lock. *Reverse:* Usually seen with break from the border upwards through U and wreath, along C in CENT to left above. This last crack is seen in many stages of progression, finally splitting and distorting the U so that it looks like a Greek ψ.

R-2. Basal $1.50. 60-50 (60-60-50-50-45-40). Two are known in MS-60: the Ellsworth-ANS coin and one that turned up in the T. J. Clarke collection in 1949. Probably there are a full

1794

half dozen in the bracket between 50 and 40. Yet three or four of the numismatically best ones have been recolored or otherwise tampered with in some way. This is a difficult variety in which to find an attractive coin above the VF level.

		Short Bust	
44	19·S	LARGE BERRY OPPOSITE C	HAYS 33 CHAPMAN 36

Obverse 19. Here obverse 19 is *always* cracked, the breaks are heavier, and examples are known on which the two cracks extend and meet, in the lowest hair locks. The die has been slightly injured, and on most specimens traces of the wreath can be seen under the cap, between cap and head, and near the juncture of pole with bust.

Reverse S. Seven berries on the left branch: *the third (opposite* C *in* CENT*) extra large, and the fourth without a stem.* Six on the right. The right ribbon end is weak, split, and seems short. *A berry is directly under the left upright of* M. The upper part of O in OF is struck up strongly (always weak on reverse R).

Die break variations. *Obverse:* Many stages of the breaks seen. *Reverse:* The perfect die is not rare, but usually a conspicuous crack is seen running downward from the border, near the O, to the N of ONE, and (in some instances) continuing to the bow. In practice, reverses R and S are recognized "across the room" by their die breaks.

R-2. Basal $1.50. 55-50 (55-55-50-45-40-40). The Proskey-Hines and Sargent-ANS coins are AU-55 but in this review we have failed to bring to light an MS-60. The Newcomb coin is a nice AU-50. After this there are at least a dozen which can be called EF or about EF. Like the preceding variety, quite a number of the better Hays 33's have been tampered with—usually darkened to an undesirable blackish brown.

		Short Bust	
NC·5	19·T	"BERRY" IN LEFT LOOP OF BOW	NEW NOT IN CHAPMAN

Obverse 19. Cracked as on the last specimens of No. 44.

Reverse T. Injured as on all known examples of No. 45, the Hays 47.

1 7 9 4

R-8. Unique. 4-0. A previously unreported variety discovered by John Pawling, 1951. The existence of this coin provides confirmation of the order of varieties presented in EAC.

45	20·T	Braided Hair	HAYS 47
		"BERRY" IN LEFT LOOP OF BOW	CHAPMAN 33

Obverse 20. Called by Maris *The Plicae*, referring to the fact that the hair is partially twisted or coiled into heavy, separate braids, which point out behind in quite a novel manner. There are *five heavy braids, and between the third and fourth a gap or open space leads into the nape of the neck.* LIBERTY rather distant from the border. L about 0.5 mm. from the cap, and R the same distance from the hair. *The 1 and 4 just about touch the hair and bust respectively.* The 7 is a trifle low and seems very long. The face is large and full, with what Chapman calls a "solemn expression." The first *Braided Hair*.

4 5

Reverse T. This reverse has been injured, and *the whole area across the coin from* TA *of* STATES *to the lower right branch seems peppered with a shower of minute linear marks*, evidently caused by scratches in the die. Between the end of the right ribbon and the milling is what looks like a small extra piece of ribbon. *In the left loop of the bow there is an irregular injury about twice the size of a berry*, and a smaller injury in the right loop. Several little injuries at the first T of STATES, near and in the first letters of $\frac{\text{ONE}}{\text{CENT}}$, and in and about the wreath, induced both Frossard and Chapman to describe a "continuous die break" in this region. Seven berries left and six right. Ribbon bow high, with the berries at its left close. The short fraction bar slants upward to the right and points above the end of the right ribbon.

Die break variations. *Reverse:* In addition to the injuries described, which are constant, a small crack is usually seen from the border, touching I and C, crossing the nearest leaf, and reaching the right stem.

R-6. Basal $5. 60-25 (60-35-30-30-20-20). Lower range of R-6, formerly rated R-5. No important new ones have appeared, and the consensus of opinion strongly supports elevation to R-6. The Gilbert-Hines coin appears to stand alone at MS-60, with

1 7 9 4

the Dr. French piece probably second at VF-35. To complete the top half dozen it seems necessary to include two 20-coins.

46	20·U	Braided Hair	HAYS 48
		CROSSED E	CHAPMAN 34

Obverse 20. In this marriage a straight crack is always seen beginning at the tip of the third denticle to the left of the pole, and extending across the bust to the hair.

Reverse U. Six berries left, four of them on the inside, and six right. Ribbon distant above the knot, and no injuries or die breaks within the bow (contrast with reverse T). *A heavy, short break crosses the* E *of* CENT, *and extends only 1 or 2 mm. beyond that letter. This break is constant and diagnostic.* By means of it collectors identify the die at a glance. The rather short fraction bar points directly at the end of the right ribbon. The berries are more distant from the left side of the bow than on reverse T. The *Crossed E* variety.

Die break variations. *Obverse:* In addition to the crack already noted, another starts at the border below the 4, extends up through that numeral, and sends a branch nearly at right angles to join the first crack. Another branch starts in the opposite direction, runs along the bottom of the bust and across the lowest lock, and curves upward to the border. This obverse is seen in many stages of progression of the cracks, but oddly enough the final state, with all the breaks heavy, is rather common. Hundreds of coins must have been struck with the die shattered, but how it held up in such a condition is quite a mystery.

R-2. Basal $1.50. 60-55 (60-55-55-55-50-50). Probably in the lower range of R-2, yet in this review we have been able to unearth only a single MS-60—a Gilbert-Proskey-Hines coin. There are at least three 55's, possibly four. The current book rating on one of these would be 55×$1.50×2, or $165.

47	21·V	Short Bust	HAYS 6
		BOW SKEWED LEFT	CHAPMAN 29

Obverse 21. Resembles both obverse 19 and obverse 20. It has

1 7 9 4

the short, loopless bust of obverse 19. The hair is similarly short, but not so wavy, and presents a semi-braided appearance which suggests obverse 20. LIBERTY is very low, the uprights of L and I are double cut, and R almost touches the highest point of the forelock. In the date the two central figures are close but the 1 and 4 are more distant, almost touching the hair and bust respectively. *The upper two locks are braided,* as on obverse 20, *and they end abruptly. Immediately beneath these is an end of a lock entirely severed from the hair.* The lowest locks are thin and wavy. The plump, full face induced Maris to name this the *Young Head.* It might be called the *Braided Upper Locks.*

Reverse V. Six berries on each side, *with four of them on the inside on each branch,* and this is diagnostic, since on all of the other six-six reverses, at least three of the berries on the right branch are outside. *The bow is badly to the left of center. The right ribbon is split at the end,* with the inner part extending 1 mm. beyond the outer part. Right ribbon shorter than the left. Fraction bar a little short.

Die break variations. *Reverse:* On most specimens a small crack extends from the border past the first A in AMERICA to the nearest leaf, but Chapman is incorrect in the statement that this crack is always present. I have seen four or five examples without it.

R-5. Basal $4. 55-30 (55-30-30-30-25-25). The Clapp-ANS coin, AU-55, is the only one known to us near Mint State. It was incorrectly graded MS-60 in EAC. After this one, the Hines coin, the Newcomb coin, and one unearthed by Downing in 1950 can all be graded about alike at VF-30.

48	21·W	Short Bust	HAYS 8
		STARRED REVERSE	CHAPMAN 30

Obverse 21. Now retooled. The double cutting of L and I has been removed.

Reverse W. The famous reverse with the *circle of ninety-four minute five-pointed stars* seen just inside the border and between the points of the denticles. The stars are not quite equally spaced, and the denticles partially cover some of them. They are put in with a light punch, and since they are far too light to have been intended as a border, it is perhaps more likely that they are the result of the whim of an idle hour at the Mint. The R has a tail, as on reverses H and FF. The *Starred* reverse.

Die break variations. None seen.

R-6. Basal $10. 25-15 (25-25-15-12-10-10). The Miller-ANS piece and the Jackman-Hines coin, both VF-25, are well-known numismatic landmarks. The Brand hoard remnant, already several times mentioned, produced a new Hays 8 in 1951 which can be graded F-15. The Gilbert-Würtzbach coin is an F-12. The French piece and a somewhat eroded Hays 8 from the Winsor collection are about VG-10. Both of these last two have been often sold during recent decades as "finest known." Each time this happens there is a fine tremor in the earth as all the great cent collectors turn over in their graves with angry grunts. The Starred Reverse variety is in the lower range of R-6 but its great fame ordains a high basal value. Collectors mention it with religious awe.

49

| 49 | 21·X | Short Bust / CLOSED WREATH | HAYS 7 CHAPMAN 31 |

Obverse 21.

Reverse X. This reverse die is famous as the "tough old lady of the big cents." She outlasted six husbands and even at the end showed not a die break and scarcely a scratch. Leaves large and spread rather widely, *one leaf ending within 0.5 mm. of the bottom of* O *in* OF. *The two branches of the wreath touch at the top, closing the circle,* and this is practically diagnostic, for the only other reverse on which it occurs is the preceding one (W). The piece of ribbon connecting the bow to the knot is defective, and connects only with the *right ribbon end, which in turn is so far out of place that it practically touches the last* 0 *of the fraction,* and this also is diagnostic, occurring on no other reverse. *The Closed Wreath.*

Die break variations. *Obverse:* Found perfect, and with many stages in the progression of a crack from the border through the upright of E, and ultimately over the head to a side lock of hair. Obverse sometimes seen with double profile.

1 7 9 4

R-2. Basal $1.50. 55-45 (55-50-45-45-40-40). No MS Hays 7 has appeared, but one from the Brand hoard (1940) can be graded AU-55 and at least a half dozen more are rather bunched in the 50 to 40 bracket.

		Short Bust, Detached Lower Lock	
50	22·X	CLOSED WREATH	HAYS 57 CHAPMAN 32

Obverse 22. Very similar to obverse 21. The hair is shorter, and more delicately or minutely engraved, like that of obverses 19 and 20 but even more remarkably fine than they. Here the engraver seems to have tried to represent each single hair, and the face also is more delicately executed than perhaps any other in the series except obverse 23, which shows the same quality. The pole is twice its width from the bust. *The 4 touches the bust but the 1 is clear of the hair.* Seven locks can be counted, *the lowest detached from the hair,* the second a mere line, and *the uppermost lock only a short little nub which points nearly at the center of the cap.* This last, and the detached lower lock, are the easiest diagnostic points.

Reverse X. *The Closed Wreath.*

Die break variations. None seen.

R-6. Basal $5. 45-25 (45-40-35-25-20-15). The Miller-Newcomb coin, EF-45, is now generally regarded as finest of the variety. This is a 50-coin with a planchet defect which grades it down a little. The Proskey-Hines piece, now ANS, can be called EF-40, and the Gilbert-French coin is VF-35. The condition census 40-35, given in EAC, resulted from two badly exaggerated gradings from what should have been excellent sources. The difficulty lies in standardization of description, and a scale is only an effort to make a description more exact.

		Short Bust, Long Locks	
51	23·X	CLOSED WREATH	HAYS 10 CHAPMAN 37

Obverse 23. As on the last, the hair is very finely engraved, and this die closely resembles obverse 22 except that *the locks are much longer, particularly the second and fourth* from the bottom, which project out into the field well beyond the others.

1 7 9 4

The coin is readily recognized by these long lower locks. *The 4 touches the bust and the 1 almost touches the hair.*

Reverse X. *The Closed Wreath.*

Die break variations. *Obverse:* Usually found perfect. A few examples are known with a crack which arises from the border between 1 and 7, turns across the top of the 7, crosses the bust, and curves down to the end of the pole. I have seen four or five specimens on which another crack extends almost horizontally from the border at the left, through the second lock and into the hair.

R-5. Basal $4. 55-40 (55-50-50-40-30-25). The Miller-Hines coin can be graded AU-55, almost MS. The Newcomb-Downing and the Clapp-ANS coins are about on a par at AU-50, and a new EF-40 was turned up by Gaskill in Philadelphia about 1949. This variety, the Closed Wreath with the Long Locks, has been a cherished one among cent people.

52   24·X   1 and 7 Distant   HAYS 9
CLOSED WREATH   CHAPMAN 50

Obverse 24. With this obverse we leave behind the fine engraving of the hair and henceforth encounter less delicate execution of the dies. The head and hair are in lower, although not yet flat relief, and the hair ends in seven locks, of which the lowest is coarse and comparatively heavy. *This lock continues upward over the back part of the neck in a manner not seen on any other die.* The 4 touches the bust and the 1 *is rather distant from the* 7 but is clear of the hair by about 0.5 mm. The third lock from the bottom is the longest and it curves down a little, over the second.

Reverse X. *The Closed Wreath.*

Die break variations. *Obverse:* Only two examples of perfect die known to me. Usually, a crack starts from the border about 2 mm. below the top of the cap, crosses the cap and disappears in the hair.

R-7. Basal $12.50. 25-10 (25-12-12-12-10-8). There appear to be eight of these now in collectors' hands, and two more in ANS. The Hays-Gilbert-Hines coin stands out in lonely position at VF-25. The ANS coins are a 12 and a 10. Two more 12's and an

1 7 9 4

8 complete the condition census. Among these last the most famous is the Dr. French piece, F-12.

53 25·X Severed Sixth Lock / CLOSED WREATH HAYS 58 / CHAPMAN 47

Obverse 25. General style like the last. Moderately low relief. Locks rather coarse. The features not so delicately engraved as on earlier obverses, leaving the face somewhat "hard" or expressionless. Seven locks, the lowest heavy and ending in a short hook. The third lock is the longest but does not bend down over the second, as it does on obverse 24. *The sixth lock (second from the top) is chopped off short* and its severed tip is seen 0.5 mm. out in the field. LIBERTY low, the R and T not over 0.5 mm. from the forelock. In the date the 1 and 7 are close, and the 4 just touches the bust.

Reverse X. *The Closed Wreath.*

Die break variations. None seen.

R-7. Basal $12.50. 50-25 (50-45-45-15-10-10). Probably seven now available to collectors, and one in ANS. This last, AU-50, is perhaps the finest one although closely seconded by the Newcomb and French pieces, both of which can be graded EF-45. The Dr. French coin, thought to be discolored and corroded, and graded VF-30 in EAC, produced a pleasant surprise when it turned out to be merely coated with some kind of black, gummy substance which could be removed, revealing beneath it an EF-45 coin. This is the kind of numismatic anecdote that usually ends in a different fashion.

54 26·X Slanting 7 / CLOSED WREATH HAYS 11 / CHAPMAN 43

Obverse 26. Maris called this the *Crooked 7*. One of the easiest of the obverses to recognize, as *the 7 is tipped markedly to the right*. The relief of the coin is a little flatter than the last two, and the general outline of the head of Liberty, with the long straight sweep down the hair on the left, suggests a pyramid. The seven locks are comparatively heavy, and the *three upper ones are more widely spaced than on any die yet consid-*

1794

ered. The third is the longest, turning slightly downward at the tip. (Chapman suggests that the second and third locks form a figure like a bird's beak.) *The uppermost lock points into the cap.* LIBERTY is low, with the L close to the cap. The 1 and 4 are very close to the hair and bust, but neither touches.

Reverse X. *The Closed Wreath.*

Die break variations. *Obverse:* Usually seen with perfect die. On some specimens a light crack runs from the border to the hair, below the cap.

R-3. Basal $2. 40-35 (40-35-35-35-30-30). The Dr. French coin, at EF-40, is still considered slightly the finest among a half dozen or so of very nearly equal condition rating. This is the last appearance of the Closed Wreath reverse, which bore up heroically under six marriages in one year, and for a century and a half afterward has provided cent collectors with one of their best clues to attribution.

5.5

| 55 | 26·Y | Slanting 7
LARGE BERRIES | HAYS 13
CHAPMAN 44 |

Obverse 26. In this marriage, the crack noted is always seen.

Reverse Y. *The ribbon bow has two knots and they are not connected.* The right ribbon connects with the upper knot, the left with the lower one. The right stem is disconnected from the ribbon. Six berries left and five right, the upper one on the right lying against the wreath stem, having no stem of its own. *The berries are cut in high relief and are unusually large.* A in STATES *high and toppling to the left.* N of CENT high; T very high. The *Big Berries* variety.

Die break variations. *Obverse:* On some specimens a second crack branches off from the first, curving down through the hair to the shoulder.

R-3. Basal $2. 65-40 (65-50-40-40-35-30). No new ones of high condition. The Shumway-Hines piece appears to stand alone at MS-65, with the Newcomb coin an excellent second at AU-50. The Slanting 7 with the Large Berries.

[117]

1 7 9 4

		Slanting 7	
56	26·Z	OFFICE BOY REVERSE	HAYS 12 CHAPMAN 45

Obverse 26. The cracks are more strongly developed.

Reverse Z. Clapp calls this the *Office Boy* reverse. The wreath is unsymmetrical, with some of the leaves too deeply cut. TA of STATES joined at the bottom. AM of AMERICA too widely spaced. *The N of ONE was first cut upside down and then recut.* Two knots to the ribbon bow and no connection between them. Short fraction bar sloping up to the right. *The right ribbon end seems to fall inward toward the fraction, and then to turn back, making an angle.* The tip of the ribbon is detached and pointed. Eight berries left and seven right, the two upper ones at the left almost microscopic and lying against the wreath stem. Lowest leaf on the right points to the right foot of A.

Die break variations. None seen.

5 7   **R-4.** Basal $3. 55-35 (55-45-35-35-35-30). The Newcomb coin, showpiece of the variety, is an AU-55, almost MS. The next finest seen is the Dr. French piece, EF-45, and then follow perhaps a half dozen between 40 and 30. The Slanting 7 with Office Boy reverse.

		Pyramidal Head,	
57	27·AA	Button on Cap	HAYS 14 CHAPMAN 46

Obverse 27. In even flatter relief than obverse 26, and presenting the same straight sweep down the hair at the left which suggests the outline of a pyramid. Maris names this variety the *Pyramidal Head. At the lower corner of the cap a diecutter's slip left a minute crater in the die which on the coin looks like a button,* about the size of a berry, and has given rise to the name *Button Variety.* LIBERTY very low. Date compact and well spaced, nearer to hair than bust but close to both. Seven rather coarse locks with the three upper ones widely spaced, as on obverse 26. The third lock much like the longest (forming a "bird's beak" with the second) and the tip of the fifth severed.

Reverse AA. Seven large berries on each branch, with four on the inside and three outside. *The lowest berry on the left is merged with the ribbon bow,* while another berry is very close, and this is diagnostic. The lowest leaf on the right nearly

1 7 9 4

touches C. Long fraction bar and wide denominator.

Die break variations. *Obverse:* Found perfect, and with two faint parallel cracks or shallow troughs from the nose and lower lip to the border; crack about 2 mm. in length connecting top of cap to the hair, and a fainter crack curving above this one, between cap and hair. In the more advanced stages of the first cracks mentioned, the lower one develops into the "image of a snake projecting his tongue" (Chapman), and another very faint crack extends into the mouth, through the upper lip, to cheek, and to temple.

Reverse: There is an injury to the die over CA, which on some specimens looks like a crack, and several other injuries are seen faintly near the center of the reverse.

R-1. Basal $1. 55-55 (55-55-55-55-55-50). We have not been able to defend the earlier impression that at least one of this famous variety is an MS-60. Not less than five of them, and possibly six, seem to be grouped at AU-55. Probably this is the third commonest variety of 1794, surpassed only by Nos. 22 and 65.

58

58	28·BB	Thick Hair, Wide Date	HAYS 16
		RIGHT RIBBON HIGH	CHAPMAN 39

Obverse 28. Thick hair, thick planchet, wide date. Called by Maris the *Many Haired,* because of the *luxuriance of the hair.* Very similar to obverses 26 and 27, but the upper locks of hair are much longer, and so the head has lost its pyramidal effect. Seven large but well-defined locks, with 3 mm. of distance between the points of the sixth and seventh. The fourth and fifth locks slope downward, and the second and third present the "open bird's beak" appearance mentioned by Chapman. LIBERTY midway between hair and border, *with* L I B *very widely spaced. The date is wide,* curving, with the 1 near the hair and the 4 nearly a millimeter away from the bust.

Reverse BB. Six berries left and seven right. Four on the inside of each branch. *The right ribbon end emerges from the top of the knot and is much closer to the stem than is the left.* The rather long fraction bar seems shifted to the right, covering the last cipher but failing to reach beyond the center of

1 7 9 4

the 1. A berry under the right edge of the left upright of M.

Die break variations. *Reverse:* Usually found perfect, but not infrequently seen with a crack through UNIT, and on some specimens the crack has become a heavy break involving the border. The cracked die is not much rarer than the perfect die. This variety and the next three to follow are always found on extra thick planchets.

R-3. Basal $2. 55-40 (55-45-40-35-30-30). In this review the rarity of both Hays 16 and Hays 15 is reduced from R-4 to R-3, although both are maintained at the old basal value of $2. For the Hays 16 the Gilbert-Hines coin, now corrected to AU-55, is far the finest seen. The next half dozen or so are fairly well strung out between 45 and 30.

5 9

| 59 | 28·CC | Thick Hair, Wide Date
LEFT RIBBON BOW DOUBLE CUT | HAYS 15
CHAPMAN 40 |

Obverse 28. Thick hair, thick planchet, wide date.

Reverse CC. Berries as on reverse AA (four inside and three outside on each branch). *The left side of the ribbon bow is double cut,* and there is a diecutter's slip on the right wreath stem near its crossing with the ribbon. The inside leaf, right, points just under the foot of T. A berry under the left edge of the left upright of M.

Die break variations. *Obverse:* Found perfect, and with a small crack back of the 9 to the bust. *Reverse:* Found perfect, but usually has a crack starting at the border under the end of the left ribbon, slanting across the fraction and the right ribbon end, and curving down through the A to the border. Examples are known in which this crack has developed into a heavy break obliterating the entire area between the original crack and the rim. ANS has a collection of five, illustrating progressions of the break. Thick planchets, often with rich color.

R-3. Basal $2. 60-40 (60-60-40-35-30-30). Rarity reduced from R-4 to R-3. The two finest seen are an MS-60 from ANS and another from the Clarke collection. At least four more are now known between 40 and 30.

[120]

1794

60   29·DD   Thick Hair, Close Date   HAYS 35
　　　　　RIGHT RIBBON HIGH   CHAPMAN 41

Obverse 29. Thick hair, thick planchet, close date. Similar in general to obverse 28. Broad head with coarse locks and thick hair, but *the date is compact,* the last three figures particularly so. LIBERTY evenly spaced and low, almost touching the *forelock, which has a peculiarly square top.* Some collectors have called this the *Square Forelock* variety. The 1 touches the lowest lock, and the 4 almost touches the bust. The hair has seven ends, or points, with the "bird beak" formed by the second and third well marked, but the *fifth from the bottom is entirely detached and looks like a minute island out by itself.* The cap practically touches the milling, and the L is a full millimeter from the cap. The chin is small and the lower lip is a little pursed, suggesting to Maris, for some reason, a Patagonian profile, and this is Maris' *Patagonian* obverse.

Reverse DD. *Edgewise Leaf* reverse. *The right leaf of the lowest inside pair on the right is a mere line* and so seems to be edgewise—a characteristic which is diagnostic. The A's are peculiarly thin or slender. Six berries left and five right, three on the outside on both sides. T in CENT low and leaning a little to the right. Ribbon bow emerges from the knot to the left, and the right ribbon end is high, connecting with nothing.

Die break variations. *Obverse:* Many specimens show part of a double leaf, a stem end, and a ribbon end incused between the hair and LIB. Chapman states that these "suction marks" are always present, but some examples do not show them. A faint crack is frequently seen, starting at the border below the cap, running nearly parallel with the border, crossing the cap near its top, and terminating at the top of LIBE. *Reverse:* Complex injuries to the reverse die have left traces which are sometimes seen on the left side of the coin. Examples showing these injuries are scarce. Thick planchets.

R-4. Basal $3. 55-40 (55-45-40-40-35-30). In this variety the two presently finest known are both new discoveries or rediscoveries since EAC was written. The aforementioned Brand hoard remnant produced an AU-55 in 1951, and an EF-45 turned up in the Dupont collection, sold in 1954. These two outstanding coins change the condition census from 40-35 to 55-40.

1 7 9 4

61   29·EE   Thick Hair, Close Date   HAYS 36
SHORT RIGHT STEM   CHAPMAN 42

Obverse 29. Thick hair, thick planchet, close date.

Reverse EE. Short right stem. *The right stem reaches only half way from the ribbon to the right foot of* A. Fraction bar short, last cipher high. N of CENT leans to the left and has the center dot imbedded in the angle where the left upright joins the cross-bar. The die has been injured so that there is an incused impression of a border under UNITED, under the fraction, and sometimes under part of AMERICA. Also there are complex faint injuries in the central part of the die. Seven berries on each side.

Die break variations. *Obverse:* The faint crack noted on the preceding die combination is slightly more developed but still inconspicuous. Another crack is sometimes seen, from the rim to the hair, left of the 1. The marks of injury to the die, between the hair and LIBERTY, are present on all coins that I have seen. Thick planchets.

R-4. Basal $3. 60-50 (60-60-55-55-45-40). The Dr. French and ANS coins, both MS-60 (and both listed as MS-65 in EAC) appear to stand alone in the MS class. There are at least four others between 55 and 40 but this variety is poorly represented at the VF level. There may be no more than another half dozen between 40 and 20.

62   30·EE   Heavy, Stubby Lower Lock   HAYS 49
LARGE RIM BREAK (Usually)   CHAPMAN 51

Obverse 30. The highest lock is wide at the base and of peculiar shape. Just above it, about opposite the center of the cap, *there is a marked depression in the hair* that is distinctive of this variety. Dr. Maris, a medical man, named it the *Trephined Head. The lowest lock is stubby, and thicker than that of any other 1794 die.* The second lock is fused to the third in a manner which to some has suggested the open mouth of a serpent, and I have known collectors who called this die the *Serpent Mouth.* LIBERTY a trifle nearer to the hair than to the border. In the date the 7 and 9 are somewhat closer to each other than to the other figures. *The fifth lock from the bottom*

1794

is detached and widely separated from the hair. On most specimens *a large break is seen at the rim behind the neck.*

Reverse EE.

Die break variations. *Obverse:* Found perfect (rarely), and with the heavy rim break mentioned. This break extends about 9 mm. along the rim, is of almost oblong shape, and protrudes for 2 mm. into the field.

R-5. Basal $4. 40-35 (40-35-35-35-30-30). The finest H-49 known to us was pictured in the catalogue of the Pearl collection and also on the Chapman plate. This is an EF-40, with the heavy obverse die break. Immediately behind it at least six more of the variety range as 35 and 30 coins, three of them oddly enough appearing in one auction in 1954. Perhaps this supplement will bring an MS-60 out of hiding.

The Fallen 4

63   31·FF   HAYS 32   CHAPMAN 38

Obverse 31. *The 4 seems much too low*, although if a ruler be applied to the coin it will be seen, as Chapman says, that actually the 9 is more displaced than the 4, and is much too high. All the figures of the date are "recut" (double punched). LIBERTY *is flush against the border*, with L farther from the cap than on any other variety. *On the lowest corner of the cap there is a button-like appendage similar to that on obverse 27.* Both LIBERTY and the date are badly spaced. I B and E R are far apart, with BE close. Clapp calls this the *Drunken Diecutter's* obverse. The hair ends in seven locks, but the second and seventh are small enough to be considered vestigial. *A spur from one of the denticles under the bust points at the 4*, and other minute spurs are seen on some of the denticles above the end of the pole.

Reverse FF. *The long fraction bar connects with the end of the right ribbon. The R has a long tail*, like that of reverses H and W. The legend is very close to the border, which is made up of *heavy, coarse denticles.* Many letters of the legend badly formed. Six berries left and five right, *the two berries under the left half of the ribbon bow so small and weakly cut that they are barely visible.* The bottom leaf of the lowest pair on the right is so faint that it has been called the "ghost leaf." The right stem droops, or curves downward a little.

Die break variations. None seen. Traces of injury are seen on both dies.

R-3. Basal $2. 60-50 (60-55-55-50-45-45). Since EAC was written the Winsor coin, MS-60, has come out of hiding, and also an AU-55 came to light in the Ryder collection in 1953. It was stated in EAC that "at least 15 or 20 are known which reach EF condition." We should have said *About* EF condition (VF-30). The Fallen 4 variety is one of the famous numismatic landmarks.

64	32·GG	Shielded Hair	HAYS 46
		FRACTION BAR MISSING	CHAPMAN 48

Obverse 32. The *Shielded Hair.* So named by Maris because *the border milling on the left side of the coin is always deep and heavy*, thus protecting the hair, and the whole left side, from wear. This high border occurs on both obverse and reverse, and the coin sometimes seems to be much thicker on the left side. The bust is in relatively high relief, like some of the earlier ones, and the detail of the face and hair is more delicately treated than it is on those we have last been considering. Yet the primary *arrangement* of the hair is that of the later style, in seven coarse locks, and *the ends of the five highest locks are almost in a straight line.* The hair is thick and in high relief above the ear. LIBERTY well spaced and nearer to hair than to the border. The date is compact, with the 1 touching and the 4 close. *The milling is invariably weak, and often missing, in the upper right portion.*

Reverse GG. The *Missing Fraction Bar.* No fraction bar. The left ribbon terminates in a sharp point. Seven berries on each branch. This is a beautifully executed reverse, with excellent spacing throughout and fine engraving of the leaves. All the detail about the ribbon bow and fraction is perfect and symmetrical, except for the strange omission of the fraction bar.

Die break variations. *Reverse:* On about half the specimens seen there is a break from the border through D to the wreath. In some instances this crack is heavy, extending to the C of

1 7 9 4

CENT. On some coins, a light crack from the rim to the right top of M.

R-5. Basal $4. 70-45 (70-60-50-45-45-35). It is felt that the Bement-Newcomb coin, which is pictured in Chapman, can be called MS-70. The French-Clarke piece is a full MS-60. Coins from this beautiful die are always in demand, and the Hays 46 may still be an R-6. It certainly is in the upper range of R-5.

| 65 | *32·HH* | Shielded Hair
SHORT STEMS | HAYS 45
CHAPMAN 49 |

Obverse 32.

Reverse HH. *The right stem reaches less than half way from the ribbon to the right foot of* A. Right ribbon short, ending abruptly in a point. Seven berries left, six right. The two upper outside berries on the left are very small. Fraction bar rather long. Ribbon bow imperfectly connected with the knot. *Of the two berries adjacent to the left side of the bow, the upper one is much the larger.*

6 5

Die break variations. *Obverse:* Found perfect and with delicate cracks. Between the border and the bottom of the cap; between the border and the bust, through the 9, and also through the 7; along the lower margin of the bust and across its tip to the border. All of these cracks are delicate and hairlike. *Reverse:* Found perfect and with cracks: From the border to the wreath, touching the left side of the last s in STATES—this is the first crack to appear; from the border through the left foot of the last A to the lowest leaf on the right.

R-1. Basal $1. 55-45 (55-50-50-50-45-40). Commonest 1794 without a doubt, and we are rather embarrassed to have to report failure in the current search for an MS example. The Gilbert-Hines coin is an AU-55. The best ANS piece is a 50, rather than 60 as formerly reported, and there are several Hays 45's that can be graded 50 or very near it, but this is the best we can do in 1957 for the commonest 1794.

| NC·6 | *32·LL* | Shielded Hair
FIVE BERRIES LEFT
SEVEN RIGHT | NEW |

Obverse 32. Perfect die.

Reverse LL. *Five berries left, seven right,* four inside each

[125]

branch. The lone outer berry on the left is stemless and detached from branch. The lowest outside berry on the right has a very long curving stem. Pair of leaves under T in CENT peculiarly formed, the right one only a fragment. Wide fraction with the denominator extending beyond the bar. Top of F in OF very thin. C in AMERICA is above the base arc line of RI-A.

Die break variations. Reverse: The only specimen known is raised and has buckled at the center as in Reverses K and O. There is also a die break extending from the border between D and S into the field.

R-8. Unique. 12-0. Discovered by WB in August, 1957. He found it in a consignment of cents from England.

| 66 | 33·II | Distant 1, Heavy Figures | HAYS 44 |
|----|-------|DOUBLE LEAF UNDER O| CHAPMAN 52 |

Obverse 33. *Extremely wide date*, even wider than that of obverse 16. *The 1 is distant from the 7 and the figures are of the large type,* as all are, beginning with obverse 19. The relief is the flattest yet encountered in the series, although not quite so flat as will be seen on the seven obverses to follow. LIBERTY wide, well spaced, close to cap and to the border. The seven locks are of singularly unequal size, and are irregularly spaced. *The fifth lock, greatly overgrown, projects far beyond the ones above and below it.* The lowest lock is one of the heaviest in the series, and it has a long, heavy hook. *Usually seen with a heavy die break from the border up the pole,* which seems to split the pole—hence often called the *Split Pole* variety.

Reverse II. *Double leaf under* O *in* OF. On all other reverses except JJ this leaf cluster is triple. AM in AMERICA too large, and the right side of A double cut. Short fraction bar. The ribbon ends much nearer to the fraction than to the letters of the legend. Stems long, and the arrangement of the bow, ribbon ends, fraction, and stems is excellently symmetrical. Six berries left, seven right. The three upper berries on the left are outside, and the middle one has a very long stem.

Die break variations. *Obverse:* Found perfect and with the break already noted. On some specimens the crack extends across the neck to the hair, and these coins also show a light crack from the bottom of the bust across the lowest lock and

1 7 9 4

into the field. A third light crack curves down from the middle of the forehead to the border opposite the chin. Traces of injury to the die are seen above and below the cap, and in front of the forehead. *Reverse:* Traces of injury are seen above the wreath and below the ribbon knot.

R-7. Basal $12.50. 35-15 (35-30-20-15-12-10). No new ones have appeared. The same twelve examples that were known in 1947 are still accounted for, but no more. Three of these are in ANS, leaving but nine in collectors' hands. Ten years ago the writer (WHS) "guessed" that there must be more of them somewhere, and so rated the variety R-6, but with only nine available to collectors it now must be called R-7. Finest seen is the Gilbert-French coin, VF-35, pictured on the Chapman plate. The next three—VF-30, VF-20 and F-15—are all in ANS. This variety is a little hard on collectors who desire only Mint State coins.

6 7

		Five Braided Locks, Large Circular Curl, Marred Face	
67	*34·II*		HAYS 54 CHAPMAN 53

The final six obverses of the 1794's, beginning with this one, are in quite a distinctive style—Chapman's Style 6. The heads are a little larger, broader, and the whole design is executed in a "hard, inartistic style, as continued in 1795." *The relief is now almost entirely flat, the hair is braided into five heavy, coarse locks*, there is little evidence of fine engraving, and the features suggest no expression other than a grim stare, or as Maris put it, a Roman stare. He called these the *Roman Plicae*.

Obverse 34. *Marred hair and cheek.* Near the juncture of cap with hair, on a level with the eye, there are two little elevated patches, or die breaks, about 1.5 mm. in length. These can almost always be seen. On the cheek are four more little oblong marks in relief, which can be seen on a Fine coin. The die has been injured by contact with a reverse die, and *the projecting end of a leaf is seen at the juncture of the forehead with the front roll of the hair*; another from the end of the nose, and others from the chin. *The lowest lock ends in a rather full and almost circular curl* about 0.5 mm. from the 1. The

1 7 9 4

topmost lock has a peculiar shape, suggesting the head and fore part of a bird. The stand of the T is exactly over the top of the front roll of hair. The date is wide and evenly spaced, with the 1 and 4 about the same distance from hair and bust.

Reverse II.

Die break variations. *Obverse:* Found perfect, and with three faint die cracks; from the upper lip, across the face and hair to the field; from the rim to the left top of Y; along the tops of RTY and a short distance into the field beyond. Coins showing all of these cracks are rare. In addition to the injuries noted, still other traces of the wreath are often visible.

R-3. Basal $2. 60-45 (60-55-50-50-40-40). Only one MS-60 accounted for. This is the Ellsworth-Newcomb coin, pictured on the Chapman plate. The Dr. French piece is the only AU-55 we can now be sure of. Between 50 and 40 there are probably half a dozen, perhaps more, and the Hays 54 is not rare in the 30's and 20's.

6 8

68   *35·II*   The Bisecting Die Break   HAYS 55 CHAPMAN 54

Obverse 35. Five braided locks. The die break variety. *A conspicuous straight line die break bisects this obverse,* running diagonally across the head from border to border, crossing the hair between the third and fourth locks, and the nose about 1.5 mm. from its tip. No examples are known without this break. The fifth lock is more slender or delicate at the tip than the other locks. Date compact and curved, with the 4 almost touching and the 1 distant from the curl. BERTY close, L I B normally spaced. The foot of T is entirely over the forelock.

Reverse II.

Die break variations. None seen. The break noted is found in various stages from very light to heavy. On some specimens the upper portion of it shows as a mere crease, or depression.

R-6. Basal $5. 55-35 (55-50-45-35-35-20). No new ones. This variety may fall near the middle range, rather than the lower range, of R-6. The finest one seen is the Saltus-ANS-Downing coin; graded MS-60 in EAC, it is here corrected to AU-55. There are at least four, perhaps five other excellent examples,

[128]

between 55 and 35, and then a rather sharp drop. The Bisecting Die break is another well-known landmark. Bidding is always brisk when a Hays 55 is offered.

69 *36·II* Five Braided Locks, Small Circular Curl HAYS 50 CHAPMAN 55

Obverse 36. The R of LIBERTY over the forelock, and the T almost entirely clear of it. L distant from the cap. *The curl on the end of the lowest lock forms a circle, but a smaller one than is seen on obverse 34.* Date wide and well spaced. Double cutting shows at the upper right corners of the 1 and the 7. The die has been slightly injured and the faint impression of a leaf can usually be seen growing out of the forehead just above the eye.

Reverse II.

Die break variations. *Reverse:* The original Hays coin shows a straight line break diagonally across the coin, passing through the first T in STATES, through E in CENT, and through the last A in AMERICA. The break is faint, and I have never seen it on another example of the variety. It may account for the final retirement of this tough old die during its fourth marriage.

R-4. Basal $3. 60-40 (60-60-50-40-35-35). Upper range of R-4 but in the present review opinion is unanimous against elevating this variety to R-5. The Ellsworth-Hines piece is graded MS-60. A new one, competently reported as at least MS-60, was discovered in Britain and is known as the Donovan coin. The original Hays coin, pictured in both Hays and Chapman, and now ANS, is called AU-50 in the present review. We can account for only four or five in full EF condition.

70 *36·JJ* Five Braided Locks, Small Circular Curl, Die Break Between T and Y TRIPLE LEAF UNDER D HAYS 51 CHAPMAN 56

Obverse 36.

Reverse JJ. *Double leaf under* O *in* OF, *and triple leaf under* D *in* UNITED. This is diagnostic, since the only other reverse with double leaf under O is II, and that that reverse has a double leaf under D. On II, the two leaves under o are parallel; on JJ, they cross, like a pair of shears. Six berries left and seven right, the lowest one on the left lying close to the wreath stem and barely formed. Ends of wreath stems long and club-shaped. The numerator touches the fraction bar. First T of STATES leans to the left.

Die break variations. *Obverse:* Found perfect but nearly unique in that condition. Usually seen with a break extending from the border between T and Y, across the forehead and back of the eye to the cheek. Reverse shows faint traces of injury in the lower right portion of the wreath.

R-2. Basal $1.50. 55-45 (55-50-50-45-45-40). The Ellsworth-Macallister coin, called MS-60 in EAC, is now graded AU-55. This one resided in the T. J. Clarke collection between 1942 and 1952. The original Hays cent, now ANS, and the Gilbert-Hines cent, are both fairly graded as 50-coins. This variety is decidedly more rare in the higher condition grades than it was thought to be in 1947 when EAC was written.

		Five Braided Locks, Small Circular Curl		
71	37·JJ	TRIPLE LEAF UNDER D	HAYS 52	CHAPMAN 57

Obverse 37. About one third of the base of the T of LIBERTY projects beyond the forelock. The curl at the end of the lowest lock forms a slightly larger circle or ovoid than is seen on obverse 34. The 1 is closer to the curl than to the 7. The 9 and 4 are high, and are farther from the border than is the 1. LIBERTY is wide and well spaced, with L close to the cap. *Three short lines, probably from a die injury, cross from the bridge of the nose to the eye.*

Reverse JJ.

Die break variations. *Obverse:* Found perfect and with a light crack from the border across tip of cap and tops of LIBE; on some specimens a faint crack extends from E to the forelock; a few examples are known with an advanced break between R and T of LIBERTY. On all examples I have seen there are traces of the reverse wreath at the chin and in front of the neck. On some, traces of the word AMERICA and other parts of the reverse show plainly in the upper field of the obverse.

Reverse: No die cracks seen. Those reported by Frossard were later shown to be planchet flaws. Traces of injury from contact with an obverse die are sometimes seen.

R-2. Basal $1.50. 55-45 (55-50-50-50-45-40). Upper range of R-2, probably close to R-3. Condition census 50-50 in EAC, and this is almost correct. In the present review one formerly owned by Dr. French has received the grade AU-55, and one earlier called 45 now appears to be a 40.

		Head of 1795, 1 Almost Touches Under the Lower Lock	
NC-3	38·KK		HAYS 60 CHAPMAN 58

Obverse 38. *Five braided locks. The topmost lock is of the same length as the three immediately below it, so that the four tips or points are practically in a straight line. The curl on the end of the lowest lock is smaller and thicker than any other in this group.* Almost the head of 1795. The figure of Liberty is low in the field, with the bust and the end of the pole close to the border and the date rather crowded. *The 1 almost touches UNDERNEATH* the lower lock—another diagnostic feature. The bottom of the 7 nearly touches a denticle. I B of LIBERTY very widely spaced.

7 2

Reverse KK. *Triple leaf under* O, *double leaf under* D— distinctive for this later group, although characteristic of several of the earlier reverses. The stems droop, or curve downward a little, particularly the right one. Six berries left and seven right. Short fraction line with the numerator almost touching it. ST of STATES very close. T of CENT leans to the left.

Die break variations. None seen. Only a single example known.

R-8. Unique. 8-0. Dr. French to WHS, and to ANS in 1945. No whisper of another has been heard.

		Head of 1795, No Curl	
72	39·KK		HAYS 56 CHAPMAN 59

Obverse 39. *The Exact Head of 1795. The lowest lock does not form a curl, but ends in a short downward pointing stub*

1 7 9 4

such as is seen on the cents of 1795. L touches the cap, and T almost rests on the hair. The first three figures of the date are very widely spaced, with the 4 closer to the 9 and too high. All figures but the 4 are close to the border. This die nearly always has a *conspicuous break from the border through the top of* Y *diagonally to the base of* T at the junction of hair and forehead, and across the hair to the cap.

Reverse KK.

Die break variations. *Obverse:* Only two examples seen without the die break, and possibly a half dozen on which the break is faint. *Reverse:* Found perfect and with a crack from the border diagonally through D to the stem of the wreath.

R-2. Basal $1.50. 65-45 (65-60-50-45-40-35). Head of 1795. The Winsor-Bement piece, MS-65, and the Würtzbach-Clarke coin, MS-60, appear to stand alone in the MS class. The Dr. French coin, pictured in Chapman, and the Proskey-Hines example probably are third and fourth. In the statement, "I have probably seen twenty that are VF-30 or better," on p. 133 in EAC, change VF-30 to VF-20.

Considered as a whole, the Liberty Cap cents possess a charm not often exceeded among the things made by man. To no small degree the charm inheres in the great variability and individuality of these dies, of which there are no less than 105 —53 obverses and 52 reverses (in 1793, 3 obverses and 2 reverses; in 1794, 39 obverses and 38 reverses; in 1795, 5 obverses and 6 reverses; in 1796, 6 obverses and 7 reverses). About three fourths of the Liberty Caps are dated 1794, and among these nearly all of the variation occurs, since the first of the 1794's are practically duplicates of the 1793's, and the last of them are virtually duplicates of the 1795's and 1796's. A collection of 1794 cents reflects much of the story of one of the most pioneering and romantic struggles in American history. In the little Mint building on Seventh Street in Philadelphia, during the middle of the last decade of the eighteenth century, history seems almost to have held her breath for a time, and we find the marks of her desperately clenched teeth engraved deeply on the soft copper pennies of those years.

1 7 9 4

The real charm of our early coins lies in the fact that each die was cut directly on steel by the hand of the diemaker. After the Draped Bust cents were introduced, in 1796, the figure of Liberty was merely stamped into the dies from hubs or large punches which carried the head in relief, so the heads on the different varieties become exactly alike, and only the legends and dates vary, for these still were punched in separately. Later, the whole process was mechanized, and after 1833, American coins were made as modern buttons are made, and are of about comparable interest.

Robert Scot is generally credited with being the engraver of the 1794 cents, although the "degradation of style" between the earliest and latest ones is remarkable. He may have yielded gradually to a demand for coins in lower relief (for better stacking), and the factor of durability of the dies may have been an important one—the simpler dies in lower relief may have stood up better than the more finely engraved ones, or it may have been discovered that the latter required more time and attention than could be given to them.

Chapman presents the cents of 1794 in six groups or styles. Of these the first, second, and sixth are clearly well taken and defensible. Style 1 included only our first three obverses, which are close copies of the 1793's. Style 6 is made up of our last six obverses, which are practically the head of 1795. Chapman's Style 2 also fits the presentation here, for it includes only obverses 4 through 18, or those on which (besides Style 1) the small figures are used in the date. Chapman's Styles 3, 4, and 5 are more artificially designated, and I should prefer to lump these three into one group, the large-date-prior-to-the-1795-head group, which would include our obverses 19 through 34.

It should be noted that Chapman says there are 44 obverse and 42 reverse dies among the 1794's. This was merely a careless error which failed to get corrected. There are 39 obverses and 38 reverses.

So many collectors and dealers mention the divagations of edge lettering on the lettered edge cents that even a repetitive comment on the subject may be in order. We have now reviewed three varieties which have true subvarieties arising from differences in the edge device. These are the 11-J of 1793, and

1 7 9 4

the 2-A and 2-B of 1794. Since edges were lettered separately, and before the coins were struck, which way you hold the coin to have the edge legend right side up is a matter of chance, and errors in the edge legend, such as leaving out a word, double striking, or even omission are matters of interest mainly to a collector of freak coins—not to the collector of die varieties.

Similarly with respect to the question of indented and perfect letters in obverse and reverse legends. The indentation is not in the dies, but is a product of the mechanics of striking the coin. Sometimes, when the timing or pressure or temperature was not quite right, the metal failed to flow into the letters sufficiently to fill them properly. As Chapman points out, the metal has to flow centrifugally toward the periphery of the coin, therefore generally filling the tops of the letters but often failing to fill the bottoms, and thus leaving little central indentations in the bottoms. Later in the series we often encounter the problem of "double and triple profiles" and the like. This too, is of course not in the dies but is a product of the mechanics of striking the coin.

The records of the Mint give the coinage of 1794 cents as follows:

Jan. 13	11,000	'93 Heads, Hays 1 to 4
To Nov. 12	807,500	48 var. Dies by Scot
Dec. 16-24	80,000	7 var. Gardner heads
Dec. 30	20,021	Exact Head of '95, Hays 56
	918,521	(Calendar year was Mint's fiscal year)

The above division is based on documents in the National Archives. John Smith Gardner entered the Mint as Assistant Engraver late in November 1794 and was put to work on cent and half-cent dies; he left at the beginning of 1796, mainly on account of inadequate salary. The Hays 56 is from the hub Gardner made which was used throughout the 1795 coinage. The Mint's fiscal year was the calendar year until the Act of February 21, 1857.

The modern collector would be more interested in knowing how many 1794 cents *now exist* than how many were coined, and oddly enough it is possible to answer this question almost as accurately as the latter one. At any rate it is easily possible to make an estimate within which a nucleus of factual observation exists. About a dozen years ago, after receiving and attributing the lot of 300 1794 cents from Henry Chapman which was mentioned on page 126.* I enlisted the aid of Mr. Chapman and two other dealers to extend the "observation series" to 1000. This series of 1000 worn 1794 cents taken at random was then attributed and it was possible to construct a

TABLE 4. COMPARATIVE POPULATIONS OF THE DIFFERENT RARITY GROUPS AMONG ONE THOUSAND 1794 CENTS

Rarity Group	Number of Coins Found Among 1000
R-1 (Hays 14, 26, 37, 43, 45)	438
R-2 (Hays 5, 7, 17, 21, 24, 33, 34, 39, 48, 51, 52, 56)	377
R-3 (Hays 11, 13, 22, 23, 32, 54)	96
R-4 (Hays 2, 3, 12, 15, 16, 19, 35, 36, 50)	59
R-5 (Hays 1, 6, 10, 18, 20, 46, 47, 49)	20
R-6 (Hays 4, 8, 25, 29, 31, 41, 42, 44, 55, 57)	8
R-7 (Hays 9, 27, 28, 40, 58, 59)	2
R-8 (Hays 30, 60, 61)	0
	1000

table showing the relative frequencies of occurrence of the R-1's, R-2's, and so on.

Of course it is not maintained that the 1000 coins used in this experiment constituted quite an accurate sample of the present 1794 population, especially at the rare end of the distribution, but except for the rarities it was perhaps reasonably accurate, and probably yields a rough idea of the percentages actually prevailing. If now we disregard the extreme rarities, and consider just the R-5's, recalling that by definition R-5 means "probably not over 75 known," the predicted total population of the eight varieties falling in this group might be about eight times 75, or 600. Now among the sample of 1000 I actually found 20 R-5's, or roughly 3 per cent of the predicted population. Thus *if* the sample had been known to be a truly representative one, and *if* the rarities were known to be accurately stated, *it would follow that the sample of 1000 must be*

* EAC

1794

about 3 per cent of the total population of 1794 cents. We should then know that the total population of cents of this date is somewhere in the neighborhood of thirty to thirty-five thousand.

Two fairly large "ifs" were just now included in the calculation, and the question is, exactly *how* large are those ifs. That cannot be answered with finality, but we can reflect a little more light on the question. Turning to the R-4's, where the assumed maximum is 200 examples of each of the nine die varieties, we find a predicted total population of 1800, and a sample population of 59, which again is a little over 3 per cent. The analysis of the R-4's then agrees closely with that of the R-5's, in its prediction of the probable total population of 1794 cents.

By now permitting the further assumption that the progression from R-4 to R-3 should be proportionally about the same as that from R-5 to R-4, from R-6 to R-5, and from R-7 to R-6, in short, a geometric progression involving a constant of about the order 2.5, we can assume that 500 examples ought to be approximately the maximal population for each of the six varieties of the R-3 group. Then 3000 will be the predicted *total* population for the R-3's, and the sample population of 96 is 3.2 per cent, which again yields close agreement.

TABLE 5 KEY TO THE 1794 CENTS

Starred Reverse—94 tiny stars around border 48
"Shielded hair"—very deep left obverse border. Rev. stems very short 65
Same obverse. Reverse five berries left, only one outside. Break,
 border to field between D S; bulged in center NC-6
Exact head of 1795 72
No fraction bar 64
Fallen 4; spurs from denticles, LIBERTY rests on border 63
Heavy, stubby lower lock, usually with large rim break at left 62
Left ribbon bow double cut 59
Tiny button on lower corner of cap 57
N in ONE first cut inverted then recut properly 56
A in STATES far too high, tilted left; ONE CENT ascend to right 55
Two berries outside each branch, four berries within each branch 47
"Crossed" E in CENT. Hair braided in flat twists 46
"Berry" in loop of left ribbon bow. Obverse as last 45

1 7 9 4

TABLE 5. KEY TO THE 1794 CENTS—*Continued*

Same reverse. Crack down from cap through curls and 17 to border....NC-5
Tremendous rim break at ED obliterating the D...................NC-2
Date very wide and spaced 1 794; single berry left of bow............37
Date very wide and spaced 1 794; two berries left of bow.............66
Single berry left of bow; break over LI..............................34
Single berry left of bow; extremely delicate lower lock..............35
Single berry left of bow; PLLR almost touches A; bust rests on 4.....NC-1
Single berry left of bow; inner berries above O E of ONE; same obverse.....36
Single berry left of bow; "Marred Field" (chips behind curls).........38
"Marred Field"; long tail to right ribbon and R in AMERICA............30
"Marred Field"; very long fraction bar extending beyond 1 and 0.......31
"Marred Field"; sprawled ribbon ends close to U and A.................39
"Marred Field"; die cut from r. ribbon end; usually buckled in center....40
Hook shaped defect from O in OF; date 17 94..........................26
Tall numerator; "apple cheek" obverse, 4 almost touches bust..........24
Tall numerator; date midway bust and border. Usually break from cap
  to pole end...23
Left ribbon severed from knot. Usually, mound above ONE...............22
End of pole wide and flat, upper part much thinner...................21
1793 Head. Date straight, 4 distant. Stem about touches A............20
1793 Head. Double chin, date well curved. Same reverse...............19
1793 Head. Same obverse. N in CENT first inverted, then corrected....18
1793 Head. Date straight, widely spaced. Reverse as last.............17
Note: On the last three (possibly all four) there are edge sub-varieties.
Double leaf at OF, crossed like scissor blades; triplet at D:
  L about touches cap..71
  L far from cap. Usually, break between TY........................70
Double leaf at OF, the two parallel:
  JHF almost midway TY; usually, cracked across the obverse.........68
  JHF under upright of T; impression of leaf just below.............67
  JHF left of upright of T; L far from cap..........................69
Head of 1795 but small tight loop to lowest curl; 1 about touches it....NC-3
Wide date, divided 17 94; very short fraction bar....................25
Five ends of curls are in straight line:
  Long tails to right ribbon and R in AMERICA......................29
  Curled tail to R in AMERICA; single leaf at I in AMERICA.........28
  Reverse identical to last, with obverse bulged across............27
5th lock from bottom double, 4th and 6th turn up:
  Berry directly under r. edge of upright of R in AMERICA..........32
  First berry touches bow. Buckled in center; several breaks.......33
Seven very minute berries at right. Usually cracked from D to tops of
  CE...41
Weak OF; date 1 79 4, figures just about rest on the border..........42
Weak OF; close date, 1 and 4 touch above. No loop under bust.........43

[137]

1 7 9 4

TABLE 5. KEY TO THE 1794 CENTS—*Continued*

Right ribbon end split, short, weak; large berry at c in CENT............44
Thick hair, wide date; 1 about touches above, pole touches border.......58
Edgewise leaf (right one of pair) under T in CENT; narrow A's...........60
Right stem short; obv. "suction marks" between hair, cap and LIB.......61
"Closed Wreath"; fraction crowded against right ribbon:
    7 tilted markedly to right and close to 1 at base....................54
    Rather widely spaced date, 17 close; RT both very close to hair........53
    Date 1 79 4; B E R T well apart. Usually cracked through cap.........52
    Very finely engraved hair, 2nd and 4th locks very long...............51
    Very finely engraved hair, LI, BE and RT close, R leans right..........50
    Very finely engraved hair; JHF just left of upright of T...............49

Following the same reasoning, each of the twelve varieties in the R-2 group ought to have a maximal population of about 1250, or 15,000 for the whole group. The sample population of 377 is 2.5 per cent of this number. Finally, if 3000 is taken as the approximate maximal population for each of the five R-1 varieties, 15,000 will be the predicted population for that group, and the sample population of 438 is 2.9 per cent of the total.

This remarkable agreement at five levels of rarity does not necessarily prove that 1000 is approximately 3 per cent of the total population of 1794 cents, but it *does* prove, apparently, that the levels of rarity as described are well taken, and it indicates that the quantitative estimates of rarity are at any rate in about the right proportions with one another. For what this experiment is worth, we may suggest, then, that the total present population of 1794 cents may be in the neighborhood of thirty to thirty-five thousand.

The varieties of the cents are known and cherished more for their obverses than for their reverses, but in the actual work of identification, I think that the greater use is made of the reverses. A few years ago, Mr. Clapp worked out a key for quick identification of the 1794's from their reverses. Although never published, this key has proved useful to some of Mr. Clapp's friends, and the accompanying table is an adaptation of the same method.

It has also developed that the approximately 35,000 extant

1 7 9 4

1794 cents represent just about 3 per cent of the original mint age. In 1953, WB performed a similar experiment on 100 unattributed cents of 1793 and 100 of 1795 Lettered Edge; the results confirmed the interrelations of the rarity levels as given in EAC. From this he proceeded to compute the estimated total populations of these dates as given by the assumption that twelve specimens exist of every R-7, thirty of every R-6, etc. This yielded the following "characteristic ratio" (100×Estimated Extant Population / Number Coined) for the various issues: 1793 Chain, 3 per cent; Wreath, 4 per cent (evidently these were hoarded as first year of issue); Liberty Cap, 2.9 per cent; 1795 Lettered Edge, 2 per cent. These nearly constant results—sometimes referred to as the "3 per cent Rule"—seem to verify what may be called a natural law of numismatics, one implicitly appealed to whenever a collector looks up the number minted of a coin for information on its probable scarcity. This may be summarized by saying that the ratio Number Extant / Number Coined (or its approximation, the characteristic ratio) is practically constant for a particular issue barring either "finds" or destructive forces acting selectively on particular varieties. The figure of 2 per cent for the 1795 Lettered Edge coins bears closer examination in this context. A check through the Archives reveals no record of the disposition of these coins—apparently most of them were held in the Mint. Elias Boudinot, then Director, had stopped their coinage on December 1, 1795, and in his annual report (issued Dec. 3) he petitioned for a reduction of the weight of the cent to 168 grains. It seems that copper coinage at the old weight involved a loss of about 22 per cent because copper prices were so high that the cents were worth more as metal than as coins. It is therefore quite unlikely that many of them were released in December 1795. Recoinage would have been feasible as soon as the requested reduction was authorized, since the Mint made its own planchets; and profitable, as every $10 in thick cents would yield $12.38 in thin ones. Moreover, the melting would have affected most of all No. 76a, and this variety actually is very rare. We may therefore assume that a large number, perhaps more than one third, of the thick 1795's never left the Mint and were in fact recoined after December 27, 1795. The characteristic ratio

1 7 9 4

and its implications are more extensively followed up in WB's various monographs.

TABLE 6. RARITY AND VALUE: 1794 CENTS

Number	Obv.-Rev. Designation	Rarity	Basal Value (Dollars)	Hays No.	Chapman No.
17	1-A	6	9.	4	4
NC-4	1-A	8	—	4	4
18a	2-A	7	7.50	3	3
18b	2-A	4	3.50	3	3
19a	2-B	7	7.50	2	2
19b	2-B	5	5.	2	2
20	3-B	5	6.50	1	1
21	4-B	3	2.	5	5
22	5-C	1	1.	43	6
23	6-D	5	4.	18	7
24	7-D	2	1.50	17	8
25	8-E	4	3.	22	17
26	8-F	2	1.50	21	18
27	9-G	6	5.	25	19
28	10-G	2	1.50	23	20
29	10-H	3	2.	24	21
30	11-H	1	1.	37	22
31	12-I	2	1.50	39	23
32	13-J	1	1.	26	11
33	13-K	7	15.	27	12
34	13-L	7	12.50	28	13
35	14-L	6	6.	29	28
NC-1	15-L	8	—	30	15
36	15-M	6	6.	31	14
37	16-M	7	15.	59	16
38	17-M	6	5.	41	24
39	17-N	7	12.50	40	25
40	17-O	6	5.	42	26
NC-2	17-P	8	—	61	27
41	18-Q	4	3.	19	9
42	18-R	5	4.	20	10
43	19-R	2	1.50	34	35
44	19-S	2	1.50	33	36
NC-5	19-T	8	—	—	—
45	20-T	6	5.	47	33
46	20-U	2	1.50	48	34

1 7 9 4

TABLE 6. RARITY AND VALUE: 1794 CENTS—*Continued*

Number	Obv.-Rev. Designation	Rarity	Basal Value (Dollars)	Hays No.	Chapman No.
47	21-V	5	4.	6	29
48	21-W	6	10.	8	30
49	21-X	2	1.50	7	31
50	22-X	6	5.	57	32
51	23-X	5	4.	10	37
52	24-X	7	12.50	9	50
53	25-X	7	12.50	58	47
54	26-X	3	2.	11	43
55	26-Y	3	2.	13	44
56	26-Z	4	3.	12	45
57	27-AA	1	1.	14	46
58	28-BB	3	2.	16	39
59	28-CC	3	2.	15	40
60	29-DD	4	3.	35	41
61	29-EE	4	3.	36	42
62	30-EE	5	4.	49	51
63	31-FF	3	2.	32	38
64	32-GG	5	4.	46	48
NC-6	32-LL	8	—	—	—
65	32-HH	1	1.	45	49
66	33-II	7	12.50	44	52
67	34-II	3	2.	54	53
68	35-II	6	5.	55	54
69	36-II	4	3.	50	55
70	36-JJ	2	1.50	51	56
71	37-JJ	2	1.50	52	57
NC-3	38-KK	8	—	60	58
72	39-KK	2	1.50	56	59

1 7 9 4

TABLE 7. FINDING LIST FOR THE HAYS NUMBERS

Hays	New Serial Number	Obv.-Rev. Designation	Hays	New Serial Number	Obv.-Rev. Designation
1	20	3-B	31	36	15-M
2	19	2-B	32	63	31-FF
3	18	2-A	33	44	19-S
4	17	1-A	34	43	19-R
5	21	4-B	35	60	29-DD
6	47	21-V	36	61	29-EE
7	49	21-X	37	30	11-H
8	48	21-W	39	31	12-I
9	52	24-X	40	39	17-N
10	51	23-X	41	38	17-M
11	54	26-X	42	40	17-O
12	56	26-Z	43	22	5-C
13	55	26-Y	44	66	33-II
14	57	27-AA	45	65	32-HH
15	59	28-CC	46	64	32-GG
16	58	28-BB	47	45	20-T
17	24	7-D	48	46	20-U
18	23	6-D	49	62	30-EE
19	41	18-Q	50	69	36-II
20	42	18-R	51	70	36-JJ
21	26	8-F	52	71	37-JJ
22	25	8-E	54	67	34-II
23	28	10-G	55	68	35-II
24	29	10-H	56	72	39-KK
25	27	9-G	57	50	22-X
26	32	13-J	58	53	25-X
27	33	13-K	59	37	16-M
28	34	13-L	60	NC-3	38-KK
29	35	14-L	61	NC-2	17-P
30	NC-1	15-L			

1795

For this date the obverse-reverse designations are the same as those established by Clapp and Newcomb (p. 24), but with the Jefferson cents added to the series. The cents of 1795 (except the Jeffersons) are of the same general design as the last variety of the 1794's.

		Lettered Edge,	
		Hyphen Variety	NOT IN D
73	1·A		CN 1

Obverse 1. Always seen with a *short, hyphen-like break between* R *and* T. The break curves downward under the R, and there is a mound or swelling under ER. LIBERTY wide. L distant from the cap. R high. Date wide, curved, and distant from the border. 1 and 5 close to lower lock and bust, but not touching.

Reverse A. Both branches of the wreath terminate with single leaves. Fraction low, almost touching the border, with the fraction bar moderately long, *touching all figures of the fraction except the first cipher*, and pointing to both ribbon ends. Fifteen leaves on the left branch. Double leaf under D.

Die break variations. *Obverse:* Found with additional crack starting at rim above left top of Y, crossing the top of that letter, down past the face and (sometimes) almost reaching the pole. Examples showing this crack are very rare. *Reverse:* Found perfect, and with crack from left top of U to N, to the base of 1, below TE to D and beyond; another, delicate, from

1795

center of F to A, to the base of ME, to R, to top of I, to rim over C. Always found with lettered edge.

R-6. Basal $6. 45-15 (45-25-20-15-12-10). Middle range of R-6. A few low grade examples have turned up in recent years with which we were not previously acquainted. The earlier impression was that the Hyphen variety belonged in the upper range of R-6. The finest one, now corrected to EF-45, is the Lardner-Hines coin. Next is the Dr. French piece, later owned by Downing, VF-25. The Gies-ANS is an excellent third at VF-20.

| 74 | 2·A | Lettered Edge SINGLE LEAVES | D-68 CN 2 |

Obverse 2. *Top of 5 almost entirely lost in the bust.* Date heavy and wide. Juncture of forelock with forehead immediately below the center of T. *The pole touches the bust.*

Reverse A. Both branches terminate with single leaves.

Die break variations. *Obverse:* Found perfect, and with crack from rim below 95 to the top of the 9, to the bust. *Reverse:* The cracks are more advanced, and on some examples a new one is seen across TES and beyond. Occasionally, cracks extend almost entirely around the legend. Always found with lettered edge.

R-4. Basal $4. 70-60 (70-70-65-60-50-50). Two 70-coins are known in this famous, much-sought variety, with a 65 for an excellent third. The Winsor-Würtzbach and the Newcomb-Clarke coins are brilliant 70's. The Beckwith-ANS piece at 65 is equally perfect although not so brilliant. This is the first variety in the list for which two 70's are recorded.

| 75 | 2·B | Lettered Edge DOUBLE LEAF ON RIGHT | D-67 CN 3 |

Obverse 2.

Reverse B. Recognized easily because it is the *only lettered-edge 1795 on which the right branch of the wreath terminates in two leaves.* A berry on each side of the bow, below each loop. The right stem points to the center of the bottom of A.

Die break variations. *Obverse:* As on No. 74, and with a fine crack across the tops of RTY to the rim opposite the mouth.

1 7 9 5

There are a number of minute defects on obverse and reverse (poor steel in this die, Clapp says). Always found with lettered edge.

R-3. Basal $3.50. 70-65 (70-65-65-65-60-60). At least seven or eight are known in full Mint State, 60 or better, and this is the only Lettered Edge variety of any date which has more than four or five representatives at that level. The 70-coin is one which Jimmy Clarke used to exhibit often at conventions as a "proof." Clarke loved the Lettered Edge '95's; at one time he had five of this variety, all MS-60 or better.

76a	3·C	Lettered Edge SINGLE LEAVES, ONE CENT HIGH	D-66 CN 4

Obverse 3. *About half of the top of the 5 is imbedded in the bust.* The pole is close to the bust but does not touch. The juncture of hair and forehead is just below the right foot of T. LIB lower than RTY. L almost touches the cap.

Reverse C. $\frac{ONE}{CENT}$ *high in the wreath,* and by this characteristic the die is generally known. Seventeen leaves on the left branch, and *three leaves under D.* Both branches of the wreath terminate with single leaves. Short fraction bar. Right stem points to the right foot of A.

Die break variations. On the lettered edge coins, none seen.

R-6. Basal $6. 70-30 (70-60-30-20-20-15). The 70-coin came from the Brand hoard in 1940 but was there misattributed and sold as a sleeper. The MS-60 was from Ellsworth-Newcomb, and was sold to ANS privately before the Newcomb sale. After these two, there are only four or five known to us in better than Fine condition. Middle range of R-6.

7 6

76b	3·C	Plain Edge ONE CENT HIGH	D-66 CN 4

Early in this marriage the lettered edge device was discontinued, the weight of the coins was reduced from 208 grains to 168 grains (see p. 15), and a thinner, plain-edge planchet was introduced. Apparently the change to the thin planchets preceded the abandonment of the edge lettering, as a few examples

[145]

1 7 9 5

are found with a comparatively thin planchet and lettered edge. One such coin is known in MS-70 condition.

Since the Proclamation by President Washington authorizing the change in weight of the cents was made on December 27, 1795, it is evident that the plain edge 1795's must have been actually coined in 1796. This confirms the supposition that many of the early cents were struck in a year other than that of their date.

Die break variations. *Obverse:* Found perfect and with a fine crack from rim at left of 1 to the tip of the second hair lock, to the cap, and back to the rim. Swellings often seen in the left and right fields, from die sinking. *Reverse:* Found perfect and with die crumbling at OF, at the N of ONE, and back of CENT. On some (rare) examples a rim break obliterates part of R and all of IC.

7 7   After most of the "D-66's" had been struck, the obverse was reground, leaving the pole weaker and severing the second lock from the hair, together with the upper half of the third lock.

R-1. Basal $0.75. 70-65 (70-70-70-65-65-65). Possibly twenty or so are known in full Mint State. Commonest 1795, and perhaps the highest condition census (if all of them were listed) of any eighteenth-century cent.

		Plain Edge	
77	3·D	FIVE THREE-LEAF CLUSTERS ON LEFT BRANCH, ONE CENT CENTRAL	D-69 CN 5

Obverse 3. After regrinding. Pole weak, second and third locks now partially severed.

Reverse D. Twenty-one leaves on the left branch and twenty on the right. Five clusters of three leaves each on the left branch. Both branches terminate with single leaves. *Legend close to the wreath, touching in two or three places.* The right stem points well to the right of A. Fraction rather high, near the knot. The border milling is finer than on other varieties of this date. ONE/CENT in the center of the wreath.

Die break variations. *Obverse:* Found perfect and swollen in the left and right fields; also with a crack extending from the shoulder above the date to the cap and border. Always found

1795

with plain edge. *Reverse:* Found perfect and with many delicate cracks; also with marked weakening at OF, at NI and CENT, and with flattening of most of the leaves of the wreath. The die must have been injured severely by contact with some hard object.

R-4. Basal $2.50. 60-50 (60-60-55-50-40-35). Upper range of R-4 but not quite R-5. The two 60-coins are the Newcomb-Würtzbach and the Ellsworth-ANS pieces. The Dupont coin, just about equal to these but not brilliant and here graded AU-55, is clearly second finest in collectors' hands. By our current rules its book rating would be $55 \times \$2.50 \times 2\frac{1}{2}$, or $343.75. At the Dupont sale, 1954, it brought $325.

		Plain Edge Free Date		
78	4·E	ONE CENT CENTRAL	D-70 CN 6	7 8

Obverse 4. *The top of the 5 barely touches the bust, and the full curve of the upper stroke of that figure is visible.* This is diagnostic, for on the only other plain-edge 1795 (obverse 3) the 5 is partly buried in the bust. The pole is long, reaching to the border. LIBERTY is closely spaced, with the left foot of Y over the juncture of hair with forehead. The border milling is deep, and is usually even (coin well centered). Considered the most finely executed of the 1795 obverses.

Reverse E. ONE CENT central in the wreath. *Only three berries on the right branch and four on the left.* This is diagnostic, since there are no other 1795 cents with a total of less than nine berries. Both branches of the wreath terminate with single leaves.

Die break variations. *Obverse:* Found perfect, and with a faint crack under the jaw, near the neck. On some specimens the die has crumbled a little at the top of the 5, uniting it to the bust.

R-1. Basal $1. 70-65 (70-70-65-65-65-65). Distinctly less common than 76b, but still R-1. A coin of great beauty and perhaps responsible for an early interest in cents on the part of more discriminating people than one or two. There may be more than two 70-coins around. We know at least two—the Dr. French-

1 7 9 5

Clarke and the Beckwith-ANS coins. Possibly half as many of these are available in Mint State as is the case with 76b.

The Reeded Edge Variety

79   5·F   NOT IN D
              CN 7

Obverse 5. LIBERTY very closely spaced. Juncture of hair with forehead a little *to the right of the center of the stand of the* Y (diagnostic). The date entirely free of the bust, and widely spaced except for the two central figures, which are close together.

Reverse F. Same as reverse U of 1796. Seven berries left and right. Fourteen leaves left and eighteen right. The right branch terminates with a double leaf. The stems droop, or curve downward a little. The bottom leaf on the right points to the inner corner of the right foot of A.

Die break variations. None seen. The edge is *milled*, or *reeded*, like our modern silver coins, and this was apparently an experiment which did not meet with favor, since it was immediately abandoned.

R-8. Basal $20. 10-6 (10-8-6-5). The best of the four, which is the McGirk-ANS piece, can be called VG-10. The Book-Newcomb coin, VG-8, is finest in collectors' hands. This coin brought $660 at auction in 1953. Downing found one among a junk lot in New York in 1947, G-6. The Proskey-Hines piece, which was the discovery coin for the variety, is about G-5. Many years ago WHS found in Chicago, in another junk box, what is almost half of a fifth example of this variety. It is a freak coin, with a nice obverse but struck without a reverse. It is holed and the obverse is also incused on the reverse. WHS bought it for a few cents, carried it as a pocket piece for years, and gave it to Homer Downing about 1945. It was one of Downing's first Early Cent acquisitions, was later sold with the Downing collection. In the present condition census review, however, it was decided not to include holed or freak coins. On Plate 12 in EAC the wrong reverse is pictured as Reverse F, although the description on p. 147 is correct. Reverse F of 1795 is the same as Reverse U of 1796.

1 7 9 5

Lettered Edge Jefferson Cent

NC-1 6·G   CN X-1

By some, the *Jefferson* cents have been regarded as contemporary counterfeits, but others have thought it more likely that these coins were the result of a sort of whimsical experiment on the part of some Mint employee who may have been caricaturing, or may merely have been "idly trying his hand." I am inclined to this latter view. At any rate the coins are of entirely different design from any of the regular cents, and they possess quite a personality of their own. Moreover, they certainly circulated as cents, for many of the specimens are in well worn condition, and for a long time the Jefferson has been looked upon with favor by cent collectors—at least as a mystery and a curiosity. That they are contemporary with the early cents is certain. However questionable their antecedents, they have by adoption at least, like the strawberry leaf cents of 1793, long been regarded as "members of the family."

Obverse 6. Hair combed out almost straight. No hair ribbon. Pole thin and distant from the bust. Cap small. Date small, with crude figures, which seem to have been engraved rather than punched into the die. Profile almost a straight line from hair to point of the nose. Lips pouting, chin pointed. The lowest lock forms a long double curl under the bust. LIBERTY in large letters, widely spaced.

Reverse G. Coarse, heavy letters in the legend. Large, "lobster claw" leaves. Ribbon bow in three loops instead of two. Large fraction, with fraction bar extending beyond the denominator at both ends. The right stem points to the center of final A. Nine berries left, four right. Seventeen leaves left, eighteen right.

Die break variations. None seen. Edge lettered ONE HUNDRED FOR A DOLLAR. The one example known is struck on a large planchet with completely milled obverse border.

R-8. Unique. 30-0. No rumor of another has been heard. This is the Newcomer-Hines-Downing coin. Graded F-15 in EAC because of apparent wear, it has been found on closer examination to have the sharpness of EF. The "worn areas" on the hair and on the reverse (see Plate 12 in EAC) are the result of imperfect striking, not of wear. In 1945 Mr. Clapp commissioned the writer (WHS) to try to buy this piece at $1,000. The effort was unsuccessful.

80   6·H   Plain Edge Jefferson Cent   CN X-2

Obverse 6. Milling incomplete on obverse border.

Reverse H. Similar to reverse G in general appearance. Heavy letters, lobster claw leaves, and triple loop in the ribbon bow. Much shorter fraction bar. Right stem points to right foot of final A. Eleven berries left, twelve right (the *many berries* reverse). Nineteen leaves left, eighteen right.

Die break variations. None seen. A number of counterfeits or molded reproductions of this variety are in numismatic circulation. These have crude, more or less porous surfaces, and their edges are "too good." The genuine, struck pieces show the crude edge-cutting that is characteristic of all plain-edge 1795 cents. Mr. Downing has a struck piece struck over a Liberty Cap Lettered Edge cent.

R-6. Basal $10. 35-15 (35-25-15-15-12-10). Upper range of R-6. Probably less than 20 genuine Jeffersons known. The Randall-Fewsmith-ANS piece, here graded VF-35, has been famous for more than a century. The Proskey-Hines cent is here called VF-25, and probably the Dupont coin is third at F-15. The Chase Manhattan Bank owns one which is perhaps also a 15.

The Jefferson cents apparently received their name from Ebenezer Mason, a coin dealer of the eighteen sixties and later. So far as is now known the sobriquet first appeared in *Mason's Coin Collector's Magazine,* December 1867. The stated basis was an alleged resemblance of the profile to that of Thomas Jefferson; whether the resemblance was intentional or not Mr. Mason did not conjecture. The frequently seen electrotypes of the Randall cent originated with Mason. He advertised them at 50¢ each, as late as December 1881. At that time 50¢ was a liberal price for electrotypes, but in later years we have seen them offered at a thousand times that figure, without mention that they were electrotypes.

1 7 9 5

The *Coiner's Copper Account Book* together with *Bullion Journal A,* both in the National Archives, establish that 37,000 thick cents were delivered on December 1, 1795; George Washington's executive order of December 27, 1795, authorized cent coinage at 168 grains, and 45,000 thin-planchet coins (No. 76b) were struck December 28-31. These were delivered January 1, 1796. From January 16 to March 31 five more deliveries took place totaling 456,500 cents, or 501,500 thin-planchet coins of 1795 in all; and immediately afterward came a long hiatus during which new dies were engraved, presumably for the 1796 Liberty Caps, which are entirely unlike the Gardner dies of 1795.

TABLE 8. RARITY AND VALUE: 1795 CENTS

Number	Obv.-Rev. Designation	Doughty Number		CN No.	Rarity	Basal Value (Dollars)
73	1-A	—		1	6	6.
74	2-A	68		2	4	4.
75	2-B	67		3	3	3.50
76a	3-C	66	Lettered Edge	4	6	6.
76b	3-C	66	Plain Edge	4	1	.75
77	3-D	69		5	4	2.50
78	4-E	70		6	1	1.
79	5-F	—		7	8	20.
NC-1	6-G	—		X-1	8	—
80	6-H	—		X-2	6	10.

The 1795 cents were sent to banks throughout the country for general distribution. Prior to this, all the U. S. Mint coins, according to Stewart, had been issued only locally in Philadelphia, and had for the most part circulated locally.

1796

CLAPP AND NEWCOMB (5) HAVE SHOWN THAT FOR 1796 THE Gilbert designations are altogether inadequate, since they present the varieties in no systematic order, omit four known varieties, and include fifteen that are mere duplications. Students of the cents have long felt the need of a *systematic* presentation of the 1796's.

When I set about preparing to write this book, Clapp said he thought the 1796's "ought" to be listed in a straight-through series by the Crosby obverse-reverse designations, as the 1793's are, but he felt that for his own monograph this step would require too much rewriting and reorganizing. To me it seemed easier and in the long run better to systematize this date once and for all at the outset, since in the end it surely would have to be done. Accordingly, I have employed the Crosby method of nomenclature, arranging the forty-four known varieties in a continuous progression of obverses and reverses.

It is of course not maintained that the order here fixed upon is the *exact* order in which the coins came from the Mint. I have merely done with this date as I did with the 1794's, as Crosby did with the 1793's, and as Clapp-Newcomb have done with the 1795's and other dates—arranged the varieties in an uninterrupted progression of obverses and *as nearly as possible* in an accompanying uninterrupted progression of reverses. As has been the case with the other dates, the list starts with what seem to be the earliest varieties, most closely resembling the preceding date, and closes with varieties most nearly resembling the succeeding date.

1 7 9 6

To the descriptions of the various dies I have added but little. This is mainly the work of Gilbert, Clapp, and Newcomb, aided by many contemporary collectors and numismatists.

THE LIBERTY CAPS

All of the 1796 Liberty Cap dies were made from the same hub. The head of Liberty is therefore virtually the same on all of them, and differences are to be found only in the arrangement of LIBERTY, the pole, and the date, and in the reverses. The style of the head follows that of 1795, but the five braided locks are a little finer, the cheeks are fuller, the engraving of the features is more delicate, and the head possesses a degree of rounded relief which falls about half way between that of 1793 and the flatness of the 1795's.

81 1·A   Pole Attached to Bust   GILBERT A
          DOUBLE LEAF UNDER N   CN A

8 1

Obverse 1. L *touches the cap.* The top of 1 touches, or practically touches, the hair, *the pole is in contact with the bust for about half its length,* and the JHF (junction of the hair with the forehead) is below a point halfway between T and Y.

Reverse A. Left "19-5," right "18-4" (the left wreath has nineteen leaves and five berries, the right eighteen leaves and four berries). Fraction bar curved upward a little, last cipher too high. AME connected at their feet. *Lowest right leaf points to the center of the bottom of final* A. *Double leaf under* N.

Die break variations. *Obverse:* Usually seen with a faintly roughened ridge or die failure, from the rim back of the center of the cap, through the cap to the uppermost curl. Found with faint break from under nose to rim; another faint and curved crack from the rim past Y to the bridge of the nose. Planchets have been found as small as 28 mm. and as large as 30.5 mm.

R-3. Basal $3.50. 65-55 (65-60-60-55-50-50). The French-Clarke coin is a 65. The Proskey-Hines and Deets-ANS coins are full 60's; and there may be others recently in hiding. There are so few of these Cap '96's in Mint State that the one-of-a-date collectors and the "type" collectors tend to buy them up, and

[153]

1796

then they may drop out of sight for a generation or two. This variety is in the lower range of R-3; called R-2 in EAC.

| 82 | 1·B | Pole Attached to Bust
TRIPLE LEAF UNDER AM
AND UNDER UN | GILBERT B
CN B |

Obverse 1.

Reverse B. Left 21-5, right 20-5. Letters in AMER touch, with A a little higher than the other letters. *Cluster of three leaves under* AM *of* AMERICA *and under* UN *of* UNITED. *A leaf almost touches* F. NE of ONE touch at the top. ENT of CENT practically touch, with N highest. Lowest right leaf points to the left foot of final A.

Die break variations. *Reverse:* Small break always seen from the right foot of E to the upright of R in AMERICA.

R-5. Basal $5. 65-30 (65-50-45-25-25-15). The Dr. French coin stands alone. A 50-coin appeared early this year. The Jones-ANS piece is graded EF-45. These three are the only ones we know clearly surpassing the VF-25 Newcomb and Sawicki examples. Lower range of R-5 as a variety but extremely rare in the higher condition states.

| 83 | 2·B | End of Pole Connected to
Bust by Die Break | GILBERT E
CN E |

Obverse 2. Wide date, *the first three figures very widely spaced,* with the 6 closer to the 9 and high. The 1 and 6 are close to the hair and bust, but do not touch. Pole lightly cut, except between hair and cap, ending opposite the point of the bust, and on nearly all specimens *a short die break connects the end of the pole to the bust.* JHF below a point halfway between T and Y.

Reverse B.

Die break variations. *Obverse:* I have seen only two examples of this variety without the break between the end of the pole and the bust. Examples are known with a rim break from the left of B, running along the top of RTY, to the rim. Die scaling is seen across the lower edge of the cap and in front of the mouth.

1 7 9 6

R-5. Basal $5. 65-40 (65-60-55-35-35-25). The 65: French-Würtzbach. The 60: Ellsworth-ANS. The 55: Dupont, 1954. Then a sharp drop. Lower range of R-5. Rarity somewhat underestimated in EAC.

84	3·B	The Low 6 TRIPLE LEAF UNDER **AM** AND UNDER **UN**	GILBERT D CN D

Obverse 3. The *Open Mouth* obverse. The lips are unfinished. The 6 is low, about 1 mm. from the bust, and too close to the 9. It seems to slant to the right (it really fails to slant to the left and thereby to fit the curve of the other figures). JHF below the right side of the upright of T. End of the pole lightly cut and distant from the bust. For the benefit of the man with a magnifying glass, Miss Liberty lacks a nasal septum as well as most of her lips, and a small comma-shaped mark is seen (chip out of the die) in line with the point of the third lock and 2 mm. from it.

Reverse B.

Die break variations. *Obverse:* There is always a swelling under the bust involving the last figure of the date and making it weak, so that on slightly worn specimens the 6 is often partially obliterated. *Reverse:* Found perfect, and with a crack through the top of OF.

R-3. Basal $3.50. 65-60 (65-65-60-60-60-60). At least a half dozen are known in full Mint State, and there is no outstanding candidate for first honors. In this review we have called the French-Clarke and the Ellsworth-ANS coins 65's. There may be another one or two at that level. In 1948 T. J. Clarke had four Gilbert D's, all MS-60 or better. Probably half of the "uncirculated" 1796 Caps that are offered for sale are of this beautiful variety. In the French catalogue the MS-65 was misattributed and listed as "Gilbert J."

85	3·C	The Low 6 TRIPLE LEAF UNDER **AM**, LEAF DISTANT FROM **F**	GILBERT G CN G

Obverse 3.

Reverse C. Left 21-4, right 20-4. First S of STATES low, and

[155]

the first T joined to A at the bottom. AME connected at their feet. Cluster of three leaves under AM of AMERICA. Nearest leaf more than 1 mm. distant from F in OF. Lowest leaf on the right points to the right foot of final A. All figures of the fraction rather distant from the fraction bar. *Double leaf under* T *of* CENT.

Die break variations. *Reverse:* There is a small chip out of the die below the center of N in ONE.

R-6. Basal $7.50. 55-25 (55-45-30-20-15-15). The 55: French-Sternberg. The 45: Gies-Clapp-ANS. One of the famous rarities and almost prohibitively scarce above Fine.

86	3·D	The Low 6	GILBERT L
		GHOST LEAF UNDER T	CN K

Obverse 3.

Reverse D. Left 19-5, right 19-4. *The leaf immediately under the first* T *of* STATES *is a mere line,* or "ghost leaf." *Two defective leaves on the left branch, and seven on the right.* D leans to the right, and is distant from E at the top. First s of STATES low. Stems point to the right of final A, and to the left of U. AMERICA closely spaced, AME touch at their feet, and RI almost touch.

Die break variations. None seen. Highly defective reverse. In addition to the nine defective leaves, the bow is incomplete, a fragment of stem is cut across the left ribbon at the wrong level, and most of the legend is badly spaced. "Office boy" reverse.

R-6. Basal $6. 50-35 (50-50-50-35-20-15). The three 50's: Dr. French, Clapp-ANS, and a coin of unknown pedigree shown to WHS by Mehl in 1944. Mehl later reported that he sold this one to "somebody on the West Coast." Barely R-6; rated R-5 in EAC. At the time of writing EAC we called the Dr. French coin MS-60. It had been examined in a poor light. Later, when examined properly, it turned out to be a very nice 50-coin with a coat of paraffin. Text error in EAC: On the reverse, the right branch has 19 leaves and four berries, not 18-4. This error was inadvertently repeated from the Gilbert-Elder text.

1 7 9 6

		The Low 6	GILBERT C
87	3·E	DOUBLE LEAF LEFT OF ONE	CN C

Obverse 3.

Reverse E. Left 19-4, right 18-4. AME connect at their feet. *Compact fraction with numerator too far to the right.* Lowest leaf on the right points to right foot of final A. A and second T of STATES almost touching at their feet. *Double leaf to the left of* ONE (all other reverses of the Liberty Caps except reverse F have a triple leaf here). Triple leaf cluster under T of CENT.

Die break variations. *Obverse:* Found perfect and with a light crack which describes a nearly perfect arc, from the border under 7, through that figure, across the bust and the end of the pole, and back to the border. *Reverse:* Found perfect and rusted between U and the end of the left stem, also between E of ONE and T of CENT.

R-3. Basal $3.50. 60-40 (60-50-45-40-40-35). The 60: Dr. French. The 50: Book-ANS. In the French catalogue this 60-coin was misattributed and called Gilbert M. It should begin to be apparent that Dr. French showed a certain fondness for 1796 Liberty Cap cents. In eight of the eleven varieties he had a finest or unexcelled coin.

8 8

		The Club Pole, Balanced Date	GILBERT H
88	4·E		CN H

Obverse 4. L touches the cap. T almost a millimeter above the forelock, and JHF just to the right of center of space between T and Y. The pole is long, almost reaches the border milling, is *club shaped at the end*, and distant from the bust. The date is evenly spaced, perfectly balanced, and sharply curved, with the 1 *and* 6 *high* and free from hair and bust.

Reverse E.

Die break variations. *Obverse:* Found perfect and with a short crack along the right side of 7, from rim to bust.

R-6. Basal $7.50. 55-15 (55-20-20-20-15-12). The 55: Proskey-Hines-Downing. The 20's: Newcomb-ANS, Dr. French, and perhaps we can call the Dupont coin a 20. The last was a former 30 or 35 which had been tampered with—tooled, polished and

[157]

1796

recolored. Had that coin been left alone it might now have a book rating of 35×$7.50×2½.

89	5·E	**The Crowded Head** TRIPLE LEAF UNDER T	GILBERT K CN J

Obverse 5. L, 1 *and* 6 *almost touch the cap, hair, and bust respectively.* On any but Very Fine specimens the 6 does seem to touch. T is very low over the forelock. The low LIBERTY and high date seem to crowd this obverse and to give it the appearance of having a large head. The end of the pole is about even with the bust, and JHF is just below the right foot of T.

Reverse E. Triple leaf cluster under T of CENT.

Die break variations. None seen.

R-3. Basal $3.50. 35-25 (35-30-30-25-20-20). The 35: Proskey-Hines. The 30's: Dr. French and Newcomb-Clapp-ANS (sold to Clapp before the Newcomb sale). One of the least scarce of the date in low grade condition but a great frustration to the kind of collector whose happiness is invested overmuch in "gem" coins.

90	5·F	**The Crowded Head** DOUBLE LEAF UNDER T	GILBERT I CN I

Obverse 5.

Reverse F. Left 18-5, right 17-3. *Numerator of the fraction much too far to the right.* The right stem points to the right foot of final A, and lowest leaf on the right terminates under the extreme left edge of that letter. Letters of UN of UNITED almost touch. *The leaf cluster adjacent to* T *of* CENT *is double and touches that letter.*

Die break variations. *Reverse:* Found perfect and with a short vertical crack above the right top of N in ONE. In this marriage, the reverse is usually seen upset, or upside down.

R-7. Basal $8.50. 60-30 (60-55-55-15-10-10). The 60: Dr. French. The 55's: Miller-Gies-ANS and Brand-Downing. The last-named coin was not listed in EAC. It came to light in 1949 after a long sleep somewhere, was bought by Downing and sold with the Downing collection in 1952. The variety is just barely R-7, as the present review accounts for exactly 12.

1 7 9 6

91   6·G   The Wide Date   GILBERT F
DOUBLE LEAF LOWER RIGHT   CN F

Obverse 6. *Very wide date, with the 6 high, but the 1 and the 6 are each a good 0.5 mm. from the hair and bust respectively.* Pole long and close to the bust but not touching. The stand of T sits close above the forelock and JHF is below the center of TY. The L does not quite touch the cap.

Reverse G. Left 19-5, right 16-5. The lowest leaf on the right terminates near the bottom of c but points to the middle of the upright of I. *This lowest cluster of leaves on the right is double, whereas on all other Liberty Cap reverses it is triple.* AMERICA very closely spaced, with AME connected at the bottom, and RI almost touching.

Die break variations. *Obverse:* A bend or failure of the die is always seen between the rim and the end of the nose, from the rim toward the lower middle portion of the neck, and in the left field from the rim toward the lowest locks. This failure is advanced on some examples. A break is sometimes seen back of the lower locks, and there is a small break through the middle portion of the 6. In the last stages, the field becomes roughened along the front of the face. *Reverse:* Found perfect and with a break through the final s of STATES; also from rim to the right top of I in AMERICA.

R-3. Basal $3.50. 65-55 (65-60-60-60-55-50). A 65-coin came over from England in 1956. The Proskey-Hines, French, and Gies-ANS coins can all be called 60's. Perhaps one or two others would so qualify. This is the last Liberty Cap cent. It ends an era.

1796 FILLET CENTS

General description of the type

Obverse: A draped bust of Liberty to the right. Hair fastened by a narrow band ending behind the head in a ribbon knot, then flowing downward over the shoulder and terminating in small, well-defined ringlets. Above, in large letters, the legend LIBERTY. Below, the date. The same head punch was used for all the Draped Bust dies of 1796. **Reverse:** Same general pat-

1 7 9 6

tern as that of the Liberty Cap coins. The planchets usually measure 29 mm. in diameter, but occasional variation is encountered.

		Close 96,	
		6 Leaning Right	
92	7·H	SINGLE LEAVES	GILBERT 1 CN 1

Obverse 7. ER touch at the bottom. *The 9 and 6 are very close, with the 6 leaning sharply to the right.* PC (the point of the curl which runs along the top of the head) exactly under the inside curve of B. HWH (the highest wave of hair) is just to the right of the center of R. JHF (the junction of the hair with the forehead) is central under TY.

Reverse H. Left 18-3, right 17-5. *Both branches of the wreath terminate with single leaves.* AME joined at the bottom. The uppermost berry on the left, small and stemless, might be mistaken for a mere enlargement from the stem of the wreath. Very wide separation of ONE and CENT. Right stem points to right foot of final A, and lowest leaf on the right points to left foot of that letter. The fraction has a wide denominator and long fraction bar.

Die break variations. *Obverse:* Found perfect, and with a light crack along the base of RTY, extending nearly to the rim; another, curving down the field in front of the face, to the rim opposite the base of the neck; a small crack from the mouth joining this last one; another, from the rim to the 6 and across to the 9, with a little spur projecting to the right from the upper part of the 9. Frequently seen with a double profile. *Reverse:* Found perfect and with a heavy rim break at the end of the right ribbon.

R-3. Basal $3.50. 50-45 (50-50-50-50-45-40). Lower range of R-3; in 1947 we thought it was R-2. Three of the top six coins are in ANS.

		Close 96,	
		6 Leaning Right	
NC-1	7·I	DOUBLE LEAF	GILBERT 18 CN 18

Obverse 7.

Reverse I. Left 16-5, right 19-4. *The Right branch terminates*

1 7 9 6

with a double leaf. Fraction too far to the right, with a long bar. Denominator closely spaced. Stems short and heavy, the left pointing to the left bottom of U, and the right to the center of A. E in UNITED too high. The last s of STATES distant. ONE too far to the left, and closely spaced. CENT crowded, left top of N overlapping the E.

Die break variations. Obverse breaks as noted.

R-7. $12.50. 30-10 (30-15-12-12-10-6). Six now accounted for, five of them in collectors' hands. *NC*-1 should therefore be read Now Collectible-1. If one or two more are found, the basal value will automatically drop.

		Hyphenated 7-9	GILBERT 2
93	8·J	THE CIRCLE WREATH	CN 2

Obverse 8. *Hyphen-like break between 7 and 9*—always present. Likewise always present is a *rough spot below the ribbon knot, in the left field,* as if the die had rusted. The spot is about 4 mm. long, and is a conspicuous landmark for this important obverse die (which outlived six marriages). All the figures except the 6 seem to slant a little to the right. The 6 is high and close to the drapery. PC just right of B. HWH below the center of R. JHF under the right foot of T.

9 3

Reverse J. Left 20-5, right 18-4. Both branches terminate with single leaves, *the two leaves pointing directly toward each other in such a manner as to give the wreath the appearance of being a perfect circle.* AM joined at the bottom, while the other letters of AMERICA are well separated. The stems are long, somewhat club-shaped, and they define an extremely wide angle. The left stem reaches almost to the bottom of U, and the right almost to the right foot of A.

Die break variations. *Obverse:* In addition to the defects noted, some specimens show a light crack through the date, and weakening of the die over ER. *Reverse:* Found perfect and with a crack over RICA to the rim, which increases and becomes heavier until the tops of ER and CA are connected to the rim by heavy breaks. Several other minor cracks develop across the lower reverse.

R-3. Basal $3.50. 65-60 (65-65-65-60-60-55). Except for No.

119, the commonest 1796 Fillet in Mint State. There are possibly eight or ten of these between 65 and 50, but two of them are in ANS.

94   8·K   Hyphenated 7-9
           ———————————
           DOUBLE LEAF   GILBERT 33
                                                     CN 26
Obverse 8.

Reverse K. Left 16-5, right 19-5. *Right branch terminates with double leaf. The lowest leaf on the right touches, or practically touches the left foot of the final* A. Stem ends short, ribbon ends long, fraction low. TAT connected at the base line, as are AME.

Die break variations. None seen.

R-6. Basal $7.50. 45-15 (45-25-20-15-15-12). Rarity underestimated in EAC. In 1945 Hines had five of them, Clapp four. We thought the variety must be R-5.

95   8·L   Hyphenated 7-9
           ———————————
           SINGLE LEAVES,   GILBERT 34
           TRIPLE LEAF LEFT OF ONE   CN 27
           AND RIGHT OF CENT
Obverse 8.

Reverse L. Left 19-5, right 18-4. *Both branches terminate with single leaves. A cluster of three leaves at the left of* ONE, *and a cluster of three at the right of* CENT—*distinctive.* I *of* UNITED *distant from both* N *and* T. The stems form a very wide angle, but they are rather short.

Die break variations. *Obverse:* Cracks as noted. Die failing at ER.

R-7. Basal $10. 40-25 (40-35-30-25-15-10). This was a proof reader's error in EAC. The original typescript had it R-6, but even that was wrong. The variety is in the middle range of R-7, with only seven or eight in collectors' hands.

NC-2   8·M   Hyphenated 7-9
             ———————————
             SINGLE LEAVES, LOWEST RIGHT   GILBERT 35
             LEAF NEARLY TOUCHES A   CN 28
Obverse 8.

Reverse M. Left 19-4, right 17-5. *Both branches terminate*

with single leaves. *The lowest leaf of cluster of three on the right almost touches the right foot of* A—*diagnostic, not seen on any other Draped Bust reverse of 1796.* TAT *connected at the base, and also* AME. *Fraction closely spaced. Stems long, somewhat club-shaped, the left pointing to the left side of* U, *the right to a point slightly beyond the right foot of* A. N I T *widely separated.* NE *in* ONE *connect at the top.*

Die break variations. None seen.

R-8. Basal $15. 40-5 (40-10-5-5). Only four reported, three of them in collectors' hands, including the 40-coin. If another one turns up, this variety like *NC*-1 will become R-7.

		Hyphenated 7-9	GILBERT 36
96	8·N	SINGLE LEAVES, TRIPLE LEAF UNDER A	CN 29

Obverse 8.

Reverse N. Left 18-4, right 18-5. *Both branches terminate with single leaves. Cluster of three leaves under the first* A *of* AMERICA. TAT *joined at the base, also* AMER. N I T *widely spaced. Wide fraction, extending nearly across the space between the ribbon ends. Numerator close to the knot and central under it.*

Die break variations. *Reverse:* Found perfect and with a heavy break from the rim down the left side of T in UNITED, across CENT, across the right side of M to the rim. Of the eight examples of this variety that I have seen, five were perfect, and three had the die break.

R-7. Basal $12.50. 12-6 (12-8-8-7-4-4). Six now known to us in collectors' hands, and two in ANS.

		Hyphenated 7-9	NOT IN GILBERT
NC-3	8·O	DOUBLE LEAF, NT JOINED	CN 31

Obverse 8.

Reverse O. *Right branch terminates with double leaf. Three leaves under* F. *Pair of leaves directly under the first* A *of* AMERICA. *First berry at the left a mere lump on the wreath stem.* CENT *low, with* NT *touching. Short fraction bar. Stems short, the left club-shaped, the right straight. Left stem points to the center of the bottom of* U, *the right to the center of* A.

1 7 9 6

Die break variations. None seen.

R-8. Basal $15. 8-7 (8-8-6). Two now in collectors' hands. One more will make it a collectible variety, R-7.

| 97 | 9·P | 6 High and Close to Bust SINGLE LEAVES | GILBERT 4 CN 4 |

Obverse 9. *First three figures of the date almost in a straight line, with the 6 much higher and very close to the bust.* PC under the right side of B. HWH under the center of R. JHF under center of TY. Closely resembles obverse 8, but no hyphen between 7 and 9, no rough spot under the ribbon knot, the date is more closely spaced, and the 1 is more than a millimeter from the hair.

Reverse P. Left 19-4, right 18-4. *Both branches terminate with single leaf.* TAT *and* AME *joined at their bases. Lowest leaf on the right terminates under the left foot of the final* A. Of the pair of leaves to the right of T in CENT, the right one is a mere outline while the left terminates on a line even with the top of that letter.

Die break variations. *Obverse:* Found perfect and with a crack along the top of TY; also with crack along the top of BER; with heavy rim break over TY; with rim break along the margin in front of the face.

R-3. Basal $3.50. 60-40 (60-50-45-40-35-35). Middle range of R-3. Two of the first six are in ANS.

| 98 | 10·P | Date Slants Right SINGLE LEAVES | GILBERT 3 CN 3 |

Obverse 10. *All figures of the date slant to the right.* The 6 close to the 9. TY *very closely spaced.* Base line of ERT above that of the other letters. PC below the center of the space between B and E. HWH to the right of center of R—almost under the tail of that letter. JHF under the center of TY.

Reverse P.

Die break variations. *Obverse:* A short break is always present from the rim to the right top of Y. *Reverse:* Found perfect and with a diagonal crack through the top of the first A of AMERICA.

1 7 9 6

R-3. Basal $3.50. 60-45 (60-60-50-45-35-30). Apparently a little more scarce than No. 97, but still near the middle range of R-3.

| 99 | 10·Q | Date Slants Right
SINGLE LEAVES,
TRIPLE LEAF LEFT OF CENT | GILBERT 38
CN 30 |

Obverse 10. In this marriage, the die is breaking down a little at the throat, under the jaw.

Reverse Q. Left 19-4, right 17-5. *Both branches terminate with single leaf. Right stem points to and nearly reaches the right foot of* A, the left stem points to the bottom of U. Cluster of three leaves at the left of CENT. AME joined. ERI, and AT of STATES touch.

Die break variations. *Obverse:* As noted, short break from rim to right top of Y, and slight crumbling at the throat. Also found with a crack from the rim back of the shoulder, through the hair ribbon to B, to the rim. This obverse seems to have failed quickly in its second marriage.

R-7. Basal $8.50. 40-15 (40-25-15-12-12-8). Eleven accounted for in this review. Probably just barely R-7. Two of the six best are ANS.

| NC-4 | 11·Q | Close, Curved Date
SINGLE LEAVES,
TRIPLE LEAF LEFT OF CENT | NOT IN GILBERT
CN 32 |

Obverse 11. E and R of LIBERTY almost touch the hair. Engraver's scratch into the field from the lowest point of the upper hair ribbon. *Compact, curved date,* with the 1 and 7 separated by no more than 0.5 mm. *The 1 and 6 are high, and the former is closer to the hair than the 6 is to the bust.* PC under the inner curve of B. HWH under the left foot of R. JHF central under T.

Reverse Q.

Die break variations. None seen.

R-7. Basal $12.50. 10-3 (10-5-4-3-2-2). Now a collectible variety, R-7, with seven accounted for, six of them in collectors' hands. The 10-coin, however, is ANS.

1 7 9 6

| 100 | 11·R | Close, Curved Date
DOUBLE LEAF,
TRIPLE LEAF UNDER O | GILBERT 20
CN 20 |

Obverse 11.

Reverse R. Left 16-5, right 19-5. *Right branch terminates with double leaf. Lowest leaf on the right points to* C, right stem points to right foot of A, and the left stem to the bottom of U. AT and AM united at the base. The denominator distant from the fraction bar. *Triple leaf under* O *in* OF.

Die break variations. *Reverse:* Found perfect as a rule. One example seen with heavy crack from the rim above A in STATES along top of TES OF and back to the rim. This coin was found by the writer years ago in a junk dealer's shop, and is now in the ANS collection.

R-6. Basal $7.50. 45-15 (45-25-20-12-10-8). Upper range of R-6, probably, but not R-7. Two of the condition census coins in ANS.

| 101 | 11·S | Close, Curved Date
DOUBLE LEAF,
DOUBLE LEAF UNDER O | GILBERT 24
CN 22 |

Obverse 11.

Reverse S. Left 14-6, right 17-7. *Right branch terminates with double leaf. A double leaf under* O *in* OF, and a single leaf under C of CENT—the former diagnostic. First A of AMERICA leans to the left, with its right foot high. The numerator of the fraction is merged with the short fraction bar, which slants upward to the right. The two ciphers of the denominator are distant from the fraction bar.

Die break variations. None seen.

R-6. Basal $6.50. 60-30 (60-50-45-25-20-15). Middle or lower range of R-6.

| 102 | 12·S | Defects over Date
DOUBLE LEAF,
DOUBLE LEAF UNDER O | GILBERT 7
CN 7 |

Obverse 12. IB and ER of LIBERTY closely spaced. *Dotlike defects* between the bust and 79, another through the top of 6, and another at the right of 6, under the bust. Date well spaced with the 1 and 6 about equidistant from hair and bust. PC under the right side of the curve of B. HWH under the center of R. JHF central under TY.

1 7 9 6

Reverse S. The double leaf under o is diagnostic. Right branch also terminates in a double leaf.

Die break variations. *Obverse:* Found perfect and with a diagonal crack from the rim through BE to the hair. *Reverse:* Found perfect and with a light crack along the top of AMERI.

R-4. Basal $4.50. 45-30 (45-40-35-30-20-20). Upper range of R-4.

		LIHERTY	GILBERT 9
103	*13·S*	DOUBLE LEAF UNDER O	CN 8

Obverse 13. *The* "LIHERTY" *obverse*. The B was first cut reversed, and after being corrected it looks like an H. PC just to the right of the center of B. HWH below the upright of R. JHF under the right side of the upright of T.

Reverse S. Double Leaf under o in OF.

Die break variations. On all specimens seen, the reverse shows the light crack along the top of AMERI.

R-6. Basal $8.50. 50-30 (50-50-45-30-20-15). The rare "LIHERTY."

1 0 4

		LIHERTY	GILBERT 10
104	*13·T*	TRIPLE LEAF UNDER O	CN 9

Obverse 13. The "LIHERTY" obverse.

Reverse T. Left 16-6, right 19-5. *Right branch terminates with double leaf.* The denominator of the fraction very widely spaced and the fraction bar extends to the right ribbon end. *Larger figures in the fraction.* The fraction bar itself is short, the extension of it to the right caused by an engraver's scratch. *The final A of the legend practically touches the right ribbon.* No letters of the legend are touching one another. *Triple leaf under o in OF.*

Die break variations. *Obverse:* Found perfect, and with a heavy break across the drapery near the point of the bust. Examples showing this break also give evidence of a considerable amount of rusting of the die. *Reverse:* Found perfect, and with several breaks, from the rim to the top of the second T in STATES; rim to o in OF, to the wreath, to the top of E in ONE; rim to M; and other minor cracks. When in combination with the rusted obverse die, this die also shows evidence of rusting. Evidently the two dies were "resurrected" after having been retired, and the fact that the reverse is found in another marriage (14-T) *without* the die breaks supports such a speculation.

R-3. Basal $4. 50-35 (50-45-45-40-30-25). The commoner "LIBERTY."

105	14·T	Double Cut 6	GILBERT 16 CN 16

Obverse 14. The double cut 6. *The lower part of the 6 is conspicuously double cut*, and this is diagnostic. Date well spaced, except that the 6 is a little high, and a little too close to the 9. PC under the center of the right side of B. HWH under the center of the upright of R. JHF under the right side of the upright of T.

Reverse T.

Die break variations. Found with traces of minor injury to the reverse die, but without the reverse die breaks mentioned for the preceding variety. The 14-T appears to have resulted from a brief interim marriage, or possibly from an indiscretion at the Mint, and that may account for its rarity.

R-6. Basal $7.50. 65-12 (65-25-15-10-10-7). Upper range of R-6; possibly 15-20 known.

106	15·U	Date Slants Right DOUBLE LEAF, CHIPS UNDER E	GILBERT 25 CN 23

Obverse 15. *The figures seem to slant to the right*, as on the next, but the date is more evenly spaced. The greatest distance is between the 7 and the 9, the 9 and 6 are a little too close, and the 6 is somewhat high. The 1 points directly into the angle formed by the hair and curl, and is only about 0.5 mm. from the apex of that angle. (On obverse 20 the 1 points similarly, but is about 1 mm. distant.) PC under the inner curve of B. HWH under the center of R. JHF under the right foot of T.

Reverse U. *This is reverse F of 1795* (found on the rare Reeded Edge cent), now resurrected and beginning a series of six more marriages with 1796 obverses, all but two of which are rare. There seems to have been a certain amount of whim-

[168]

1 7 9 6

sicality, or intermittency in some of these marriages, and there is no way of "guessing confidently" at the true order in which this group of coins was issued from the Mint. I have presented them here merely in what seems to be one of the less illogical sequences.

Left 14-7, right 18-7. *Right branch terminates in double leaf. The right stem points to the right foot of the right stand of the final* A *while the lowest leaf on the right points to the left foot of the same stand of that letter.* In all of the marriages with 1796 obverses there is a small lump and other *imperfections under* E *of* UNITED, and another to the right of E in ONE; these apparently result from loss of little chips from the die.

At some time during the career of this die it was apparently ground down a little, to remove imperfections. The imperfections remain, but one result of the effort seems to have been a severing of the right ribbon from the knot (thus producing what has been called the Gilbert 5 reverse, as distinguished from the Gilbert 6). On this present variety, and on others, *both* states of the reverse are encountered.

Die break variations. *Obverse:* Found perfect and with light cracks, through T to the forehead, and down the nose to the rim opposite the point of the bust; from the rim to the left of L across the head to the rim; from the rim past 7, up through the neck and face; from 1 to the top of 7.

R-5. Basal $6. 60-35 (60-55-50-45-20-15). Upper range of R-5. Two of the top six in ANS.

1 0 7

107	*16·U*	Date Wide and Slanting Right DOUBLE LEAF, CHIPS UNDER E	GILBERT 17 CN 17

Obverse 16. *The figures of the date slant decidedly to the right,* and they are widely and evenly spaced. On the lower part of the back of the 9 there is a light spike pointing to the 6. 1 points well below the apex of the angle formed by the hair and lowest curl. PC under the center of the curve of B. HWH under the center of R. JHF under the right foot of T.

Reverse U.

Die break variations. *Obverse:* Usually found perfect. One

1 7 9 6

example is known with a heavy rim break which starts over the Y and extends 8 mm. to the right. The Gilbert-Elder monograph refers to this break as extending along the milling to R, which is misleading. The example with the die break was the discovery specimen, and was apparently the only one known to Gilbert. *Reverse:* Found in both states, with the right ribbon attached and detached, although I have seen only one example of the latter state.

R-7. Basal $10. 20-10 (20-12-12-10-8-8). We now account for just seven in collectors' hands, and one in ANS.

| 108 | 17·U | Widest Date
DOUBLE LEAF,
CHIPS UNDER E | GILBERT 23
CN 21 |

Obverse 17. *Extremely wide date, the widest of the 1796's.* Measured at the top, it is a little over 8 mm. in width. The 6 high, and the 9 6 a little closer than the other figures. The 1 points straight into the angle formed by hair and curl. LIB widely spaced. PC under the inner curve of B. HWH under the center of R. JHF midway between T and Y.

Reverse U.

Die break variations. *Obverse:* Found perfect and with light cracks, along the top of LIBERTY; from the rim across the hair, through the date and the point of the bust into the field; from the nose to the rim opposite the bust; from the back of the drapery through the hair. This die seems also to have been used in rusted condition, and the obverse-reverse combination is probably another of the "resurrected" ones. *Reverse:* Found in both states, with the right ribbon attached and detached, the latter in combination with the rusted obverse die.

R-5. Basal $5. 65-35 (65-45-35-30-30-25). Lower range of R-5. Three of the leading six are ANS coins.

| 109 | 18·U | Close, Curved Date
DOUBLE LEAF,
CHIPS UNDER E | GILBERT 6
CN 6 |

Obverse 18. *Date compact, closely spaced, with the 6 leaning to the left.* The 1 points into the angle of hair and curl, but is distant 1 mm. from the apex. PC slightly right of the center

[170]

1 7 9 6

of B. HWH under the center of the upright of R. JHF slightly left of the extreme right foot of T.

Reverse U.

Die break variations. *Obverse:* Found perfect and with light cracks, from the rim to the head, passing through the upright of T; and from the lowest curl across the upper parts of all figures in the date. *Reverse:* Found in both states, with the right ribbon attached and detached, and about equally common in the two states.

R-3. Basal $3.50. 60-35 (60-50-35-30-30-25). Probably in the middle range of R-3, although formerly considered R-4. Two of the listed six are in ANS.

110	19·U	96 Close and Connected DOUBLE LEAF, CHIPS UNDER E	GILBERT 5 CN 5	1 1 0

Obverse 19. *The last two figures of the date very close, and always connected by a crack.* The 6 leans to the right. Date straight on top. The top of the 1 is close to the hair and on some specimens is connected to the hair by a die break. L and I are recut along the left sides of their uprights, but this is evident only on fine specimens. R of LIBERTY leans to the right, T is high. Many examples have a heavy rim break over TY and extending 3 mm. to the right. PC under the center of the right side of B. HWH under the center of R. JHF central under TY.

Reverse U.

Die break variations. *Obverse:* Found perfect and in many stages of die breaks. Fine crack through the top of LIBERTY and into the field to the left; through the lower curl and the lower part of the date; from the rim to the top of the highest ribbon end; from the rim across T to the forelock, and this crack apparently starts the heavy rim break mentioned; from the forelock down past the face near the nose, then curving to the rim opposite the angle of neck and jaw; from the throat to the rim. There are several small chips out of the die in front of the neck. *Reverse:* Found in both states, with the right ribbon attached and detached, and this marriage of dies must

1796

also have been terminated and renewed at least once, for the variety is found with both the obverse and reverse dies in early and late stages of die break progression. Some of the reverses show extensive breaking down of the die under E of UNITED. The lump becomes nearly as large as the letter itself, and is joined at the top of the letter by a crack. The break to the right of E in ONE also develops, and these advanced breaks are found only on coins with the ribbon detached (later state of the reverse). Some examples show evidence of heavy rusting of both obverse and reverse dies.

R-2. Basal $3. 70-45 (70-55-50-40-35-35). Clearly the least scarce of the 1796 Fillets, and the only variety other than No. 119 (Nichols Find) which offers a 70-coin. Two of the condition list in ANS.

1 1 1

111	20·U	Date Leans Right, 9-6 Close DOUBLE LEAF, CHIPS UNDER E	GILBERT 29 CN 24

Obverse 20. *All the figures seem to lean to the right. The first three are widely spaced, with the 96 rather close.* The 1 and the 6 are distant from hair and bust. PC under the center of the curve of B. HWH under the right side of the upright of R. JHF under the right foot of T.

Reverse U.

Die break variations. *Obverse:* Light cracks usually seen from the rim past 1 to the hair; from the chin to the rim; from the point of the bust to the rim; from 9 to 6 and across the top of 6 to the bust. Small chip out of the die opposite the neck. I have seen but one example without any of the cracks mentioned. *Reverse:* Both states of the reverse are encountered, and apparently with about equal frequency.

R-5. Basal $6. 55-15 (55-20-15-12-12-10). Upper range of R-5. Two of the six are ANS.

NC-5	20·V	Date Leans Right, 9-6 Close DOUBLE LEAF, TWO BERRIES AT LEFT LOOP	NOT IN GILBERT CN 33

Obverse 20.

Reverse V. *Left 14-7. Right 18-7. Right branch terminates*

1 7 9 6

with double leaf. Two berries adjacent to the left loop of the bow—diagnostic. The tip of the leaf under T in CENT just touches the tip of the right foot of that letter. C low and T high in CENT. "This reverse is a close copy of the reverses of the 1794 cents, having the high ribbon bows, knot and pendant ends, and the fraction bar near the milling. It is the only variety of 1796 to have two berries immediately at the left of the bows"— from Ebenezer Gilbert's notes, and reproduced in Gilbert-Elder.

Die break variations. *Obverse:* On the finest example of this variety that has been reported, there are light cracks as noted in the description of the preceding variety. *Reverse:* Perfect die.

R-8. 25–4. Only two reported. The 25-coin now ANS.

112	*19·V*	96 Close and Connected / DOUBLE LEAF, TWO BERRIES AT LEFT LOOP	GILBERT 14 CN 13

Obverse 19.
Reverse V.

Die break variations. *Obverse:* Not seen with perfect die. All of the fine cracks mentioned are found on perfect specimens of this variety, but I have not heard of one with the heavy rim break. The 19-V combination seems to have been an intermediate one, coming between the early and the late coins of the 19-U marriage. The reverse shows many faint traces of injury. On most examples there is a faint crack from the rim along right side of second T of STATES to near the tip of leaf below.

R-6. Basal $6.50. 60-40 (60-50-50-45-30-25). Probably in the middle range of R-6, although it seemed to be R-5 when EAC was written.

113	*21·W*	Crack Through 17 / WIDE DENOMINATOR	GILBERT 11 CN 10

Obverse 21. *Always seen with a conspicuous crack from the rim across the bottom of the lowest curl,* across the 1 and the 7 to the rim beneath the 9; also with a break connecting the top

[173]

of the 6 to the bust. LIBERTY widely spaced, the L leaning a little to the left. The date is moderately wide, with the greatest distance between 1 and 7. The 6 practically touches the border milling.

Reverse W. Left 16-6, right 19-5. *Right branch terminates with double leaf.* Fraction bar short, *the denominator very wide,* with the 1 leaning to the right. The ribbon bows are imperfect and are detached from the ribbon ends. There is only a faint trace of a knot. Stems short, the right one pointing to the left stand of the final A, and the right stand of that letter almost touches the ribbon. The "die break" described by Gilbert-Elder turned out to be a cut.

Die break variations. *Obverse:* Have not heard of an example without the breaks described. ANS has four, showing progression of these breaks. *Reverse:* Always seen perfect in this marriage, so far as I know.

R-6. Basal $7.50. 40-25 (40-35-30-30-20-15). Upper range of R-6, and the condition census is in this instance a bit misleading, since four of these six finest coins are impounded in ANS—among them the 40-coin.

114   22·W   6 in the Drapery   GILBERT 30
                                    CN 25

Obverse 22. *The top of 6 merged with the drapery, and it is punched in OVER the latter,* so that the top of the figure shows instead of the drapery. The B is defective, lacking its left top. PC just left of center of B. HWH under the extreme left foot of R. JHF under the center of T.

Reverse W.

Die break variations. *Obverse:* Found perfect, and with cracks from the rim to T, along TY and back to the rim; heavy rim break to the left of L; a few examples with heavy rim break touching the tops of TY. *Reverse:* In this marriage a break is always seen from the rim to the second T of STATES. A defect over the adjacent A develops, on some specimens, into a small rim break.

R-5. Basal $6. 50-30 (50-45-40-30-25-15). Upper range of R-5.

1 7 9 6

		6 High, Tilted Left	GILBERT 12
115	*23·W*	WIDE DENOMINATOR	CN 11

Obverse 23. LIBERTY widely spaced and even, with the R high, leaning to the right. *The first three figures of the date are widely spaced, with the 6 very high, tilted far to the left, and almost touching the drapery.* The 1 points below the apex of the angle of the hair and curl. PC under the extreme right side of B. HWH under the right foot of the upright of R. JHF under the right foot of T.

Reverse W.

Die break variations. *Obverse:* Found perfect and in many stages of progression of die breaks. A curved crack which is almost an arc of a circle starts at the rim just to the left of the curls, touches the lowest curl, crosses 1 and the top of 7, passes near the top of 9, and down through the 6 to the rim; light crack over BERTY; crack from the rim to the left top of T and from the right top of Y to the rim—on some specimens this becomes a heavy rim break; the letters BER often weakened, sometimes entirely obliterated (failing die). Heavy "suction marks" are usually seen at the chin. ANS has five, showing progression of the breaks. *Reverse:* In this its last marriage, the break over the second T of STATES is heavier, on some specimens appearing as a small rim break, and the defect over the adjacent A also becomes heavy. Fine engraver's scratches are seen from the rim to the C of AMERICA.

R-4. Basal $4.50. 45-25 (45-40-25-25-20-15). Four of the six finest in ANS, including the 45-coin. Possibly in the upper range of R-4, although we formerly thought it was R-3. Perhaps we were misled by the array of them in ANS.

		6 High, Tilted Left	GILBERT 19
116	*23·X*	SINGLE LEAVES	CN 19

Obverse 23.

Reverse X. Left 19-5, right 18-4. *Both branches terminate with single leaves. A large berry on each side of the bow.* AT of STATES touch. AME joined at the base. UN almost touch. The fraction bar almost touches the left ribbon. Left stem points to the left side of U, the right stem to the extreme right foot of

1796

A. *Triple leaf clusters on the outside under* UN, D, *and* R.

Die break variations. *Obverse:* Always found perfect, except for "suction marks," or traces of injury to the die. The later coins of 23-W were certainly struck after the 23-X coins, but *some* of the 23-W coins were apparently struck earlier, for there are examples of this die that do not show either die breaks or "suction marks." This seems to be another case of separating and later reuniting a pair of dies, while a second marriage is meanwhile consummated by one of the dies.

R-6. Basal $6.50. 25-15 (25-25-20-15-12-12). Lower range of R-6 but rarer than we formerly suspected.

117   **24 · Y**   Straight Date with Figures Leaning Right
NO RIBBON KNOT   GILBERT 13 CN 12

Obverse 24. RT widely spaced, and above the arc of E—Y. *Date almost evenly spaced, straight on top, and all figures seem to lean a little to the right.* The 1 and the 6 equidistant from the hair and drapery. PC under the center of the curve of B. HWH under the right side of the upright of R. JHF under the right foot of T.

Reverse Y. Left 16-5, right 19-5. *Right branch terminates with double leaf.* The ribbon bows are connected to the ribbon ends, but *without a knot.* The fraction is centrally located in the space between the ribbon ends, the *figures are large* and widely spaced, and the *fraction bar is very short.* On all examples seen, *a short hook-shaped break connects the top of* E *in* AMERICA *to the rim.* The final A nearly touches the right ribbon end, and the right stem points to the left foot of the left stand of that letter. *The only cluster of three leaves on this reverse is under the* O *in* OF.

Die break variations. *Reverse:* On some examples a short crack connects the right side of D to the rim.

R-7. Basal $8.50. 15-12 (15-15-15-12-10-8). Just twelve accounted for, two of them in ANS. Barely R-7.

1 7 9 6

118 **25·Z** Closest Date, 6 in Drapery / BERRY UNDER D NOT IN GILBERT CN 14

Obverse 25. *The most compact, or closely spaced date of the series. The top of the 6 is lost in the bust,* and the 1 almost touches the hair. The 9 is a little low. The 6 leans to the left. The stand of R nearly touches the hair. PC very lightly cut, but when it can be seen, it is under the center of B. HWH about central under ER. JHF under the left foot of T.

Reverse Z. Left 16-6, right 19-6. *Right branch terminates with double leaf. The only cluster of three leaves is under* O *in* OF. *Directly under* E *of* UNITED *there is a double leaf which does NOT also extend under the upright of* D, and this is distinctive. *An outside berry directly under the upright of* D, with no leaves between—also distinctive. A leaf cuts off the right foot of T entirely. Wide fraction. The final A almost touches the right ribbon end. The right stem points to the left foot of the right stand of A.

Die break variations. *Reverse:* Found perfect and with a rim break under the left ribbon end, extending below 1 of the denominator. I have seen only six examples of this variety, four with perfect die reverses and two with the rim break.

R-7. Basal $7.50. 55-20 (55-40-30-25-10-7). Middle to lower range of R-7. Ten accounted for, two of them in ANS, including the 55.

119 **25·AA** Closest Date, 6 in Drapery / DOUBLE LEAF UNDER D GILBERT 15 CN 15

Obverse 25.

Reverse AA. Left 16-6, right 19-6. *Right branch terminates with double leaf.* On this reverse there is a *double leaf directly under the* D, *and an outside berry directly under the stand of* E. The single leaf at the top of the left branch terminates under the space between E and S. The lowest leaf on the inside of the left branch touches C of CENT, and the lowest on the inside of the right branch touches the right foot of T. The last O of the denominator is high, and the left ribbon end terminates about 1 mm. from U.

[177]

1 7 9 6

Die break variations. *Obverse:* On all the examples I have seen, there is a crack from the rim back of the curls, along the lower curl, touching the bottoms of 1 and 7, to the rim; another, starting at the rim under 6 and extending across the point of the bust into the field. *Reverse:* Above TA of STATES two denticles are connected by a crack; rim break sometimes seen over AT, extending across five or six denticles; light crack across the top of F to near the bottom of the right stand of A; light crack from the right top of N in ONE to the left foot of E, to the left top of T in CENT, and other minor cracks. This reverse is always seen with the leaves more or less "blunted" or flattened, from some injury to the die.

R.-3. Basal $3. 70-65 (70-70-70-65-65-65). These Mint State coins are from the Nichols Find (see p. 189). Probably more than one hundred of No. 119, near Mint State, are in numismatic circulation. It might be supposed that so large a number would force downward the market value of the variety, but nowadays date collectors gobble up Nichols Find coins as fast as they are offered.

The variety formerly designated CN 34 (26-BB in EAC) is now generally acknowledged to have been a fraudulent coin. It should never have been listed. Probably the coin was originally No. 143 of 1797, since it has that reverse. The entire obverse was removed by a remarkable job of retooling, and a new bust re-engraved; also a new LIBERTY and date, complete with a singular "die break," added as an extra fillip. The retooling reduced the weight of the coin from the normal 168 grains to 151.7 grains. It was listed in EAC as a gesture of deference to Mr. Clapp, who had included it in his own excellent monograph.

In view of the extreme rarity of some of the varieties of this date, and the relative newness of any systematic knowledge of the date as a whole, it is altogether probable that the present list is inadequate—that other varieties will turn up, to fill some of the gaps in the series. As this happens, a more desirable order of presentation will perhaps make itself manifest. Meanwhile it can go without saying that some of the estimates of rarity will need correction downward. The quickest way to discover how common a coin is, is always to "put your neck out" that it is rare.

1796

In first-rate condition the Liberty Cap cents of 1796 are decidedly rarer than the Draped Bust cents. Therefore the former have somewhat higher basal values.

The change-over from the Liberty Cap to the Draped Bust type took place, in the cents, in July 1796, according to *Mason's Magazine,* December 1867, quoting a Mint official who presumably had it originally from Adam Eckfeldt. This agrees well with the breakdown given below:

May 12 to June 8	109,825	Liberty Caps
Oct. 12 to Nov. 24	363,375	Draped Busts
	473,200	Coined in 1796 with that date

Nevertheless, this is not the total number of cents dated 1796, as die break progression proves that some were struck after varieties dated 1797. *NC*-5 of 1797 has for reverse a new die which in a broken state appears on Nos. 113-114-115 of 1796; and No. 119 of 1796 was evidently coined around the same time (December 6 to 8, 1797) as Nos. 123 and 135 of 1797, as these varieties were made from the same lot of planchets and two of them share the same reverse die. These "Nichols Find" varieties are discussed at considerable length on page 189

1 7 9 6

TABLE 9. KEY TO THE 1796 CENTS

Liberty Caps

Double leaf at UN, and at ICA...91
Double leaf at UN, triple at ICA; close date..........................81
Leaf about touches left tip of F in OF:
    Close even date, 6 about touches bust............................82
    Date 1 7 96 with the 6 high.....................................83
    Date 1 7 96 with the 6 low and far from bust....................84
No berry immediately right of ribbon bow
    Double leaf at T in CENT; PLLR between CA.......................90
    Triple leaf at T in CENT; PLLL almost touches U
        Date 1 7 96, 6 low and far from bust........................87
        Club pole; JHF about midway TY.............................88
        L, 1 and 6 practically touch cap, hair and bust.............89
PLLL nearly touches center of base of U; "Low 6" obverse.............86
Leaf nearly touches upright of E in UNITED; "Low 6" obverse..........85

Draped Busts, or *Fillet Heads*

Reverse Type of 1794: Leaves 14 left-17 right, or 14–18; single leaf at
    C of CENT
    Double leaf at OF
        LIHERTY...103
        JHF under center of T...................................101
        JHF midway between TY..................................102
    Two berries just left of ribbon bow
        LI recut; 9–6 joined by crack...........................112
        I B widely spaced, L low............................NC-5
    Chip under E of UNITED
        LI recut; 9–6 joined by crack...........................110
        I B widely spaced, L low. Usually, crack past I to hair.....111
        Close, well curved date, 6 leans left...................109
        Very wide coarse denticles; wide date rests on them.....108
        ER close, E low; LI low and far from B..................106
        IBE evenly spaced, ER very close and even..............107
Reverse Type of 1795: Single leaves at top of both branches
    ONE far from CENT; berries 3 left, 5 right......................92
    Stem almost touches U..93
    Outermost leaf of triplet ends right of center of E in UNITED
        Wide even date, 1 far from curl.........................97
        Date 1 7 96, TY almost touch............................98
    Triple leaf at final A, PLLR close to right foot............NC-2
    Triple leaf right of E in ONE...................................116
    Leaf close to tip of tail of R; D too high......................95
    Leaf close to base of E in AMERICA; E D apart...................96

1796

Triplets left of ONE CENT; stem nearly touches foot of A:
  Close curved date, 6 leans left; T Y apart.....................NC-4
  Date spaced 1 7 96 and almost straight.........................99
Reverse Type of 1797: Leaves 16–19
  Small fraction; berries 5–4...................................NC-1
  Small fraction; berries 6–5, PHL almost midway S O.............NC-3
  Small fraction; berries 5–5, PHL under center of S..............94
  Small fraction; berries 5–5, PHL slightly right of S............100
  LIHERTY..104
  The double cut 6..105
  Closest date, imbedded 6. Berries 6–6, berry under D.............118
  Closest date, imbedded 6. Berries 6–6, leaf under D..............119
  Berries 5–5. Hook-shaped defect over E in AMERICA................117
  Berries 6–5, PLO far right. Date 1 7 96, break through 17........113
  Berries 6–5, PLO far right, Imbedded 6...........................114
  Berries 6–5, PLO far right. RT close, T Y apart; high 6..........115

TABLE 10. RARITY AND VALUE: 1796 CENTS

Number	Obv.-Rev. Designation	Gilbert Number	CN Number	Rarity	Basal Value (Dollars)
		Liberty Caps			
81	1-A	A	A	3	3.50
82	1-B	B	B	5	5.
83	2-B	E	E	5	5.
84	3-B	D	D	3	3.50
85	3-C	G	G	6	7.50
86	3-D	L	K	6	6.
87	3-E	C	C	3	3.50
88	4-E	H	H	6	7.50
89	5-E	K	J	3	3.50
90	5-F	I	I	7	8.50
91	6-G	F	F	3	3.50
		Draped Busts			
92	7-H	1	1	3	3.50
NC-1	7-I	18	18	7	12.50
93	8-J	2	2	3	3.50
94	8-K	33	26	6	7.50
95	8-L	34	27	7	10.
NC-2	8-M	35	28	8	15.
96	8-N	36	29	7	12.50
NC-3	8-O	—	31	8	15.

1 7 9 6

TABLE 10. RARITY AND VALUE: 1796 CENTS—Continued

Number	Obv.-Rev. Designation	Gilbert Number	CN Number	Rarity	Basal Value (Dollars)
97	9-P	4	4	3	3.50
98	10-P	3	3	3	3.50
99	10-Q	38	30	7	8.50
NC-4	11-Q	—	32	7	12.50
100	11-R	20	20	6	7.50
101	11-S	24	22	6	6.50
102	12-S	7	7	4	4.50
103	13-S	9	8	6	8.50
104	13-T	10	9	3	4.
105	14-T	16	16	6	7.50
106	15-U	25	23	5	6.
107	16-U	17	17	7	10.
108	17-U	23	21	5	5.
109	18-U	6	6	3	3.50
110	19-U	5	5	2	3.
111	20-U	29	24	5	6.
NC-5	20-V	—	33	8	—
112	19-V	14	13	6	6.50
113	21-W	11	10	6	7.50
114	22-W	30	25	5	6.
115	23-W	12	11	4	4.50
116	23-X	19	19	6	6.50
117	24-Y	13	12	7	8.50
118	25-Z	—	14	7	7.50
119	25-AA	15	15	3	3.

1796

TABLE 11. GILBERT-ELDER "VARIETIES" WHICH ARE EITHER DUPLICATES OF OTHER VARIETIES OR UNKNOWN
(After Clapp)

G-E Number	
J	Same as D.
M	Same as C.
N	Same as B.
8	Unknown. Probably same as GE-25.
21	Same as 5.
22	Probably same as 35.
26	Probably 16.
27	Probably 19.
28	Probably 25.
31	Unknown. Possibly 25 or 29.
32	Same as 6.
37	Probably 19.
39	Probably 23.
40	Same as 5.
41	Same as 12.

Numbers higher than 40 are not to be blamed on either Gilbert or Elder, but appear to be a product of inventive imagination on the part of cataloguers, dealers, collectors, and others.

1797

THE 1797 OBVERSES ARE ALL EXACTLY ALIKE SO FAR AS THE head of Liberty is concerned. The dies evidently were prepared from a single hub, or "head punch," and obverse variations depend on the manner in which LIBERTY and the date were punched in, on the border milling, on die breaks and injuries, or on the way the coins were struck.

Many of the varieties are more or less marked or "milled" on the edges, with faint diagonal lines in patches, but never evenly, and never entirely around the edge. Since the process probably had to do with the preparation of the planchets, and not with the striking of the coins themselves, the presence or absence of traces of milling is a condition of no great concern to the student of die variation.

Two varieties of 1797, 2-A (usually) and 3-A (always), are found *heavily* marked around their edges with "gear-tooth bites," as if they had been gripped in some sort of collar with teeth in it. These are the "gripped edge" coins.

No overdates are encountered until 1798. It is of interest to note, however, that reverses which saw use on 1796 coins are found on no less than six of the 1797 varieties.

With the completion of the Clapp-Newcomb work on this date, twelve new varieties have been added to the original Proskey-Doughty list, making twenty-nine, and the new descriptions have helped change the study of 1797's from a guessing game to the unfolding of a meaningful sequence. The descriptions here in nearly all instances agree closely with those given by Clapp-Newcomb.

1 7 9 7

NC-1   1·A   Close Date, Perfect B;
Crack at BERT
REVERSE OF '96   NOT IN D
CN 1

Obverse 1. LIBERTY rather widely and evenly spaced. *The date even and compact, close to both hair and drapery, but not touching either.* PC under the left side of the upright of B; HWH between E and R; JHF under the left foot of T. The B of LIBERTY is perfectly formed.

Reverse A. *Reverse F (Gilbert I) of 1796. Single leaves at the top.* Left 18-5, right 17-3. PLLR (point of lowest leaf on the right) very close to the left foot of the final A.

Die break variations. On the only example I have seen, the one in the ANS collection, there is an obverse crack from the top of B through the top of E and down to about the middle of R and T.

R-8. Unique. 2-0. No rumor of a second one has yet been heard.

1 2 0

120a   2·A   Wide Date
REVERSE OF '96   PLAIN EDGE   D-94
CN 2

Obverse 2. First three figures of date widely spaced. 97 much closer. The 7 almost touches the drapery. The 1 is 0.5 mm. from the hair, and it points into the angle formed by hair and curl. PC under the center of the curve of B; HWH under the center of R; JHF under the right foot of T.

Reverse A.

Die break variations. *Obverse:* Found perfect, but this die began to fail early in front of the face and around the knot, with resultant roughness. Found with an irregular or rough crack which starts at the milling left of L, extends to that letter and along the top of LIBERTY to the rim over Y. In later stages the die is crumbling along BERTY. The upper part of I crumbles and becomes misshapen. A delicate crack from the rim opposite the knot extends to the curls and date. *Reverse:* Found perfect, and with a crack from the rim past the left side of U.

R-4. Basal $2. 60-45 (60-55-45-45-40-35).

[185]

1 7 9 7

120b   2·A $\dfrac{\text{Wide Date}}{\text{REVERSE OF '96}}$ GRIPPED EDGE   D-94 CN 2

Same as No. 120a but heavily marked around its edge with "gear-tooth bites." The *Gripped Edge* subvariety.

R-2. Basal $1.50. 65-50 (65-65-55-50-45-40). Wide date and Gripped Edge.

121   3·A $\dfrac{\text{Close Date, Defective B}}{\text{REVERSE OF '96}}$ GRIPPED EDGE ALWAYS   D-93 CN 3

Obverse 3. Date compact and even, the 1 close to both hair and curl, and pointing directly into the angle of hair and curl. 7 close to the drapery but not touching. *The B is defective at the top,* and on many specimens is weakly struck. PC under the left side of the upright of B; HWH between E and R; JHF under the center of T.

Reverse A.

Die break variations. *Obverse:* Found perfect and in many stages of die break progression. Crack from the rim to the center of the knot; from this crack another branches up to the rim; a third curves down through the field, across the curls, and into the bust; through 97, across the bust and into the field to the rim; rim through ERTY. The perfect die is rare, and the crack from the rim to the ribbon knot is nearly always seen. *Reverse:* Light crack from the rim past the left side of U, and other minor light cracks are seen. *Always found with Gripped Edge.*

R-3. Basal $2. 60-45 (60-55-50-50-45-35). Close date and Gripped Edge. There are half a dozen or so examples of this variety on which the grip marks are weak or missing. Two or three of these coins show clear evidence that their edges were turned down, probably on a lathe, to remove the grip marks. Occasionally a D 93 is offered as a "Plain Edge" variety. When the Clapp-Newcomb monograph on 1797 cents was under construction, about 1940, Clapp, Newcomb, Macallister, Hines and Würtzbach made a systematic examination of the available examples with alleged plain edges. Their opinion at the time was that there was no good evidence on which to postulate the existence of a true sub-variety. All of the plain edges they saw were on rather worn coins which might well have been tampered

1 7 9 7

with. In our present review of this question we agree in substance with the "Clapp committee" but would add that even if perchance there *are* a couple of coins of this variety with true plain edges such coins are in all likelihood imperfectly processed products of the mint—freaks like the dozen or so 1794's whose edges failed to get lettered—and we do not feel that there is any evidence for an intended sub-variety of this number.

122	4·B	Closest Date / 1 TOUCHES LEFT RIBBON	NOT IN D / CN 4

Obverse 4. Obverse of D-106. *The closest date of the year*, measuring 6 mm. at the bottom. PC under the center of the upright of B; HWH between E and R; JHF under the left upright of T. *The first 7 leans a little to the right.*

Reverse B. Left 16-5, right 19-5, as are all of the 1797 reverses except five, which will be noted later. Fraction bar short. The denominator widely and evenly spaced, *with the 1 touching or practically touching the left ribbon*. The right stem points to the right foot of the left stand of the final A, and its continuation would just touch the serif of C. The left stem points to the right side of the bottom of U. PLLR below the center of of C; PSL (point of seventh leaf) below the center of the curve of D; PHL (point of highest leaf) left of right side of S.

1 2 2

Die break variations. *Reverse:* Found perfect, and with crack through top of MERI. This crack extends to C and to rim between AM; another crack develops from rim to right top of M. One is known with a rim break over IC; another with this break heavier and accompanied by a lighter rim break over M.

R-6. Basal $5. 15-10 (15-12-12-12-8-8). Listed as R-7 in EAC, fifteen examples now accounted for. Upper range of R-6. Usually seen on imperfect, rough planchets. These planchets, coming as they probably did just before the highly polished Boulton planchets were used (for the Nichols Find coins and some others), appear to have been of uniformly poor quality. Presumably, most of the 1796 Fillet cents and some of the 1797's were struck on planchets from two shipments which arrived in October 1796. The Mint complained bitterly about these two shipments, and during the next nine or ten years placed most of its planchet orders with Boulton.

1 7 9 7

NC-2   4·C $\dfrac{\text{Closest Date}}{\text{RIM BREAK OVER D ST}}$ NOT IN D
CN 5

Obverse 4.

Reverse C. Very similar to the last. Fraction bar short and to the left. 1 of the denominator clear of the left ribbon. 00 closer than 10. Final 0 half under the right ribbon. *Left stem ends in a long engraver's scratch running to the right bottom of* U. Right stem points to the right foot of A. PLLR below the left foot of A; PSL just below the inner curve of D; PHL under right side of S. Second berry on the left attached to the point of the leaf below.

Die break variations. *Reverse:* Faint crack through tops of ED; rim break above D ST, later extending above all of STATES and a little beyond last S.

R-8. Basal $15. 20-10 (20-15-5). Three now known, two in collectors' hands. The 20-coin is ANS. Discovery of one more will make the variety collectible. Two more will make it R-7. If one is interested primarily in profit it is dangerous to hold these extremely rare coins, for of course the basal value falls sharply with the discovery of new examples.

123

NC-3   4·D $\dfrac{\text{Closest Date}}{\text{PHL RIGHT OF S}}$ NOT IN D
CN 28

Obverse 4.

Reverse D. Fraction bar short, covering only half of the second 0. 00 closer than 10. Stems short, the left pointing to the center of the bottom of U, the right to the right foot of A. TAT high. PLLR under the left foot of A; PSL to the right of the center of D; PHL to the right of S. N below E and T of CENT. Second berry on the left touches the stem of the leaf above.

Die break variations. None seen.

R-8. Basal $15. 20-5 (20-5-5). Two new ones have turned up, both 5-coins. ANS has the 20. Same comment as for the preceding variety.

123   4·E $\dfrac{\text{Closest Date, Cut on Cheek}}{\text{LAST O HIGH}}$ D-106
CN 6

Obverse 4. There is always a small cut on the cheek below the eye.

[188]

1 7 9 7

Reverse E. *This is reverse AA of 1796.* Left 16-6, right 19-6. Double leaf directly under D, and an outside berry directly under the stand of E. *Last 0 of the denominator high.*

Die break variations. *Reverse:* The minor cracks mentioned (p. 174) are seen, with no apparent further advancement.

R-4. Basal $2. 70-65 (70-70-70-65-65-65). Grading one of these reddish uncirculated Nichols Find coins, struck on its polished Boulton planchet, may amount to something of a quibble. Perhaps they are all 60's, or all 65's, or possibly more of them should be called 70's. In any case they are all much alike, and rather uninteresting coins.

It is curious to note that a number of specimens of this variety are now known without the rim break or any of the minor cracks described for No. 119 of 1796 (p. 174 in EAC), which has the same reverse. Evidently No. 119, despite the date on the coin, was struck *after* No. 123.

The Nichols Find

Some time before 1863 there was dispersed a quantity of Mint State 1796 and 1797 cents, probably numbering as many as a thousand in all, which are traced to a bag brought in December 1797 from the Mint to his daughters by one Benjamin Goodhue, formerly of the Continental Congress. The name of Nichols Find was attached to these coins in the eighteen sixties and apparently arises from the fact that they were the property of the Nichols family at the time of their dispersal to collectors, perhaps just prior to 1863. According to report, David Nichols of Gallows Hill, near Salem, Mass., passed them out at face value.

Three varieties of cents are traditionally ascribed to this find, their identity of fabric, similar preservation and similarity of dies, and frequent appearance in the identical red MS-65 condition, pointing to a common source. They are Nos. 119, 123 and 135. A lengthy account of this find was presented (by WB) in the January 1952 *Numismatist*. If the facts there set forth are accepted, it follows that the coins were all made in the latter part of 1797, despite the fact that the commonest one (No. 119) bears date 1796.

To the best of anyone's knowledge, these Nichols Find cents represent the surviving Mint State coins from the first Boulton planchet shipment (April 26, 1797; 9,856 pounds, per H.M.S. *Adriana*), which the Director of the Mint pronounced "perfect and beautifully polished." Before any of the planchets were actually stamped and released, however, the yellow fever epidemic in Philadelphia intervened and the Mint shut down. In November 1797 the Mint reopened, and between November 22 and December 18 there were coined some 486,000 cents. Exactly 69,437 of these came from the Boulton shipment, and hence they included the cents we know as Nichols Find varieties. Planchets from the same Boulton lot have been seen on occasional examples of other varieties, which presumably appeared in small numbers in the Nichols hoard. These varieties include No. 118 of 1796, No. 104 of 1796 (rusted dies only), and Nos. 136 and 137 of 1797. The reverse N of No. 137 was made at the same time as Reverse Z of No. 118, as Clapp pointed out, and the single AU-55 of No. 118 is on a Boulton planchet. Die break evidence proves, moreover, that this must have been struck before the common Nichols Find variety, No. 119. Reverses M and N of Nos. 136-7 usually come blunted, as do those of the three traditional Nichols Find varieties. It is therefore very probable that the original hoard included examples of all seven varieties named, which could then be all dated to the period November-December 1797. The presence among them of the rusted-die No. 104 (at least three examples of which have been seen on Boulton planchets) gives a valuable clue as to when the rusted-die or "resurrected" examples of Nos. 106, 107, 108, 109 and 110 were struck, even though no specimens of these have yet been noted on Boulton planchets. A ready explanation for all this mixing up of dated dies in the winter of 1797 can be found in the chaotic conditions that must have prevailed after the reopening of the Mint. It is not to be expected that all would have been left in perfect order at the Mint when the primary thought of everybody that summer was to escape the epidemic and avoid the fate of some of his colleagues.

124	5·F	Compact date, Last 7 high, R nearly touches Hair	NOT IN D
		VERY WIDE DENOMINATOR	CN 7

Obverse 5. The upright of R nearly or practically touches the hair. Clapp says it does touch. On my coin, which came from the Newcomb collection, it does not quite touch. B E R and T Y rather widely spaced. 1 closer to hair than to curl. *Two denticles are directly below the foot of the first 7; one denticle directly under the foot of the second 7:* PC under the right side of the upright of B; HWH under the end of the left foot of R; JHF under the left side of the upright of T. There is a swell in the die across the point of the bust. Date compact with the last figure high, the 1 7 a little more widely spaced than the other figures, and the 9 slightly higher than the first 7.

1 7 9 7

Reverse F. Short fraction bar and *very wide denominator* measuring 5 mm. from the center of the last 0 to the point of the 1. 1 0 more widely spaced than 00, and the last 0 a little high. The right stem points to the left foot of A, and its continuation would bisect C diagonally. The left stem points to the middle of the left stand of N. PLLR under the center of C; PSL below the inner curve of D. There is a small defect near the rim to the left of the first A of AMERICA, and another between the tops of M and E.

Die break variations. None. Swellings on obverse become heavier, on two examples nearly as severe as on most examples of No. 125. Reverse becomes swollen at OF and sometimes shows extensive rusting at ES of STATES, upper wreath, and ITE of UNITED.

R-7. Basal $7.50. 12-9 (12-12-10-10-8-6). At least 8, possibly 9 now accounted for. Only one in ANS. Middle range of R-7. 1 2 5

		Obverse as last, with Heavy Swelling	NOT IN D
125	5·G	SHORT FRACTION BAR	CN 8

Obverse 5. There has now been *extensive sinking of the die, with resultant heavy swelling* across the point of the bust and upward along the rim. The swelling somewhat resembles that seen on the comparatively common 18-P variety (D-104), but is more advanced. It extends all around the head, most pronouncedly from the nose to the throat and around the bust. On two of the specimens I have seen the die is heavily swollen through the right side of the date, across the point of the bust, and up the field to a point opposite the nose, as well as in the field behind the hair ribbons. There are "suction marks" from the angle of the chin to the point of the bust. On the reverse, F and A are weak because of the obverse swelling opposite them.

Reverse G. Reverse of D-107. *Short fraction bar* and wide denominator, measuring 4.5 mm. from the center of the last 0 to the top of the 1. The fraction bar starts just half way between the 1 and the first 0. The right stem points to the middle of the bottom of A, and its continuation would just touch the top of the serif of C. The left stem points to the middle of the left stand of N, and about 1 mm. from its tip there is a dotlike defect. PLLR even with the left of foot of A; PSL under the inner curve of D. A leaf terminates under the left side of the right stand of M.

Die break variations. None seen.

R-7. Basal $6.50. 20-10 (20-20-8-8-7-7). About 11 now identified, 10 of them in collectors' hands. Therefore in the lower range of R-7.

126   6·G Both Tops of 7 Touch the Drapery; Crack, Rim to Throat (Usually)   D-107 CN 9

1 2 6

Obverse 6. *Defective* B. The upper serif of that letter is missing. Both tops of the second 7 touch the drapery, and the 1 is distant from the curl. *Opposite the nose there is a long denticle, with a "tail" which curves upward*, and the two denticles above this one are united by a break. PC under right side of upright of B; HWH just left of left foot of R; JHF a little right of left side of upright of T.

Reverse G.

Die break variations. *Obverse:* Found perfect (rarely), and with a heavy, irregular crack from the rim to the throat. This crack looks like a connected series of defects, and becomes almost solid near the rim where (on some specimens) it involves four denticles. Another smaller crack starts from the rim four denticles above the first, and (sometimes) extends to a point near the bridge of the nose, where the die is crumbling. A light crack runs from a point below the lowest curl up the field to a point opposite the lowest ribbon end. *Reverse:* Found perfect and with a fine crack from the right foot of the first A to the left pendant of the second T of STATES. A light crack slants from the rim above M, across the right top of E and through the upper part of RI.

R-3. Basal $1.50. 60-55 (60-60-55-55-55-50). Middle range of R-3.

1 7 9 7

127 7·G The Peaked Hair Wave NOT IN D / CN 10

Obverse 7. Date wider than the preceding, and about evenly spaced, with the 7 entirely clear of the drapery. *The second wave of hair comes up to a sharp peak* under the left lower serif of E. PC under the center of the upright of B; HWH between E and R; JHF slightly left of the center of T.

Reverse G.

Die break variations. *Obverse:* Found perfect and with a crack from the rim opposite the knot, extending 2 mm. into the field and then turning downward almost at right angles to a point about opposite the lower hair ribbon. This is the break described in Doughty as occurring on the D-107, but it does not occur on that variety. Proskey must have confused this with his No. 107. *Reverse:* Shows the two light cracks mentioned.

R-6. Basal $4. 30-15 (30-20-20-15-12-12). Lower range of R-6, although rated R-5 in EAC.

128 8·H The 1 and Both Points of the 7 Touch / M CUT OVER AN E D-109 / CN 11

Obverse 8. Easily recognized, as *both points of the 7 touch the drapery and the 1 touches the hair.* This is true of no other variety. The R touches the hair. PC just to the right of the upright of B; HWH touches the left foot of R; JHF under the left side of the upright of T.

Reverse H. Also easily recognized, as *the M is cut over an E.* Loops of the bow disconnected from the knot, which is defective. The right stem points to the right foot of A, and the left to the tip of the left lower serif of N. PLLR under the center of the left foot of A; PSL beneath the outer curve of D.

Die break variations. *Obverse:* Found perfect and in many stages of die break progression. Crack from the rim at the left through the curls, to the top of the 9; from the rim at the right of the 7, a heavy crack to the top of the bust, with a branch going off to the rim at the right; from the upper curl up through the ends of the hair ribbon to the rim; along the top of LI to the center of B, to the hair; other minor cracks around

1 7 9 7

TY, the ribbon, the point of the nose, and behind the curls. *Reverse:* No die breaks, but heavy traces of injury in the upper right portion, and there is a defect at the base of I in AMERICA.

R-3. Basal $1.50. 60-45 (60-55-50-45-40-35). Just about midrange R-3. No more than three seen above EF.

| 129 | 9·H | Curved Break Behind Hair Ribbon, Early State
M CUT OVER AN E | D-108
CN 12 |

Obverse 9. *Defective* B, with the upper serif missing. The 1 is 0.5 mm. from the hair and curl, and the 7 is nearly that distance from the drapery. There is a minute defect or projection on the upper right portion of the 9. PC under the right side of the upright of B; HWH under the left foot of R; JHF central under T.

Reverse H.

Die break variations. *Obverse:* At the rim behind and just above the hair ribbon, a faint injury or break begins, curves out into the field and back toward the rim, traversing a distance of about 5 mm. I have seen only two examples without the break. Through the three marriages of this obverse the break becomes in general heavier and more massive, but does not extend in length. A slight depression can always be seen in the field, running from the rim opposite the bust to the rim opposite Y.

R-7. Basal $7.50. 45-15 (45-45-12-10-8-7). Called R-6 in EAC but this was a proof reader's blunder. Middle range of R-7. Three new ones have appeared and there appear to be eight now available to collectors. One in ANS.

| 130 | 9·I | Curved Break Behind Hair Ribbon, Middle State
BROKEN LEFT RIBBON END | D-99
CN 13 |

Obverse 9.

Reverse I. *Highly defective left ribbon end,* the lower half disconnected and the upper half broken up. A leaf touching the back of C in CENT is a mere outline (ghost leaf). The leaf opposite T in UNITED is fragmented. PLLR between C and A, and these two letters are very close. PSL beneath the inner curve of D.

Die break variations. *Obverse:* The break behind the hair ribbon is usually more developed, and on some specimens has begun to unite with a couple of defects which have appeared adjacent to it. I have seen one example (now ANS) without the break. There is usually a short diagonal crack across the upright of R.

R-2. Basal $1.25. 60-50 (60-55-50-50-45-45). One of the three commonest 1797's but a tremendous favorite because of the progression of the die break behind the hair.

131   *9·J*   Curved Break Behind
Hair Ribbon, Late State
STEMLESS WREATH   D-98
CN 14

Obverse 9.

Reverse J. *Stemless wreath,* and easily distinguished from the other stemless reverse (T) by the position of the PSL beneath the right side of the upright of D (on reverse T it is under the curve of D). A line is seen on the left side of the right ribbon, below the knot and at the end.

1 3 2

Die break variations. *Obverse:* In this marriage the break behind the ribbon ends is heavily developed; there is usually a small break on the forelock below the tail of the R, and a faint break from the end of the nose. On some specimens the weakness of the die in the right field has developed into a conspicuous ridge or break, from the rim near the point of the bust to the rim at the right of Y.

R-3. Basal $3.50. 60-30 (60-50-35-25-25-20). The relatively common Stemless Wreath variety but always in demand because listed as a "type." (Actually, they all are types, as people are.)

132   *10·J*   Defective B,
No Curved Break
STEMLESS WREATH   NOT IN D
CN 15

Obverse 10. *Defective* B—*upper serif missing,* and the lower serif of B is double cut. The date is unequally spaced, with a little more distance between the 1 and the 7. PC beneath the center of the upright of B; HWH between E and R; JHF beneath the center of the upright of T.

Reverse J.

[195]

1 7 9 7

Die break variations. *Reverse:* Found perfect and with a rim break over IC.

R-7. Basal $6.50. 30-12 (30-20-15-10-8-7). In the present review we can account for just about 12. Lower range of R-7, instead of R-6.

		Perfect B, No Curved Break	
133	11·J	STEMLESS WREATH	NOT IN D CN 16

Obverse 11. *The B is perfect*, and a light scratch extends from its top to the rim above 1. The foot of R almost touches the hair. Date rather compact and equally spaced. PC below the center of the upright of B; HWH between E and R; JHF under the left side of the upright of T. To distinguish obverse 11 from obverse 10 at a glance, look at the uprights of 1 and B. On obverse 11 they are about parallel; on obverse 10 they converge or diverge markedly.

Reverse J.

Die break variations. *Obverse:* Found with heavy traces of wreath at the throat, and around the head and knot; a light V-shaped break from the rim through the top of T to R. *Reverse:* Usually seen with a light rim break over IC, and with an irregular crack along the top of STATE.

R-6. Basal $4. 35-15 (35-20-20-15-15-12). Middle range of R-6, instead of R-5. Probably there are about twice as many of these as of No. 132.

134	12·K	Period Before Throat	D-95 CN 17

Obverse 12. One of the easy ones. Upper serif of B missing. *Right foot of E touches the hair* (diagnostic), and R almost touches. The curl at the top of the head has no point (no PC). *The 1 touches the hair and the right top of 7 touches the drapery. There is a conspicuous triangular chip (period) out of the die in front of the throat.* The top of the second wave is between B and E; HWH between E and R; JHF under the left foot of T.

Reverse K. *Small figures in the fraction,* and these are seen

1797

on no other 1797 reverse except A, which is a second appearance of reverse F of 1796. Right stem points to the middle of the right stand of A, the left stem to the bottom of U. *The lowest leaf on the right is a mere fragment found under the left foot of* A. PSL under the tip of the serif (left foot) of D.

Die break variations. *Obverse:* There is *always a swelling of the die behind the lower curls and the neck.* Several small scratches through the date, a heavy one connecting 9 7; a swelling at the rim under the 9, and a defect at the rim to the right of the 7. The edge is often slightly gripped, and the obverse milling is broad. *Reverse:* Found perfect, and with a crack from the rim through E of AMERICA to the wreath stem. On some specimens the crack begins as two separate cracks from the milling, but the two converge at E. The perfect die is rare.

R-4. Basal $2.50. 50-45 (50-50-50-45-45-40). Upper range of R-4, and this may possibly be an R-5. One of the favorites among old collectors.

		7 Touches,	
		R Almost Touches	D-100
135	13·L	SIX BERRIES ON EITHER SIDE	CN 18

Obverse 13. Upper serif of B missing. The right corner of the 7 touches the drapery. The stand of the R almost touches the highest wave. PC under the right side of the upright of B; HWH under the left foot of the upright of R; JHF under the center of the upright of T.

Reverse L. *Left 16-6, right 19-6, and this is true of no other 1797 reverse except E,* which is also a 1796 reverse. Wide fraction. Right stem points to the center of the right stand of A, and the left to the left side of the bottom of U. PLLR between C and A; PSL beneath the inner curve of D.

Die break variations. *Reverse:* A slight crack or defect is always seen connecting the top of C in AMERICA to the rim; some specimens show a faint crack connecting the adjacent I to the nearest leaf.

R-4. Basal $2. 70-65 (70-70-70-65-65-65). Another Nichols Find variety. Lower range of R-4, probably.

1797

On these three varieties the planchets have a high polish or "prooflike" luster; all show the same finish on the rims; the denticles are deep and heavy; two of the reverses are identical and the third varies only triflingly from them; in all cases the dies had been slightly injured or blunted, especially the reverse dies.

Clapp has raised the question whether these coins may not have come from the shipment of "highly satisfactory" planchets referred to in the Old Mint records as received from England in April, 1797, after a long series of shipments of a "very disappointing" nature (see Stewart, 22, pp. 69-75).

NC·6	13·M	Evenly Spaced Date	NOT IN D
		FOUR BERRIES RIGHT	NOT IN CN

Obverse 13. Date almost evenly and rather closely spaced.

Reverse M. Four berries on the right branch; for full description see No. 136.

Die break variations. None seen. Reverse without the injuries of No. 136.

R-8. Unique. 4-0. Discovered by Raymond Chatham as the revision of this book was going to press.

136	14·M	Wide Date with 97 Close	D-102
		FOUR BERRIES RIGHT	CN 19

Obverse 14. *The 7 9 widely spaced; the 97 very close, almost touching.* Rather wide date, close to the milling, the last 7 only a hair's breadth from touching a denticle. PC under the center of the curve of B; HWH under the tail of the R; JHF between T and Y. The die is lightly flaked above IB, between T and Y, in front of the face, near the point of the bust, between 1 and 7, and diagonally across the final 7 ("probably poor steel"—Clapp).

Reverse M. Found uninjured and in an injured state where several letters and some of the leaves are more or less flattened, especially in the central and upper right portions of the coin. The die must have been injured by coming into contact with some smooth object. *Left 16-5, right 19-4,* and this is diagnostic as no other 1797 reverse has four berries on the right branch.

1797

PLLR even with the left foot of the left stand of A; PSL under the center of the upright of D. The right stem curves downward and points to the center of the bottom of the right stand of A, the left stem to the left side of U.

Die break variations. *Reverse:* Found perfect and with light crack from the rim through U to the wreath; from rim to F, then down the wreath to R and back to the rim; from rim to left foot of E in AMERICA, to the wreath, then curving back of C to the rim.

R-4. Basal $2. 60-55 (60-60-55-50-50-50). High condition census but nearly all of the finest examples are struck from a heavily rusted reverse die.

| 137 | 14·N | Wide Date with 97 Close SPRAWLED RIBBON ENDS | D-101 CN 20 | 1 3 7 |

Obverse 14.

Reverse N. *Left 16-6, right 19-5,* and this is almost diagnostic since the only other 1797 reverse with six berries left and five right is the unique or nearly unique reverse R, a resurrected reverse of 1796. *Under the first s there is an outline of another s. The ribbon ends sprawl widely and the right one touches the right foot of A.* PSL between E and D of UNITED. There is a berry below the center of D. PLLR under the center of C.

Die break variations. *Obverse:* The die is more flaked and the defects mentioned are more prominent. *Reverse:* Several irregularities of surface and minor defects are seen. This die also seems to have been made of poor steel. *Swellings at* UNI *and* RICA. Crack on some examples through the end of the right ribbon and AC to the rim near I. Light crack from rim between 00 crossing the ribbon and stem. Examples are seen with these swellings and cracks heavy. On some coins all of IC and part of A are gone.

R-3. Basal $1.50. 50-35 (50-50-45-35-30-20). Now rated R-3 instead of R-2, but even for an R-3 it is hard to find in VF condition.

1 7 9 7

NC-4　　15·O

Crack from Point of Bust to Milling Opposite Nose

NOT IN D
CN 29

Obverse 15. LIBERTY comparatively high, and about equidistant between rim and hair. B perfect. R leans a little to the right. Date equally and moderately spaced, with the 1 and the 7 comparatively distant from hair and drapery. PC under the center of the upright of B; HWH between E and R; JHF under the center of T.

Reverse O. Continuation of the right stem would just miss the final A and would bisect the C diagonally. The left stem points to the left foot of the left stand of N. PLLR under the right side of C; PSL under the inner curve of D. Fraction bar short, starting about half way between 1 and the first 0.

Die break variations. *Obverse:* On the only example seen, a light crack curves from the drapery at the point of the bust to the milling opposite the middle of the nose. *Reverse:* Perfect, and showing no trace of the swellings and irregularities which are always seen in its later marriage (16-O).

R-8. Unique. 15-0. The lone example is comfortably housed in ANS.

138　　16·O

R Touches and 7 Touches
SWELLING ON UPPER RIGHT REVERSE

D-103
CN 21

Obverse 16. *Left foot of* R *touches the HWH.* Perfect B, and from the upper serif of B an engraver's scratch, which looks like a light break, extends over the I. The 1 is close to the hair and the right top of the 7 just touches, or practically touches, the drapery. PC under the center of the upright of B; HWH under (touching) the left foot of R; JHF under the center of the upright of T.

Reverse O. In this marriage *a swelling is always seen in the upper right portion of the coin,* weakening or obliterating the last letters of STATES, OF, and the first letters of AMERICA. Another swelling, or weakening of the die, at NITED. These swells become much heavier as the die is used.

Die break variations. *Obverse:* On some examples a light wavy crack extends from the right foot of Y into the field oppo-

[200]

1 7 9 7

site the upper lip. Slight defect near the ninth denticle to the left of L. *Reverse:* Light cracks seen on some examples, from the left of first s along its top to adjacent T; from the right top of E and second s to the rim.

R-2. Basal $1.25. 70-55 (70-65-65-55-50-50). By a small margin the highest Condition Census for a 1797 other than the Nichols Find coins. Probably R-2, although called R-3 in EAC.

139	17·P	R Touches, 7 Does Not; Heavy Crack at Left (Usually) FRACTION BAR CONNECTED TO RIGHT RIBBON	D-105 CN 22

Obverse 17. *Left foot of R touches the HWH.* The 7 is close to the drapery but is entirely clear of it. Usually seen with a heavy crack from the border to the hair, and from the same point on the border through the lowest curl to the middle of 1. PC under the center of the upright of B; top of the HWH between E and R; JHF under the left side of the upright of T.

Reverse P. *An engraver's scratch connects the extremely short fraction bar to the right ribbon. The left stem ends with a similar scratch which nearly touches the bottom of U.* Right stem points to the left foot of the left standard of A. Continuation of the left stem would touch U and the upper left serif of N. PLLR under the right side of C; PSL under the center of D.

Die break variations. *Obverse:* Found with perfect die, but usually seen with heavy cracks mentioned. The first crack often runs horizontally across the hair and (sometimes) across the neck. On some examples there is a heavy swell in the left field between the two cracks. Found with light crack along the top of LIBERTY. Row of impressed denticles sometimes seen under the date and to the right, past the bust. *Reverse:* Die swollen a little at S OF A, but never badly so in this marriage.

R-1. Basal $1. 65-55 (65-65-55-55-55-50). Far the commonest 1797, and a familiar, well-loved variety.

140	18·P	Imperfect T; Swelling at Point of Bust FRACTION BAR CONNECTED TO RIGHT RIBBON	D-104 CN 23

Obverse 18. Upper serif of B missing, and top of T unfin-

[201]

1 7 9 7

ished, with the left pendant imperfect and the right disconnected. R is clear of the hair. PC under the right edge of the upright of B; HWH under the center of the upright of R; JHF under the right side of the upright of T. Point of 1 close to the hair and the right top of 7 close to the drapery but not touching it. *Always seen with the die more or less swollen across the point of the bust* and (less markedly) in back of the hair.

Reverse P. The swelling in the upper right portion much heavier. OF often obliterated.

Die break variations. *Obverse:* Usually seen with a light crack from the rim below 1, curving up the field close to the border and rejoining the rim at a level just below the ribbon knot. Some examples show a light crack from the bottom of Y down the field to a point opposite the chin. The 7 of the date is often obliterated by the swelling. In its last stages this variety is seen in "bad shape."

R-3. Basal $1.50. 70-55 (70-60-60-55-50-50). Probably in the lower range of R-3, possibly R-2.

141   19·Q   Compact Date, 7 Distant from Drapery / RIGHT STEM POINTS TO C   NOT IN D / CN 24

Obverse 19. Liberty well spaced and "comfortably clear" of the hair. The date compact except for the 1 7, which are of average spacing, and the 7 is almost a millimeter from the drapery. PC under the center of the upright of B; HWH between E and R; JHF under the right side of the upright of T. The knob of the 9 is usually weak or not struck up.

Reverse Q. Engraver's scratch between the fraction bar and the right ribbon. *Very short fraction bar, reaching less than half way from the first 0 to the 1.* Right stem points to the bottom of the left stand of A, and its continuation would nearly bisect C. Continuation of the left stem would touch U and the upper left corner of N. PLLR between C and A; PSL under the right side of the upright of D.

Die break variations. *Reverse:* Traces of injury at several places around the wreath. Usually but not always seen with a conspicuous crack from the rim through the left ribbon across the left stem and wreath and left side of bow to the right side of C in CENT. Crack also seen from the point of the numerator to the left of ribbon near the knot.

R-6. Basal $4. 45-20 (45-35-30-15-15-15). Lower range of R-6.

NC-5   20·R   VERY WIDE DENOMINATOR; RIBBON BOWS DETACHED, IMPERFECT   NOT IN D CN 25

Obverse 20. Upper serif of B missing. LIB close. Left foot of R close to the hair but not touching. The date has 179 evenly and rather widely spaced, 97 closer. Point of 1 closer to the hair than to the curl. Final 7 leans somewhat to the left and the right top touches the drapery. Next to lowest curl unfinished.

Reverse R. A reappearance of reverse W of 1796 (Gilbert 12). Left 16-6, right 19-5.

Die break variations. None seen.

R-7. Basal $7.50. 30-15 (35-35-30-8-7-5). At least eight now known, seven in collectors' hands. A Now Collectible variety.

142   21·S   7 Imbedded in Drapery / RIGHT STEM POINTS THROUGH C   D-96 CN 26

Obverse 21. On this obverse a new set of letter punches appears for the first time. They are heavier, and all the serifs or endings and cross strokes at the top and bottom, are more solidly attached. The serif at the tip or toe of L is prolonged almost halfway to the top of that letter, the serifs of B are longer and heavier, and the right foot of the upright of R almost touches the tail of the letter. The date is compact, with both sides of the top of the 7 touching the drapery—the right top being well imbedded. PC under the inner curve of B; HWH under the upright of R; JHF under the right side of the upright of T.

Reverse S. Torpedo-shaped fraction bar, pointed at the left end, with an engraver's scratch connecting the right end to the ribbon. Continuation of the right stem would touch the left foot of A and would bisect C. Continuation of the left stem would cut off the right side of the bottom of U and the upper left corner of N. PLLR between C and A; PSL under the center of D.

1 7 9 7

Die break variations. None seen.

R-6. Basal $5. 25-12 (25-15-15-12-10-8). Upper range of R-6. The 25-coin, from the Newcomb collection, is in ANS. When Mr. Clapp acquired it he said it gave him as much satisfaction as "almost any coin I've got, outside of the 1794's."

143   21·T   7 Imbedded in Drapery   D-97
                      STEMLESS WREATH   CN 27

Obverse 21.

Reverse T. *Same as Reverse BB (NC-6) of 1796.* Left 16-5, right 19-5. *Stemless wreath.* The 10 is more widely spaced than 00, and the 1 leans to the right. Loop disconnected from the knot at the left. PLLR half way between center and right side of C; PSL even with the right side of D.

Die break variations. None seen.

R-7. Basal $6.50. 40-20 (40-40-25-15-15-12). Exactly twelve accounted for in this review. Barely R-7 but highly prized as one of the rare Stemless Wreath varieties.

TABLE 12. KEY TO THE 1797 CENTS

Single Leaves at top of both branches (Type of 1795):
  Date spaced 1 7 97..120
  Close date.
    Perfect B, very wide L I B E R T Y............................NC-1
    B defective at top..121
Double Leaf at top of right branch (Type, 1796–1807):
  Berries 6 left, 6 right
    Final 0 in fraction high; very close date.....................123
    PHL a trifle past right side of final S........................135
  Berries 6 left, 5 right
    Berry under D. Date 1 7 97....................................137
    Leaf under D. PHL right side of final S.......................NC-5
  Berries 5 left, 4 right (none at T in CENT). Date 1 7 97.........136
  Same reverse. Date close, about evenly spaced....................NC-6
  Berries 5 left, 5 right. Style 2 letters (curly tail to R in LIBERTY)
    Stemless. The 7 imbedded in drapery...........................143
    With stems. The 7 imbedded in drapery.........................142
  Berries 5 left, 5 right. Style 1 letters (straight tail to R)
    Stemless. PSL under upright of D
      Break into field behind hair ribbon........................131
      B defective; date weak.....................................132
      B perfect; TY low, IB lean right...........................133

1 7 9 7

TABLE 12. KEY TO THE 1797 CENTS—*Continued*

Small fraction. Crude ONE CENT............................134
Left ribbon end in fragments..............................130
M cut over E; PHL far right
   1 and both points of 7 touch hair and drapery.................128
   1 and 7 do not touch; defective B...........................129
Berry far above top line of CENT; "knobless 9"..................141
Date extremely close-spaced:
   1 of 100 about touches left ribbon..........................122
   Leaf under center of F....................................NC-2
   Leaf under left tip of F...................................NC-3
E in ONE directly over T in CENT
   3 defective denticles in r. obv. border.......................126
   I B apart; 7 well away from drapery.........................127
   Swellings through 97 and drapery...........................125
Berry below upper serif of E in ONE
   7 quite distant from drapery..............................NC-4
   7 and R touch drapery and hair; swells at OF..................138
Final A extremely close to ribbon
   Broken T in LIBERTY......................................140
Leaf point left of center of M. Part of r. ribbon end hollow........124
   Leaf point right of center of M..............................139

1 7 9 7

TABLE 13. RARITY AND VALUE: 1797 CENTS

Number	Obv.-Rev. Designation	CN Number	Doughty Number	Rarity	Basal Value (Dollars)
NC-1	1-A	1	—	8	—
120a *Plain Edge*	2-A	2	94	4	2.
120b *Gripped Edge*	2-A	2	94	2	1.50
121	3-A	3	93	3	2.
122	4-B	4	—	6	5.
NC-2	4-C	5	—	8	15.
NC-3	4-D	28	—	8	15.
123	4-E	6	106	4	2.
124	5-F	7	—	7	7.50
125	5-G	8	—	7	6.50
126	6-G	9	107	3	1.50
127	7-G	10	—	6	4.
128	8-H	11	109	3	1.50
129	9-H	12	108	7	7.50
130	9-I	13	99	2	1.25
131	9-J	14	98	3	3.50
132	10-J	15	—	7	6.50
133	11-J	16	—	6	4.
134	12-K	17	95	4	2.50
135	13-L	18	100	4	2.
NC-6	13-M	—	—	8	—
136	14-M	19	102	4	2.
137	14-N	20	101	3	1.50
NC-4	15-O	29	—	8	—
138	16-O	21	103	2	1.25
139	17-P	22	105	1	1.
140	18-P	23	104	3	1.50
141	19-Q	24	—	6	4.
NC-5	20-R	25	—	7	7.50
142	21-S	26	96	6	5.
143	21-T	27	97	7	6.50

1798

THE MATERIAL HERE PRESENTED ON THE CENTS OF 1798 follows closely Clapp's monograph on that date. The obverse-reverse nomenclature is the same as that established by Clapp, but as he himself has now discarded the device of assigning letters to different "states" of the die breaks, that has been omitted here. Since the Clapp Nos. 3 and 4 are from the same dies, the only difference being a slight retooling of the obverse (for No. 4), these are here presented as a single variety.

For this date, the study of obverses is more fruitful than the study of reverses, for the obverses present four distinct "variables" which, once mastered, yield a satisfactory key to classification. These four variables are as follows.

1. Perfect date or overdate
2. Large 8 or small 8
3. Two styles of letters in LIBERTY
4. Two styles of hair

1. There are but two overdate obverses, and they are easily distinguished.

2. On the obverses with "large 8" that figure is so much larger than the other figures that a glance suffices for identification.

3. In LIBERTY all but the first six obverses have the "style 2" letters described in the discussion of obverse 21 of the 1797's (heavier letters with more massive serifs, a long tip or toe to the L, and a short, heavy tail for the R which almost closes in the bottom of that letter). After this difference in lettering has

1 7 9 8

once been noted, the two styles can be recognized about as far as the letters can be read.

4. Finally, the two styles of hair: Two head punches or hubs were used in 1798, and on style 2 there is a *conspicuous extra curl superimposed on the mass of hair,* about 3 mm. from the edge of the lowest curl and on a direct line between the latter and the forelock. Once this extra curl has been noted it can never be overlooked. On style 1 no such curl appears. There are other minor differences in the hair, but this one is sufficient for our purposes. The style 2 head punch of 1798 was continued without change to the end of the series of Draped Bust cents in 1807, except for the first obverse of 1800, an overdate, on which the style 1 punch was used.

Using these four variables, Clapp divides the 1798 cents into six groups.

GROUP 1. Diagnostic characteristic: *Style 1 lettering.* Also has large 8's and style 1 hair. Obverses 1-6.

GROUP 2. Diagnostic characteristic: *Overdates.* They have large 8's, style 1 hair, and style 2 lettering. Obverses 7-8.

GROUP 3. Diagnostic characteristic: *Large 8's with style 2 lettering and style 1 hair.* Obverses 9-10.

GROUP 4. Diagnostic characteristic: *Small 8's with style 2 lettering and style 1 hair.* Obverses 11-20.

GROUP 5. Diagnostic characteristic: *Large 8's with style 2 lettering and hair.* Obverse 21.

GROUP 6. Diagnostic characteristic: *Small 8's with style 2 lettering and hair.* Obverses 22-34.

With the frame of reference which such a primary grouping offers, it is almost as easy to classify 1798 cents, after a little experience, as to classify 1793's. 34 obverses and 34 reverses of 1798 are known, and these occur in 46 marriages.

GROUP 1

(Large 8's, style 1 lettering and hair)

144   1·A   Large Close Date / BUCKLED REVERSE   NOT IN D / C 1

Obverse 1. Obverse of D-115. *Date very compact.* ER close. 8 equidistant from bust and margin. Point of 1 closer to hair

1 7 9 8

than to curl. PC under the left side of upright of B; HWH between E and R; JHF below left side of upright of T.

Reverse A. *Long, heavy fraction bar, ending in a point on the right* (engraver's slip). Wide fraction. Right stem points to the left foot of the right stand of A; left stem to the bottom of U. Straight tailed R in AMERICA (style 1 lettering). Point of leaf under T of CENT left of the point of the right pendant of T. This leaf cuts off the right foot of T. PLLL (point of lowest leaf on the left) below the right side of N; PHL (point of highest leaf) midway s and o.

Die break variations. *Reverse:* On all known specimens a "buckle" or raised ridge runs from A of STATES across the coin to the region of R in AMERICA, and this is really the hallmark by which No. 144 is recognized. Apparently caused by a bend in the die, the buckle is faint on early specimens, heavy on later ones. As it develops, cracks appear: From the rim through left ribbon and stem to E of CENT, and later to the right foot of N in ONE; from the rim to the right arm of first T in STATES, through pendant to stand of that letter, branching to A and continuing to wreath stem, joining the buckle; from rim between s and o through the top of OF and to the rim above A. Other minor cracks are seen on perfect specimens.

R-7. Basal $6.50. 50-15 (50-35-12-12-10-8). Eight now known to be available to collectors, and two in ANS. A 50-coin turned up in the Brand hoard remnant which was sold in 1953. This piece had formerly been reported to us merely as "a fine one"; it was therefore included in the condition census for EAC as an F-12—perhaps an excusable error.

1 4 5

145	1·B	Large Close Date	D-115
		FRACTION BAR CONNECTED TO RIGHT RIBBON	C 2

Obverse 1.

Reverse B. *Short fraction bar,* starting between 1 and 0 and *ending in a long point which connects it to the right ribbon.* There is a period-like defect over the numerator, just below the knot. Right stem points to the left foot of A; left to the bottom of U. Leaf touching the back of C in CENT is a mere

[209]

1 7 9 8

outline. Leaf under T just touches the right foot. PLLL almost central under N; PHL to the right of center of S.

Die break variations. *Obverse:* Found perfect, and with a crack between neck and rim halfway from point of bust to chin. *Reverse:* Found perfect, and with the die beginning to sink at S OF A. Later, a crack appears over OF and the lower curve of O in ONE is broken. Other minor cracks sometimes seen on perfect specimens. Always seen with wide milling.

R-3. Basal $1.50. 50-35 (50-45-40-40-30-20). About a midrange R-3. No more than a half dozen seen above VF.

		Island at Left Lower Corner of E	
146	2·C	.	NOT IN D C 3, C 4

Obverse 2. LIB close, E R widely separated. *The top of the hair is unfinished,* the wave under R is present only as an outline seen on fine coins, and *the second wave shows only a little triangular island* nearly touching the left bottom of E. PC absent and HWH not clearly discernible. JHF below the left side of the upright of T. The date well spaced, equidistant from bust and rim, the 1 close to hair and curl.

This obverse is found in several states, apparently because of excessive retouching or grinding down of the die. Clapp presents two of these states (here called *State a* and *State b*) as different obverses. *State a* is the obverse of the Clapp No. 3 variety; *State b* is the obverse of his No. 4 variety. But intermediate states are known, and since they are only variations in the condition of a single obverse die it has seemed best to present them here as a single variety.

State a: The usual line under the shoulder part of the bust can be seen, although very faintly, and only on fine specimens. *The detail at the point of the bust is sharp, with the drapery normal or clearly defined.*

State b: The die has been ground down, perhaps to remove rust. *The bust is now almost flat at the point, the drapery ends in distinct and isolated points, and the line under the shoulder part of the bust is entirely gone.* Various defects have developed and appear as "masses of heavy rust" about the lower part of the date and across the lower part of the bust.

1798

Reverse C. Fraction bar short; 1 distant from 0. Right stem points between the feet of A, the left ends in a long point which runs through the bottom of U to the right side. Leaf heavily merged with back of c in CENT. Leaf touches the right foot of T and its point ends just to the right of the pendant. PLLL right of center of N; PHL between E and S.

Die break variations. None seen.

R-6. Basal $3.50. 55-25 (55-50-25-20-12-12). Mid-range of R-6. No new ones have appeared in the higher brackets of condition.

Note: In describing the obverse of his No. 3, which is here called *State a*, Mr. Clapp writes (3, p. 23), "To the right of Y there is a row of straight lines, ½ mm long, running from the denticles into the field and continuing to opposite the point of the bust. These appear to have been made on the die blank for the guidance of the engraver in cutting the denticles." In describing the obverse of his No. 4, which is here called *State b*, he says, "This is the same (as the previous obverse) after it had been ground down to remove engraver's marks."

The "engraver's marks" thus appear to constitute a principal point of differentiation between the two dies, for Mr. Clapp.

These marks have later turned out to be not in the die at all, but only scratches on the particular coin which Mr. Clapp owned. The coin is now in the museum of the ANS.

This is a minor point and I have hesitated to make the correction, but to make it without further apology is perhaps as high a tribute as we can offer to Mr. Clapp's well known scientific objectivity and love of accuracy.

| 147 | 2·D | FRACTION SKEWED TO THE RIGHT | D-116 C 5 |

Obverse 2. After still further regrinding and retouching. (Clapp presents this also as a new obverse.) LIB now weak, but the top of the hair has been finished. HWH now seen between E and R, and touching the left foot of R. PC is below the right side of the upright of B. The defects have been removed and *the line under the shoulder side of the bust has been re-engraved.*

Reverse D. The skewed fraction. *Fraction too far to the right, and the final 0 is practically touching the right ribbon. Extremely short fraction bar.* Right stem points to the bottom of

1 7 9 8

c, the left to the left foot on N. AM touch. Leaf not quite touching c of CENT. Leaf cuts off right foot of T entirely, and its point is inside the right pendant. PLLL almost under right side of N; and PHL under the right side of E.

Die break variations. None seen.

R-6. Basal $4. 40-20 (40-30-25-20-15-12). Upper range of R-6 and not far from R-7. Second rarest of the varieties known to Doughty—No. 149 was the rarest.

Horned 9 Variety

148   5·E*   D-117
                                                                  C 6

Obverse 5. The horned 9 variety. *There is a small spur on the back of the* 9, by which this variety is easily recognized. The R a little high. PC below the right side of upright of B; HWH almost touches both E and R; JHF below the center of the upright of T.

Reverse E. Wide fraction. Right stem points to the inner serif of the left foot of A, left stem to the right side of U. AM touch. Leaf touches back of c; point of leaf almost touches right pendant of T. PLLL right of center of N; PHL just left of center of S.

Die break variations. *Obverse:* Found perfect and with crack along the top of LIBERTY; another from the rim past 8 to the bust. Later, rim heavily broken over ERTY. Finally, an additional triangular break, the left top of which just touches the bust, extends along the rim about 5 mm. to the right. Other faint cracks seen on perfect specimens. *Reverse:* Faint crack along top of UNITED, and along ST, then through upper part of A and along TES. This crack always seen on specimens fine enough to show it. Another, sometimes seen, through top of AMERICA.

R-2. Basal $1. 60-45 (60-60-55-45-40-30). The only variety in Group 1 (Style 1 letters) that is not scarce, and the only one of which a mint state example exists.

---

*In order to make the remaining obverse-reverse designations for this date correspond with those used by Clapp, I have simply omitted the obverse designations 3 and 4.

1 7 9 8

		Large Date,	
		9 8 More Distant	D-114
149	6 · F		C 7

Obverse 6. The date has 179 rather closely spaced, *the* 8 *more distant.* E a little high and leaning slightly to the left. Bottom of R below E and almost touching the hair. 1 close to hair and curl. PC below left edge of upright of B; HWH between E and R; JHF below left edge of upright of T. Closely resembles obverse 2, but has greater space between 9 and 8.

Reverse F. Moderately long fraction bar with wide fraction. 00 closer than 1 0. Right stem points between the feet of A, left to the bottom of U. Leaf attached to the back of C, leaf under T close to the upright, with the point almost touching the right pendant. PLLL directly under center of N; PHL left of the center of S. The second berry on the left is on a long stem and free from leaves.

Die break variations. *Reverse:* Sometimes found with die sunken from S across OF to A. Usually a little weak at the center.

R-7. Basal $6.50. 15-10 (15-15-12-7-7-5). Both of the 15-coins are new discoveries since EAC, and nine now known in collectors' hands. But this famous variety remains R-7.

1 5 0

GROUP 2

(The overdates. Large 8's, style 1 hair and style 2 lettering)

		Close Overdate	D-111
150	7 · F	LONG FRACTION BAR	C 8

Obverse 7. The large 8 has been cut over a 7, *both of the upper points of which show above the top of the* 8, and the lower end shows as a point in the bottom of the lower curve. IB close. PC below center of curve of B; HWH under center of upright of R; JHF below right side of upright of T. Compact date, with 1 close to hair and distant from curl. The 7 has a heavy top and slender stem. *The right top of the overcut 7 touches the drapery.*

Reverse F. In this marriage, on all specimens seen, a delicate crack starts at the bottom of the right upper leaves, runs down

1 7 9 8

the stem and passes between A and M to the rim. Other delicate, minor cracks are sometimes seen, and the sinking of the die at and below OF becomes pronounced. It has also begun to sink over ER.

Die break variations. Reverse as noted.

R-5. Basal $3.50. 40-25 (40-40-25-25-15-15). Upper range of R-5, possibly R-6. Another somewhat distressing variety for collectors of "gem cents only." Rarest overdate.

| 151 | 7·G | Close Overdate
SHORT FRACTION BAR | D-112
C 9 |

Obverse 7. In this marriage, *always seen with a curved crack* from the rim back of the knot through the field half-way to the lower curls.

Reverse G. Fraction bar rather short and heavy, not extending to the 1 and covering less than half of the final 0. Right stem points to inner serif of the left foot of A, the left to the left side of the bottom of U. Left foot of M slightly above the foot of adjacent A. Leaf just touches the back of C, and leaf just touches the right foot of the stand of T. PLLL under center of N; PHL nearly under the left side of S. Chip out of the die below the end of the left ribbon.

Die break variations. *Obverse:* On some, a crack parallels the first crack, from the lower ribbon to the hair; two parallel cracks from rim to knot cross the first crack at right angles; a crack starts at the lower end of the first crack and crosses hair and shoulder to near the top of 8; crack from the rim near L runs down to bow. These delicate cracks are visible only on the finest specimens. *Reverse:* Found perfect and with several delicate cracks. From the rim between F and A, through right wreath and across the tips of the two highest leaves; from the rim running back of E in AMERICA to the stem; from the lowest group of leaves on the left through both ribbons and numerator to the rim near top of final A; on some specimens further extensions of these cracks are seen.

R-4. Basal $2.50. 45-25 (45-40-30-25-15-15). Commands a premium as an overdate. Rarity underestimated in EAC. This and the preceding variety are always struck in very low relief. Their condition therefore tends to be underrated.

1 7 9 8

152   8·H   The Wider Overdate   D-113
C 10

Obverse 8. Date moderately wide. The 8 cut over a 7 and the left top of the 7 shows distinctly, but *the right top is not seen.* 1B high. PC below right side of upright of B; HWH between E and R; JHF below left side of upright of T. Date evenly spaced and closer to the milling than to the bust. The 1 is nearer to the hair than to the curl.

Reverse H. *Fraction very wide, with both numerator and denominator distant from the bar,* which is pointed at the left end. Right stem points to the inner serif of the left foot of A, the left misses U and points to the tip of the left foot of N. *The crossbar of E in* AMERICA *is connected with the upper pendant, which ends in a sharp point.* Leaf merged with the back of C. Leaf under T just touches the right stand and its point passes to the right of the point of the pendant. PLLL is almost under the right upright of N; PHL under right side of S. The stem of the second berry on the left rests on the point of leaf, and the berry projects well beyond it.

Die break variations. *Obverse:* Always seen with a light crack from rim to hair, just below the knot. On some examples this crack is visible at the curls below the ear, and another delicate crack runs from the rim through the outer ends of the knot.

R-3. Basal $2. 60-40 (60-50-40-35-35-30). Lower range of R-3 rather than R-2 as given in EAC. Commonest overdate and therefore a difficult one for the variety collector because of the pressure from type collectors.

GROUP 3

(Large 8's and style 1 hair, style 2 lettering)

153   9·E   Large Wide Date,
7 Touches Denticle   D-120
C 11

Obverse 9. *Wide, curved date* with the figures close to the milling and *the bottom of the 7 touches a denticle.* Point of 1 close to curl but distant from hair. L I B widely spaced, ERT

1 7 9 8

close. PC below right side of upright of B; HWH below left side of upright of R; JHF below right side of the upright of T.

Reverse E. Crack now seen along the tops of the letters practically around the legend, with other minor, branching cracks.

Die break variations. *Obverse:* Found perfect and with a crack along the top of LIBE; along the bottom of 17; from the rim to the left of the point of the bust, running across the point and a short distance into the field; from the lowest curl, running close to the rim and parallel with it, to the level of the middle of the knot. Finally, the crack at the point of the bust develops into a heavy rim break, connecting the rim to the bust.

R-4. Basal $2. 55-35 (55-50-40-35-35-25). Probably in the upper range of R-4, and under some pressure from type collectors because of the large numerals in the date.

154   10·1   The Imbedded 8   NOT IN D
                                            C 12

Obverse 10. *Large 8 with its top imbedded in the bust*—diagnostic. PC just right of upright of B; HWH between E and R; JHF below center of upright of T. Date wide, with 8 high. 1 close to curl and hair.

Reverse I. Wide fraction, with the bar starting halfway between 1 and first 0. Right stem points to the middle of the left foot of A, left stem to the middle of the left standard of N. Leaf just touches back of C; leaf cuts off the right foot of the upright of T. PLLL to the right of center of N; PHL under the right side of S. Reverse legend has style 1 lettering, although the obverse has style 2.

Die break variations. *Obverse:* Found perfect and with crack from upper point of drapery to the rim. *Reverse:* Always seen with a swell in the die under ITED S, and under AMERI, extending into the wreath. On some specimens, after a little circulation, these letters are wholly or partially obliterated. The faint outline of the head of Liberty is incused on the reverse die.

R-4. Basal $2. 70-45 (70-50-50-45-45-30). Upper range of R-4. Sometimes called a type because of the large numerals, with the

[216]

1 7 9 8

8 imbedded in the bust. The 70-coin was discovered in England by Sears and was sold to Hines in the early 1930's.

GROUP 4

(Small 8's and style 1 hair, style 2 lettering)

155 *11·J*   Widest Date   D-110
               SINGLE LEAVES,   C 13
               REVERSE OF '96

Obverse 11. Extremely wide, evenly spaced date—the widest by far. The 1 is close to the curl and rather distant from the hair; the 8 touching or practically touching the drapery. PC under right side of upright of B; HWH between E and R and almost touching both letters; JHF just to the left of the left foot of T.

Reverse J. Reverse E (Nos. 87, 88, and 89) of the 1796 Liberty Caps (see p. 155). *Both branches of the wreath terminate with single leaves.*

Die break variations. *Obverse:* Found perfect and with a crack from the rim through the center of L, through I and bottom of B to the hair; from the rim through the 7 and through the lower curls, with a branch crack from the top of the 7 to the bust above 8; crack from the drapery down along the back of the 9, and another from the drapery diagonally through the 8. *Reverse:* In this marriage always found with the rust spots mentioned, and with a light crack from the right top of N to above E in ONE.

R-3. Basal $2. 70-45 (70-60-50-45-35-30). Under great pressure from type collectors because it is the only one of the three varieties with reverse of '96 that is not R-7. The 70-coin is a famous one from the Mickley, Winsor, Earle, Beckwith, Newcomb and Clarke collections. The 60-coin was sold in the Dupont collection, 1954.

156 *12·K*   Compact Date   NOT IN D
               SINGLE LEAVES,   C 14
               REVERSE OF '96

Obverse 12. Date compact, but *spacing increases from left*

1 7 9 8

to right, so that the 9 and 8 are well separated. The 8 is high and seems to touch the drapery, although it does not quite actually touch. The point of 1 almost touches the hair. LIB close. PC below center of upright of B; HWH between E and R; JHF below left side of upright of T.

Reverse K. Reverse **B** (Nos. 82, 83, and 84) of the 1796 Liberty Caps (see p. 153). *Both branches of the wreath terminate with single leaves.*

Die break variations. *Obverse:* Found perfect and with a light crack from the rim near the point of the bust, which splits, one branch continuing upward, and the other running to the left through drapery and hair, into the field. *Reverse:* In this marriage there is always a fine crack from the top of F to the top of 0 and into the field to the left.

R-7. Basal $7.50. 20-10 (20-15-12-10-8-6). Another Reverse of '96 variety. Eleven now appear to be accounted for, three of them in ANS. Prohibitively rare in fine condition. Yet the third Reverse of '96, No. 178, is even rarer.

157

		Small, Close Date; Crack, Rim Through TY to Forelock	
NC-1	*13 · H*		NOT IN D C 15

Obverse 13. Small, compact date, the first two figures a trifle more widely spaced than the last three. Point of the 1 distant from curl and close to hair. LIBERTY close to the hair. PC below right side of upright of B; HWH below left side of upright of R; JHF below right side of upright of T. *On the two that have been reported, there is a crack from rim through left top of Y and foot of T to forelock.*

Reverse H.

Die break variations. None seen.

R-8. 10-5. Only two reported. No new ones. The 10-coin is in ANS.

		The Fused Denticles. Wide Fraction	
157	*14 · L*		D-122 C 16

Obverse 14. The date has 179 closely spaced with the 8 a little more distant and midway between bust and milling.

1 7 9 8

Point of the 1 equidistant from hair and curl. *Below the 9, three denticles are united or fused together*—diagnostic. PC below the center of the curve of B; HWH under the right side of the upright of R; JHF slightly right of right foot of T.

Reverse L. Wide fraction, with *great distance between 1 and first 0*; the 1 leans a little to the right. There is a short vertical break or defect through the center of c in AMERICA. AME touch. Stems heavy, blunt, the right one pointing to the bottom of the left stand of A, the left to the bottom of U. Leaf welded to the back of c; leaf touches the right foot of T, with the point to the right of and below the right pendant. PLLL to the left of the center of N; PHL left of center of S.

Die break variations. *Obverse:* Found perfect, but usually seen with an irregular break, in the form of a series of dots, from the rim to the neck; with the die crumbling along the neck and the upper part of the bust. These dots become heavier, uniting into what is almost a solid line, and the die becomes pitted around them. Another crack runs through 798 and to the rim below the point of the bust. *Reverse:* Found perfect, and with light crack along top of ITED to the rim between D and S; crack from foot of second T in STATES to bottom of O. Both of these cracks develop branches and become heavier, and coins are seen with the die badly rusted and scratched through the center.

R.-2. Basal $1. 65-55 (65-65-60-55-50-45). The Rusted Die variety. Usually seen struck with heavily rusted dies, both obverse and reverse.

NC-2 *15·M* Wide LIBERTY, Heavy Rim Break at ERTY   NOT IN D C 17

Obverse 15. *LIBERTY very widely and evenly spaced.* The widest LIBERTY. Date close and even. Point of 1 equidistant from curl and hair. 7 slightly below top of 19, and 8 equidistant from bust and border. PC under center of B; HWH below left edge of left foot of R, and almost touching; JHF below left foot of T. On the only example reported, a *heavy rim break from above E slants downward, touching top of* RTY, then up to rim a short distance right of Y.

[219]

1 7 9 8

Reverse M. Fraction bar short and square at the ends. Denominator wide, with the first 0 low. The denominator and fraction bar are too far to the left. Right stem points between the feet of A, left to the bottom of U. AMERICA shows extremely wide spacing. *Six berries on the left branch.* Leaf rather distant from the back of C, and leaf cuts off the right foot of T. PLLL below center of N, and PHL midway between S and O.

Die break variations. None.

R-8. 10-7. A second example was found in Chicago a few years ago, this one VG-10. It has the same heavy obverse die break shown in the picture of the first one (Plate 27, EAC).

158   **158**   **16·M**   Y Low and Distant, Three Parallel Cracks Behind Head (Usually)   D-126
SHORT SQUARE-ENDED FRACTION BAR   C 18

Obverse 16. Y *distant from* T *and low.* Well spaced date with the 9 leaning to the left. Point of 1 equidistant curl and hair. *Line under the bust is light and ends 2 mm. from the hair.* PC below center of curve of B; HWH below center of R; JHF to the right of T.

Reverse M.

Die break variations. *Obverse:* Found perfect, but more often with three parallel cracks in the field back of the head, the inner one passing through the hair ribbons and bottom curl. *Reverse:* Found perfect and with weakening in the upper left portion; also with crack from the rim to top of T in UNITED, through T, then as a double crack to the leaves, and finally across AT to the rim. Later, a heavy rim break covering ITE to the stand of D. In final stages, other branch cracks and all cracks heavier.

R-4. Basal $2. 55-45 (55-55-45-40-40-35). R-4 instead of R-3, and now believed to be in the upper range of R-4. Mr. Hines at one time had a collection of nine of this variety, all showing different stages in the die breaks.

1 7 9 8

159   *16·N*   Parallel Cracks Behind Head (Always) / WIDE FRACTION, LONG BAR   D-127   C 19

Obverse 16. In this marriage *always seen with heavy parallel cracks.*

Reverse N. Wide fraction with great distance between 1 and first 0. Fraction bar rather long, and ends in an engraver's scratch which almost reaches the right ribbon. Stems long, the right pointing between c and a, the left to the upper left corner of N. Leaf connected with the back of c, and leaf just touches the right foot of T, with its point to the right of pendant. PLLL just past the center of N; PHL right of center of s. There is a minute triangular cut in the die joined to the outside leaf under I in UNITED, and two more on the upper side of the left stem.

Die break variations. *Obverse:* Cracks heavier, the middle one extending to rim back of lowest curl; the inner one to rim left of L and continuing along top of LIB; on some examples a branch crack runs from the upper ribbon to left top of L, joining the crack along top of LIB; rim becomes heavily broken over L. *Reverse:* Found with crack from rim above A in STATES, through T to tip of right terminal leaf; arc crack from rim between D and S through left branch to join first crack; from rim between F and A to right branch; other minor cracks and defect at right top of M.

R-4. Basal $2. 60-35 (60-55-40-30-30-25). Upper range of R-4, with some possibility that it may be R-5.

160   *17·O*   The Leaning 7 / ER OF AMERICA CONNECTED TO DENTICLES   D-130   C 20

Obverse 17. LIBERTY wide and evenly spaced. Date rather wide, with the 9 and 8 most distant. The 7 leans to the right. Point of 1 distant from curl and rather distant from hair. On fine specimens, faint engraver's marks can be seen running into the field from denticles opposite the point of the bust. PC below right side of upright of B; HWH between E and R; JHF below left side of upright of T.

[221]

1798

Reverses O through Y, together with CC, FF, GG, and HH form a group of very similar reverses which were lumped by Doughty as "reverse H." Yet all these show distinct and recognizable differences. Clapp believes that many if not all of them were struck from the same hub die, and that the differences were introduced by the engravers in finishing the dies. The description to follow is a general one for the group.

Short fraction bar. Fraction evenly spaced between the ribbon ends, and both numerator and denominator distant from the bar. Right stem points to the inner serif of the left foot of A, left to the upper left serif of N. Ribbon ends wide, the right one less than 1 mm. from A. PLLL just to the left of right side of N; PHL between the left side and center of s. Point of seventh leaf under right side of D. D tilted to the right. OF closer to A than to S. AMER close and ICA more widely spaced. Left 16-5, right 19-5. N in ONE wide with the top imperfect; N in CENT narrow, perfect.

161

Reverse O. The problem with this reverse is to distinguish it from reverse P, which occurs with the same obverse. Three characteristics will make the distinction: (1) The second lowest outside double leaf on the right does not touch the wreath stem. (2) The first berry on the left has a short stem which points to the left side of C; the first and second berries on the right have short stems and the second touches the wreath stem. (3) *Above* ER *of* AMERICA, *a pair of short lines run from adjacent denticles to the adjacent upper corners of the letters.* Two mm. left of the upper curve of first s there is a dotlike defect.

Die break variations. *Obverse:* Found perfect, and with a faint crack from the rim across the neck and upper part of drapery into the hair; light chip out of the die near rim back of hair, and a small defect to left of 1.

R-6. Basal $3.50. 60-35 (60-55-40-40-25-20). A much-sought coin. Lower range of R-6.

		The Leaning 7, with	
		Advanced Cracks	D-130
161	*17·P*	LUMP ON RIGHT SIDE OF O	C 21

Obverse 17. Cracks more advanced.

Reverse P. Four characteristics distinguish this from reverse

1 7 9 8

O: (1) The o in ONE has a small lump, or fragment from die crumbling, on its right side; (2) The second lowest outside double leaf on the right touches the wreath stem; (3) The first berry on the left has a stem whose length is nearly equal to the diameter of the berry, and the stem points into the right side of the leaf above. The lowest berry on the right has a longer stem, and the second lowest does not quite touch the wreath stem; (4) The R has a "straight tail," somewhat like that of the style 1 lettering, although this is not style 1 lettering.

Die break variations. *Obverse:* Always has the crack mentioned, and several other cracks develop: Rather heavy crack across the bust from point of drapery; faint diagonal crack across L; crack from rim opposite neck, curving down toward point of bust; another from near the same point to the nose; another from the rim, paralleling the last up the field; from rim opposite top of knot, running down the field 10 mm. and curving into the hair. These cracks become heavier and minor branches develop. *Reverse:* Found perfect and with several cracks: Light crack from rim to center of the curve of D; from above top of first T in STATES to top of A and along tops of TES; from back of D through top of wreath to bottom of o in OF; the crack above STATES becomes a heavy rim break, and continues as a crack to the top of o; crack from rim below 1 of denominator through left ribbon and UNIT to rim. Other minor cracks and branches sometimes seen on perfect specimens.

R-1. Basal $0.75. 65-60 (65-65-65-60-60-55). An excellent variety for young collectors. Common, and seen with a tremendous progression of die break variations. Third or fourth commonest 1798.

162 *18·O* Unfinished Top, Straight Date, Blunt 1 NOT IN D C 22

Obverse 18. *Top of the hair unfinished.* E R T Y widely spaced. *Date almost straight on top* and evenly spaced. *The top of the 1 is almost square.* This is the only 1798 with blunt 1 and a round, perfect knob on the 9. PC and HWH are more or less *in absentia;* JHF below right side of upright of T. Die swollen in the left lower field, and sometimes in right central field.

[223]

1 7 9 8

Reverse O.

Die break variations. *Reverse:* Found perfect and with light crack starting at rim between s and o, running above OF to near the top of A; also seen with injury to the die, or incusations, between upper leaf and s.

R-5. Basal $3. 65-30 (65-60-40-25-20-15). Upper range of R-5, not far from R-6.

163 *19·N* Unfinished Top, Straight Date, Pointed 1   D-131
C 23

Obverse 19. E R T wide, and the R leans a little to the right. Y *very heavy,* and its bottom is low. *Top of the hair unfinished,* like the preceding obverse. JHF below right side of upright of T. The line under the shoulder side of the bust connects with the hair. *Date almost straight on top* and evenly spaced. The 1 is pointed and the knob of the 9 slightly flattened. *Always seen with a faint crack connecting* RTY *at the top.*

Reverse N.

Die break variations. *Obverse:* In addition to the crack mentioned, most specimens show a conspicuous crack starting at rim below hair, running into the field about 1 mm. and then turning sharply right, under 17, and back to the rim at a right angle; a long straight crack runs from the end of the last, up through 7 and through the bust and hair, and curves to the left at the level of the curl under the ribbon ends; light crack from rim above R and through R to the hair; from rim opposite nose, through upper lip, cheek, ear, and hair, then curving downward through lowest ribbon to rim; heavy traces of injury under the ribbon knot, and on some specimens the cracks are much heavier, with minor branches. This die cracked up. *Reverse:* In addition to the cracks mentioned, additional crack from rim to top of first A in AMERICA, down right side and across wreath and top of ONE to left branch; from rim to left top of M. Examples seen with all cracks heavy.

R-5. Basal $3. 20-15 (20-20-20-15-15-15). Rated R-6 in EAC. Now thought to be in the upper range of R-5. A dozen or so examples of which we were previously unaware have come to light, nearly all of them in low grade condition.

1 7 9 8

164 **20·Q** Die Sinking at Date D-123 / C 24

Obverse 20. LIBERTY moderately wide and even, with B high. Date even, slightly curved, 1 nearer to hair than to curl, and the 8 a little more than 0.5 mm. from the drapery. PC below right side of curve of B; HWH below center of R; JHF below right foot of T.

Reverse Q. Same hub as reverse O. Inside pair of leaves under T rather distant from wreath stem; adjacent outside pair close to stem but not touching. First berry on left has short stem pointing to leaf; the second has a short stem which starts from the leaf stem above; first two berries on right have long stems starting directly opposite one another. This reverse sometimes found upset.

Die break variations. *Obverse:* Found perfect, but nearly always seen with sinking of the die, which causes a swell, at first to the right of 8, then extending through date and the curl and into the left field. Sometimes the lower curls and 17 are obliterated. Also seen with die-scaling in front of the face, and a series of flaked spots, starting opposite the nose, runs in a curve downward into the bust.

R-5. Basal $2.50. 65-35 (65-55-40-30-30-30). Probably in the lower range of R-5, although called R-4 in EAC.

GROUP 5

(Large 8, style 2́ lettering and hair)

165 **21·R** Whisker Variety, the Common Large Date D-118 / C 25

Obverse 21. Y distant from T and low. 179 are on the same top line, with the 8 large, high, and about 0.5 mm. from the drapery. Point of 1 a little closer to hair than to curl. Slight defect, or "whisker" in the die, under the chin; another under the drapery 2 mm. to the right of 8. PC below inner curve of B; HWH under the center of upright of R; JHF just right of the upright of T. This is the only large date obverse that is

[225]

common, and the only one except the Horned 9 that is not scarce.

Reverse R. Same hub as reverse O. Above the left foot of the second T in STATES there is a dotlike chip out of the die. Inside pair of leaves under T widely separated from the wreath stem, *with the adjacent outside pair overlapping the stem*. First berry on left has long stem pointing to leaf; second berry just touches leaf and stem; first two berries on right have medium stems and are not quite opposite.

Die break variations. *Reverse:* Found perfect and with heavy crack from rim between I and C to the first outside berry on the right.

R-5. Basal $3. 35-20 (35-30-20-15-15-12). Upper range of R-5.

166 21·S — Whisker Variety — ARC CRACK, E TO FINAL O — D-118 C 26

Obverse 21.

Reverse S. Same hub as reverse O. R has a lump at its upper left corner. *First A in AMERICA always weak, has left leg small and shorter than the right. Both pairs of leaves under T free from the stem.* First two berries left and right have long stems.

Die break variations. *Reverse:* All examples seen have a *conspicuous arc crack* starting at the rim to the right of E in UNITED, extending in a curve through that letter, through leaves, stem, ribbon, numerator, and right side of final 0 to the rim. The crack becomes heavy. Some specimens have a small rim break over the first T in STATES, and a small break connecting C of CENT with the adjacent leaf.

R-1. Basal $0.75. 70-60 (70-65-60-60-60-55). Clearly the second commonest 1798.

167 21·T — Whisker Variety, Crack Through 8 — D-118 C 27

Obverse 21. In this marriage, *always seen with a crack from rim through right side of 8 into the drapery*, where it turns sharply to the right and runs to the point of the bust.

Reverse T. Same hub as reverse O. Inside pair of leaves under T distant from the stem; the adjacent pair on the out-

1 7 9 8

side just touch. All examples seen have a *short break starting at the center of* E *in* UNITED, pointing toward the right terminal leaves, where another short break crosses these leaves and ends at the middle tip of the triple leaf under o and OF. Thus the three different reverses of "D-118" can be distinguished by the presence or absence of die breaks.

Die break variations. *Obverse:* The crack mentioned forks, the new crack runs across the bust and the old crack continues into the field from the point of the bust; a crack runs from rim to eye, and later across the head past the knot, meeting just above the ear another crack which runs up through the hair to B and the rim; back of the lower curls there is a faint, curved crack in the field. *Reverse:* Another crack starts at rim between T and A, curves to right top of T, then down across the wreath to o in ONE and on to the center dot; rim broken above NI and TE in UNITED, and heavily broken above first T in STATES, involving the whole top of that letter. Other minor branch cracks on perfect specimens. This is one of the most heavily cracked coins in the series.

R-1. Basal $0.75. 65-50 (65-60-55-50-50-45). Third or fourth commonest—apparently about tied with No. 161. These last three varieties, this one and Nos. 165 and 166, were all embraced in the old Doughty 118 designation. If all three were again to be lumped together as a single variety, that would perhaps be the commonest variety of 1798.

1 6 8

GROUP 6

(Small 8's, style 2 lettering and hair)

168	22·E	8 High and Left CRACKS AROUND OUTER LEGEND OF REVERSE	D-134 C 28

Obverse 22. LIBERTY high, close to the border. B high. Date fairly wide and evenly spaced. *The 8 a little high and tilted left.* Point of 1 almost equidistant from hair and curl. PC below inner curve of B; HWH below upright of R; JHF below right foot of T.

[227]

1 7 9 8

Reverse E. In this marriage, *always seen with the crack along the tops of* UNITED *and* STATES, and nearly always with other cracks.

Die break variations. *Reverse:* In addition to the cracks listed (p. 203), crack starts at rim below left ribbon and extends to top of U. Some examples show small pits, particularly around UNI and AME.

R-3. Basal $1.50. 60-50 (60-60-55-50-50-45). Middle range of R-3.

| 169 | 22·U | 8 High and Left / SHORT FRACTION BAR | D-119 C 29 |

Obverse 22. Often seen in this marriage with small rim break or lump on the border below 98.

Reverse U. Same hub as reverse O. C *of* CENT *leans markedly to the right and almost touches* E. Pair of leaves under T close to wreath stem but free; the adjacent pair outside just touch the stem. Second berry on the left stemless, and held between point of leaf below and stem above. First berry on the right has a rather long stem; the second a short one. *Fraction bar very short*, with the final 0 almost entirely to the right of it. No center dot.

Die break variations. As noted. On all reverses I have seen there is a faint impression of an obverse, seen especially through the ribbons and left stem, and through the numerator.

R-5. Basal $2.50. 50-40 (50-50-45-35-35-30). Middle range of R-5.

| 170 | 23·U | Date Curved, Well Spaced; Arc Crack at Left (Often) / SHORT FRACTION BAR | D-128 C 30 |

Obverse 23. LIBERTY high, evenly and widely spaced. Date moderately wide, curved, and close to the border, with the point of 1 equidistant from hair and curl. PC below inner curve of B; HWH below right side of upright of R; JHF below right side of upright of T.

Reverse U.

Die break variations. *Obverse:* Found perfect, but more often seen with an arclike crack which starts at rim opposite knot

1 7 9 8

and runs almost in a perfect arc through the ribbon ends and to the rim back of the lowest curl; there is a swell in the die between this crack and the rim; sometimes a second crack runs from the rim through the left side of T to the forelock; dotlike defect in the field to the right of Y. The perfect die specimens of this variety are difficult to distinguish from the preceding variety.

R-4. Basal $2. 60-35 (60-45-40-35-35-25). Rarity underestimated in EAC. Upper range of R-4.

		Rim Break Left of L	
171	*24·U*		D-133 C 31

Obverse 24. LIBERTY even and moderately high. Date well spaced with the 8 rather high, slanting to the left, and 0.5 mm. from the drapery. Point of 1 a little closer to hair than to curl. PC below inner curve of B; HWH below right side of upright of R; JHF below right foot of T. *Easily recognized by rim break described below.*

Reverse U.

Die break variations. *Obverse:* Perfect die not known to me, although reports of its existence recur. On all examples seen, a heavy rim break starts close to the left top of L, extends 7 mm. to the left, and from 1 to 2 mm. into the field. On some specimens an additional crack runs from the rim over the right top of T, through the bottom of Y to rim opposite chin. *Reverse:* Found perfect and with a slight die injury over ER, so that the tops of those letters have a sawtooth appearance.

R-5. Basal $2.50. 60-35 (60-50-45-35-30-25). Mid-range R-5. A single example has recently come to light with a perfect die obverse.

		Die Injury Over Y and Right, Recut 7	
172	*25·V*		D-129 C 32

Obverse 25. LIBERTY high, close to the border. IB close, E large and leans right. Date even and curved, 7 *recut on top*. Point of 1 equidistant from hair and curl. PC below center of B; HWH below left side of upright of R; JHF below right side

[229]

1 7 9 8

of upright of T. Usually recognized by injuries at upper right rim (see below).

Reverse V. Same hub die as reverse O. Crossbar of E of STATES connected with top. Both pairs of leaves under T close but free (the lower pair practically touches). Second berry on the left stemless and held between point of leaf and stem above. M *first started too low, and the upper points show on both uprights.*

Die break variations. *Obverse:* Found perfect, but usually with a row of impressed denticles extending from above I to Y; rim break to the right of Y, and the die has been injured below this break; a series or shower of slight defects appears in the field, between the injury and the neck, and from left of 7 to the rim; delicate crack through the field between RTY and hair; below the ear, two small pits in the die; small defect left of L, and a rim break (later) over the defect. In later stages the rim break covers top of Y and the die is heavily sunken over TY. *Reverse:* Found perfect, and with light crack from left ribbon to right foot of A, passing just above the fraction bar; rim lightly broken, then heavily broken over ICA.

R-2. Basal $1. 60-55 (60-60-55-55-50-45). ANS has five of these, including at least three of the condition census pieces.

	Straight Compact Date, Rim Break Over RTY (Usually)	
173 26 · W		D-132 C 33

Obverse 26. LIBERTY rather high, B E R widely spaced. Date compact with the 9 a little high so that the top of the whole date is nearly on a straight line; the 8 almost a millimeter from the drapery. There is a minute point on the upper left corner of 7. Point of 1 nearer to hair than to curl. PC between B and E; HWH below right side of upright of R; JHF slightly right of foot of T. *Usually identified by rim break over* RTY.

Reverse W. Same hub die as reverse O. Both pairs of leaves under T free from stem, the lower pair almost touching. Second berry on left touches point of leaf and stem above. Second berry on right has very short stem, almost stemless. Center dot clearly visible, and on fine specimens a more minute dot can be seen to the right of and slightly above it.

1 7 9 8

Die break variations. *Obverse:* Found perfect, but usually with a heavy rim break over RTY, touching the tops of those letters; on some specimens this break extends above the top of E, and the rim is also broken above LI. *Reverse:* Usually found perfect, but seen also with a crack running along the top of NITE.

R-2. Basal $1. 60-55 (60-60-60-55-55-50). The reverse of this variety reappears on the unique NC-1 of 1799. The die breaks show, actually, that the 1799 cent was struck before the 1798 cent.

174	27·X	Projection at Top of 1 VERY SHORT FRACTION BAR, HEAVY INCUSATION IN LOWER WREATH (Usually)	NOT IN D C 34

Obverse 27. *There is a clearly visible point or projection from the middle of the top of* 1 (diecutter's slip), and this is diagnostic. 17 closer than the other figures. Point of 1 about equidistant hair and curl. PC right of center of B; HWH below left side of upright of R; JHF below right side of upright of T.

1 7 4

Reverse X. Same hub die as reverse O. Fraction bar extremely short, measuring exactly 2 mm. Lower part of C in CENT is a flat curve ending in a sharp point. *Both pairs of leaves under* T *are free and the lower pair is the farther from the stem* (almost diagnostic). First berry on the right has a long stem. The left top of M is vestigial, almost missing.

Die break variations. *Obverse:* Several slight defects usually seen: A small dotlike defect 2 mm. from the left bottom of L; another the same distance below and right of Y; several just under the ribbon knot near the uppermost curl. *Reverse:* A light crack is always seen running from the rim into the field between the end of the left ribbon and 1. *On most examples the outline of an obverse die is heavily incused in the lower part of the die.*

R-2. Basal $1. 65-45 (65-60-50-45-35-35). Commonest variety "Not in Doughty." Called R-3 in EAC. Perhaps we were influenced by its history of usually being called "Very rare—not in Doughty."

1 7 9 8

175   **27·Y**   Projection at Top of 1 / HEAVY RIM BREAK OVER U   NOT IN D / C 35

Obverse 27. In this marriage, the die is sinking above LI, caused by rim break above U.

Reverse Y. Same hub die as reverse O. Fraction bar 2.5 mm. long. Both pairs of leaves under T free from the stem, but the lower pair almost touches. First berry on the left has short stem and is very close to wreath stem. The second on the right has practically no stem and lies against the wreath stem. M perfect. *Left top of* E *in* AMERICA *long and heavy, and connected with the crossbar. Always seen with rim break over* U, usually covering the top of that letter and from above the center of N almost to the I; always seen with crack along tops of inside pair of leaves back of O in ONE past outside pair and a short distance into the field.

Die break variations. *Reverse:* Second crack from rim through right side of A in STATES, across terminal leaves and through outside leaves in right branch to M; crack from tip of leaf under ST to A; from rim through back of C in AMERICA to the wreath. Other branch cracks on perfect specimens.

R-4. Basal $2. 65-35 (65-50-35-35-30-25). In the upper range of R-4; nearly R-5.

176   **28·O**   Vertical Crack in Right Field   NOT IN D / C 36

Obverse 28. LIB closer than the other letters. Y imperfect ("home made"). The figures of the date also seem crude or home made. Date evenly spaced, following the curve of the border, and equidistant from bust and border. PC below inner curve of B; HWH below left side of upright of R; JHF below right side of upright of T. *Usually recognized by vertical break in right field.*

Reverse O.

Die break variations. *Obverse:* Found perfect, although very rarely so. Usually seen with a crack which starts at the point of the bust and runs perpendicularly up the field to about the level of the mouth, reappearing at the right of Y. On some examples this crack is heavy, covering the point of the bust;

1 7 9 8

light crack connecting 7 and 9, and another down the right side of R. *Reverse:* Found perfect, but rare in this condition. Usually seen with the crack described on p. 224, and the defect near the first s is larger.

R-5. Basal $3. 60-35 (60-55-40-30-25-25). Mid-range, or possibly upper range of R-5. Rarity underestimated in EAC (R-4). Vertical crack usually seen in the right field.

		Vertical Crack in Right Field	
177	28·Z	IMPERFECT RIBBON ENDS BELOW WREATH	NOT IN D C 37

Obverse 28. In this marriage, *the crack described is always seen.*

Reverse Z. Moderately long fraction bar and wide fraction. Short stems, the right pointing to the center of the left stand of A, the left to the middle of the left stand of N. The left ribbon is weak in the upper half, and the right in the lower half. R has a straight tail—the reverse lettering is of style 1. PLLL just past center of N; PHL to the right of center of s. First berry on left has a very long stem, the second is attached to the leaf above. First berry on the right is opposite the bottom, and the second is opposite the top of T of CENT.

Die break variations. *Obverse:* The vertical crack continues to increase in size; another crack starts at rim below point of bust, runs through date and into the field beyond the lowest curl; finally, the vertical crack extends past Y and reaches the rim.

R-6. Basal $3.50. 35-25 (35-30-30-25-20-15). Middle or upper range of R-6. The vertical crack is heavier, and always present.

		Vertical Crack in Right Field	
178	28·AA	SINGLE LEAVES, REVERSE OF '96	NOT IN D C 38

Obverse 28. In this marriage, *all cracks are heavier,* and the original vertical crack extends to the rim opposite the point of the bust.

Reverse AA. Reverse A (No. 81) of the Liberty Caps of 1796

1 7 9 8

(see p. 152). *Both branches of the wreath terminate in single leaves.* This is the third and last, and rarest, of the 1798 cents with reverse of 1796.

Die break variations. None seen.

R-7. Basal $7.50. 30-12 (30-25-12-12-10-6). Rarest of the three Reverse of '96 varieties. The vertical crack is still heavier, with several subsidiary cracks, and most of the known examples show heavy rusting of the obverse die. Eight of these now accounted for; only one of them in ANS.

179   29·BB   The High 98   D-135
C 39

Obverse 29. The figures 98 are high. Actually the top of the date is almost in a straight line, but the bottoms of the 9 and 8 are high, and the variety is recognized by the high appearance of the last two figures. LIBERTY even, wide, and close to the milling. PC below center of the curve of B; HWH below center of upright of R; JHF below right side of upright of T.

Reverse BB. Same hub die as reverse O, although Clapp does not so indicate in his description. *The E of AMERICA was first cut reversed, and the lower point and upright of the reversed letter show*—diagnostic. Inside pair of leaves under T distant from wreath stem, outside pair merge with the stem and obliterate it for more than half the length of a leaf.

Die break variations. *Obverse:* Found perfect, and with a very light crack from between I and B to the hair; also a dot defect below the upright of L, about halfway to the hair. *Reverse:* Found perfect, and with a number of minute defects and flaking, principally around final S, the fraction, and 1C.

R-2. Basal $1. 70-55 (70-60-60-55-50-50). The familiar variety with the high 98.

180   30·CC   Horizontal Crack in Left Field
HEAVY RIM BREAK OVER ATE   NOT IN D
C 40

Obverse 30. IB close, and LIBERTY very close to the border. Date evenly spaced and curved, *with the 9 low,* and the bottoms of the figures are usually fused with the border. Just below the ear there is a "bald" spot, where the hair was omitted. PC

[234]

slightly right of curve of B; HWH below center of R; JHF below right foot of T. All reported examples have a nearly horizontal crack from rim just below knot, running almost to the hair, and a delicate crack connects tops of ER.

Reverse CC. Same hub die as reverse O. Inside pair of leaves under T free from wreath stem, and the outside pair touch. Clapp says that R has a "straight tail," but this is not style 1 lettering, and the R is similar to that on reverse P. This reverse *always seen with a heavy rim break over* ATE, *which includes the whole top of* T—and the break is diagnostic.

Die break variations. *Reverse:* On some examples a second rim break is seen, 8 mm. long, covering the top of U and left top of N. The first break is heavier, and sends out a little tongue to the left top of E.

R-7. Basal $6. 35-15 (35-35-15-12-6-6). Still R-7 but almost an R-6. Exactly twelve accounted for in this review, two of them in ANS. One of the newly discovered ones has a perfect die reverse. All examples with the broken reverse die are very weak under the date, the weakness being directly opposite the rim break and doubtless resulting from it. Both of the 35-coins are new discoveries since EAC. The 15-coin is the piece formerly graded VF-20—this one in ANS.

181 $30 \cdot DD$ Horizontal Crack in Left Field, with Other Cracks   D-136
HIGH NUMERATOR, LARGE DENOMINATOR   C 41

Obverse 30. In this marriage, *always seen with the cracks mentioned, and with an additional crack from rim opposite point of bust into the drapery.* The crack originally connecting tops of ER now runs along the tops of LIBER.

Reverse DD. *Six berries left and five right. Numerator of the fraction high,* closer to the ribbon knot than to the fraction bar. *Figures of the denominator unusually large,* filling almost the entire space between the ribbon ends, and *inside the ciphers outlines of smaller ciphers* can be seen. Fraction bar heavy and cut square at the ends. Right stem points to the middle of the bottom of A. The left stem ends in a short engraver's scratch and points to the upper left corner of N.

1 7 9 8

ONE too far to the left and leaf nearly touches o. PLLL below the right side of N; PHL just right of the left side of s.

Die break variations. *Obverse:* On some specimens the crack from the rim opposite the point of the bust extends across drapery and hair to the rim; other cracks from rim to upper and lower ribbon ends; rim break over L; cracks from HWH through base of T, from forelock through Y, and from the tip of the nose diagonally to the rim; from the rim to the right of 8 through bust and back to rim.

R-5. Basal $2.50. 70-45 (70-65-55-40-40-35). The Large Fraction reverse. Probably in the lower range of R-5. Called R-4 in EAC.

182 31·EE   REVERSE: DIE CUT ACROSS A FROM RIGHT RIBBON   NOT IN D   C 42

Obverse 31. This is the first of three obverses which look very much alike, and as the first two are very rare, while the third is common, the differential diagnosis among the three constitutes a pleasant numismatic nicety. Date evenly spaced and slightly curved, *with the 8 a trifle higher.* B and E are more widely spaced than the other letters. PC below the center of the curve of B; HWH below the center of R; JHF below right foot of T. Point of 1 equidistant from hair and curl.

Reverse EE. Easily recognized by a *short cut in the die, or break, which crosses the right ribbon* to the center of A and ends between A and C. This is possibly an engraver's scratch upon which a break has been superimposed. It is present on all known examples, and is diagnostic. Continuation of the right stem would about bisect C diagonally; left stem points to the middle of the left stand of N. R has a straight tail and the lettering of this reverse is style 1. The leaf under T cuts off the whole of the right foot, and the point is above and left of the right pendant. PLLL between center and right side of N; PHL below center of S. N in ONE low. C and E of CENT almost touch at the top.

Die break variations. *Obverse:* Some of the specimens have a double profile. *Reverse:* Examples are known showing traces of injury from contact with an obverse die. OF is often weak.

[236]

1798

R-5. Basal $3. 55-40 (55-55-45-40-35-30). For this review, upper range of R-5 although called R-6 in EAC.

		Peaked HWH	NOT IN D
183	32·EE	REVERSE: DIE CUT ACROSS A FROM RIGHT RIBBON	C 43

Obverse 32. Resembles the last, *but* IB *almost touching at the bottom*, and HWH comes up to a comparatively sharp peak left of the center of the upright of R; the highest point of the second wave is under the center of E; PC below the inner curve of B; JHF slightly right of the upright of T. Date evenly spaced and slightly curved, with the 8 a little high and leaning slightly to the left. On this obverse and the next to follow, *the 7 is comparatively short*, or about the same length as the 1, and the short 7 is seen only on these two dies, but unfortunately the bottoms of the 1 and 7 are usually weak and difficult to make out.

Reverse EE.

Die break variations. None seen. One of the examples that I have examined has a fine double profile.

R-7. Basal $6.50. 30-10 (30-20-12-12-8-5). At least eight now in collectors' hands, and one in ANS. Middle to lower range of R-7. Only four were known when EAC was written. Oddly enough, the five new ones have not changed the condition census.

		The Low 9	D-124
184	33·EE	DIE CUT ACROSS A FROM RIGHT RIBBON	C 44

Obverse 33. LIBERTY rather widely and evenly spaced. B high and leaning somewhat to the right. Date spaced like the last except that *the 9 is lower*. Short 7. *A die defect* is usually present, apparently growing "like a faint spray of flowers" *from the upper left corner of the* 7, and this is diagnostic. Close to the front of the neck a dotlike defect is always seen on fine specimens. PC below inner curve of B; HWH under left side of upright of R; JHF below right side of upright of T.

Reverse EE.

Die break variations. *Obverse:* On some specimens the die is rough between the forelock and RT, and a faint diagonal crack can be seen in front of the face; additional minute flakes out of the die in front of neck and back of head. Often the profile is faintly double.

R-2. Basal $1. 65-60 (65-65-65-60-60-55). This variety and No. 187 are the two 1798's most frequently seen in Mint State.

		The Low 9, With Cracks in Right Field	
185	33·FF		D-125 C 45

Obverse 33. In this marriage, *various stages in a succession of cracks are seen:* Faint crack from base of T into the field to opposite the nose, where it bends and curves to rim opposite neck; between the bend and the neck a "loop crack" connects the two sections; the defect from the upper left corner of the 7 is heavier, becoming a "fungous mass." Crack from rim through left side of Y to forehead; crack from rim opposite point of bust to the throat continues across the neck and up through the hair to the bottom of B.

Reverse FF. Same hub die as reverse O. The two pairs of leaves under T are equidistant from wreath stem and close to it but not touching. All the berries on the left except the fourth have rather long stems. Stems of first two berries on the right form a right angle. Fraction bar longer than usual for this hub, cut square at the ends and too far to the right. First 0 a little low. *Usually seen with point of bust incused at* OF.

Die break variations. *Obverse:* As indicated. *Reverse:* In earlier stages, a row of impressed denticles between ERICA and the border; later, die fails over ICA and the denticles disappear or have been worked out; part of LIBERTY seen incused at the fraction; Finally, rim break over IC, touching top of I.

R-3. Basal $1.50. 55-45 (55-50-45-40-40-40). Familiar to collectors as the Many Die Breaks variety.

		Arc Crack From Rim Through Left Top of T	
186	34·GG	REVERSE: ARC CRACK, M TO FINAL O	D-121 C 46

Obverse 34. LIBERTY evenly spaced except T Y, which are distant. Date even and curved with the border. Point of 1 a little

closer to hair than to curl. PC below outer curve of B; HWH below center of R; JHF slightly right of the foot of T. Always seen with a *faint crack from rim above the left top of* T *through* T *and the foot of* Y *to rim opposite the chin.*

Reverse GG. Same hub die as reverse O. Inside pair of leaves under T distant from wreath stem, outside pair overlap stem and cover it for two-thirds the length of the leaf. First berry on left has long stem, second short. *The third outside and third inside pairs of leaves on the right are stemless and disconnected from the wreath*—diagnostic. *Always seen in this marriage with a rim break under* 100, *and with a crack from the rim break* through the last 0, right ribbon, first two pairs of outside leaves, left foot of E and right top of M to rim. This is the same as reverse B of 1799—the second reverse of the 1799 overdate, *and on the latter the die breaks are always seen less advanced*, indicating that the 1799's must have been struck before this variety of 1798 was struck.

Die break variations. *Reverse:* The rim break becomes much heavier, touching the bottom of the first 0 and covering half of the second; crack from top of first 0 through fraction bar and (later) through left ribbon to the end of the stem; crack from the first (main) crack along base of C through the top of I and (later) to the rim; crack from below left ribbon diagonally through the top of 1 to join the crack which runs from top of first 0 to end of left stem.

R-3. Basal $1.50. 70-40 (70-60-40-40-35-35). Barely R-3, yet peculiarly scarce at the higher condition levels.

187	34·HH	Arc Crack, Rim Through Left Top of T: Additional Cracks	D-121 C 47

Obverse 34. In this marriage, always seen with the crack mentioned, and with an *additional crack starting from it opposite the nose and extending to the rim opposite the point of the bust.* A defect 2 mm. in front of the eye has developed into prominence, and a series of faint scratchlike defects are seen above the main crack, and on the neck below the ear.

Reverse HH. Same hub die as reverse O. Inside pair of leaves under T distant from wreath stem, outside pair very close but

1 7 9 8

not quite touching. *The uppermost berry on the left hangs down*—diagnostic.

Die break variations. *Obverse:* In later stages, the rim is broken at the lower end of the main crack—opposite the mouth; a light crack extends from 2 mm. in front of the nose to the lower end of the crack ending at the rim near the point of the bust; light crack on the neck parallel to the throat. *Reverse:* Found perfect and with a light crack from the rim below the final 0 through the top of A; from the bottom of the right ribbon through the base of A to the back of C (and later) through top of I to the rim; the die begins to sink above IC, and later from the top of A to above I; small break connects end of right ribbon to the right foot of A; right side of the wreath shows light injury from contact with another die.

R-1. Basal $0.75. 70-60 (70-65-65-60-60-55). Clearly the commonest 1798 cent, and perhaps also commonest in Mint State. However, we can account for only one 70-coin.

TABLE 14. KEY TO 1798 CENTS

Group 1. Large 8, style 1 letters (straight tailed R), *style 1 hair* as in 1796–97.
Closest date of the series. Rev.: Fraction bar too far right, joins ribbon..145
Same obv. Rev.: Fraction centered, PSL right of D; die "sprung" from A in STATES to about R in AMERICA.........................144
E R far apart. Fraction skewed far r., crowded against ribbon.........147
Same. "Island" under E in LIBERTY. PSL almost touches D; long point to left stem..146
Horned 9. PHL about center of final s.........................148
Date 179 8; base of R below E, T below R......................149

Group 2. Overdates.
Close date; JHF about under r. upright of T. ED in UNITED close, D a bit low..150
Same obv.; E D apart, D a trifle high........................151
Date a bit wider; left top of 7 distinctly shows, 1 far below B, JHF below left upright...152

Group 3. Large 8, style 2 letters (curled tail to R), *style 1 hair*.
8 imbedded in bust; 100 skewed well to left....................154
8 away from bust..153

Group 4. Small 8, style 2 letters, style 1 hair.
Extremely wide date, rev. of '96 (single leaves at top of wreath)........155
Close date with 9 8 apart, rev. of '96.........................156

1 7 9 8

TABLE 14. KEY TO 1798 CENTS—*Continued*

Six berries left, widest A M E R I C A; widest L I B E R T Y, break at RTY.NC-2
Six berries left; LIB close..158
Four vertical cracks in left field; PSL almost touches D.............159
Top of hair unfinished; same rev. as last. Dies usually shattered.......163
Top of hair unfinished; rev. like 1800, die scratches from adjacent corners
    of ER to border...162
Wide date and L I B E R T Y with same rev. as last.................160
Obv. as last. Rev.: Like 1800, lump on right side of O in ONE........161
Close date. Rev.: Bar from top towards bottom of C in AMERICA. Usually,
    dies rusted and scratched in centers...........................157
Close date. Rev.: No features of previous Group 4 dies; PHL r. side of
    final s...NC-1
Close date. Die usually sinking right of 8, scaling in fields. Rev.: Like
    1800, fragmented ribbons.......................................164
Group 5. Large 8, style 2 letters, style 2 hair (large extra curl 3 mm. above
    lowest curl).
Rev.: Lump at upper left corner of R, stunted left leg of first A in AMERICA.
    Usually, heavy arc crack, final zero to E in UNITED..............166
Rev.: Small break below E in UNITED pointing to F; chip out of die at
    triple leaf. Usually, obv. crack, 8 to drapery; rev. often shattered..167
Rev.: Inner pair of leaves under T of CENT away from wreath stem, outer
    pair overlaps stem...165
Group 6. Small 8, style 2 letters, style 2 hair.
Six berries left, large fraction.......................................181
Upper berry on left wreath droops................................187
Heavy arc crack, final zero to ME..................................186
Vertical crack in r. obv. field. Rev. of 1796, single leaves at top of
    wreath...178
Same obv. Rev.: Style 1 letters....................................177
With or without vertical crack as above. Rev.: Like 1800, die scratches
    from adjacent corners of ER to border.........................176
Bald spot below ear; usually, horizontal crack in field just below knot.
    Rev.: Like 1800, upper left wreath stem weak; usually, rim break
    over TATE...180
In date 98 high. Rev. like 1800; E in AMERICA first cut reversed, then
    corrected...179
In date 98 a bit high; usually, die break at RTY. Rev. like 1800, double
    center dot..173
Top of 7 recut; usually, die injuries at Y and right. Rev. like 1800, M first
    cut too low, then corrected; points show on both uprights........172
Spur up from top of 1 in date. Rev.: Crack slants up from border towards
    numerator, between left ribbon and fraction. Incusation from head
    through lower wreath...174
Same obverse. Reverse: Rim break over U.........................175

1 7 9 8

TABLE 14. KEY TO 1798 CENTS—*Continued*

Defect sprouts from left top of 7. Rev. like 1800, long heavy fraction bar slanting down... 185
Rev.: Style 1 letters; die cut joins final A and r. ribbon.
    Low 9 in date, usually with defect from left top of 7. I B apart...... 184
    IB almost touch at bottoms.. 183
    Not matching either of above. JHF under r. foot of T............. 182
Cracks join tops of most letters on rev............................. 168
Heavy rim break left of L... 171
Arc crack from border to border through ribbon and left obv. field.... 170
Small lump on border below 98. Rev. like 1800..................... 169

If your coin cannot be identified by any of the above criteria, it is probably a perfect-die example of No. 169, 170 or 171. These can be identified through careful comparison with the plates. I B are farther apart on No. 170, ER closer together on 171.

TABLE 15. RARITY AND VALUE: 1798 CENTS

Number	Obv.-Rev. Designation	Clapp Number	Doughty Number	Rarity	Basal Value (Dollars)
144	1-A	1	—	7	6.50
145	1-B	2	115	3	1.50
146	2-C	3,4	—	6	3.50
147	2-D	5	116	6	4.
148	5-E	6	117	2	1.
149	6-F	7	114	7	6.50
150	7-F	8	111	5	3.50
151	7-G	9	112	4	2.50
152	8-H	10	113	3	2.
153	9-E	11	120	4	2.
154	10-I	12	—	4	2.
155	11-J	13	110	3	2.
156	12-K	14	—	7	7.50
NC-1	13-H	15	—	8	—
157	14-L	16	122	2	1.
NC-2	15-M	17	—	8	—
158	16-M	18	126	4	2.
159	16-N	19	127	4	2.
160	17-O	20	130	6	3.50
161	17-P	21	130	1	.75
162	18-O	22	—	5	3.
163	19-N	23	131	5	3.
164	20-Q	24	123	5	2.50
165	21-R	25	118	5	3.

1 7 9 8

TABLE 15. RARITY AND VALUE: 1798 CENTS—*Continued*

Number	Obv.-Rev. Designation	Clapp Number	Doughty Number	Rarity	Basal Value (Condition 1)
166	21-S	26	118	1	.75
167	21-T	27	118	1	.75
168	22-E	28	134	3	1.50
169	22-U	29	119	5	2.50
170	23-U	30	128	4	2.
171	24-U	31	133	5	2.50
172	25-V	32	129	2	1.
173	26-W	33	132	2	1.
174	27-X	34	—	2	1.
175	27-Y	35	—	4	2.
176	28-O	36	—	5	3.
177	28-Z	37	—	6	3.50
178	28-AA	38	—	7	7.50
179	29-BB	39	135	2	1.
180	30-CC	40	—	7	6.
181	30-DD	41	136	5	2.50
182	31-EE	42	—	5	3.
183	32-EE	43	—	7	6.50
184	33-EE	44	124	2	1.
185	33-FF	45	125	3	1.50
186	34-GG	46	121	3	1.50
187	34-HH	47	121	1	.75

1799

NC-1   *1·A*   <u>Overdate. LIBERTY Far Left</u>   NEW
           OUTSIDE LEAVES OPPOSITE T FREE   NOT IN CLAPP
           FROM THE STEM OF THE WREATH

Obverse 1. The 1799 overdate. *The second 9 has been cut over an 8*, and the knob is connected to the upper part of the figure. The small 7 used on obverses 32 and 33 of 1798 reappears here, but this obverse does not match any of the known obverses of 1798. LIBERTY evenly spaced except for IB which are close. LIBERTY *farther to the left than on any of the 1798 cents*. PC to the right of B; HWH slightly right of center of R; JHF almost under left foot of Y. Date wide and even with the second 9 high. Point of 1 long and about equidistant from hair and curl.

Reverse A. Same as Reverse W of 1798. Easily distinguished from Reverse GG of 1798, which is also Reverse B of 1799, by the following points: 1) *Both pairs of leaves under* T *of* CENT *are free from the stem of the wreath.* On Reverse GG the outside pair overlaps the stem. 2) *The lowest berry on the left has a short stem*, only about as long as the diameter of the berry. On GG the length of the stem of this berry is nearly twice the diameter of the berry. 3) *The berries are notably larger* than those of Reverse GG. 4) *All leaves and pairs* of leaves have stems. *On Reverse GG the third outside and third inside pairs of leaves on the right are stemless.* 5) A center dot is present (above the upper left serif of the N in CENT) on both of these reverses. On this reverse *a second and more minute dot* can be seen with a hand lens just to the right of and slightly above the center dot.

1799

Die break variations. On the single example of this variety that has been reported both dies are perfect.

R-8. 20-0. No duplicate has yet appeared, although many 1799 overdates have been hopefully examined since 1948.

188 **1·B** Overdate. LIBERTY Far Left / OUTSIDE LEAVES OPPOSITE T OVERLAP THE STEM OF THE WREATH   D-137 C 1

Obverse 1. The 1799 overdate.

Reverse B. Reverse GG of 1798. In this marriage *always seen perfect* except in the case of the four known examples which have a heavily cracked obverse. On only these four coins does the reverse show the main crack which is *always* seen on the 1798 coins. This fact seems to indicate, as Mr. Clapp has pointed out, that the 1799 overdates must have been struck before the 1798's with the same reverse were struck. The reverse crack occurs directly opposite the heavy obverse crack and was doubtless caused by the latter.

Die break variations. *Obverse:* Usually seen perfect, but four examples are known with a heavy triple break: From rim above left side of T through bottom of Y to rim opposite nose; from rim above center of R through right top of R and bottom of T, joining the first crack at about its middle; third crack from rim above left top of R runs diagonally through R, touches second crack and then runs parallel with the combined first and second cracks till it curves in to rim near the end of the first crack. Die heavily sunken right of Y, between cracks and rim, and in the sunken area there are incused marks which probably come from RIC. *Reverse:* On the examples with cracked obverse, a crack starts at the rim below final 0, runs through the right side of that figure, the right ribbon, first two pairs of outside leaves, through left foot of E and right top of M, to rim, the whole course of the crack corresponding directly to that of the obverse break.

R-5. Basal $20. 35-30 (35-35-35-25-25-20). Rarity raised to R-5, perhaps in part because collectors find it so hard to believe that such a highly advertised "extreme rarity" could be R-4. In the present review we have been unable to sustain the earlier impression that a 40-coin exists. There are three examples of the

1 7 9 9

variety which are usually called "finest" whenever they are discussed. One of these is in ANS now. One is the Proskey-Hines piece. The third was last heard from in an Eastern collection a few years ago. Apart from these three, the next best we have seen is a VF-25. There are still only the four examples previously listed of the broken die obverse.

Perfect Date,
Close Date

189   2·C   D-138
         C 2

Obverse 2. LIBERTY evenly and somewhat closely spaced, and back in its usual position (not to the left as on obverse 1). 179 evenly spaced, but the 9's are closer, the second a little high and also slightly larger and heavier than the first. Point of 1 closer to hair than to curl. PC below outer curve of B; HWH below center of R; JHF just right of right foot of T.

Reverse C. Same hub die as reverse O of 1798. Inside pair of leaves under T distant from stem, outside pair touch. Point of leaf under T short, extending only slightly above the foot of T. All berries have medium stems, second at left touching point of leaf. Denominator rather close and *heavier* than on any of the 1798 editions of this hub die. E of CENT has a heavy, recut crossbar which joins the upper serif of the letter. The first T in STATES has a heavy right pendant. The crossbar of F is heavy and recut. There is a small chip out of the die between E of ONE and T of CENT, and this is the "mint mark" by which many recognize the die. However, this chip is of variable size, and on some coins is very faint.

Die break variations. *Reverse:* A few examples are known which do not show the so-called mint chip between E of ONE and T of CENT except as a faint trace. Later, with the chip small but plain, a small rim break shows on the denticles over the space between F and the first A of AMERICA. Later yet, this break extends and another, smaller, develops over AM. These breaks gradually become a little heavier along with increasing size of the chip. *Obverse:* One example is known, about VF-30, with the reverse breaks at their heaviest, and with a straight line obverse crack running from the border at the right to the bust point, through the bust, drapery and curls, extending into the

1799

field past the third curl from the bottom, and to the left border, there appearing as a bulge or buckle in the die. Rust marks from the die show plainly beneath the chin. The crack is heavy and unmistakable.

There is one minor mystery which might possibly lead to the discovery of a new variety. Several 1799 electrotypes are in existence with the regular Obverse 2, but with Reverse X of 1798, cracked as on all known of that variety. The original of these electrotypes has not been identified, but there may be a possibility that both the electrotype obverse and the reverse came from the same coin. In that event the coin would represent a new variety of 1799.

R-3. Basal $15. 50-30 (50-35-35-30-30-30). More than twice as common, probably, as the overdate. The famous Hines coin, referred to on p. 236 of EAC, is a 50. At any rate it was a 50 when last seen by WHS in 1945. The ANS cent and at least one other, formerly in the Würtzbach collection, can be called 35's. Several of the known examples present claim to the grade VF-30. Among these latter is the Abbey cent, incorrectly credited to the Gaskill collection in EAC. Mr. Gaskill had one he had bought as the Abbey cent, right enough, but this turned out to be the Parmelee-Beckwith coin. The Abbey cent came from the Lorenzo H. Abbey collection, about 1850. Later it was sold in the Mackenzie, Winsor, Earle and Bement collections.

Second in fun only to the practice of selling genuine 1799's to collectors at high prices, is that of selling altered date, mutilated, or faked 1799's, of which there are a large number in numismatic circulation, and among these are a few masterpieces. But careful study of the reverse will always give away the fake. On the reverse there is too much to alter. When in doubt, get out the glass and study the reverse. Watch out also for "improved" or mutilated (retouched) coins. These, even if genuine, are worth only a fraction of the value of untouched coins.

1800

THE CENTS OF THIS YEAR HAVE BEEN REGARDED AS THE HARDEST of all to identify, and they are among the hardest to find in fine condition. Prior to the completion of the Clapp-Newcomb work, reliable information on identification of 1800's was not to be had. Perhaps no more tantalizing experience can be found in numismatics than that of trying to identify 1800 cents from the Doughty descriptions. Of the twenty-seven varieties now known, the Doughty book deals with seventeen, but several are incorrectly or confusingly described, and one Doughty number (D-144) is unknown.

A major difficulty resides in the fact that there is really only one 1800 reverse. The reverses are all from the same hub die, and such reverse differences as can be made out result only from die breaks, from injuries to the die, and from minor recutting by the engraver. The copper used in the 1800 (and 1799) cents must have been exceptionally soft, for the coins are usually seen well worn, and they dent most easily (drop one on a hard surface and see!).

Yet the coins of this year are among the most interesting of the series, and the obverses more than make up for the paucity of reverse variation. There are six different 1800 overdates, nine varieties in all with overdate obverses. Also there are several bizarre, extreme, or unusual die breaks and injuries. The availability of the date in general, the softness of the metal with its consequent rich coloring, the difficulty in finding fine specimens, the richness in overdates and in heavy die breaks, and the extreme rarity of several of the varieties—all

1 8 0 0

these characteristics combine to render the 1800 coins especially attractive to the lover of cents.

On all except the first obverse, the head of Liberty is from the same head punch as style 2 of the 1798's. The first obverse is from the head punch of style 1 of that date, and this is its last appearance, as all the rest of the Draped Bust series, through 1807, are from the style 2 punch. It is a curious fact that of the six different overdate obverses, none can be identified as having been used in a previous year, and it is even more curious that the same is true of all the other fourteen overdate obverses among the large cents. The overdates seem always to be new dies, not revivals of previously used ones.

In the presentation here, the exact obverse-reverse nomenclature of Clapp-Newcomb is followed, and the descriptions usually follow the CN work closely.

1 9 0

190 **1·A** Overdate with Missing Curl D-140
LEFT SIDE FINAL A DOUBLE CUT CN 1

Obverse 1. *Style 1 hair. The curl just above and back of the shoulder is missing*—diagnostic. *The 8 cut over a 7*, and both the upper points of the latter figure show. *The lower part of the loop of a 9 appears in the first 0, and the outline or "ghost" of an 8 in the second.* Close, even date. Point of 1 distant from hair and curl. PC under inner curve of B; HWH under right side of upright of R; JHF under the tip of the right serif of T.

The following *general* description applies to all the 1800 reverses: Left, 16-5, right 19-5. Heavy, conspicuous berries. Close general resemblance to reverse O of 1798. Center dot missing. Right wreath stem slightly longer than left.

Reverse A. Fraction bar rather long and thin. U *double cut on inside left* (faintly). First S low. *In* AMERICA, *bottom of* E *and left side of final* A *double cut.* Lump on top of R. RT *incused under right ribbon and final* 0. Defect under foot of first T in STATES.

Die break variations. *Reverse:* Found perfect and with light break from left ribbon through fraction; from bottom of I in AMERICA toward nearest berry. Numerous small chips out of die. Roughness around the wreath.

[249]

1 8 0 0

R-5. Basal $4. 65-40 (65-65-60-40-25-20). Upper range of R-5. These 1800 overdates are sometimes in feverish demand. One of the 65-coins of this variety brought $600 at auction in 1954, but even this seemingly high price was below its present book rating of 65×$4×3, or $780.

| 191 | 1·B | Overdate with Missing Curl
INJURED REVERSE | D-139
CN 2 |

Obverse 1. In this marriage, ERTY is frequently weak, especially at the top, because of reverse die sinking and breaks at the fraction, and at ICA.

Reverse B. *Long fraction bar.* Numerator left of center. D higher than E. O in OF low. *Second berry on left has no stem.* Die more or less sunken at fraction, and a triangular shaped mound is usually present there.

Die break variations. *Reverse:* Always more or less injured. Found with row of impressed denticles over STAT. Die heavily sunken between ONE and CENT, and at the fraction. On some specimens the fraction is nearly obliterated, a mound obscuring the fraction bar and the two ciphers. Irregular crack from rim through center of final A, then in V-shape to end of right ribbon; from center of I through C to left of A. O in ONE broken at inner top, and connected to N by a break at the bottom. Crack from 1 of denominator to rim; from left ribbon to rim. Leaves under ST crumbling. Other minor cracks, and flakes out of the die. Heavy injury above and to the left of CENT, also through left stem, ribbon, and the numerator. Usually recognized by the break or mound at the fraction.

R-2. Basal $2.50. 60-40 (60-55-45-40-30-25). Almost common but in especial demand because of the 1800/1798 overdate and also because this is the last appearance of Style 1 Obverse (see p. 199 in EAC)—the obverse with the missing curl.

| 192 | 2·C | Compact Overdate, Both Points of Overcut 7 Show
LONG FRACTION BAR SLANTING DOWN TO RIGHT | D-141
CN 3 |

Obverse 2. Second overdate. Rather close, even date, but slightly wider than the preceding. *The points of the 7 show*

[250]

1 8 0 0

more distinctly above the 8 *than on obverse* 1. The first 0 is cut over a clearly visible 9, and in the center of the final 0 just a trace of another figure can be seen, but not made out. By "numismatic license," often called 1800/1799. The tops of RTY always seem to be weak. PC right of inner curve of B; HWH under the extreme left foot of R; JHF under center of T.

Reverse C. *Long bar which slants down to the right.* Final 0 high. T of UNITED very uneven at the top. Left foot of E in STATES missing. ME united at bottom. Inner side of upright of E recut. Lump above the left top of R. *Always seen with scaling* (or flaking or light breaks) *connecting the bottom of* O *in* OF *to adjacent leaf top, and right of* E *in* ONE; also through left ribbon bow, and through U.

Die break variations. *Reverse:* Found with crack, describing almost an arc of a circle, from rim through center of fraction through right ribbon, bottom of C and top of I to rim. Later, branch cracks appear and run to R and E. The scaling mentioned becomes more prominent and extensive.

R-4. Basal $3. 60-40 (60-60-55-40-30-20). Upper range of R-4. Two examples in the neighborhood of Mint State have appeared, or reappeared, since EAC was written.

193	2·D	Compact Overdate, Both Points of Overcut 7 Show FIRST INSIDE PAIR ON RIGHT STEMLESS	D-142 CN 4

Obverse 2. RTY often weak at the top, and usually some obliteration of the border over these letters.

Reverse D. Fraction bar a little shorter, high above 100, *square at left end and pointed at right. First inside pair of leaves on right stemless.* RTY incused under CA and ribbon end.

Die break variations. *Reverse:* Usually found with crack, from left end of fraction bar through left ribbon, bottom of U and left side of N to rim; from rim to left side of E in AMERICA, to leaves. Sometimes seen with heavy rim break under fraction.

R-5. Basal $3.50. 65-25 (65-40-30-25-15-15). Rarity lowered from R-6. In the middle range of R-5. Quite a flurry of low grade examples have been brought to light by the intensive hunt of recent years. Also an MS-65 coin has re-emerged from the

1 8 0 0

Brand hoard. This is one of the cents brought over here in the eighteen nineties from the stock of Lincoln of London. Even so, we can account for only four examples of the variety better than VF.

		Compact Overdate, Only the Left Top of 7 Shows, Last 0 Leans Left	
194	3·E	RIM BREAK UNDER FRACTION (Usually)	D-143 CN 5

Obverse 3. Third overdate. *Only the left top of the 7 seen above the 8*, and the upper loop of the 8 is more than half filled up by the 7. The 9 shows strongly under the first 0, and the second 0 is perfect, *but leaning sharply left*. This is one of the obverses referred to by the expression 1800/179. Date close, with the 80 very close. *The 1 and the 8 appear to lean somewhat to the right.* The die is injured over RTY, and on perfect specimens (which are not often seen) a row of impressed denticles can be made out extending from above RTY along the rim to a point opposite the nose. On fine specimens, 100 can be seen incused under ERT.

Reverse E. Fraction bar moderately long and heavy, beveled a little at either end, and distant from the denominator. Second 0 higher than the first. Left top of F long. Lump on left top of R. *Nearly always seen with rim break from opposite last 0 to final* A.

Die break variations. *Obverse:* Frequently seen with rim failing badly over RTY. *Reverse:* The rim break becomes heavier, finally extending from under the left ribbon end to between C and A. A small rim break appears over C. A crack is usually seen from the rim below the left ribbon, along the fraction bar, across the right ribbon to right foot of final A, and across A to the top of C. Under 100, ERT can sometimes be seen incused. For practical purposes, the variety is recognized by the heavy rim break, *with incused letters under the fraction.*

R-3. Basal $2.50. 65-55 (65-65-60-60-50-50). Probably in the lower range of R-3 but it is one of the nine overdate varieties of this year and is always in demand.

1 8 0 0

		Compact Overdate, Only the Left Top of 7 Shows, Last 0 Leans Left	
195	3·F	THIN, HIGH FRACTION BAR	NOT IN D CN 6

Obverse 3. In this marriage, crack from rim through center of T and base of Y to rim opposite nose. *The rim is broken and incused letters are seen right of* Y.

Reverse F. *Fraction bar thin, long, and high* above 100. Base of E in STATES recut. Left top of F long. ME touch. Lumps on M E R. *First inside berry on right small and weak.*

Die break variations. *Obverse:* Found with rim break covering Y and half of T. *Reverse:* Found with crack from rim through final 0 and right ribbon, along base of CA, and up to the middle of I. Die sinking under fraction and under CA.

R-6. Basal $6. 60-20 (60-30-25-15-12-12). Very close indeed to R-7. We have been able to account for just 13 with two of them, including the MS-60, in ANS. The condition census is lowered —one EF-40 from the earlier review turned out to be misattributed.

		Wide Overdate, Last 0 High	
196	4·G	SECOND INSIDE PAIR ON RIGHT STEMLESS	D-145 CN 7

Obverse 4. Fourth overdate. *Final 0 high*—the hallmark of the die. The left corner of the 7 shows clearly under the 8, and the right corner faintly. There is little if any encroachment on the inner space of the upper loop of the 8. Date a little wider than the three preceding overdates. 9 seen distinctly under first 0; second 0 perfect. PC under outside curve of B; HWH under center of R; JHF midway between T and Y.

Reverse G. *Fraction bar very short.* First T of STATES rough on left side. Lump under right foot of first A of AMERICA. *Second berry on left stemless and second inside pair of leaves on the right stemless.*

Die break variations. *Reverse:* Found with light crack through right top of E to bottom of adjacent s in STATES.

R-1. Basal $1.50. 60-45 (60-55-50-45-45-40). The commonest

[253]

1 8 0 0

overdate of the year, and not much less common than No. 197 —the other R-1.

		Compact Overdate, Only Left Top of 7 Shows, Last 0 Upright	
NC-1	5·H	LOOK AT THE FIRST E	NOT IN D CN 8

Obverse 5. Fifth overdate. *Only the left top of 7 shows above the 8.* The 7 also appears slightly in the upper loop of 8. *Faint traces of 9 in the first* 0; second 0 perfect and upright. Date evenly spaced and moderately compact. LIB close; Y distant from T. PC left of inner curve of B; HWH under center of upright of R; JHF under right side of upright of T.

Reverse H. Fraction bar long, spindle-shaped. Numerator heavy, lacking the top point. Second berry on the left stemless, held between point of leaf and stem above. *First E has center cross-stroke high and misshapen, with lower part of down stroke twice as long as the upper part.* O of ONE crumbling on the right. Light break from fourth leaf on left across third leaf. Heavy "suction line" from left stem across leaf past first berry.

Die break variations. Only one example seen, and now in the ANS collection. A second specimen has been reported.

R-8. Unique. 8-0. A second one has been rumored but never verified. The only example positively known is now in ANS.

		Overdate, Both Points of 7 Show, Rim Break at Lower Right Obverse	
NC-2	6·I	HOOK AT RIGHT BOTTOM OF FINAL S	NOT IN D CN 9

Obverse 6. Sixth overdate. *Both points of the 7 show above the top of* 8. Part of the curve of 9 seen in first 0; second 0 perfect. Moderately wide date with 18 closer than other figures. Point of 1 distant from hair and curl. LIB close, R slightly high, TY close. PC under the outer curve of B; HWH under the center of upright of R; JHF under extreme right end of foot of T. *Rim break opposite bust and neck runs up about 1 cm.*

Reverse I. Fraction bar short, bevelled at both ends. *A hook at the right bottom of final* S. D tilted slightly to the right. Left top of M *long*. F in OF usually weak.

1 8 0 0

Die break variations. Only a single example reported.

R-8. Basal $15. 10-7 (10-10-7-5). Four now extant, three of them in collectors' hands. One more will make this R-7.

		Q Variety; First 0 of Date Looks Like a Q	
197	7·I		D-146 CN 10

Obverse 7. The so-called Q variety. There is a *break in the center of the first 0*, another from its lower right side, and another under the final 0. With the breaks, the first 0 looks somewhat like a Q. There is also a *V-shaped break starting at the rim between* I *and* B, and extending down between these letters. Heavy, irregular *break connects bottoms of* B *and* E, filling much of the space between these letters and the hair. PC under center of B; HWH under left foot of R; JHF under center of upright of T.

Reverse I.

Die break variations. *Obverse:* The breaks at IB become heavy, and connect with the top of the hair. Crack across upper part of hair; another from hair above tip of 1 to 8. *Reverse:* Usually seen with light crack from top of T to center of A in STATES, then to base of TE and up to middle of S. Many small defects around and under ES. Small break in center of left upright of N in CENT. Light rim break over AT.

R-1. Basal $1.25. 65-55 (65-60-60-55-50-50). The Q variety. Commonest 1800 cent.

		Rounded Right Top of 1	
198	8·J	JAGGED BREAK CONNECTING 1 OF DENOMINATOR TO LEFT RIBBON	D-147 CN 11

Obverse 8. Y slightly high and left foot missing. Date even and wide. *Point of 1 very close to curl. Right top of 1 rounded*, and adjacent to the rounded area there is a chip out of the die; also a small defect at the upper right side of first 0. PC under center of curve of B; HWH under right side of upright of R; JHF just left of center of space under TY.

Reverse J. An identifying feature is a short, rather jagged *break connecting the 1 of the denominator to the left ribbon immediately above it.* The break touches the point of the 1,

[255]

1 8 0 0

runs along the left side of the figure, and peters out between the bottom of the 1 and the rim. No examples are known to me without this break. Fraction bar short, right end slightly high. Left side of final A faintly recut. All berries have very short stems. *Lowest pair of berries on the right stemless and welded directly to the very thick wreath stem*—also diagnostic. *Third and fourth outside right pair of leaves stemless* and welded directly to the wreath stem.

Die break variations. *Obverse:* The two fine examples that are known to me show a row of impressed denticles above and to the right of TY. *Reverse:* Light crack seen from center of I in AMERICA, through center of CA and past the end of the right ribbon. Chips are out of the die between 100 and end of right ribbon, and between I and C.

R-7. Basal $7.50. 20-10 (20-15-15-10-8-6). In this review we account for eleven, which makes the variety just barely R-7, but in view of the low condition census the basal value is continued at $7.50.

199	9 · K	Thin, Unfinished Ciphers	D-149
		CRACK ACROSS LEFT TOP OF D TO RIM	CN 12

Obverse 9. *Figures of the date thin, unfinished at the bottom, especially the two ciphers,* which are sometimes almost open at the bottom. Point of 1 long, nearly touching curl. LIBERTY rather close. IB almost touch. PC under center of B; HWH under center of upright of R; JHF under tip of right foot of T.

Reverse K. Easily recognized by its die breaks, some of which are almost always present. Short fraction bar. I of UNITED and first T of STATES high. *First outside berry on left stemless (or stem merged with leaf stem) and caught between point of leaf and stem above.*

Die break variations. *Obverse:* Some examples show several light flakes out of the die in a line, in front of the neck. *Reverse:* Found perfect but usually seen with crack from right top of E in UNITED across left top of D to rim about midway between D and S; die failing over F—later, a heavy break connects top of F to rim. Crack from E to base of T in UNITED, and most examples show a light chip under adjacent I, to which

[256]

this crack finally extends; crack down right side of first s; from top of F to left foot of first A in AMERICA; from F through o to middle tip of triple leaf under o; from base of left terminal leaf down left side of o, past c, through left bottom of E to the ribbon loop; crack from between T and E to terminal leaf to pair below; from tip of second outside pair of leaves on right through base of M. The die at last fails badly in the upper left and right central portions.

R-5. Basal $4. 60-15 (60-20-15-15-12-12). Rarity underestimated in EAC. This variety is mid-range or even upper range R-5. The MS coin is in ANS and the next best one mustered for this review is a VF-20.

200	9·L	Thin, Unfinished Ciphers	D-148
		THE LONG-STEMMED BERRY	CN 13

Obverse 9. The flakes in front of the neck are more conspicuous. Most examples show a slight crack starting at the rim opposite the lower curls, and from this point to the date the die is beginning to sink. Coins showing no trace of the crack or die sinking are rare. *The last cipher is crumbling along the inner left side and at the bottom;* the first cipher is crumbling in the upper right portion.

Reverse L. Short fraction bar. Second cipher high and both ciphers perfect. *Left lower serif of E in STATES very short,* almost missing. Same is true of left lower serif of F. Die sinking usually seen at STA. First outside berry on the left has a short, thick stem. *Second outside berry on the right has a stem about twice the length of that of any of the other berries.* ("Long stem variety.")

Die break variations. *Reverse:* Found perfect and with crack through top of O, joining that letter to top of F. Later, top of F becomes heavily broken. Crack from bottom of second T to top of E in STATES; from rim above same T to top of E; break above E in AMERICA; crack from base of same E along leaves to right stem; crack from below right foot of A through ribbon and final 0 to rim; rim break over AT. The die sinking at STA becomes very pronounced. The perfect die reverse is scarce.

R-3. Basal $2.50. 50-35 (50-45-40-35-35-30). About a mid-range R-3.

1 8 0 0

NC-3   9·V   <u>Thin, Unfinished Ciphers</u>   NOT IN D
SPIKED I VARIETY   NOT IN CN

Obverse 9. The crack from the rim now continues to the hair, with another crack branching off from it almost to the ribbon end. The ciphers show further crumbling. A light, wavy crack starts from the rim three denticles to the left of 1, passes through the bottom of that figure and through the other figures to the tip of the bust beyond.

Reverse V. Very similar to reverse L but differing from it in the following respects: *Projecting from the center of the top of* I *in* AMERICA *there is a conspicuous spike, or point, about 0.5 mm. in length. The second outside berry on the right has a stem of normal length,* or of the same length as that of its neighbor below. The second cipher of the fraction is badly formed or unfinished in its upper right portion. The first cipher shows this same characteristic to a lesser degree. The left lower serif of the E in STATES is too short, as on reverse L, but the F is correctly formed. In other respects the description of this reverse agrees with that of reverse L. The *Spiked* I *variety*.

Die break variations. None seen.

R-8. Basal $15. 50-15. Semi-unique. Only two reported but both are in collectors' hands and the variety therefore merits a basal value of $15.

201   9·M   <u>Thin, Unfinished Ciphers</u>   NOT IN D
STEMLESS LEAVES VARIETY   CN 14

Obverse 9. All of the examples I have seen show the same stage of the die breaks as that just described for the NC-3 variety.

Reverse M. Fraction bar moderately long and high, with the right end a little higher than the left. *The second inside pair of leaves on the left, and the first inside pair on the right are stemless*—diagnostic. This is one of the easy ones. *Stemless Leaves* variety.

Die break variations. None seen.

R-6. Basal $6. 20-10 (20-15-10-10-8-6). The present review accounts for fifteen of these, only one of them in ANS. No longer R-7, but in the extreme upper range of R-6.

[258]

1 8 0 0

Thin, Unfinished Ciphers.
Heavy Break Behind Curls

202 **9·N** BUST INCUSED AT OF A   D-150 CN 15

Obverse 9. *Crack from rim now very heavy, and it turns down along the curls,* causing sinking of the die. Another crack from the rim joins the vertical branch crack, which is heavier. *Last cipher crumbling badly,* and other figures of the date are weakening.

Reverse N. Fraction bar shorter than the last, and level. First T in STATES recut at left top, but STATES *is frequently obliterated,* because of the obverse break. Left foot of F short. Point of bust incused at OF A. Small projection on right side of right ribbon, 2 mm. from the end.

Die break variations. *Reverse:* Examples are found with TATE entirely gone, and the two s's just visible, the swell extending as far as T in UNITED. Crack from the leaves over O in ONE to the triple leaf under OF; crack from right terminal leaf to bottom of final s.

R-3. Basal $2.50. 65-35 (65-50-45-35-30-25). Middle or upper range of R-3. The Winsor-Hines-Downing coin is MS-65.

Die Cut Before Nose

203 **10·O** BUST INCUSED AT S OF   D-151 CN 16

Obverse 10. Left foot of Y missing. E tilted to the left and distant from R at the top. There is a *diagonal "saw-tooth cut" in the die, about 3 mm. in front of the nose.* Date wide and curved, with the point of the 1 practically touching the *top* of the lowest curl—diagnostic. PC under the inner curve of B; HWH under center of upright of R; JHF to the right of right foot of T.

Reverse O. Easily recognized by *heavy incusation of point of bust* from final s across OF, and 1800 incused under TES, with the last cipher just to the right and above the s. Only a single example is known without this injury, and that one is in the ANS collection. Fraction bar long. First T in STATES very heavy, especially the right top. The *Incused* variety.

Die break variations. *Obverse:* Except on the one specimen with uninjured reverse, the face, forelock, and back of the hair

1 8 0 0

are somewhat flat, showing that the obverse die also was injured by the "collision."

R-3. Basal $2.50. 60-35 (60-50-35-30-25-25). R-3 rather than R-2, and probably in the middle range of R-3. The previously reported condition census of 60-50 resulted from gross overgrading of coins on the part of two collectors whose probity remains otherwise above reproach. This reverse reappears in 1801 on the variety NC-1.

204   11·P   Wide Date, 1 Nearer the 8 at the Top than at the Bottom
PERFECT DIE REVERSE   D-153   CN 17

Obverse 11. This die is always seen injured. Fine specimens show a row of impressed denticles through BER and above TY. There is usually a light crack in the field running from right of Y toward the rim opposite the chin, and between this crack and the rim the die is sunken. Fine specimens show the *tops of incused letters in the sunken area* (raised area on the coin). Some examples have a heavy rim break directly in front of the face. LIB close; I slightly high, Y low. *Fairly wide date with the 1 tilted to the right and too close to the 8 at the top.* PC under the right side of the curve of B; HWH under right side of upright of R; JHF under right foot of T.

Reverse P. Fraction bar rather long, square at the ends, and high above 100. ME touch. Lumps at tops of E and R and trace of lump at left top of M. Fine specimens show recut base of E in STATES, and a light scratch in the die between S and O. Very close indeed to reverse F, but the first inside berry on the right is of normal size—not small as on F. One of the few 1800 reverses not characterized (in this marriage) by any breaks or injuries. The *Perfect Die* Reverse.

Die break variations. *Obverse:* As noted.

R-6. Basal $5. 40-25 (40-40-30-25-25-15). Lower range of R-6, probably, but clearly R-6, and we hope that no reader has missed a "nice one" because of our earlier underestimate of rarity. This variety is hard to find. Perhaps we were misled by two little hoards of them; three examples in ANS, and four in the Hines collection.

1 8 0 0

205   *12·P*

Wide Date, Period
Before Neck, Blank
Lower Curl

NOT IN D
CN 18

Obverse 12. Y low, distant from the T, and with its left foot missing. Date fairly wide with 18 more distant than 80. The 8 leans a little to the right. Point of 1 equidistant from hair and curl. *A period-like defect is always present about 4 mm. in front of the middle of the neck*, and a smaller one half way between it and the neck. *Lower curl unfinished—its inner part almost blank.*

Reverse P. In this marriage, a light crack is nearly always found, along the base of final A to the lower point of C, and from the back of C to center of I.

Die break variations. *Obverse;* On most examples, although not all, *a light horizontal crack extends from the hair above the lower curls, two thirds of the distance to the rim.* For practical purposes, this crack is the hallmark of the die, since it is always present on the more frequently seen variety which follows.

R-5. Basal $3.50. 65-55 (65-60-60-55-50-50). Rare, but eight or ten are known at the AU-50 level or better. One example has turned up with extended die breaks which nearly duplicate those found on No. 206, and this necessitates a sharper differentiation between the two reverse dies than was given in EAC. Reverse P: The stem of the uppermost berry on the left is horizontal; its continuation would hit the first A near its right foot. On Reverse Q this continuation would pass between F and A. It should be mentioned too that on the example of No. 205 seen with the advanced obverse die break, Reverse P shows cracks across both zeros of the fraction, and across the ribbon end and ICA. This may appear to be a straining at a gnat but it may prevent a bit of perplexity somewhere.

1 8 0 0

206   12·Q   Wide Date, Period Before Neck, Horizontal Crack Behind Hair, Perfect Lower Curl   D-152 CN 19

Obverse 12. *Lower curl now finished,* and *the horizontal die break to the left heavier, as are the defects in front of the neck.* Meanwhile the die has been injured over LIBERTY, and fine specimens show a row of impressed denticles above the letters and to the right.

Reverse Q. Extremely close to reverse P, but as a rule easily recognized by its die breaks. Below the fraction the die is sinking, probably following the obverse injury, and most examples have a small triangular rim break beneath the first 0. A crack extends from the rim or from the rim break, across the first 0 and the top of the second, across the ribbon end and both feet of A to C, and from the back of C to the center of I. Another light crack from the rim touches the left top of U and the end of the ribbon, and passes along the fraction bar. There is a minute point, or imperfection, on the top of the first outside berry on the right. A continuation of the stem of the uppermost berry on the left would pass between F and A. This same continuation, on reverse P, would about hit the right foot of A.

Die break variations. *Obverse:* On some examples, the horizontal break extends nearly to the border.

R-4. Basal $3. 45-35 (45-40-40-35-30-30). Lower or middle range of R-4, not R-3. Another 1800 for which our earlier census estimate was a bit too liberal. These 1800's are very educative when one comes to close quarters with them.

207   13·Q   Obverse: No Horizontal Crack
REVERSE: RIM BREAK UNDER FRACTION   NOT IN D CN 20

Obverse 13. This variety can be recognized in two glances: (1) *It always has the triangular rim break under the fraction on the reverse;* (2) *It of course lacks the horizontal obverse break seen on the preceding obverse.* These two observations identify the coin. IB a little high. Y perfect. Date well spaced, with the 8 equidistant from 1 and 0. PC under the center of

[262]

1 8 0 0

the curve of B; HWH under center of upright of R; JHF between T and Y. Nearly always seen with some sinking of the die over B, a result of the rim break on the reverse. Row of impressed denticles seen faintly over Y and to the right.

Reverse Q. With the rim break below the fraction always present.

Die break variations. *Obverse:* Some examples have a light crack from the forelock to the foot of T. *Reverse:* In the later stages the rim break extends to the final 0 of the fraction, covers most or all of CA, and the upper half of 1.

R-4. Basal $3. 35-25 (35-30-25-25-20-15). Probably in the middle range of R-4, and same comment as for the preceding variety. During the past decade we have encountered at least a dozen coins misattributed to No. 207. This may help account for the earlier impression that the variety is much commoner than it is. ANS has three of them, as did the Hines collection.

208

208   **14·R**   Break Over TY and Right, 1 Almost Touching Curl   D-154 CN 21

Obverse 14. LIBERTY even. Date even and curved. Point of 1 almost touches curl. *Often seen with heavy rim break over TY and right. Nearly always seen with break over TY obliterating part of top of Y.* PC under inner curve of B; HWH under center of upright of R; JHF under the right foot of T. Dot-like defect about 0.5 mm. from lowest ribbon end.

Reverse R. Short fraction bar. Top of F uneven. Both upright and top of T in UNITED irregular. Usually seen with light crack from middle of right side of R in AMERICA to the bottom of I, to base of C and up through the middle of A to the rim.

Die break variations. *Obverse:* The obverse rim break, in its advanced stage, extends from the left of T to a point about opposite the chin, obliterating half of T and all but the bottom of Y. A light crack also develops from the foot of T to the foot of Y and through Y to the rim break.

R-3. Basal $2.50. 40-20 (40-25-20-20-20-15). Probably in the lower range of R-3, although previously regarded as R-2. At the time of writing EAC we had been spoiled by close association with Mr. Hines, Mr. Clapp, Mr. Würtzbach and Mr. Newcomb.

[263]

1 8 0 0

These four, between them, had almost a monopoly on the desirable 1800's and 1796's—those being the two "difficult" dates on which they had been working for years.

		Widest Date 1800, Figures Bold at the Bottom, Prominent "Suction Marks"	
209	15·R		NOT IN D CN 22

Obverse 15. LIBERTY close, measuring 14 mm. at the bottom. Left foot of Y missing. *Date wide, well curved, and perfectly spaced.* Point of 1 about 0.5 mm. from both hair and curl. Prominent "suction marks" always seen back of head, under hair ribbons, and below chin. Nearly always seen with die sinking above Y and this progresses down the rim to opposite the neck. *The figures of the date are all perfectly cut, and they stand out in a bold manner, particularly at the bottom, which is not seen on other 1800 cents.* PC under inner curve of B; HWH under right side of upright of R; JHF midway under TY.

Reverse R.

Die break variations. *Obverse:* The die sinking progresses, there has been an injury, and on some of the finer specimens incused letters are seen in front of the face near the border. The die becomes rough in that area. *Reverse:* Found perfect and with very light rim break under 00 to right ribbon end; also light crack from rim to top of AM, through center of ER, near the bottom of ICA, and from right foot of A to ribbon end.

R-5. Basal $3.50. 55-40 (55-50-45-40-40-35). Probably in the lower range of R-5. Widest date 1800 and one of the aesthetically most pleasing varieties.

		The Comma Variety, Die Chipped Above BE	
210	16·R		D-155 CN 23

Obverse 16. LIB close, B slightly high, left foot of Y missing. Date even, rather straight, and distant from the bust. Point of 1 closer to curl than to hair. *Always seen with comma-shaped chip out of the die extending down between B and E from the rim.* Die injured and sinking from TY along rim, and faintly

1 8 0 0

incused letters can sometimes be seen in the injured area, as on the preceding obverse. PC just left of center of B; HWH under left foot of R; JHF under right side of upright of T.

Reverse R. In this marriage, *always seen with the light crack through* AMERICA.

Die break variations. *Obverse:* Found with a crack from rim to left top of E and foot of R, past forelock and almost to the rim opposite the nose. The die fails progressively from TY down along the rim.

R-7. Basal $7.50. 40-15 (40-35-15-10-10-8). Nine now reported, eight in collectors' hands, and two of the new ones are the 40-coin and the 35-coin. The example previously graded VF-20, and previously finest known, is now called F-15. But five were known when EAC was written, and two of those were then rather new discoveries. This famous variety came near to being R-8 in the earlier book. Mr. Clapp "never saw one" until he got the Gillette coin, VG-10, in 1937 after some decades of collecting. Two of the new examples have reverse rim breaks over AME.

		Crack From L to Hair, Swollen Areas on Obverse	
211	17·S	LARGE PLANCHET	NOT IN D CN 24

Obverse 17. LIBERTY evenly spaced. Date well spaced with last 0 a little high. The figures are thin and of imperfect shape, as on obverse 9, but are nowhere broken down. *A light crack or die injury always seen from the hair to the lower left corner of* L, and there is usually *a swell above the point of the bust, through which a light crack runs from the rim two thirds of the way toward the angle of the jaw.* PC under inner curve of B; HWH under right side of upright of R; JHF midway under TY.

Reverse S. Short fraction bar. T of UNITED even more badly shaped than usual. Slight die crumbling at the inner right top of O in OF. C of CENT has a short bottom point and a down-pointing spike at the top.

Die break variations. *Obverse:* The swell in the die increases, and some examples have an additional swell opposite the face. Another swell behind the lower curls. Crack from rim below

1 8 0 0

1 touches bottom of first 0. In the last stages, there is a crack from the rim along the bottoms of 18. *Reverse:* On some examples, there is a light, irregular crack from the center of E to the bottom of adjacent s in STATES. This coin is usually well centered, with a sharply defined obverse rim, and is generally struck on a large planchet.

R-3. Basal $2.50. 70-40 (70-60-45-40-30-30). Lower range of R-3. Clearly second commonest perfect date, third commonest 1800.

| 212 | 18·T | The Chips Variety, Defects Below the Ciphers LONG HEAVY FRACTION BAR | NOT IN D CN 25 |

2 1 2

Obverse 18. LI very close, ER high. Left foot of Y defective. 18 a little more distant than the other figures, last 0 high. *Chips out of the die at rim between the two ciphers and under the last cipher;* hence often confused with the Q variety. There is also a chip near the point of the bust, above the drapery. PC under center of curve of B; HWH under right side of upright of R; JHF to the right of right foot of T.

Reverse T. Fraction bar long, heavy, beveled down at both ends. *C in CENT has a point or heavy whisker, at the center of inner curve*—diagnostic. There is a *linear chip out of the die under the first T of STATES*, and a dotlike chip almost touching the right side of the crosspiece of the same letter. These last three defects easily identify the coin. Small lump or point on the ribbon loop pointing at first berry on the left. The *chips* variety.

Die break variations. *Obverse:* The chips or defects become heavier. A crack develops from rim to hair, just above knot; from rim to forehead near JHF; from forehead across hair.

R-4. Basal $3. 55-45 (55-55-50-40-40-35). The defects below the ciphers sometimes cause it to be confused with No. 197. Lower range of R-4, not R-3.

| NC-4 | 19·U | The Variety with the Heavy Rim Breaks | NOT IN D CN 26 |

Obverse 19. LIBERTY high, IB very close, and both letters lean

[266]

1 8 0 0

to the right. On both examples known, there is a *heavy rim break* starting just left of L and extending 5 mm. down the rim. At its point of origin the rim break combines with a heavy crack which curves to the bottom of the ribbon knot. Another *extremely heavy break* starts opposite the center of the knot and runs down the rim 12 mm. to opposite the lowest curl. This break appears to prevent STATES from striking up on the reverse. Date very wide and well curved. PC about under center of curve of B, and rather blunt; HWH under right side of upright of R; JHF barely right of right foot of T.

Reverse U. Numerator heavy and blunt, as on Reverse H, and slants to the left. Outer pair of leaves under ME apparently stemless. First s of STATES low. Lumps at left tops of MER. Fraction bar short and rather high.

R-8. 8-6. Semi-unique; two known, only one in collectors' hands. If another is found, the variety will have a basal value of $15.

TABLE 16. KEY TO 1800 CENTS

Overdate. Style 1 hair, as in 1796–7.
   Reverse: Final A in AMERICA recut on left side....................190
   Reverse: Mound under fraction; die usually shattered...............191
Overdates. Style 2 hair, as in 1799–1807.
   Close even date, both corners of 7 plain under 8. Long fraction bar slants
      down to right...192
   Same obv. Inner leaves under T of CENT stemless....................193
   Close date, 80 closer; only left top of 7 above 8. Rev.: Heavy fraction bar;
      rim break under fraction and to right...........................194
   Same obv. Rev.: Very thin, high, long fraction bar..................195
   Final zero quite high. Rev.: Inner leaves *above* T in CENT stemless......196
   LIB close, ERT wide. Rev.: Misshapen crossbar in E of UNITED........NC-1
   Long (10 mm) rim break or crack opposite bust point and neck......NC-2
Perfect dates.
   "Q" variety; V-shaped break between IB.........................197
   Chips out of die at 00; Rev. spur at center of inner curve of C in CENT..212
   Vertical crack joins 1 of denominator to left ribbon; right top of 1
      rounded...198
   Thin, imperfect 00. Spine down from upper corner of C in CENT. Wide
      planchet...211
   Similar to last; I of UNITED and first T of STATES high. Usually, crack
      through ED to border midway D s.................................199

1 8 0 0

TABLE 16. KEY TO 1800 CENTS—*Continued*

Obv. as last; chips from die before neck. Usually, crack from rim to lower curls. Rev.: E in STATES and F of OF have abnormally short left bases; die sinking at STA, chip above E in AMERICA.................200
Same. Rev.: Spine protrudes from center of top of I in AMERICA........NC-3
Same. Fraction bar slants up. Inner leaves left of ONE and below T in CENT stemless; often with buckling in center of die..................201
Same. Obv. now badly cracked at left. Bulge at ATE; bust incused at OF A...202
Diagonal saw-tooth cut in die 3 mm. from nose.....................203
Break over TY and right...208
Heavy incusations of leaves behind head, under bow................209
Comma-shaped chip just right of top of B. Crack down through AMERICA...210
Triangular rim break under fraction. Without horizontal crack on obverse..207
Wide date, "period" before neck; horizontal crack behind neck. Stem of upper left berry points between F A. Usually, with rim break under fraction..206
Same obv., with or without horizontal crack. Reverse: Stem of upper left berry points to r. foot of A..................................205
Wide date, 1 tilted r.: die injuries at BERTY and in right field.........204
IB very close, both letters lean r. Extremely heavy rim break left of L and an even larger one at lower left obverse....................NC-4

If your coin does not match any of the above, it is probably a perfect-die example of 197, 204, NC-4, 208 or 209; comparison with the plates should suffice for identification. It is also possible that a worn example of NC-1 might not show the trace of 9 in first zero, but the reverse is sufficiently distinctive.

1 8 0 0

TABLE 17. RARITY AND VALUE: 1800 CENTS

Number	Obv.-Rev. Designation	CN Number	Doughty Number	Rarity	Basal Value (Dollars)
190	1-A	1	140	5	4.
191	1-B	2	139	2	2.50
192	2-C	3	141	4	3.
193	2-D	4	142	5	3.50
194	3-E	5	143	3	2.50
195	3-F	6	—	6	6.
196	4-G	7	145	1	1.50
NC-1	5-H	8	—	8	—
NC-2	6-I	9	—	8	15.
197	7-I	10	146	1	1.25
198	8-J	11	147	7	7.50
199	9-K	12	149	5	4.
200	9-L	13	148	3	2.50
NC-3	9-V	—	—	8	15.
201	9-M	14	—	6	6.
202	9-N	15	150	3	2.50
203	10-O	16	151	3	2.50
204	11-P	17	153	6	5.
205	12-P	18	—	5	3.50
206	12-Q	19	152	4	3.
207	13-Q	20	—	4	3.
208	14-R	21	154	3	2.50
209	15-R	22	—	5	3.50
210	16-R	23	155	7	7.50
211	17-S	24	—	3	2.50
212	18-T	25	—	4	3.
NC-4	19-U	26	—	8	—

1801

Newcomb's monograph on the cents of 1801-2-3 has made these dates comparatively easy for the collector who has a copy; but unfortunately it is rare, expensive, and frequently not available.

The fifteen known varieties of 1801 make up an easy date, with a mating diagram which presents a consistent and natural order. Since Newcomb's presentation of the 1802's and 1803's is consistent with such mating diagrams, it has seemed wise to take the easy step of rearranging Newcomb's order of presentation of the 1801's, and so to fit this date also to its natural mating diagram. When the varieties follow such a mating plan it is immeasurably easier and more satisfactory to get acquainted with them. The order of 1801's, then, and consequently the obverse-reverse nomenclature, will here be found different from Newcomb's presentation.

As in the case of Clapp's work on the 1798's, the small letter designations for different stages in the progression of die breaks have been omitted as unnecessary and as somewhat misleading; the breaks do not really progress by "stages" and actually there are no two die breaks quite alike.

We know that morale must have been low at the Mint during these years (see p. 13), and it is not so very surprising to find a number of peculiar or bizarre errors on the coins; especially on those of 1801, which was possibly the darkest year at the Mint. It is these very errors and peculiarities that endear the old cents to those who know them well.

No more overdates will be encountered until 1807.

1 8 0 1

213   1·A   Four Wavy Cracks Before Face   D-161 N-1

Obverse 1. This die never seen perfect, and easily recognized by *four wavy cracks* which run diagonally in the field from rim above and through ERTY to rim in front of face. *First 1 pointed;* the second 1 is blunt, as on all 1801 obverses. PC under center of B; JHF barely right of upright of T.

Reverse A. *Perfect fraction with* 100 *equally and moderately spaced*—a description which applies to only one other reverse (reverse C, on which 100 is more closely spaced). Fraction bar high, level, close to numerator. *The three N's are perfectly formed*—diagnostic.

Die break variations. *Obverse:* Additional crack from rim through 1 and hair to forehead. RTY becomes weak, and the last two letters are obliterated as the breaks progress and the die sinks. Crack from rim below 0 in date, diagonally up through right side of 0 and curving to right through drapery and bust to rim near point of bust. *Reverse:* Always seen with a nearly straight, delicate crack from top of 1 in 100 through base of numerator, ribbon, stem, leaves, and E to rim. Later, additional crack from last 0 through bases of CA to middle of I; LIBE lightly incused about fraction and UN; crack from rim above E in UNITED through its left top and base of T into the field between N and lowest leaf on left.

R-3. Basal $2. 65-40 (65-55-50-40-30-30). Wavy cracks before the face. One example now known with perfect dies, obverse and reverse. Upper range of R-3. May possibly be R-4.

2 1 3

214   2·A   Moderately Spaced Date, First 1 Pointed, Left Stand of Y Defective   NOT IN D N-2

Obverse 2. *First 1 pointed.* 1 8 a trifle more distant than other figures. Left stand of Y defective. PC under center of right side of B; JHF just right of right foot of T. Otherwise close general resemblance to obverse 1.

Reverse A. In this marriage, seen with cracks as noted.

Die break variations. *Obverse:* Found with rim failure at RTY, and (later) with rim break over RTY.

[271]

1 8 0 1

R-5. Basal $3. 60-45 (60-60-55-50-40-35). Middle range of R-5; rarity overestimated in EAC.

		Very Close Date, First 1 Pointed, Perfect Y	
215	3·A	INJURED REVERSE	NOT IN D N-3

Obverse 3. *First 1 pointed.* Close general resemblance to obverses 1 and 2. IB and ER close. *Date very compact,* closer than the preceding two. PC below inner curve of B; JHF below extreme right foot of T.

Reverse A. Cracks heavier.

Die break variations. *Obverse:* Found with crack from rim back of lowest ribbon end, curving down toward lower curls; joined by another, which starts close to the first, in the field, and the latter crack crosses the hair and lower left tip of shoulder to top of 0 and (later) through base of last 1 to rim; rim becomes heavily broken below 01; crack from lowest curl parallels the rim, runs through date to rim near the point of the bust. *Reverse:* The die is sinking, producing a raised field on the coin above STATES; incusations from date and curls show in STATES, and the lower portion of a bust is heavily incused at S OF; die sinking between this incusation and the rim; crack through top of OF and to rim right of F.

R-6. Basal $4. 65-40 (65-55-55-35-25-25). In the middle or upper range of R-6, more than twice as rare as No. 214. The MS-65 is the Dupont coin, sold in 1954 and catalogued by WHS as MS-70. However, the present owner agrees with our current view that there is no 1801 cent in full MS-70 condition. A new discovery has turned up in AU-55 state, and the best one from the Newcomb sale, now in ANS, is also AU-55.

		Very Close Date, First 1 Pointed, Perfect Y	
NC-1	3·B	DIFFERENTLY INJURED REVERSE	NOT IN D N-14

Obverse 3.

Reverse B. A minor variant from the A reverse, discovered by H. C. Hines some years after the Newcomb monograph was published. Newcomb examined the coin and issued a supplement adding it to his list as a new variety. Fraction bar

1 8 0 1

slightly thicker than on reverse A, and a little longer. Right top of N in ONE imperfect, and this N is from a different punch from that used for the other two N's on the reverse. The bottom part of a bust is incused about the letters TES OF, but *this injury is different* from the injury seen on the last stages of reverse A, and the characteristic die breaks of reverse A are lacking.

R-8. Basal $12.50. 12-6 (12-10-8-1). Four now known, three in collectors' hands. The *NC* should be read as Now Collectible. Same reverse as that of No. 203, although this was not known when EAC was written. We then lacked a sharp enough example of the present variety to show it.

| 216 | 4·C | Blunt First 1
PERFECT FRACTION,
CLOSE DENOMINATOR | D-160
N-8 |

Obverse 4. *Blunt 1's.* The 01 higher than the 18. LIBERTY low and very closely spaced, except T Y; LIB almost touch. PC below center of B; JHF just right of right foot of T.

Reverse C. *Perfect fraction with* 100 *very close.* AM touch. Fraction bar delicate, distant from denominator, and more distant from numerator than on reverse A, which is the only other reverse with perfect, equally spaced fraction.

Die break variations. None seen, but the obverse die was heavily injured. The point of the bust is frequently found flat, with part of the drapery not struck up, and many examples are known with LIBERTY more or less obliterated. The tops of the letters in LIBERTY are lost in the rim, and not uncommonly the upper halves of these letters cannot be seen, even on Mint State specimens. On the reverse, OF is often weak or missing.

R-2. Basal $1.50. 60-55 (60-60-60-55-55-50). Not far from R-1. Usually seen with badly injured obverse die.

| 217 | 5·C | LIBERTY Far to the Right.
Injury over BERTY, and
Die Sinking (Usually)
REVERSE: PERFECT FRACTION | NOT IN D
N-5 |

Obverse 5. LIBERTY *far to the right*—diagnostic. PC below I, and JHF under the tail of R. The 1's are blunt. Always seen with an injury over BERTY, and usually with incused denticles

[273]

1 8 0 1

extending from the left top of B to a point nearly opposite the nose.

Reverse C.

Die break variations. *Obverse:* In this marriage, usually found with sinking of the die between rim and lowest curl, at left of first 1. Two examples are known with more extensive die sinking behind the curls, and with beginnings of it over the point of the bust and to the right. One example is known with no die sinking at all. Heavy traces of a wreath are usually seen before the face and neck and back of the head.

R.-7. Basal $10. 45-20 (45-40-20-15-12-6). Only five of these known to be in collectors' hands, and two in ANS. Apparently the variety is within two coins of R-8.

| 2 1 9 | 218 | 5·D | LIBERTY Far to the Right REVERSE: THE FAMOUS THREE ERRORS | NOT IN D N-4 |

Obverse 5. In this marriage, usually found *without* die sinking; but two examples are known with moderately advanced swelling between the rim and the lower curl. It is therefore probable that the 5-C marriage was an interrupted one, with the 5-D episode occurring during the interruption.

Reverse D. The famous reverse with three errors. Left stem of wreath missing; the U was first punched in upside down and then corrected, giving the effect of two I's; the fraction is $\frac{1}{000}$.

Die break variations. *Obverse:* As noted.

R.-7. Basal $7.50. 40-12 (40-20-15-12-10-8). At least nine now accounted for, eight of them in collectors' hands. Middle to upper range of R-7.

| | 219 | 6·D | First 1 Pointed THREE ERRORS REVERSE | D-156 N-6 |

Obverse 6. First 1 pointed, and with reverse D (the three errors reverse) this identifies the coin. PC below inner curve of B; JHF under the right foot of T. Date well spaced; 8 leans right.

Reverse D.

Die break variations. *Obverse:* Examples are known with die failing and sinking over ERTY, partially obliterating these letters. *Reverse:* Nearly always seen with a crack from middle

1 8 0 1

0 of fraction, touching top of first 0, through bottom of u, and curving up through n and 1 to rim. Crack from rim over t in UNITED, through t, through lowest pair of leaves on left, through ribbon and numerator to fraction line; crack connecting fraction line to first crack on the left, and to ribbon on the right; from left foot of final a to middle of adjacent c; heavy incusation or injury about lower wreath.

R-3. Basal $3. 60-40 (60-55-45-40-30-25). Lower range of R-3. The almost-common Three Errors variety. In great demand among successive generations of cent collectors.

		First 1 Pointed, 8 Leans Right	
NC-2	6·E	HEAVY RIM BREAK AT TES OF	NOT IN D N-13

Obverse 6.

Reverse E. Another minor variant from reverse A, discovered by H. C. Hines after the publication of the Newcomb monograph. This one was found a year or so earlier than the 3-B, and for it also Newcomb issued a supplement adding it to the list. Somewhat heavier and longer fraction bar than that of reverse A, with an engraver's scratch connecting the bar to the right ribbon, and with a *heavy rim break at* TES OF. The break obliterates part of the upper arm of E, the upper two-thirds of s, and extends to the right, covering part of o and ending at rim over center of F. To the left of the break, the die is sunken at the rim over AT. A fine crack connects the tops of TE; another from bottom of o runs through left tip of F to rim. Chip out of the die through c to bottom of E in CENT.

Die break variations. None seen.

R-8. Basal $12.50. 15-7 (15-8-6). Three now known, two in collectors' hands. The new discovery of this variety is a 15-coin, now owned by a famous young New Jersey collector.

		First 1 Pointed	
220	7·F	FRACTION 1/000	D-157 N-7

Obverse 7. Newcomb considered this the same die as obverse 6, but after the latter had been repaired and retooled "sufficiently to merit a new number." The lower curl has been some-

1 8 0 1

what recut, so that the first 1 is now a little further from the hair and curl than on obverse 6. The die is failing or sinking over ERTY, and there is a small rim break starting over the right arm of Y. *First 1 pointed and single reverse error.*

Reverse F. Fraction $\frac{1}{000}$. *PLLL below the center of* N. These two characteristics identify the variety.

Die break variations. *Obverse:* Found with crack from rim on the left, through curls and lower left corner of shoulder and through final 1 to rim—describing almost a perfect arc of a circle; rim break below 180, with line of impressed denticles extending from the break to point of bust; the rim break becomes heavy and extends beyond the date; letters are seen incused under the date and in field above it; traces of wreath incused before neck and behind hair. This die was mistreated. *Reverse:* Found with crack from rim over A in STATES, describing almost a perfect arc to rim between F and A; from rim through first T in STATES to join first crack midway between F and A; from rim to first crack, touching left side of O in OF; later, rim heavily broken over AM; several minor additional interconnecting cracks in this area of the coin, and some die sinking; finally, small triangular rim break above A in STATES, and two light cracks from first S and T to leaf beneath.

R-4. Basal $3. 50-30 (50-40-35-25-25-20). The rarest collectible reverse with an error in the fraction, and this also is a highly prized variety.

2 2 1

| 221 | 8·G | THE CORRECTED FRACTION | D-159
N-9 |

Obverse 8. Same die as obverse 4 but, as Newcomb says, after being set aside and then rejuvenated and remade sufficiently to merit a new number. In this marriage, it is nearly always struck up strongly and evenly.

Reverse G. The "corrected error" variety. The denominator of the fraction has a figure 1 engraved over the first of three ciphers, and both the 1 and the cipher show plainly. The first inside pair of leaves on the right is stemless. PLLL beneath center of N.

Die break variations. *Reverse:* Found with rim break extending, in its final stage, from F to cover AME; another, heavier break over STA.

[276]

1 8 0 1

R-3. Basal $2.50. 65-40 (65-55-45-40-30-25). The Corrected Fraction. Apparently in the middle range of R-3.

NC-3 $9 \cdot K$ $\dfrac{\text{Blunt 1's}}{\text{FRACTION 1/000—BLUNT STEMS}}$ NEW NOT IN NEWCOMB

Obverse 9. Same as Nos. 222 and 223. Blunt 1's, the first one away from curl.

Reverse K. Same as Reverse G of 1803, but before the fraction had been corrected. Error 1/000, as on Reverse I of 1801, but without the long point on left stem. Berry opposite center of E in ONE. CENT high above ribbon loops.

Die break variations. Both dies perfect in this marriage.

R-8. Basal $15. 8-8. Only two known, both in collectors' hands. Discovered in 1950 by Douglas Smith. The true rarity may not be as great as its present census would indicate. Both specimens were found attributed as No. 223 (Doughty 158), and the variety is deceptively similar to No. 223 since it has the same obverse and a 1/000 reverse closely resembling that of No. 223 except for the absence of the long point on the left stem. If all the readers of this description will look at the reverses of their No. 223's it is quite likely that some more NC-3's will turn up.

Perhaps this K reverse was laid aside in consternation after only a few had been struck. *Four* 1/000 reverses in a single year—not to mention Reverse G which was hastily corrected from the identical error—might have called unfavorable attention to the Engraving Department, or might even have raised the question of prohibiting rum during working hours. The offending reverse die was apparently not touched again until 1803 when it was softened (heated) and altered in the erroneous zero. In this later instance the overcut 1 is misshapen and spreads over the zero, rather unlike the similar alteration on the reverse of No. 221. This may have resulted from improper annealing of the die.

222 $9 \cdot H$ $\dfrac{\text{Blunt 1's}}{\text{FRACTION BAR TOO FAR LEFT}}$ D-162 N-10

Obverse 9. *Blunt* 1's. First 1 about 1 mm. from the curl. PC below right side of upright of B; JHF about under the right side of T. Left stand of Y defective.

[277]

1 8 0 1

Reverse H. Wide denominator; *fraction bar too far to the left and the last 0 is entirely to the right of it*—diagnostic. Point of highest leaf well to the right of S.

Die break variations. *Obverse:* Found with a small rim break over IB. Through the center of all the letters of LIBERTY, some examples show a wavy line—the edge of a line of denticles. The die is seen crumbling over the upright of R. *Reverse:* Nearly always struck weakly in the lower right central region. Sometimes T of CENT, lowest pair of leaves on the right, and right ribbon loop can only barely be made out on fine specimens.

R-1. Basal $1. 60-50 (60-60-50-45-45-40). Second commonest 1801. Weakly struck reverse, or blunted reverse die. Leaves nearly always flat.

223	9·I	Blunt 1's	D-158
		FRACTION 1/000—ELONGATED LEFT STEM	N-11

Obverse 9. In this marriage, always seen with a "cap" or slight break, above upright of R, and usually seen with heavy rim break over RT and partly over Y.

Reverse I. Again the fraction $\frac{1}{000}$ and on a third entirely different reverse. Somebody at the Mint must have skipped the grades that stress fractions. *The left stem is elongated, ending in a sharp point near the right base of* U. PLLL is to the right of right upright of N. First berry on the right very large.

Die break variations. *Obverse:* The last noted rim break progresses, becomes heavy, absorbs the tops of RT, and obliterates left arm of T. A third rim break appears, starting to the right of final 1 and ending opposite the point of the bust. This break connects with and obliterates the bust line for some distance. *Reverse:* Most of the coins show a delicate break from the rim through right side of D.

R-1. Basal $1.50. 65-55 (65-60-60-55-50-50). Commonest of the Error reverses; third commonest 1801. Highest condition census for this date.

224	10·J	Blunt 1's	D-163
		DENOMINATOR 1 00	N-12

Obverse 10. *Blunt 1's.* PC under right side of upright of B;

1 8 0 1

JHF just right of right side of upright of T. Left foot of Y very defective.

Reverse J. Recognized easily by the *very wide spacing between 1 and the first 0 of the denominator.* The two ciphers are rather close, with the second higher than the first. Left foot of T in CENT very long. PLLL just a hair left of right upright of N.

Die break variations. *Reverse:* Found with rim heavily broken over AME; crack from top of F passes over O to rim beyond; later, a light rim break appears over F.

R-1. Basal $1. 65-45 (65-60-50-45-40-35). Far the commonest 1801, yet one of the rare ones near Mint State. Both of the full Mint State coins now known are new discoveries since EAC was written. One came from the Ryder collection, one·from the Brand hoard.

TABLE 18. KEY TO 1801 CENTS

Fraction 1/000.
Three Errors—one stem to wreath, U first inverted then corrected.
  Pointed first 1 219
  Blunt first 1. LIBERTY far r.; PC under I 218
  Obv.: Blunt 1's; rev. long point on left stem 223
  Blunt 1's in date; without long point on left stem. Berry opposite center of E in ONE. CENT high above ribbon bows NC-3
  Pointed first 1 in date. Usually, shattered dies 220

Fraction 1/100 over 1/100 221

Fraction normal; blunt 1's in date.
  LIBERTY far r.; PC under I 217
  Denominator very closely spaced; LIBERTY in normal position unlike last 216
  Denominator 1 00; PSL under inner curve of D 222
  Denominator 1 00; PSL past outer curve of D 224

Fraction normal; pointed first 1 in date. Reverse like 1800.
  Low 8. Rev.: Scratch from r. end of fraction bar; heavy rim break at ES OF NC-2
  Rev.: Thin fraction bar; all N's perfectly formed. Usually, straight crack lower r.
    Obv.: PC under center of B. Usually, four wavy cracks r. of brow 213
    Obv.: Date 1 80 1; first 1 almost touches curl 214
    Obv.: Date very closely spaced, especially 180 215
  Rev.: Heavy fraction bar; N in ONE imperfect; without cracks. Heavy injury at TES OF; obv: same die as last NC-1

1 8 0 1

TABLE 19. RARITY AND VALUE: 1801 CENTS

Number	Obv.-Rev. Designation	Newcomb Number	Doughty Number	Rarity	Basal Value (Dollars)
213	1-A	1	161	3	2.
214	2-A	2	—	5	3.
215	3-A	3	—	6	4.
NC-1	3-B	14	—	8	12.50
216	4-C	8	160	2	1.50
217	5-C	5	—	7	10.
218	5-D	4	—	7	7.50
219	6-D	6	156	3	3.
NC-2	6-E	13	—	8	12.50
220	7-F	7	157	4	3.
221	8-G	9	159	3	2.50
NC-3	9-K	—	—	8	**15.**
222	9-H	10	162	1	1.
223	9-I	11	158	1	1.50
224	10-J	12	163	1	1.

1802

		1 Touches Hair, Incused Denticles Right of Date		
225	1·A	ENGRAVER'S SCRATCH AT FRACTION BAR	D-172 N-1	2 2 5

Obverse 1. *Top of 1 touches the hair above* and is very close to curl at left. This is the only 1802 obverse on which 1 touches hair. Date sharply curved, both the 1 and the 2 high. PC under center of right side of B; HWH under center of R. IB close; ERT distant. At least three, possibly four *blurred lines of impressed denticles* are to be seen through and under the date and to the right of it; across point of bust, and four or five millimeters to the right.

Reverse A. Engraver's scratch from left end of fraction bar almost to left ribbon. PHL (point of highest leaf) well to the right of s. O in OF low.

Die break variations. *Obverse:* Found with rim broken below 1802, but in this marriage usually seen without the break. *Reverse:* Nearly always seen with crack from rim over F through O to bottom of S, where it divides, one branch running to center of E and the other ending in field below T. Newcomb had not seen one without this crack, but three have now been reported, including a specimen in the ANS collection. Mr. Downing has an example in which the crack is very heavy.

R-4. Basal $1.50. 65-60 (65-65-65-60-55-50). The 1 touches the hair. Seen typically on rather rough planchets. One example is known with the described reverse crack now developed into a

1 8 0 2

large rim break obliterating most of E in STATES, all of S, and nearly all of O in OF.

| 226 | 1·B | 1 Touches Hair, Break Below 802
LOWEST INSIDE PAIR ON RIGHT
STEMLESS | D-173
N-2 |

Obverse 1. *Rim break always present below* 802. Most of the injury caused by the rows of impressed denticles now repaired or smoothed out.

Reverse B. *Lowest inside pair of leaves on right stemless.* PHL just left of center of S. The loops of the bow are incomplete. C of CENT not quite touching leaf on the left.

Die break variations. *Obverse:* Found with delicate crack from center of forehead to rim, touching right arm of Y; delicate crack curving from rim opposite chin to end of nose and (later) continuing along nose, through forehead and hair to rim over B. *Reverse:* Found with delicate crack from near top of F through tops of AMER.

R-3. Basal $1. 65-55 (65-60-60-55-55-55). Rarity underestimated in EAC. Probably in the upper range of R-3.

| NC-1 | 2·B | Crack from B across Hair and Ear | NOT IN D
N-3 |

Obverse 2. Very similar to preceding obverse. The 1 *does not quite touch* the hair, and both 1 and 2 are a little lower. PC between inner and outer curves of B; HWH below right side of upright of R. LIB wider and RT closer than on obverse 1. On the five examples I have seen, there is a crack from rim through right side of B, through hair and ear to neck. On one of these coins the crack is heavy and is continued down across the bust to the rim just to the right of 2. This last is the specimen illustrated by Newcomb.

Reverse B. In this marriage, the crack noted is present.

Die break variations. As noted.

R-6. Basal $3. 30-15 (30-25-15-15-12-12). About 16 now known, including two in ANS. Only three were known in collectors' hands when EAC was written. One perfect die obverse has

1 8 0 2

turned up. It is difficult to account for the run of new discoveries in this variety. A 10-coin today has a book rating of $30. Had none of the new *NC*-1's been discovered, such a coin would now have a book rating of 10×$10×3, or $300. This is a very easy variety to recognize, with its conspicuous die crack usually slanting across the head and bust. Perhaps that is the reason so many new ones have been found since the publication of EAC. If such is in fact the case it may follow that even yet, on the whole, examination of some of the dates among the Early Cents has been relatively superficial and incomplete. This would be particularly true of such a date as 1802, and of coins below the grade of Fine. Perhaps these *NC*-1's have turned up because, with their now familiar die break, they practically announce themselves; and it may be that more of the "hard ones" are still there but unannounced. The recent history of the *NC*-1 of this date may indicate that more rare cents are still in hiding than would ordinarily be supposed.

| 227 | 3·B | R Sits Atop HWH | D-174 N-4 |

Obverse 3. *The upright of the* R *sits squarely atop and almost touches HWH.* This is diagnostic—not seen on any other 1802 obverse. 1 close to both hair and curl. Left stand of Y defective. Heavy incusation marks from wreath show under chin, behind hair above and below knot, and in front of forehead (this coin has been known as the cobweb variety). PC below inner curve of B; HWH under center of upright of R. Dotlike defect under I.

Reverse B. The crack noted is heavier, now extending from top of F through AMERIC.

Die break variations. *Reverse:* On some examples the diagonal of N in CENT has begun to crumble.

R-3. Basal $1. (70-55-55-50-50-45). The R sits atop the highest wave of hair.

| 228 | 3·C | FRACTION 1/000 | D-164 N-6 |

Obverse 3. In this marriage, the incusations about the face and back of the head are not present. Either these have been smoothed and repaired, or it is an earlier marriage of the die,

[283]

1 8 0 2

probably the latter. The dotlike defect under I is present.

Reverse C. Same as Reverse I of 1801—fraction $\frac{1}{000}$. Here seen with crack from rim through right side of D to the leaves. This is the only example of the incorrect fraction to be encountered among the 1802's.

Die break variations. *Obverse:* Sometimes but not always seen with flaking of the die or roughness before the face and back of the head. *Reverse:* Found with crack continuing through E in ONE, through right wreath to rim between F and A; crack from rim over first T in STATES through that letter and to the right through upper leaves of both branches, through O in OF to rim; other faint cracks seen in final stages.

R-2. Basal $1. 65-50 (65-55-50-50-50-45). A rather common coin but in demand as a type because of the 1/000 fraction.

2 2 9

		8 Low, Leaning Right. Arc Crack, B to Y (Usually)	
229	4 · B	LOWEST INSIDE PAIR ON RIGHT STEMLESS	NOT IN D N-5

Obverse 4. LIBERTY *high above the hair.* IB and RT almost touching. 8 *low and leaning markedly to the right.* 02 close. PC under center of right side of B; HWH just right of center of upright of R. *Usually seen with arc crack from rim above* B, curving through E to bottom of RT, then up through middle of Y to rim. Traces of wreath seen incused in front of face down to chin.

Reverse B. Now with an additional light crack from left top of R to rim.

Die break variations. *Obverse:* Found with an additional crack through tops of LIB and extending 3 or 4 mm. into the left field.

R-5. Basal $2. 70-40 (70-60-45-35-30-30). Probably in the middle range of R-5.

		8 Low, Leaning Right	
NC-2	4 · D	ME JOINED AT THEIR FEET	NOT IN D N-7

Obverse 4. The crack through ERTY is present on the single example seen of this variety.

Reverse D. ME *joined solidly at their feet,* and on most speci-

1 8 0 2

mens AM seem to touch, although on Mint State coins these two letters can be seen to be separate. ONE high in the wreath. C in CENT low. N of CENT has imperfect right top. PHL under left side of S. Foot of N in UNITED imperfect, and PLLL is immediately beneath it.

Die break variations. None.

R-8. Basal $10. 50-12 (50-20-4). Three now known, two in collectors' hands. Unique when we last reported, in EAC. Discovery of one more will make it a collectible coin. The 20-coin now has a book rating of $600; the 4-coin, $100.

230   5·D   <u>1 Distant From Hair and Curl</u>   D-171
               CRACKS THROUGH MER   N-8

Obverse 5. Date evenly and a little more closely spaced than usual. 1 comparatively distant from both hair and curl. PC under inner curve of B; HWH under right edge of upright of R. Usually seen with light crack from top of L curving down through I to bottoms of BE, then up through R to top of T.

Reverse D. In this marriage, always seen with *delicate crack from middle of right upright of* M through top of E to rim over R; another from center of E through upper part of R to rim.

Die break variations. *Obverse:* Additional crack from point of bust to rim about opposite mouth. Roughness develops near the point of the bust, in the field above, and about 180. *Reverse:* Additional crack from rim through first S and stand of T, touching tip of leaf below A, and curving close to tip of highest leaf to rim above O in OF; crack from tops of OF to rim between F and A; from near first S to base of second leaf from top of left branch; other minor cracks in final stages.

R-2. Basal $0.75. 65-55 (65-60-55-55-50-50). Not far from the border of R-1, but difficult to find in the highest grades of condition.

2 3 0

231   6·E   <u>STEMLESS WREATH, WITHOUT DOUBLE FRACTION BAR</u>   D-165
                              N-9

Obverse 6. Y has defective left foot. PC below space between B and E; HWH beneath center of R.

Reverse E. *Stemless wreath.* All T's lack the right feet of their stands. PHL just left of right side of s. The only other stemless wreath 1802 reverse (L) has a double fraction bar and an extra s touching PHL.

Die break variations. *Obverse:* Usually found with crack through bottoms of 802 to rim 5 mm. right of 2; from rim through R and base of T and under Y, where it is generally joined by a branch crack passing 1 mm. from end of nose and curving to rim opposite angle of jaw; from this branch, a fork breaks down toward the rim at a point opposite the mouth; sometimes seen with double struck profile, most conspicuous at the chin. *Reverse:* Found in its early stage with a saw-tooth line through bottoms of ERICA to top of first cipher in fraction, and with die cut over AM, but these defects are later smoothed out. Found with faint crack from 100 to top of U and later to rim; from rim through E in UNITED to wreath, and up through right stand of A and left top of T to rim; from rim to wreath, touching E in STATES; other minor cracks.

232

R-1. Basal $0.75. 65-50 (65-60-60-50-50-45). Second commonest 1802, but the Stemless Wreath commands a premium as a type coin.

232	7·F	T Cut Over Y	D-168
		DENTICLES BETWEEN WREATH AND AMERICA	N-10

Obverse 7. *The* T *is cut over a* Y. Light incusations or defects usually seen about TY. Light rim break usually seen in the denticles under 18. PC below right edge of upright of B; HWH under left edge of upright of R.

Reverse F. Easily recognized by an *incused line of denticles which is always seen between the wreath and* AMERICA. NT of CENT fused at the top, and a small tag hangs from right pendant of T. Right feet of all T's defective. Fraction bar long, almost touching both ribbons. PHL right of s.

Die break variations. *Obverse:* Found with defects noted at TY and under 18, and with defects partially smoothed away. *Reverse:* Found with crack from top of first T to rim over A; from rim between s and o to top of OF; from rim over A to ME; with rim heavily broken over ATE; other light, minor cracks; seen with incusation of bust in upper part of reverse.

1 8 0 2

R-1. Basal $0.50. 65-55 (65-60-60-55-55-50). Far the commonest 1802. It has an attractive series of reverse die breaks.

233   7·G   T Cut Over Y
NO INCUSED DENTICLES ON REVERSE   D-167   N-11

Obverse 7. Light rim break in the milling under 18 now seen clearly.

Reverse G. PHL just right of left side of s. All the N's are perfect—unusual for this date. T's lack their right feet, and T in UNITED leans left. ME joined at the base and AM almost joined. C in CENT and leaf overlap considerably.

Die break variations. *Obverse:* A light rim break appears also under 02. *Reverse:* Found with crack from left upright of U through left ribbon to knot; from rim over O, through O and through the topmost and the lowest outside berries on the right, and through I of AMERICA to rim; other minor, light cracks.

2 3 4

R-4. Basal $1.50. 65-40 (65-55-50-40-30-25). Probably in the middle range of R-4; rarity overestimated in EAC, although we still can account for only four examples above VF-30.

234   8·H   The Injured LIBERTY Variety,
Rim Break Over B   NOT IN D   N-12

Obverse 8. LIBERTY well to the right. PC below left edge of upright of B; HWH beneath right edge of E. Date wider than usual, more curved, and the 2 high. This die was heavily injured by contact with a reverse die. Parts of fraction, ribbons and leaves are incused behind and over LIBERTY, and the lower reverse also shows many traces of injury from the blow. *Rim break always seen over* B, and from the break and the injuries the variety is easily identified.

Reverse H. *Only four berries on right branch, and no inside berry opposite* T *in* CENT. N of CENT sprawls to the right and is united to T at the top. AM united at the bottom, and ME also touch. PHL left of center of S. Injuries to the die from M of AMERICA to N of UNITED. PSL under right edge of upright of D.

Die break variations. *Obverse:* Found with heavy rim break over BERT—a progression from the break over B. *Reverse:*

1 8 0 2

Found with crumbling of the die along the lower edges of bottom pair of leaves on right branch, and along right stem.

R-6. Basal $3. 70-55 (70-70-65-60-50-30). The only R-6 variety in the whole series of Early Cents with two 70-coins. Three or four are known without the rim break over B, and on one of these the injuries at ERTY are very slight or negligible. Called R-5 in EAC, this variety now appears to belong in the lower range of R-6.

		Injured at RTY	
235	*9·H*	FOUR BERRIES ON RIGHT SIDE	D-178 N-13

Obverse 9. *The 8 a little low.* IB very close. PC beneath center of B; HWH beneath left edge of upright of R. This die also has been injured slightly. Delicate incusations are seen above RTY and to the right, as well as beneath RT.

Reverse H. The crumbling about right stem and lowest leaves on right is well advanced.

Die break variations. *Obverse:* A heavy rim break over RTY develops early, obliterating most of the evidence of earlier injury. Later, a crack from the right rim extends in a slight curve to the neck. *Reverse:* Found with crack from rim between E and S through right branch and I to rim.

R-5. Basal $2. 70-40 (70-60-55-40-40-35). Probably in the lower range of R-5; R-4 in EAC. Despite the existence of a 70-coin (Newcomb collection) and a moderately high condition census, this is a great rarity above VF. Two of the six condition census coins are in ANS.

		02 Very Close, 18 Lean Right	
236	*10·H*	FOUR BERRIES ON RIGHT BRANCH	D-175 N-14

Obverse 10. LIBERTY rather low, R close to the hair. *Close date, with 02 very close.* The 1 and 8 lean a little to the right. The 2 is thicker than usual, its curl almost touching its diagonal. PC beneath outer curve of B; HWH beneath center of R. Back of the lower curls there is usually, although not always, a sinking of the die, or swell on the coin.

Reverse H.

1 8 0 2

Die break variations. *Obverse:* Found with delicate crack from rim below 1 through base of figure and through curl at left into the field. *Reverse:* Additional cracks in this its final marriage. From rim between F and A to top outside berry; from top of S, touching left foot of adjacent T, through point of leaf under A, to join the crack between E and S; from rim through right tips of E in AMERICA to wreath; finally, heavy rim break over STA, and a number of other minor fine cracks.

R-1. Basal $0.50. 70-60 (70-65-60-60-55-55). Fourth commonest 1802 and probably in the upper range of R-1, not R-2. Highest condition census found in 1802. Many of the "uncirculated" coins offered of this date are 236's.

237   *11·1*   Widest Date of the Year   D-170
                         AND THE LARGEST BERRIES   N-15

Obverse 11. *The 1 more distant from both hair and curl than on any other 1802 die. Also the widest date of the year.* LIB close, BER distant. LIBERTY high. PC beneath center of B; HWH beneath left side of upright of R. Nearly always seen with a delicate crack starting at right top of I and curving in an arc through bottoms of ERT to the fork of Y. Have seen only one example without this crack.

Reverse I. *All berries conspicuously large.* Fraction bar ends in a short engraver's scratch at the right. N's and T's all perfectly formed. Dotlike defect on right side of both ribbon ends, at level just above the numerator. PHL just left of center of S.

Die break variations. *Reverse:* Nearly always seen with crack from rim through N of UNITED, then curving through lowest left leaf and crossing the ribbons above the knot to right wreath stem (have seen only one example without this crack); light crack connecting NITED at the tops; from rim through right side of M to leaf beneath; from rim through bottom of I to lowest right pair of leaves; from rim to left top of first T in STATES; from base of top pair of leaves on right, through upper left serif of E in ONE, through N of CENT and the ribbon loop to join the first mentioned crack; from rim through C of AMERICA to leaf directly beneath. Other minor cracks in the terminal stages of the die.

[289]

1 8 0 2

R-2. Basal $0.75. 65-55 (65-60-60-55-50-50). Lower range of R-2 but not quite R-1, and another difficult one to find in Mint State. ANS has seven examples, six of them AU-50 or better. A hoard like that makes a considerable dent in the condition census list. However, the 65 and one of the 60's are in collectors' hands.

		Widest Date, LIBERTY Injured	NOT IN D
238	11·J	FOUR BERRIES ON RIGHT BRANCH	N-16

Obverse 11. The die has now been injured, and the crack through BERTY is obscured by several rows of impressed denticles running through LIBERTY and (on some specimens) along the rim to opposite the chin. Traces of wreath seen in front of neck and under chin.

Reverse J. *Four berries only on right branch, and no inside berry opposite E of ONE*—diagnostic for the die. M shows recutting above left top and above left foot. PHL just right of center of s. Always seen with delicate cracks from foot of N in UNITED, touching bottom of U, to left ribbon; from upper right corner of U, through U, through left ribbon end and curving across last cipher to the rim; another, curving up from fraction bar through right ribbon and out its end to rim; from right stand of A to right ribbon; from rim above E in AMERICA, touching E and R, through the three lowest leaves on the right, through right stem and to right ribbon.

Die break variations. *Reverse:* Found with additional crack through top of STATES, connecting all the letters; from rim over first T in STATES, curving down through TATE, touching top of last S and to the rim; other minor cracks and branches.

R-6. Basal $3. 40-15 (40-25-20-15-15-12). Perhaps in the upper range of R-6, although certainly 15 or 18 of them are known. Of much the same rarity and condition census as *NC*-1 (Now Collectible 1).

1 8 0 2

239 *12·K*
1 Very Close to Hair and Curl; Prominent Crack Before Face (Usually)
FOUR BERRIES ON RIGHT BRANCH
D-177
N-17

Obverse 12. The 1 nearly touches the hair and is close to the curl. 180 rather widely spaced, 02 closer. Stand of Y perfect. PC beneath the center of the right side of B; HWH below right side of upright of R. Usually, but not always, seen with prominent crack from rim through R and forelock to rim opposite the mouth; another from rim through E and hair joins the first crack in front of forehead; a third fainter crack from base of Y extends downward and to the right a short way paralleling the first crack. This coin with its cracks is an old familiar friend to cent lovers.

Reverse K. *Four berries on the right branch, and no inside berry opposite* T *of* CENT. Right stand missing from all the T's. PSL under center of right side of D. PHL just left of center of S. Numerator high, much closer to ribbon knot than to fraction bar.

Die break variations. *Obverse:* Found with a fourth crack, from tip of nose curving toward rim but just before it meets the first crack it turns downward to rim near point of bust. *Reverse:* Found with a wide line of blurred denticles through RICA and 100. Found cracked from rim above AT, the crack curving down to top of N in ONE, through right top of E, through wreath and right foot of first A in AMERICA to rim. Found with a new line of impressed denticles from bottom of 1 in denominator to top of U.

R-3. Basal $1. 70-40 (70-55-50-40-35-30). Upper range of R-3 and perhaps almost R-4. Usually seen with the prominent slanting cracks in front of the face which render the variety an old familiar friend.

240 *13·K*
Diagonal Crack, Lower Right Field
FOUR BERRIES ON RIGHT BRANCH
D-176
N-18

Obverse 13. *Usually seen with crack from rim* below the point of the bust, through the end of the bust, and diagonally across the field to rim opposite the eye. PC beneath center of upright

[291]

1 8 0 2

of B; HWH between E and R. *Heavy injury from wreath shows in front of neck and below the ribbon knot.*

Reverse K. Now found with a new crack from rim through left ribbon end, across left stem, wreath, and loop, through E of CENT to join first crack at top of N in ONE.

Die break variations. *Obverse* and *Reverse* cracks become heavier, and heavy incusation of head sometimes seen on lower reverse.

R-6. Basal $3. 40-25 (40-35-30-30-20-15). Lower range of R-6; earlier rating, R-5. There may be just about 30 of them, which is the limit for R-6. Three or four examples are now known without any trace of the hitherto distinctive obverse die crack.

2 4 1

241 14·L 1 Practically Touches Hair
STEMLESS WREATH,
DOUBLE FRACTION BAR   D-166 N-19

Obverse 14. LIBERTY *well to the right.* PC beneath left edge of upright of B; HWH between E and R nearer to E, and almost touching both letters. JHF under left edge of upright of T. The top of 1 almost touches the hair. In the field near the rim, in front of the face, the letters MERIC are usually seen faintly incused.

Reverse L. *Stemless wreath.* Half of an S appears beneath last S of STATES and just touches PHL, which is under the center of the "real" S. An extra line below the fraction bar touches the top of 1 in the denominator. O much lower than F. Highest berry on the right on a very long stem and touches tip of adjacent leaf.

Die break variations. *Reverse:* Found with light crack from right top of F to rim near adjacent A. This crack develops into a heavy rim break extending 7 mm. to the right from above center of adjacent O. Crack from rim between D and S to leaf below first S. Several minor cracks develop around TATE and finally an additional rim break appears over these letters.

R-1. Basal $0.75. 65-55 (65-65-55-50-50-45). Third commonest 1802. The Stemless Wreath commands a premium as a type coin.

1 8 0 2

242 **14·M** 1 Practically Touches Hair / THREE STEMLESS BERRIES   D-169 / N-20

Obverse 14. In this marriage, the incusation marks near the right rim are not seen. Either it was an earlier marriage than 14-L, or the damage has been repaired. The injuries from the wreath are plainly seen.

Reverse M. Right stem ends in a point, the left has an *engraver's scratch extending through the bottom of* U *and into the letter. Lowest outside berry on the left and both lower outside berries on the right are stemless*—diagnostic. PHL just right of center of s. Right feet of T's defective, and this die is distinctive for the date in that the leaf adjacent to T in CENT is at least a third of a mm. clear of the base of the T (although usually connected to it by a fine die break). Always found with crack connecting tops of ERICA.

Die break variations. *Reverse:* Found with crack from rim over N in UNITED extending in a short arc through tops of NITE and back to rim.

R-3. Basal $1. 70-50 (70-65-55-55-40-40). Lower range of R-3. Almost an R-2 coin, as it was rated in EAC, but another difficult one to find in nice condition. We can now account for only four above the 40-mark, and one of these is in ANS.

Taken as a whole, the cents of this year are commoner, probably, than those of any other date before 1816. Among the twenty known varieties there are only two unobtainable rarities (NC-1 and NC-2), and these two involve but a single die (Obverse 2) which is not duplicated on commoner coins. Yet the 1802's have been largely neglected by collectors, perhaps because they contain only three varieties which may be said to possess dramatic peculiarities—the 000 denominator, which is a carry-over from 1801; the stemless wreath; and the stemless wreath with extra s and extra fraction bar. According to the Mint records, 3,435,100 cents were coined during the calendar year 1802, a record not broken until 1817.

1 8 0 2

TABLE 20. KEY TO 1802 CENTS

Fraction 1/000..228
Stemless wreath; double fraction bar, extra s under final s in STATES........241
Stemless wreath; single fraction bar, no extra s......................231
Four berries right; lacks inner berry next to E in ONE..................238
Four berries right; lacks inner berry opposite T in CENT.
    Very high numerator; PSL under curve of D. Obv.: PC under upright
        of B. Usually, long straight crack up from bust..................240
    Same rev. Obv.: PC under curve of B. Usually, cracks from ER
        through brow to border.....................................239
    PSL under upright of D; crumbling on r. stem.
        Obv.: PC under upright of B; usually, rim break over B..........234
        Obv.: PC under center of B: usually, injuries over RTY.............235
        Obv.: 02 close together; PC under outer r. curve of B..............236
Fraction bar touches or practically touches both ribbons. T in LIBERTY
        over a Y...232
Very wide denominator; die scratch from left stem runs into U.........242
Widest date, largest berries. Point from r. end of fraction bar..........237
In date 8 markedly low and leaning r. Rev.: Incomplete loops to ribbons...229
Same obverse. Rev.: PSL under upright of D; leaf almost touches top of
    E in ONE...NC-2
Rev.: Same as last. Date normally spaced..........................230
Rev.: Similar to last, but leaf not so close to top of E in ONE. Obv.: T cut
    over Y..233
In date 1 touches hair; rows of impressed denticles r. of date, sometimes
    a rim break at 802.
    Rev.: PHL r. of final s; scratch from left end of fraction bar.........225
    Rev.: Incomplete ribbon loops..................................226
Same reverse as last. Obv.: R practically touches HWH; 1 8 spaced apart.
    Usually, numerous incusations................................227
Same reverse as last. Obv.: 1 does not quite touch hair; 18 close together.
    Usually, cracked across, from B through hair and ear, eventually
    to rim r. of 2...NC-1

1 8 0 2

TABLE 21. RARITY AND VALUE: 1802 CENTS

Number	Obv.-Rev. Designation	Newcomb Number	Doughty Number	Rarity	Basal Value (Dollars)
225	1-A	1	172	4	1.50
226	1-B	2	173	3	1.
NC-1	2-B	3	—	6	3.
227	3-B	4	174	3	1.
228	3-C	6	164	2	1.
229	4-B	5	—	5	2.
NC-2	4-D	7	—	8	10.
230	5-D	8	171	2	.75
231	6-E	9	165	1	.75
232	7-F	10	168	1	.50
233	7-G	11	167	4	1.50
234	8-H	12	—	6	3.
235	9-H	13	178	5	2.
236	10-H	14	175	1	.50
237	11-I	15	170	2	.75
238	11-J	16	—	6	3.
239	12-K	17	177	3	1.
240	13-K	18	176	6	3.
241	14-L	19	166	1	.75
242	14-M	20	169	3	1.

1803

243   *1·A*   STEMLESS WREATH, DOUBLE FRACTION BAR   D-180 N-1

Obverse 1. 1 close to both hair and curl, but not touching. Close date, corner of 3 almost touching drapery. PC just left of inner curve of B; HWH below center of upright of R. Usually seen with rim break to the right of Y, which at first is very light but later extends over TY, and becomes heavy.

Reverse A. This is reverse L of 1802. *Stemless wreath, extra* s *under final* s *of* STATES, *and extra fraction bar.*

Die break variations. *Obverse:* Rim break as noted. *Reverse:* Often seen with row of faintly impressed denticles through ERICA; later these are smoothed out and then the tops of ERIC are weak. Found with crack from rim below point of bust to bottom of 3, to drapery on the right. In this marriage, the reverse is always found *without* the cracks noted for the 1802 marriage, demonstrating, as Newcomb points out, that this particular 1803 cent must have been struck before some of the 1802 cents were struck. The same thing is encountered four or five times among the early cents, and probably indicates that when a number of dies were still in good condition and not worn out, the transition from one *date* to the next was sometimes accomplished more or less gradually, with occasional returning to a die of the earlier date, perhaps in order to "use it up." They had to be thrifty at the Mint, especially with Congress in session almost next door, and many a Congressman looking for something to "correct."

R-4. Basal $2. 65-45 (65-60-60-45-30-30). Middle or lower range of R-4. Has been scarce of late. The Stemless Wreath and the Double Fraction Bar carry a premium.

1 8 0 3

244   2·B   Wide, Curved Date with the 3 in the Drapery / 1 DISTANT FROM FIRST CIPHER   NOT IN D / N-2

Obverse 2. *Right corner of 3 imbedded in the drapery. Wide, curved date. Top of hair left unfinished.* No point to the curl, and HWH an incomplete outline whose top, if finished, would have been under the upright of R. JHF even with right foot of T.

Reverse B. PHL just left of right side of S; PSL under right edge of curve of D; PLO (point of the outer leaf in the cluster of three under O in OF) under inner right curve of O. 1 distant from first cipher in fraction. PLLL just left of right upright of N. Left ribbon double cut along left edge near its end.

Die break variations. None seen. Obverse always shows injury marks from wreath under chin and in front of neck.

R-5. Basal $2. 55-35 (55-55-40-25-25-20). Mid-range R-5; rarity underestimated in EAC, as was in fact the case with the first half dozen of these 1803's. The varieties of 1803 are on the whole a little rarer than those of 1802.

245   3·C   The Unicorn Variety, Wide, Curved Date With the 3 in the Drapery   D-189 / N-3

Obverse 3. Same die as Obverse 2, but with top of hair finished and face retouched. PC now under center of right side of B; HWH under center of upright of R. Heavy traces of wreath seen in front of neck and forehead. *One of these injury marks protrudes into the field like a horn from the center of the forehead,* and this has led to the nickname "Unicorn" variety—an excellent mnemonic symbol. Slight crack connects tops of IB.

Reverse C. Reverse M of 1802, here showing the most advanced cracks noted, indicating that in *this* instance the 1803 marriage followed rather than preceded the 1802 marriage.

Die break variations. *Reverse:* In addition to cracks noted, found with a small triangular rim break over N in UNITED, and (later) with rim heavily broken down over RICA.

R-4. Basal $1.50. 70-55 (70-60-60-60-55-50). "Unicorn" variety. Lower range of R-4.

1 8 0 3

246   4·D   THE HIGH NUMERATOR VARIETY   D-181 N-4

Obverse 4. 1 close to curl and very close to hair above, although not touching. Corner of 3 almost touching drapery. T *and* Y *have defective right feet.* PC under center of right side of B; HWH under right edge of upright of R; JHF midway under TY.

Reverse D. *The high numerator.* The numerator is about its own height above the fraction bar, and close to ribbon knot. PHL under center of S; PSL under center of right side of D; PLO under inner left curve of O; PLLL just left of right upright of N.

Die break variations. *Obverse:* Found perfect, and with lump under chin which gradually increases in size and extends to junction of chin with neck. *Reverse:* Found perfect, and with crack from rim to left of first S through tops of STA. Later, the rim becomes heavily broken over STA.

R-4. Basal $1.50. 55-40 (55-50-50-40-30-30). Middle or upper range of R-4. Almost a rare coin according to recent experience.

247   4·E   The Mumps Obverse / SHORT FRACTION BAR   D-182 N-5

Obverse 4. In this marriage, always seen with *conspicuous lump under jaw.* Has been called the "mumps" variety.

Reverse E. *Fraction bar only 2 mm. in length.* Left stem ends in a point. *A peculiar saw-tooth line runs from end of right ribbon through* 100 *to top of* U. PHL between center and right side of S; PLS under center of right side; PLO under inner right curve; PLLL just right of center of N. The second inside berry on the right is opposite the top of T—distinctive of reverses E and F.

Die break variations. *Reverse:* Found with crack from rim below left ribbon to top of U, and from rim over N to right top of NIT.

R-5. Basal $2. 60-40 (60-50-50-45-35-30). Probably in the lower range of R-5, but certainly R-5. Rated R-4 in EAC. The first Mumps Obverse.

1 8 0 3

248   *4·F*   Mumps Obverse / LONG FRACTION BAR   NOT IN D / N-6

Obverse 4. In this marriage, always seen with lump noted under jaw, and also with a very small lump on forelock, just above JHF.

Reverse F. Long fraction bar, with a fine parallel line 0.5 mm. above it. PHL under center of s; PSL under center of letter; PLO under the inner left curve; PLLL just right of center of N. *First inside pair of leaves on right stemless.*

Die break variations. *Reverse:* Found with crack from rim above left side of M *running along tops of* MERI.

R-5. Basal $2.50. 55-20 (55-30-25-20-15-15). Upper range of R-5, and not impossibly an R-6.

249   *4·G*   Mumps Obverse / THE CORRECTED FRACTION   D-179 / N-7   2 5 0

Obverse 4. Lump under jaw now a little larger.

Reverse G. Corrected error in the fraction, $\frac{1}{100}$ over $\frac{1}{000}$, as on reverse G of 1801, although not the same die. The cipher is seen plainly beneath the 1. PHL under right side of s; PSL under right edge of D; PLO under center of right side of O.

Die break variations. *Obverse:* Found with crack from rim at right of 3 extending over point of bust to rim. This crack progresses and later the rim becomes heavily broken, involving the end of the bust.   *Reverse:* Found with crack from rim over E through tops of RIC, and later the rim becomes heavily broken over RIC.

R-4. Basal $2. 65-50 (65-60-60-50-45-35). Lower range of R-4. Corrected Fraction variety. This is the reverse that first appeared with NC-3 of 1801.

250   *5·H*   The Farthest 1 and 3 / MEDIUM FRACTION BAR   NOT IN D / N-8

Obverse 5. 18 close. *The 1 farther from the hair and the 3 farther from the drapery (each about 0.5 mm. distant) than on any other 1803.* PC between inner and outer curves of B; HWH under center of upright of R; JHF under right foot of T.

Reverse H. Medium or moderately short fraction bar. O in OF low and tipped to left; I in UNITED tipped to left. Numerator

1 8 0 3

midway between fraction bar and knot. PSL under outer curve; PHL under center; PLO under outer left curve.

Die break variations. None seen.

R-4. Basal $1.50. 70-65 (70-70-65-65-65-65). One of the most beautiful coins of the year and one of the three varieties most frequently seen in Mint State. Upper range of R-4 but probably not R-5.

		The Farthest 1 and 3	
NC-1	5·S	WIDEST DENOMINATOR	NOT IN D N-24

Obverse 5.

Reverse S. Easily recognized by three characteristics: (1) Small fraction with the widest denominator of the year. (2) PSL farther to the left than on any other 1803. (3) OF much nearer to first A than to last s. PSL under left edge of upright; PHL between E and s (also diagnostic); PLO under outer left curve.

Die break variations. *Reverse:* On one of the ten examples known, a light crack from rim above D connects tops of NITE.

R-7. Basal $6. 50-15 (50-25-20-15-10-8). Now near the lower range of R-7, with about ten in collectors' hands and the 50-coin in ANS. Only three were known before EAC was published.

		The Farthest 1 and 3	
251	5·I	SHORT FRACTION BAR	D-190 N-9

Obverse 5. In this marriage, always seen with a slight swelling under the chin, and a more extensive one under the lowest curl.

Reverse I. *Fraction bar only 2 mm. long.* Last s recut on right side. A short cut in the die connects outside pair of leaves under M with wreath stem. PSL under center; PHL just left of right side; PLO right of o and under left side of F—diagnostic.

Die break variations. *Reverse:* Crack from rim between D and s to wreath, curves to near highest left leaf, then turns right and crosses right wreath to rim between F and A; crack through tops of NE in ONE to berry at right; through tops of NT in CENT, across right wreath to right upright of M. Later, heavy crack from rim through left side of last s to near tip of

1 8 0 3

terminal left leaf, and other minor branch cracks and extensions.

R-2. Basal $0.75. 65-60 (65-65-60-60-50-50). Probably lower range of R-2; called R-1 in EAC.

		03 Close, Moderately Wide Date; Crack Through Bottom of Date (Usually)	
252	6·H		D-186 N-10

Obverse 6. Date moderately wide. 03 *very close*, 1 8 0 *distant*. LIB almost touching. Nearly always seen with *crack through bottoms of the figures of date*. PC below center of upright of B; HWH midway E and R; JHF beneath center of T.

Reverse H.

Die break variations. *Obverse:* The perfect die is rare. Crack usually found through bottom of date as noted. As this crack progresses, it continues left about 2 mm. and then curves down to rim beneath lowest curl. Another crack from left side of 1 touches lowest curl and continues to rim at left. LIBE connected at top by delicate crack which starts from rim over right edge of E; crack from end of bust to rim 4 mm. above. Later, rim heavily broken, the break covering part of lowest curl and lower half of 1, and touching bottom of 8. *Reverse:* Found with crack from rim through E in UNITED to wreath, later curving up through N in ONE to right wreath, to right side of O in OF, to rim. Found with incusation marks of bust at TES OF and in the left wreath.

R-2. Basal $0.75. 65-50 (65-60-60-50-50-40). About a midrange R-2.

		Close Date, 3 Touches Drapery	
253	7·J	"PERIOD" AFTER DENOMINATOR	D-183 N-11

Obverse 7. *Corner of 3 touches drapery.* 03 *close.* 1 comparatively distant from hair and curl. PC between inner and outer curves of B; HWH under right edge of upright of R; JHF between T and Y. Usually, although not quite always, a delicate crack from rim right of 3 runs diagonally up to the bust.

[301]

1 8 0 3

Examples without the crack are rare, and were not known to Newcomb when his monograph was written.

Reverse J. Period-like defect on right side of last cipher, and engraver's scratch 1 mm. long at end of right stem. PSL under left side of curve; PHL just left of center; PLO under inner left curve (incorrectly given in Newcomb as center right curve).

Die break variations. *Obverse:* Found with break connecting bottoms of 180 with the rim and the break extends below lowest curl. *Reverse:* Found perfect although rare so. Usually found with crack from rim at left of first s, passing in an arc through ST, under AT, and up through E to rim; crack from rim right of D to left wreath, through pair of leaves below first s, along stem and out the end of terminal leaf through last s to rim; TED connected lightly through tops; other faint cracks and branches in late stages.

R-2. Basal $0.75. 65-50 (65-60-55-50-50-45). Perhaps near the lower range of R-2.

254　8·K　Wide Date, 3 Touches Drapery　D-191
FRACTION BAR TOO FAR RIGHT　N-12

Obverse 8. *Wide date. Corner of 3 touches drapery.* 03 rather close, 1 8 0 distant, 1 slants a little to the right. RTY higher than LIBE. PC under inner curve of B; HWH under center of upright of R; JHF under right edge of upright of T.

Reverse K. Fraction line long and too far to the right, covering last 0 but not the 1. Always seen with light traces of incused hair from obverse, extending from lowest leaves on left, touching base of U and through fraction to end of right ribbon and final A. PSL under right edge; PHL just left of right side; PLO under center.

Die break variations. *Obverse:* Found perfect, and with light crack from rim through right side of 3 across drapery and neck to curl on neck; crack from same point on rim, running to right along end of bust to rim 3 mm. above. This crack becomes heavy and finally a massive rim break appears, involving the end of the bust.

R-1. Basal $0.50. 70-65 (70-70-70-70-65-65). Fourth commonest 1803. One of the two commonest in Mint State.

[302]

1 8 0 3

255 *9·K* $\dfrac{\text{03 Close, Very Wide Date}}{\text{FRACTION BAR TOO FAR RIGHT}}$ D-187 N-13

Obverse 9. 1 8 0 *very widely spaced, with* 03 *close.* Corner of 3 close to drapery but not touching. *Right feet of both* T *and* Y *missing, as well as part of left foot of* Y. PC between inner and outer curves of B; HWH under right edge of upright of R· JHF under the absent right foot of T.

Reverse K.

Die break variations. *Obverse:* Seen with a small period-like break under upright of B. *Reverse:* Crack from rim left of first S through tops of ST, past top of A and to rim between A and T. This crack develops into a heavy rim break over STA. Light crack also seen from rim over left side of E in AMERICA through tops of M.

R-1. Basal $0.50. 65-60 (65-65-60-60-55-50). Apparently third commonest of the date.

256 *10·L* $\dfrac{\text{03 Close, 3 Touches Drapery}}{\text{FRACTION BAR TOO FAR LEFT}}$ D-188 N-14

Obverse 10. 03 *close, corner of 3 just touches drapery, the* 1 *leans to the right more than the* 8 *does.* PC below outer curve of B; HWH under center of R; JHF midway between T and Y.

Reverse L. Fraction bar a little too far to the left. Left stand of M higher than adjacent foot of A. Right foot of first T in STATES defective, and that of second T missing. PSL between inner and outer curve; PHL just right of center; PLO under inner left curve.

Die break variations. *Obverse:* Found with fine crack which runs almost in an arc from rim through 8, across drapery and out from the point of the bust to the rim. *Reverse:* Found with crack in perfect arc from rim through D, through upper left wreath, across lower right corner of E to rim. Crack fom rim through O in OF curving across right terminal leaves to near tip of left terminal leaf; rim break involving top of first T of STATES; and extending over adjacent S and A; crack from rim between AM to wreath; crack between UN to wreath. Two or three other delicate cracks in terminal stage.

R-4. Basal $1.50. 65-35 (65-50-35-35-30-30). Probably in the lower range of R-4, but almost R-3.

1 8 0 3

257   *11·M*   Close Date / LARGE FRACTION, VERY SHORT BAR   D-192 / N-15

Obverse 11. 1 *a little more distant from curl than on any other obverse.* Moderately close date with 03 close and 8 leaning to right. Corner of 3 clear of drapery. Lower left side of upright of T recut. PC between inner and outer curve of B; HWH under center of R; JHF midway between T and Y.

Reverse M. *Large fraction,* and also there is a new set of letter punches, with the letters somewhat larger. *Fraction bar only 2 mm. long,* and with the large fraction this is diagnostic for the die. Bar starts far to right of 1. Six berries on left branch. PSL center; PHL just left of center; PLO under inner right curve.

Die break variations. *Reverse:* Found perfect, and with various cracks. From rim touching left lower side of first S to wreath beneath, through top inside pair of leaves to right terminal pair, and to rim through F; from right arm of first T in STATES to wreath; from rim through E in UNITED, through wreath to N in ONE, and joins first crack. Later, heavy die sinking around STATES, cracks heavy, minor branches and additions. The die becomes shattered.

R-2. Basal $0.75. 70-50 (70-60-55-45-45-40). Middle or lower range of R-2 but singularly rare at the higher condition levels. First of the Large Fraction reverses.

258   *11·N*   Close Date, Arc Crack in Lower Left Field (Usually) / LARGE FRACTION, SHORT BAR   D-193 / N-16

Obverse 11. In this marriage, usually but not always seen with arclike crack from rim through 1, curving left through curls and to rim after touching lowest tip of ribbon.

Reverse N. Large fraction, fraction bar 2.5 mm. in length, and this is the only large fraction reverse with bar of "moderately short" length. The bar starts under right edge of 1. *Always seen with cut or crack from rim above D to right side of letter.* PSL between inner and outer curves; PHL right of center; PLO under outer right curve.

Die break variations. *Obverse:* Swelling sometimes seen back of lower curls.

[304]

1 8 0 3

R-1. Basal $0.50. 70-70 (70-70-70-70-70-65). Second commonest 1803 and almost surely the commonest in Mint State. We can account for at least five 70's in the present review. Highest condition census of all the varieties of Early Cents.

		"Ghost 3" Obverse	D-194
259	12·N	LARGE FRACTION, SHORT BAR	N-17

Obverse 12. Close date, with the 1 8 a little more distant, and the 1 much nearer to curl than to 8. *Top of 3 comparatively distant from drapery, and its bottom is very weak, or only an outline.* PC just left of inner curve of B; HWH under left side of upright of R; JHF just right of right edge of upright of T. The two curls below the ear are connected by an engraver's scratch. Sometimes known as the "Ghost 3" obverse.

Reverse N. In this marriage, the crack noted at D is heavier and extends through the right side of the letter. Also a delicate crack starts at rim left of first s and connects tops of STATE.

Die break variations. *Reverse:* At least two examples are known with additional crack from rim over first s, joining the other crack and heavily connecting tops of TAT, then returning to rim over E.

R-5. Basal $2. 50-30 (50-50-40-25-20-15). Upper range of R-5; called R-6 in EAC. Several examples are now known with the heavy reverse crack mentioned above. On one the obverse is badly injured by contact with a reverse die. The 3 is weaker, more attenuated than ever, and this is probably what led to the retooling of the obverse die for its subsequent and lengthy use on No. 260.

		Close Date, 3 Near Hair and Curl	D-195
260	12·O	LARGE FRACTION, AVERAGE BAR	N-18

Obverse 12. The figure 3 is now strengthened at the bottom and is normally formed.

Reverse O. *Large fraction with bar 3 mm. long,* which is about average length. Leaf below T of CENT covers at least half the base of that letter, encroaching more deeply than on any other 1803 reverse. PSL under inner curve; PHL right of center; PLO between o and F (diagnostic).

1 8 0 3

Die break variations. *Obverse:* Found with die sinking, or swelling on coin, between left rim and lower curls, and above and behind 3. Also delicate crack from base of T to forelock.

R-1. Basal $0.50. 65-55 (65-65-60-55-50-50). Clearly the commonest 1803 but less common than many of the other varieties in the neighborhood of Mint State. We can now account for only three examples qualifying for MS-60 or better.

		Wide Date, 3 Touches Bust; (Usually) Arc Crack to Left, Starting Between 8 and 0	
261	13·O	LARGE FRACTION, AVERAGE BAR	D-196 N-19

Obverse 13. Rather wide, equally spaced date. *Corner of 3 imbedded in drapery.* PC between inner and outer curves of B; HWH under center of R; JHF midway between T and Y. A slight defect on forehead just above eye.

Reverse O.

Die break variations. *Obverse:* Usually found with arclike crack resembling that seen on obverse 11. This one runs from rim between 8 and 0, curves left across shoulder and hair, and through lower ribbon ends to rim. Flaking seen before the curl on neck, and this becomes quite extensive. Later, heavy swelling in field behind lower curls, and a branch curves off from main crack to run between shoulder and rim.

R-3. Basal $1. 60-50 (60-60-55-50-45-45). Lower range of R-3. Almost R-2.

		Divided Date with the Two Die Cuts	
262	14·P	FIVE BERRIES ON LEFT SIDE	D-184 N-20

Obverse 14. Always seen with a *linear die cut about 2 mm. long near the rim opposite the nose; and with another, about 7 mm. long, which starts in the field opposite the neck and runs diagonally down over the bust to the lowest fold of drapery.* 03 close, and the 8 is a little closer to 1 than to 0. 3 does not quite touch drapery. PC below inner curve of B; HWH right of center of upright of R (called center by Newcomb); JHF between T and Y, nearer T. Called by Doughty *The Divided Date.*

1 8 0 3

Reverse P. Small fraction. *Right upright of* M *conspicuously recut,* with an extra serif below upper serif. D low, and smaller than adjacent E. Short, heavy engraver's scratch from tip of leaf which supports lowest outside berry on left. PSL under right side of upright; PHL right of center; PLO center.

Die break variations. *Obverse:* Have never seen one without the two die cuts. In this marriage the coin is usually struck off center to the left. *Reverse:* Found perfect and a single example is known with heavy crack from rim left of first S, through STA, then up through top of T to rim between T and E. This broken die specimen is now in the ANS collection.

R-6. Basal $3. 45-30 (45-40-40-30-20-15). Not very far from R-7. About 18 accounted for.

263   *14·Q*   Divided Date with the Two Die Cuts   D-185   N-21

SIX BERRIES ON LEFT SIDE; HEAVY CRACKS (Usually)

Obverse 14. The crack or cut noted is now joined near the point of the bust by a crack which starts at the rim opposite the mouth, and the two form what resembles a large V.

Reverse Q. Small fraction. *Six berries on left branch,* and with small fraction this is diagnostic. PSL center; PHL *under the left side.* Always seen with light crack from rim through last 0, through fraction bar and left ribbon to near middle of left stem.

Die break variations. *Obverse:* Found with crack connecting bases of 1803, and later the rim is heavily broken below the date, touching bottoms of all figures and extending under lowest curl at left. *Reverse:* Usually found with crack from rim through left top of O in OF, through top leaves on right, left terminal leaf and pair below it, across wreath stem and adjacent outside pair of leaves to rim between D and S. Above this crack the die begins to sink, especially about STA, which is opposite the now heavy obverse rim break. Another crack appears from base of second T in STATES to near base of left terminal leaf.

R-3. Basal $1. 60-50 (60-60-55-50-50-45). Middle or upper range of R-3.

1 8 0 3

264 *15·Q* Large Date / SMALL FRACTION NOT IN D / N-23

Obverse 15. The famous *Large 3* variety. This die has a new set of punches for the figures of the date, and they are all larger. *Tall, pointed 1 nearly touching the hair, and large, round-bottomed 3 with upper corner touching the drapery.* These figures resemble those from the punches used in 1804 and later, but they appear only on this one obverse in 1803. The letters of LIBERTY are also new, and a little taller. The R is more open at the bottom, defining something of a compromise between the straight-tailed R of style 1 lettering, and style 2 (see p. 198). PC between inner and outer curves of B; HWH under center of upright of R; JHF under right foot of T.

Reverse Q. The breaks and sunken portion heavier. STA entirely obliterated on some examples, and apparently the die soon shattered, accounting for the rarity of the variety.

Die break variations. *Obverse:* Found perfect (although not in this marriage) and with crack from rim through right side of 1, through hair above and curving left through curl at back of neck and lowest ribbon into field, eventually extending to rim; crack from rim above end of bust passes bust and shoulder to hair, joining first crack. In this marriage, found only with the cracks advanced. *Reverse:* As noted.

R-6. Basal $5. 35-10 (35-15-12-10-7-6). About 18 or 19 examples now accounted for, although no more Fine ones have appeared.

The still rather abnormally high basal value is justified only by the avidity of type collectors for the Large Date-Small Fraction, and by a tendency in some quarters to exaggerate the rarity of this variety. It may not be as rare as No. 262.

265 *15·R* Large Date / LARGE FRACTION D-197 / N-22

Obverse 15.

Reverse R. Large fraction, with 3 mm. bar. PLLL under center of N; PSL left of inner curve; PHL center.

Die break variations. *Obverse:* In this marriage, found both perfect and with all stages of the breaks noted. **Reverse:** Found perfect but rare so. Arc crack from rim through E in

1 8 0 3

UNITED, left wreath, bottom o and top of N in ONE, through right wreath at base of terminal leaves to left side of o and rim. Oddly, this crack remains light while others develop and become heavy. Second arc crack from rim through D, left wreath, top of o in ONE, past tip of left terminal leaf, and across right side of E to rim; third, from rim through first s and left foot of T, through leaf under adjacent A to join second crack at lower right corner of E. Crack from rim through left foot of first A in AMERICA, across tips of double leaf beneath A and top outside berry to stem of right branch near where it is crossed by first crack. Crack connects tips of terminal leaves, and other light branch cracks seen in late stages of the die.

R-4. Basal $3. 60-40 (60-50-45-40-40-30). Another coin made famous by type collecting (although all of the varieties are types) and by exaggeration of rarity. But this fame will tend to persist and perhaps the market will continue to support a "double premium" price level for the much desired D 197.

The cents of 1803 have always been more popular with collectors than those of 1802. They present wide variations, and if a collector will once learn to look at reverses systematically he will find that the 1803's practically classify themselves for him. Furthermore, all but four or five of the twenty-four varieties are sufficiently common that a few years of careful watching of the sales will lead to the capture of a respectable collection at reasonable outlay. It is an excellent date with which to start a collection; and a good date for building up experience as to condition and value at a relatively low initiation expense.

1 8 0 3

TABLE 22. KEY TO 1803 CENTS

Stemless wreath, double fraction bar 243
Fraction 1/100 over 1/000 249
Small fraction; six berries left 263
Large date (pointed 1) with rev. as last 264
Large date (pointed 1) with large fraction 265
Large fraction; six berries left 257
Large fraction; very long fraction bar. Very wide date 261
Same rev. Close date as usual 260
Large fraction; break to top of D. Obv.: In date 1 far from curl, 3 normal 258
Same rev. Obv.: In date 1 close to curl; "Ghost 3." 259
Small fraction on all to follow. Denominator 1 00; top of hair unfinished 244
Very wide denominator; line from left stem into U, crack tops of RICA 245
Very wide denominator; PHL between ES NC-1
Numerator much too high. Usually, "mumps" obverse (small break under chin) 246
Mumps obverse. Rev: Short fraction bar; impressed denticles through fraction 247
Same obv. Fine parallel line above long fraction bar 248
PSL under r. edge of upright of D. M recut 262
Short fraction bar; final s shows recutting on r. side 251
AT in STATES about touch, with this T lacking r. base 256
Wide denominator, "period" after it. Usually cracked through STATE 253
Fraction bar long, tilted up and skewed to r.; 3 touches drapery 254
Same rev. Obv.: TY lack r. feet; 3 does not quite touch drapery 255
Rather long fraction bar, close to denominator, twice as far from numerator; final zero high. Numerator centered in space. I in UNITED leans left. Obv.: 1 and 3 away from hair and drapery 250
Same rev. Obv.: In date 3 close to drapery; usually, crack through bottom of date 252

1 8 0 3

TABLE 23. RARITY AND VALUE: 1803 CENTS

Number	Obv.-Rev. Designation	Newcomb Number	Doughty Number	Rarity	Basal Value (Dollars)
243	1-A	1	180	4	2.
244	2-B	2	—	5	2.
245	3-C	3	189	4	1.50
246	4-D	4	181	4	1.50
247	4-E	5	182	5	2.
248	4-F	6	—	5	2.50
249	4-G	7	179	4	2.
250	5-H	8	—	4	1.50
NC-1	5-S	24	—	7	6.
251	5-I	9	190	2	.75
252	6-H	10	186	2	.75
253	7-J	11	183	2	.75
254	8-K	12	191	1	.50
255	9-K	13	187	1	.50
256	10-L	14	188	4	1.50
257	11-M	15	192	2	.75
258	11-N	16	193	1	.50
259	12-N	17	194	5	2.
260	12-O	18	195	1	.50
261	13-O	19	196	3	1.
262	14-P	20	184	6	3.
263	14-Q	21	185	3	1.
264	15-Q	23	—	6	5.
265	15-R	22	197	4	3.

1804

266 1·A D-198

Obverse 1. Tall figures, although not from the same punches as those of Obverse 15 of 1803. Date evenly spaced and curved. Top of 1 blunt, close to curl and very close to hair. The 0 of the date is almost directly opposite o of OF on the reverse, and since this occurs on no other variety of the early cents, an almost infallible test for genuineness of the coin is easily at hand (for this reason, perhaps, there are relatively few altered dates of 1804, and such as there are can be recognized merely by turning the coin over). PC below inner curve of B; HWH below center of upright of R; JHF below right foot of T.

Reverse A. Large fraction. Figures of the fraction and letters of the legend from the same punches as the large fraction reverses of 1803. Wide denominator with long, slender bar. PSL right of center; PHL just right of left side; PLO between inner and outer right curves.

Die break variations. *Obverse:* Found perfect, and with heavy rim break over RTY; also with light crack along top of ER. *Reverse:* Found with light crack over MERIC, which develops into a heavy rim break *after* the obverse rim break develops.

R-3. Basal $10. 60-55 (60-60-55-55-50-45). In the present review only two Mint State cents of 1804 can be accounted for, both MS-60, and the first half dozen would have to include an EF-45. There are surely as many as thirty at VF-20 or better, and in the higher grades of condition the 1804 is much commoner than is the 1799 in both varieties combined. In the

1 8 0 4

lower condition grades the 1799's—at least the two varieties combined—seem to be as common as the 1804.

(THE 1804 MINT RESTRIKE)

"This singular example of the low moral tone of some of our public officials made its appearance about the year 1860 . . . in no (real) sense a re-strike . . . but manufactured for the sole purpose of supplying coin dealers with a cent . . . they could sell to young and ignorant collectors . . ." (Proskey-Doughty.) I think we can let this pungent comment stand without elaboration. The coin results from a marriage of obverse 13 of 1803 (altered to 1804) with a reverse of 1818.

1805

267   *1 · A*   Blunt 1 / PHL LEFT SIDE OF S   D-199 / C-1

Obverse 1. The *Blunt* 1 variety. Top of 1 blunt and very close to hair. Right top of 5 just touches drapery, and the 5 shows recutting at right top and bottom—seen only on fine specimens. PC below center of right side of B; HWH below center of upright of R; JHF below right foot of T.

Reverse A. Small fraction, with bar entirely to the right of 1. PSL under inner curve; PHL just right of left side (Clapp says left side); PLO center.

Die break variations. *Reverse:* Found with crack over AM; from bottom of first s to foot of T and wreath.

R-1. Basal $0.75. 65-55 (65-65-60-55-55-50). Far the commonest 1805.

268   *1 · B*   Blunt 1 / PHL RIGHT OF S   D-200 / C-2

Obverse 1. The traces of recutting at the right of the 5 have been smoothed out.

Reverse B. Long fraction bar almost covering the 1. PSL under outer curve; *PHL right of* s (the best hallmark for quick identification); PLO far to the right, and under left foot of F.

Die break variations. None seen.

R-5. Basal $2. 45-30 (45-45-40-30-25-20). Rarity overestimated in EAC. Quite a flurry of these have turned up in recent years, including two 45-coins.

1 8 0 5

269   2·B   Pointed 1   D-201
                          ─────────   C-3

Obverse 2. The 1 is pointed, and the whole of its top touches the hair, Right top of 5 almost touches drapery. PC below outer curve of B; HWH left of center of R; JHF below right foot of T. A cut in the die, or break, runs 3 mm. into the hair from the knot, just above the upper curl. Half a dozen short engraver's scratches from point of bust toward rim.

Reverse B.

Die break variations. None seen.

R-1. Basal $1. 70-55 (70-60-60-55-50-50). Almost an R-2 coin. Seen about half as often as No. 267. We had an earlier impression that the two varieties were of more nearly equal rarity.

1806

270   *1·A*   D-202

Obverse 1. Perfect or pointed 1, like the last. PC between B and E; HWH below center of R; JHF right of right foot of T. Always seen with crack running 2 mm. into field from a denticle on the rim opposite throat.

Reverse A. Same as reverse B of 1805.

Die break variations. *Obverse:* Found perfect and with crack from top to bottom of lowest curl and part way to rim; with heavy swell behind lowest curl, also through and to right of date.

R-2. Basal $1.50. 65-60 (65-65-65-60-60-55). Common enough as a variety but considered scarce as a date.

1807

		Perfect Date, Comet Breaks (Usually)	D-205
271	1·A	SMALL FRACTION, NO MOUND AT STA	C-4

Obverse 1. The famous Comet variety, so-called because of linear flaws in the die, which seem to trail out from left to right like the tail of a comet. On some examples, however, the flaws are very faint or virtually absent (the comet is eclipsed). The 1 is blunt. 1 and 8 more distant than the other figures. PC below inner curve of B; HWH left of center of upright of R; JHF below right side of upright of T.

Reverse A. Small fraction. U *distant nearly 2 mm. from left ribbon end. PSL under left side of upright* (diagnostic); PHL midway between E and S; PLO center. In this marriage, found only with perfect die.

Die break variations. *Obverse:* Usually seen with wide flaw in the die extending from rim to hair, touching top of knot; also with light line from mouth to rim. On some specimens there are additional flaws in front of neck, at tip of bust, at rim behind lower curls, and smaller traces elsewhere in the fields.

R-1. Basal $1.50. 65-55 (65-60-60-55-55-50). Nearly R-2. In the current review just about the same number of these as of No. 269 were seen. Examples are known lacking any traces of the characteristic "comet" die flaws. The perfect obverse die in ordinary condition is only scarce, not rare, but it is very rare above VG. In the last stage of this obverse the principal flaw behind the head has developed so that it looks like a heavy break, and die sinking under the date obliterates the 7. Use of a glass

1 8 0 7

shows that nearly the entire surface of the obverse is striated with flaws parallel to the principal one.

| 272 | 2·A | Overdate, the 1 Almost Touches Hair and Curl | NOT IN D
C-2 |

Obverse 2. Overdate. Small, narrow 7 cut over a 6, and *both tops of the 7 touch drapery. The 1 has a blunt top, and almost touches both hair and curl.* PC below inner curve of B; HWH below left side of upright of R; JHF below right side of upright of T. Date evenly spaced. Not the same obverse as the 1806.
Reverse A. Known only with perfect die.
Die break variations. None seen.
R-6. Basal $5. 55-25 (55-50-25-20-15-12). The Small Overdate. Only 15 or 20 of these known to us, and no more than a half dozen above Fine. The two AU examples are both famous ones, from the Hines and Dr. French collections. One coin is known with a heavy crack from the border through R to the brow just above the eye, with die sinking which obliterates most of RTY.

| 273 | 3·A | Overdate, 1 Distant from Curl | D-203
C-1 |

Obverse 3. Overdate. Large 7 cut over 6. *The 7 is heavy and prominent, with both upper corners close to drapery but not quite touching. The 1 is pointed* and close to hair above, but nearly a millimeter from the curl. 80 closer than other figures. Heavy traces of wreath seen at throat and under knot. PC below center of curve of B; HWH below center of R; JHF midway between T and Y. Not the same obverse as the 1806.
Reverse A.
Die break variations. *Reverse:* Found perfect, and with crack from rim through C of AMERICA, and to leaf below C—indicating that this was probably the last of its three marriages.
R-1. Basal $1. 70-50 (70-60-55-50-50-45). Large Overdate. One of the commonest Early Cents, but it commands a premium as an overdate. An example has turned up with a heavy reverse rim break over ST. The obverse develops a swell behind the lowest curl, and progressively heavy incusations to the left

1 8 0 7

and right of the head, particularly under the chin and under the ribbon.

		Perfect Date	D-204
274	4·B	MOUND AT STA	C-3

Obverse 4. Close date. 1 blunt and *very close to hair and curl.* PC below center of curve of B; HWH below right side of upright of R; JHF below right foot of T. ER *of* LIBERTY *about 1 mm. above the hair.*

Reverse B. Small fraction with engraver's scratch from right end of bar through right ribbon and to top of A. *Always seen with die more or less buckled or sunken under* STA. PSL under outer curve, or at the extreme right; PHL midway between E and S; PLO left of center.

Die break variations. *Reverse:* Found with die badly sunken, heavy swell at STA with TA sometimes obliterated; crack from bottom of first S to wreath; from rim through left side of A; from rim through D to wreath.   2 7 6

R-4. Basal $1.50. 65-35 (65-45-40-35-30-30). In the upper range of R-4, almost R-5. Rarity underestimated in EAC. The 1807 cents sold as "Small Fraction type" are always 274's or perfect die 271's.

		Perfect Date. ER Well Above the Hair	D-206
275	4·C	LARGE FRACTION	C-5

Obverse 4. ER of LIBERTY about 1 mm. above the hair.

Reverse C. *The only 1807 reverse with large fraction.* PSL under inner curve; PHL just left of center; PLO center. Second berry on left is a mere lump on stem of leaf above.

Die break variations. None seen.

R-5. Basal $2. 60-35 (60-50-40-35-30-30). Apparently in the middle range of R-5. Like No. 268, this variety appeared rarer in the earlier review than it really is.

		Perfect Date, ER Close to Hair	D-207
276	5·C	LARGE FRACTION, REVERSE UPSET (Usually)	C-6

Obverse 5. LIBERTY *lower than the last, with the* R *very close*

1 8 0 7

to HWH. E distinctly lower than B. Date more closely spaced, with 180 *much closer than on obverse* 4. PC below center of curve of B; HWH below center of R; JHF midway between T and Y.

Reverse C. In this marriage, the reverse is usually found upset, and it is rotated at every possible angle. An Eastern collector has thirty-four examples of the variety showing as many different positions of the reverse, and in fact following the rotation entirely around the clock.

Die break variations. *Obverse:* Often seen with a swell along the rim behind the lowest curl.

R-1. Basal $0.50. 65-55 (65-65-60-55-55-50). Far the commonest 1807. Last of the Fillet cents and possibly commonest of them all. Yet it is a difficult variety to find in Mint State.

1808

THE TURBAN HEAD CENTS

General description of the type: *Obverse:* Head of Liberty turned to the left. Features strongly marked and coarse, or gynandroid. Bust broad, cut nearly square in front, but short under the shoulder. A plain band inscribed LIBERTY in small letters confines the hair, which falls in short curls over the forehead and temple, and in longer curls over the shoulder. Seven stars before and six behind the head, arranged in two curves along the rim. Date under bust. There is no turban, but the band, together with the way the hair is arranged above it, gives the superficial effect of a turban. *Reverse:* A wreath of laurel, formed of a single branch, with leaves in clusters of two, three, and four, and generally bearing thirteen berries, is tied at the bottom in a short, broad ribbon. Within the center are the words $_{\text{CENT}}^{\text{ONE}}$, a center dot, and a bar under CENT. Legend around wreath. Border milled. Edge plain. Diameter 28 mm.

		Front of Hair Band Curved, First Star Weak or Absent	
277	1·A		D-208 C-1

Obverse 1. *The front of the hair band is curved,* and this is the hallmark of the die. Engraver's scratch on right upright of T. The lowest star on the left is always weak, because of the reverse die sinking, and on some examples this star is extremely faint (hence called *Twelve-star* variety). Date widely

[321]

1 8 0 8

and almost evenly spaced. Dotlike defect always seen just under the jaw.

Reverse A. PFL (point of fifth leaf) under right side of upright of D; PHL right of center of s; PLF (point of leaf under F) almost even with right foot.

Die break variations. *Reverse:* Found perfect, but usually has an arc crack from rim through D, across upper left side of wreath and through last s to rim. The die begins to sink early around TA and eventually there is swelling in nearly the whole region enclosed by the crack. Another crack runs from D to wreath below, and across ONE. The head is incused in the center of the reverse.

R-2. Basal $1.50. 70-60 (70-70-65-60-60-55). As the reverse die sinking develops, the lowest star on the left, on the obverse, becomes fainter and gradually disappears altogether.

278	2·B	Front of Hair Band Straight PHL UNDER RIGHT SIDE	D 209 C-2

Obverse 2. *Front of hair band straight.* Date spaced with decreasing distance between the figures. 18 rather distant; 80 less distant; 08 rather close.

Reverse B. PFL center; PHL under right side—and both of these characteristics are diagnostic. *Look for the point of the highest leaf even with the right side of the* s. Actually, in classifying the three 1808's it is not necessary to look at the obverses, since each of the three has a distinctive reverse.

Die break variations. None seen.

R-3. Basal $1.75. 65-55 (65-65-60-60-50-50). The most scarce of the 1808's.

279	3·C	Front of Hair Band Straight PHL NEARLY CENTER	NOT IN D C-3

Obverse 3. Front of hair band straight. In date, 180 evenly spaced, but 08 closer.

Reverse C. PFL between center and right side of upright; PHL barely right of center; PLF just left of center of the upright.

Die break variations. *Obverse:* Found perfect and with the die badly injured. After the injury, the obverse seems poorly

1 8 0 8

struck, with the stars on the right connected to the rim; figures of the date distorted; ribbon ends distorted; a pit or indentation just in front of the throat. This die must have come into violent contact with something hard.

R-2. Basal $1.25. 65-55 (65-60-55-55-50-50). Commonest 1808, and seen about twice as often as No. 277, but more rare in full Mint State.

1809

280   1·A   D-210

Obverse 1. Not an overdate, and not one of the 1808 obverses. Fine examples show that the 9 was first started a little too low, and then corrected. The middle right point of the seventh star points just above the top of the hair band. On all three of the 1808 obverses, as Clapp indicates, it points to the top of the hair.

Reverse A. PFL just right of center of upright; PHL center. Not the same as one of the 1808 reverses, although it is rather close to reverse C of 1808.

Die break variations. *Obverse:* Found perfect, but usually has a break from eleventh star toward point of upper ribbon. *Reverse:* Found perfect, but usually with crack from bottom of E in STATES through tip of leaf under s to leaf beyond; small defect or arc-shaped crack over T in CENT; later, crack from rim between T and E on STATES through E and almost parallel with first crack to wreath, where it turns down to left top of E in ONE.

R-3. Basal $2. 65-60 (65-65-60-60-60-55). Probably in the lower range of R-3, despite our earlier rating of R-2. Certainly a little more scarce than the 1806. Since these two dates and 1804 have but one variety each, the date is as scarce as that variety.

1810

		Overdate	
281	1·A		D-211 C-1

Obverse 1. Overdate, and it is impossible to make out whether the last overcut figure was originally an 8 or a 9. Doughty is wrong in the statement that the die is "the same as No. 210." It is a new die, not previously encountered in the series, and bears a closer resemblance to Obverse 2 of 1808 (D-209) than to any other. The second 1 is not only cut over a cipher, but also over another 1, or the beginning of a 1, which can be seen above the figure. This second 1 is low and leans left, destroying the symmetry of the date.

Reverse A. PFL under the inner curve; PHL nearly under right side; PLF under center of upright.

R-1. Basal $1. 70-55 (70-60-60-55-50-45). Commands a premium because an overdate, although common.

		T Low and Left	
282	2·B	PHL UNDER RIGHT SIDE	D-212 C-2

For purposes of quick and efficient classification of the four different varieties of the perfect date 1810's, I would advise that the obverses be more or less ignored until the reverses are learned. Both obverses and reverses are all different, but while the reverses can be recognized with certainty by a beginner, the obverses require a certain amount of familiarity and experience with the coins.

Obverse 2. The T in LIBERTY is low and leans distinctly to

1 8 1 0

the left. Date wide, about evenly spaced, with second 1 a little low and leaning a little left.

Reverse B. PFL between inner and outer curve; PHL under right side; PLF right of center of upright.

R-2. Basal $0.75. 65-55 (65-60-55-55-55-50). Not quite so often seen as No. 283, but by no means R-3.

283   3·C $\dfrac{\text{T in Almost Normal Position}}{\text{PHL PAST RIGHT SIDE}}$ D-213 C-3

Obverse 3. T only *very slightly low* and leaning *very slightly* left. On Y there is a rather heavy dot just below the fork (but not seen on worn coins). The hair is higher than on Obverse 2. *No center dot below the ear.* Obverse often seen unfinished: R and Y weak; lock of hair over forehead and inside of ear not finished.

Reverse C. PFL between inner and outer curves; PHL just past right side; PLF under left side of upright.

R-2. Basal $0.75. 65-50 (65-60-55-50-50-45). Commoner than No. 282 but more rare in the higher grades of condition.

284   4·D $\dfrac{\text{T Low and Left}}{\text{PHL FAR RIGHT}}$ D-214 C-4

Obverse 4. T distinctly low and leaning distinctly left. The 8 is lower than on obverses 2 and 3. If a straight edge be laid across the tops of 18 on obverse 2 or 3, the line thus determined will about bisect the 0; if this be done on obverse 4, the line will cross 0 decidedly below its center. This coin usually off center to the lower right.

Reverse D. PFL under outer curve; PHL about one third of the way between s and o; PLF under center of upright.

R-3. Basal $1.25. 65-60 (65-65-65-60-50-50). Rarest variety of the date. Mint State examples are usually found on brilliantly polished planchets which bring to mind the Nichols Find coins.

285   5·E $\dfrac{\text{The Die Crack Variety}}{}$ NOT IN D C-5

Obverse 5. Y low; I, R and T double cut; lock of hair below

[326]

1 8 1 0

ear terminates in a point just below center dot (smooth on all other varieties). Date well spaced and a little less wide. *Faint crack always present along outer points of all stars on the right and extending under 10 of date.*

Reverse E. PFL between inner and outer curves; PHL under right side; PLF under left upright. Berry below center of first A in AMERICA.

R-1. Basal $0.50. 65-65 (65-65-65-65-60-60). Far the commonest 1810. Fully twice as many of them are seen as of any other variety. The basal value for this coin in EAC was too high.

1811

286   1·A   Overdate   D-215   C-1

Obverse 1. Overdate, the last 1 cut over 0, but this is not an 1810 obverse seen before. 1 8 wide, 811 closer, with both 1's leaning left and the first of them double cut at right top.

Reverse A. Easily recognized by a dash, or defect 1 mm. long, under E of ONE. PFL between inner and outer curve; PHL nearly right; PLF under center of the base.

R-3. Basal $2.50. 55-45 (55-55-50-45-45-40). Probably in the lower range of R-3, although our earlier impression was R-2. This coin is of very nearly the same rarity as the 1809.

287   2·B   Perfect Date   D-216   C-2

Obverse 2. Perfect date, widely spaced, with the 8 high and leaning left. A scratch in the die extends from fifth star halfway to nose.

Reverse B. PFL between inner and outer curve; PHL just past right; PLF center of the upright.

R-2. Basal $1.75. 65-60 (65-65-65-65-60-60). Commoner than the Overdate by at least two to one, possibly three to one. There are seven or eight of these at full MS-60 or better, nearly all of them offered as "Finest Known" from time to time.

1812

		Large Date	D-217
288	1·A	PHL BARELY PAST RIGHT SIDE	C-1

Obverse 1. Large date, with 8 larger than other figures. Uneven spacing; 812 closer than 18. The 8 is too high and the second 1 leans too much to the left. On perfect specimens, IBE shows recutting.

Reverse A. PFL center; PHL *just barely* past right side of s; PLF right side of upright (Clapp says past right side of upright).

R-1. Basal $0.50. 60-55 (60-60-55-55-55-50). A little less common than No. 289; second most scarce of the date.

290

		Large Date	D-218
289	2·B	PHL ALMOST MIDWAY	C-2

Obverse 2. Large date, from same punches as the preceding, but more evenly spaced and nicely curved. Conspicuous recutting above right foot of T.

Reverse B. PFL under outer curve, or extreme right; *PHL almost midway between* s *and* o; PLF under right side of upright.

R-1. Basal $0.50. 60-50 (60-60-55-50-50-45). Second commonest 1812.

		Small Date	D-219
290	3·C	NO DASH UNDER E IN ONE	C-3

Obverse 3. Small date, well curved, and evenly spaced. Light engraver's scratch extending 1 mm. from hair into neck below center dot.

1 8 1 2

Reverse C. PFL under the center; PHL even with right side; PLF under right side of upright.

R-1. Basal $0.50. 65-65 (65-65-65-65-65-60). Commonest 1812. Small Date.

291   4·D   <u>The Die Crack Variety</u>   D-220
DASH UNDER E IN ONE   C-4

Obverse 4. Small date, first 1 high and distant from 8, 812 closely and about evenly spaced. *Crack from 2 connects all stars on right and extends to top of hair, ending in field above hair; another crack starts above the termination of the first and connects all stars on left.*

Reverse D. Same as reverse A of 1811, and easily recognized by the defect or dash under left side of E of ONE.

R-2. Basal $0.75. 55-45 (55-50-45-45-45-40). Far the most scarce variety of the year, and not known in full Mint State.

1813

| 292 | 1·A | Distant Star Variety | D-221 C-1 |

Obverse 1. Nearest point of the 3 about 2.5 mm. from star on right. Sometimes called the *Distant Star* variety.

Reverse A. PFL under center of upright; PHL under right side; PLF under right side of upright.

R-2. Basal $0.75. 70-55 (70-60-60-55-55-50). Perhaps just barely R-2. In the earlier review we called it R-1.

| 293 | 2·B | Close Star Variety | D-222 C-2 |

Obverse 2. Nearest point of 3 about 1.5 mm. from star on right. Has been called the *Close Star* variety.

Reverse B. PFL under outer curve; PHL almost midway between s and o.

R-2. Basal $1. 65-50 (65-55-50-50-45-45). Upper range of R-2. Much the scarcer of the two varieties of the year. The Close Star variety. Early strikings of this obverse die, when seen near Mint State, sometimes show faint traces of a 2 behind the 3 in the date; the tail of the 2 shows faintly at the right, and fragments of the curved body and lower stroke of the numeral may be visible within. Either ordinary die wear or some repolishing of the die soon obliterated the traces of the very lightly punched 2 so that most of the coins of the variety, even when seen in EF condition, are free of them. The coins showing these traces are not in any sense true overdates but should be considered variants of the

1 8 1 3

die, like die break variations. In punching in the numerals of the date for this variety, the die cutter probably picked up the 2-punch instead of the 3, tapped it lightly on the die, noticed his mistake just in time, and then punched in the 3 properly.

(*The D·223*)

Doughty's "Obverse of 221, reverse of 222." This is one of those ingenious frauds which lend color and interest to the big cents. Proskey really saw such a coin, but as Clapp has pointed out, it is a "manufactured" article, made by brazing the obverse side of one coin to the reverse side of another. Several other examples of this same fraud are known, but this is the only case, so far as I know, which has "got into print."

1814

| 294 | 1·A | The Crosslet 4 | D-224 C-1 |

Obverse 1. Small 4 with a crosslet.
Reverse A. PFL between inner and outer curve; PHL well to the right of s.

R-1. Basal $0.50. 65-65 (65-65-65-65-60-60). Less common than No. 295. In EAC we gave both of these varieties a condition census listing of 70-70, instead of 65-65 as they appear here. The change results from the observed fact that 1814's, for some reason, are not seen with the brilliant luster which by definition characterizes a 70-coin. Perhaps they never were brilliant, even when struck, owing to some alloy of the metal or peculiarity of the planchets. In any case, 1814's are fairly common near Mint State, and it may be a quibble whether the finest ones are to be called 70's or 65's. For one possible explanation, see reference 1b.

| 295 | 2·B | The Plain 4 | D-225 C-2 |

Obverse 2. Large 4 without a crosslet.
Reverse B. PFL center; PHL under right side.

Die break variation. *Obverse:* Found with break at throat, or crumbling of the die, which gradually increases until it extends entirely around the chin to the mouth—then called the "bearded variety." Arc crack from rim across bottom of eleventh star, bottom of curl and through 8 to rim. Common in all states.

1 8 1 4

R-1. Basal $0.50. 65-65 (65-65-65-65-65-65). Commonest Early Cent, apparently, and about twice as common as No. 224. But perhaps it merits its basal value by virtue of being the last of its kind.

Epilogue

On Collecting Early Cents

HERE THEN IS A GUIDE TO THE EARLY AMERICAN CENTS, AND a key to their rarity and their value. They are an intriguing family and they never die, fade, or get broken. Like good jewelry they seem to transcend human mortality and to grow richer with age. There is a time-binding quality and a sense of intrinsic full value or full integrity in an early copper cent that is often found in jewelry, and is not found at all in later money, or in tokens or in bits of postage stamp paper. The early cents carry the memory, and an indelible impress, of a little stretch of human time that was fragrant with a high hope. It was the flowering period for what might have become a great people in a land of unmatched beauty. We always live in a valley lying between the nostalgic past and an unknown future. To own a family of the early cents is in some measure to command a causeway between what for Americans is becoming a dearly remembered island of the past, and the grim urban mainland of the future.

Trying to perfect a collection of the early cents has in it much of that quality of elusive difficulty that endears the game of golf to many. Golf offers a measurable sense of progress toward an ultimate perfection which remains beautifully unattainable. The perfect golf score is imaginable, and definable, but is never realized. It is the same with the perfect cent score. For the 301 collectibles, such a score would be 301×70, or 21,070. That would be the score for the 295 known varieties and the 6 sub-varieties all in perfect Mint State. No golfer seriously aspires to tour a course in 18 strokes, and no student of early cents expects to reach the total score of 21,350. Golfers do aspire to move from the nineties to the eighties, however, and a follower of the early cents can dream of advancing from the 2000 level toward the 2500 level.

There is great allure and great satisfaction in the early cents, as in many another game. But if you are of the uninitiated I should like to advise you at the start to pay little heed to the hope of *profit* from such a game. Profit falls mainly to the professionals and to those who watch for it primarily; not to the lovers of the game. Much has been written of the steady advance in value of old coins. This advance is more apparent than real. It is true that prices of coins have advanced, in terms of dollars, but only about proportionally to the general inflation, and inflation is a sign not of an advance but of chicanery and moral collapse in the economic panel of life.

Old Cent Whist

THE LATE DR. GEORGE FRENCH, WHO BROUGHT TOGETHER ONE of the most famous collections of early cents, loved to compare and match his collection against that of others. He invented a game which he used to call old cent whist. It was a game usually played by two and the idea was to score points against an opponent's collection. Each of the known varieties, then numbering about 270, was taken up in order. You started with the Chain AMERI. variety, which is the 1-A of 1793, and you put your coin up on the table. Your opponent in turn produced his Chain AMERI. and the two pieces were compared to determine which was of superior condition. Possession of the variety, in any condition, counted one point. Possession of a piece superior to that of your opponent counted another point. So for each variety you could score one point, two points, or no points, as could your opponent. If you had the variety and your opponent lacked it, you beat him two to nothing. If he had one, but inferior to yours, you beat him two to one. If his coin about tied yours in condition, you each scored one point. Wagers could be laid both on total score, for the whole series of the early cents, and on scores by dates.

EPILOGUE

During the first decade of the century Dr. French was generally acknowledged champion at old cent whist, although he was by no means unchallenged. It was during the First World War that Howard Newcomb and Henry Hines became deeply interested in cents. By 1918 both had amassed formidable collections and Dr. French was an embattled champion.

A favorite meeting place for the cent men of those days was in Henry Chapman's old office at 333 South 16th Street, Philadelphia. There a little gathering of the hard-bitten would always accumulate after the big auctions and sometimes spirited games of old cent whist were played. I remember one particularly spirited occasion which must have been in the spring of 1918, for I was in uniform and visiting Mr. Chapman.

Dr. French, always a jolly extravert, had caught a Tartar in Mr. Newcomb who was of quiet, taciturn disposition. The two were of opposite temperaments and they provoked a little more than friendly rivalry in one another. A game of old cent whist had been arranged between them, with some wagers set. It was the onlookers who did the betting.

The score was very close, something like 122 to 119, when Dr. French began to present several of his "new varieties" of 1796. The argument which straightway broke out on those attributions would be unfit to print. Some disagreement seemed to be detectable too as to the grading of condition. The game was finally adjourned pending further research on attribution, and I am afraid it was never finished, and the bets never paid.

Dr. French and Mr. Newcomb will never meet in the little Chapman office again. Perhaps their game of old cent whist that was never finished still goes on. Or perhaps the game was only a dream and Dr. French and Mr. Newcomb themselves but shifting shadows in a changing dream. We know so little of the nature of time and of consciousness, yet have said so much, that it may not be amiss to have said this little about the old cents—those symbols of humility and integrity on which are imprinted the bright hopes of yesterday morning. Meanwhile, if you should find yourself playing old cent whist I hope this book will have added to the enjoyment of the game.

Appendix: Die Break Discoveries

This section will describe, briefly, a number of die breaks that have appeared since the publication of EAC. These are newly discovered ones—not merely extensions of those already known. Most varieties for which die breaks were earlier recorded have turned up with intermediate stages, and many with earlier or later stages, than had previously been seen.

1793   7. 8-F.   *Obverse:* One specimen shows a crack from border between RT through left foot of T to JHF.

1794   50. H-57.   *Obverse:* The Dupont specimen has a crack from crosslet of 4 through bust point to pole, extending a little distance into field above.

1795   76b. D-66, plain edge.   *Reverse:* One worn example seen with severe rim break covering tops of ED, in addition to a more advanced break obliterating most of RICA.

1796   90. G-I.   *Obverse:* Two are known with crack through tops of LIBER.

1797   140. D-104.   *Reverse:* At least one is known with a crack from rim over F through tops of AMER.
NC-5. CN-25.   *Reverse:* Perfect die as on 1796 No. 113 (21-W). Later ones show faint beginnings of the crack above second T in STATES; the last ones (with broken obverse) have this crack developed as on reverse of 1796 No. 114 (22-W). Apparently the order of emission was 1796 21-W, 1797 20-R (*NC-5*), 1796 22-W, 23-W earlier states, 23-X, 23-W with heavy breaks. *Obverse:* Perfect, and with crack through tops of RTY; two cracks from rim through arms of T to forelock; these all become heavy.

1798   173. D-132.   *Reverse:* One is known with a heavy rim break over **CA.**

1800   201. CN-14.   *Reverse:* Swellings develop, obliterating (in the last stages) most of the central regions from ED ST to lowest leaf on right, including the stemless leaves; but the swellings make identification easy even on a worn example.

1801   222. D-162.   *Reverse:* A single example shows a severe rim break over NIT touching tops of those letters.

1802   237. D-170.   *Reverse:* The Warfield coin shows a heavy rim break over STAT.

1803   249. D-179.   *Reverse:* In the last stages a second rim break appears over ED S.

1807   276. D-207.   *Obverse:* Sometimes with several small rim breaks over LIBERT.

1808   278. D-209.   *Obverse:* At least two seen with small rim breaks under date and opposite tenth to thirteenth stars.

1810   283. D-213.   *Obverse:* Several seen with small rim breaks over second to sixth stars.

PLATES

1 7 9 3

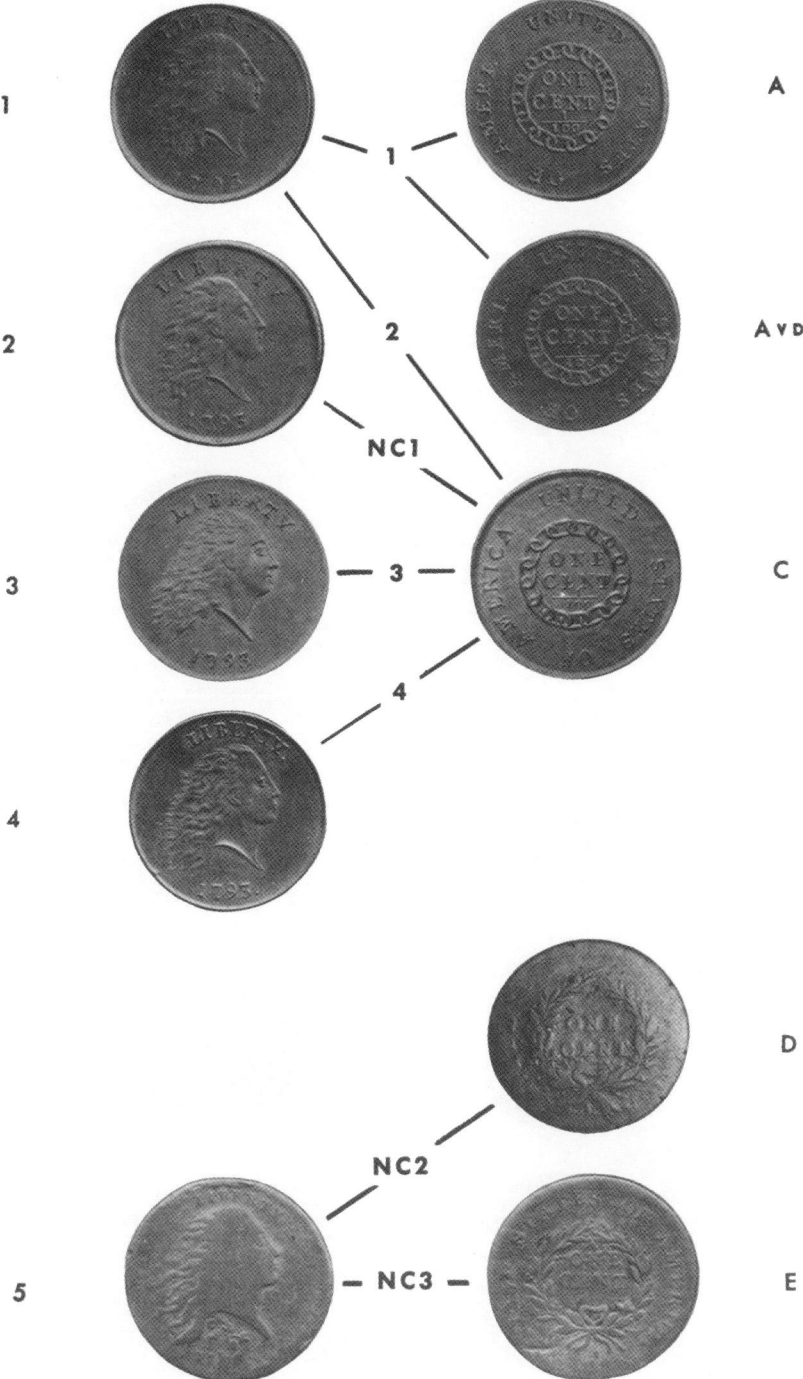

PLATE NO. 1

1 7 9 3

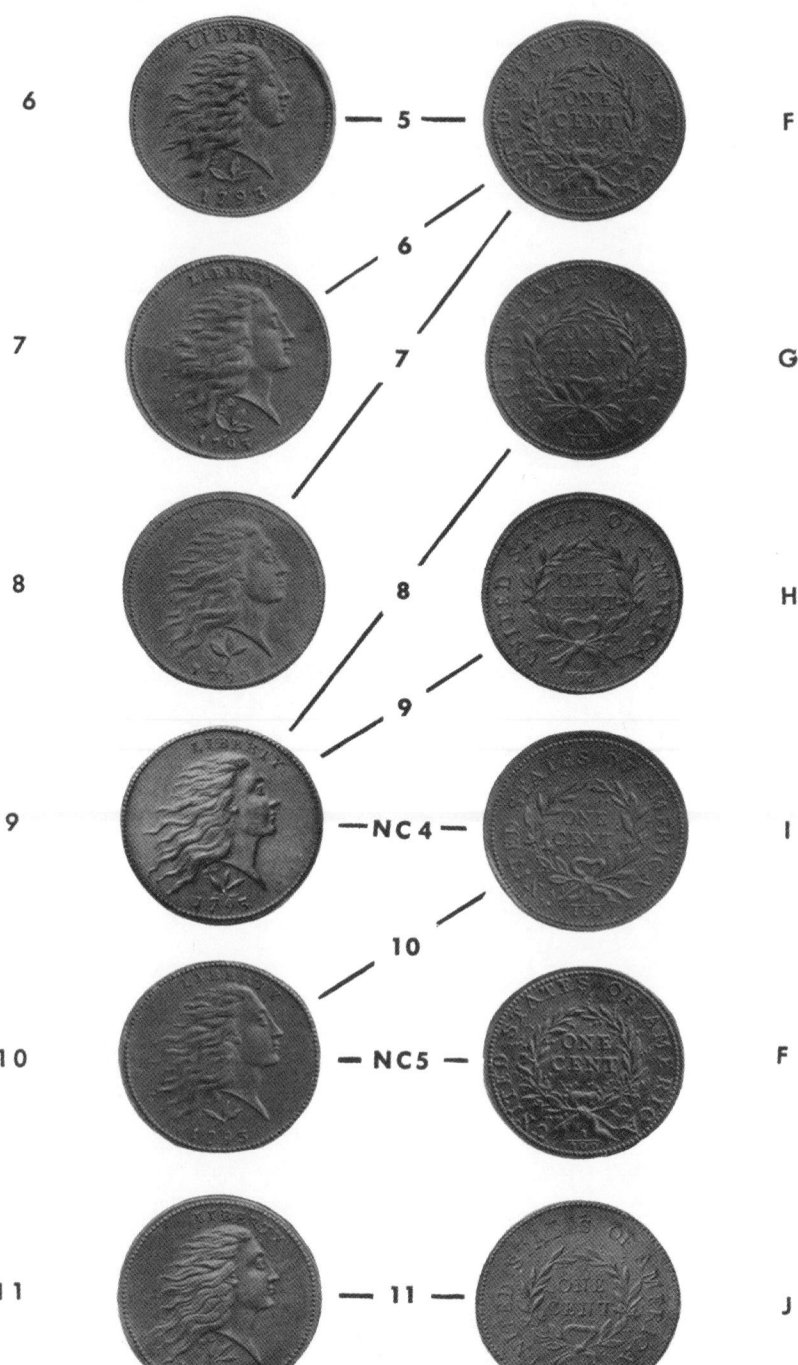

PLATE NO. 2

1 7 9 3

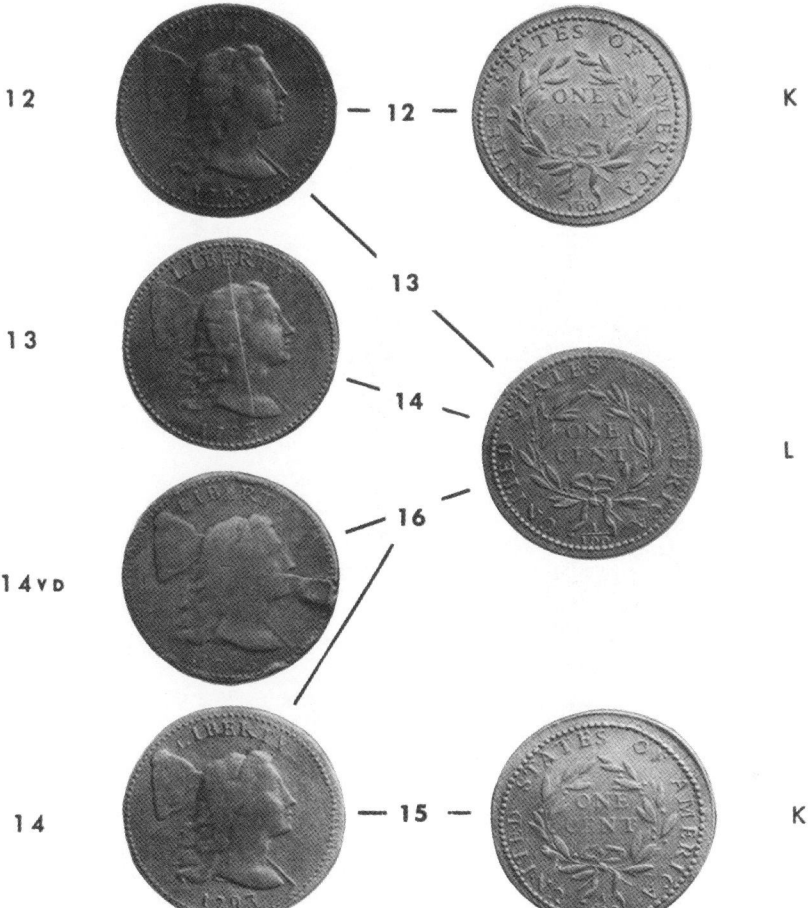

PLATE NO. 3

1 7 9 4

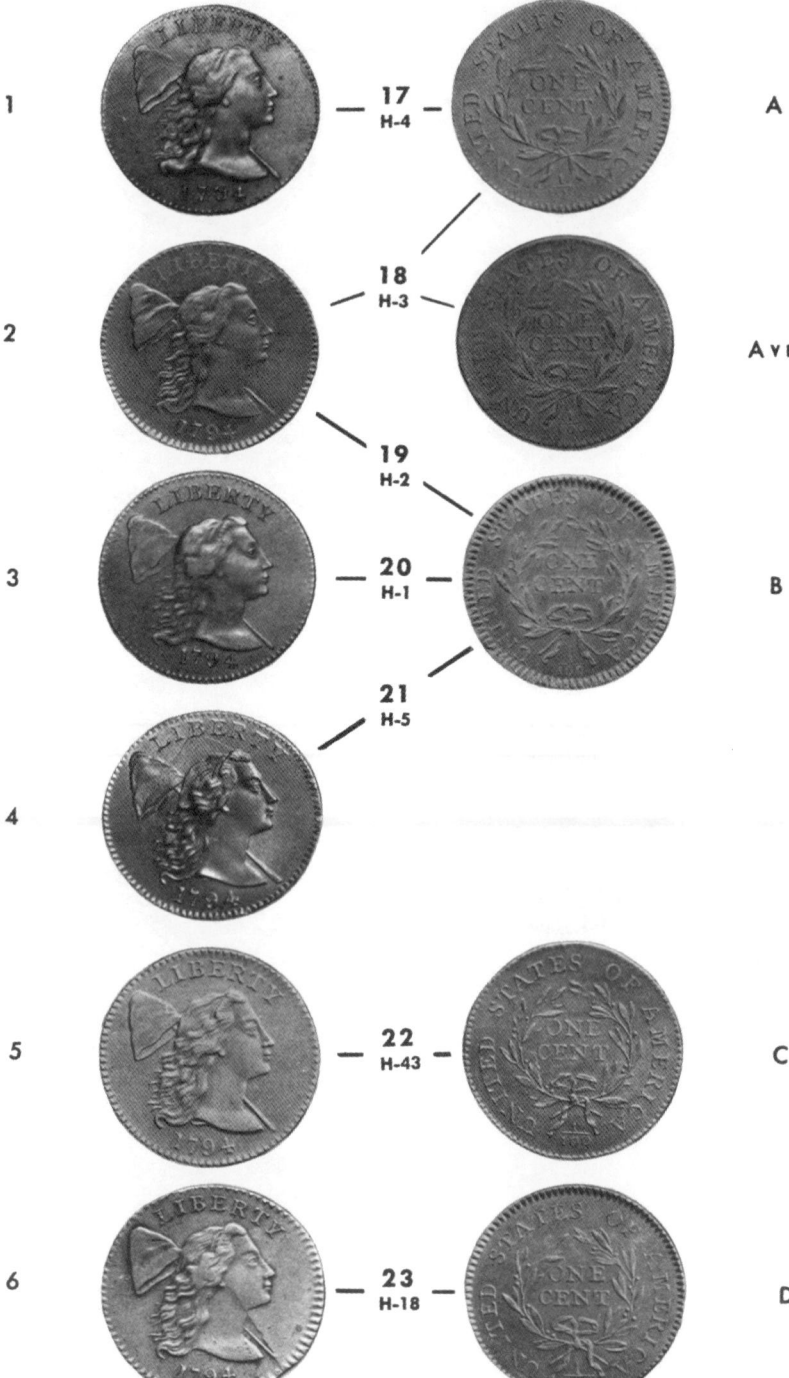

PLATE NO. 4

1 7 9 4

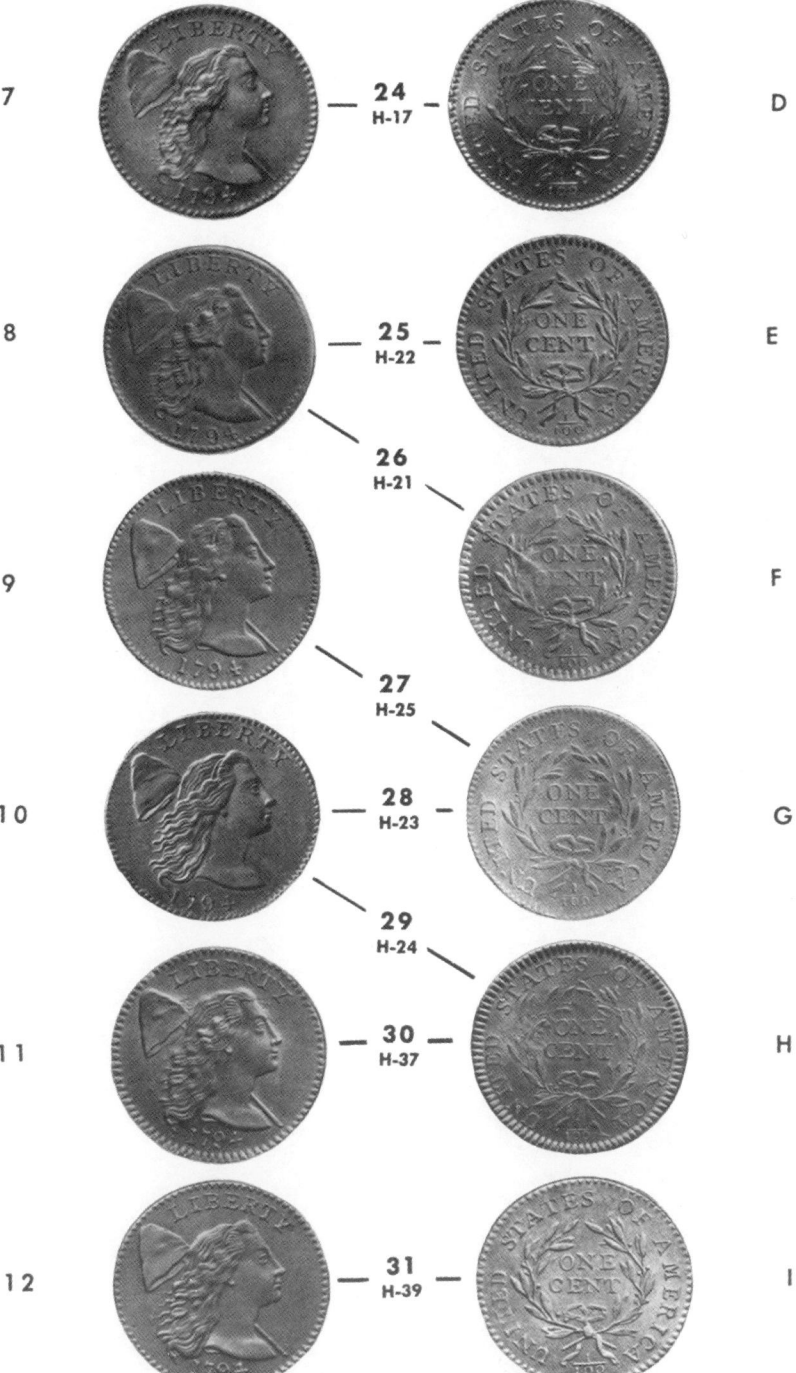

PLATE NO. 5

1 7 9 4

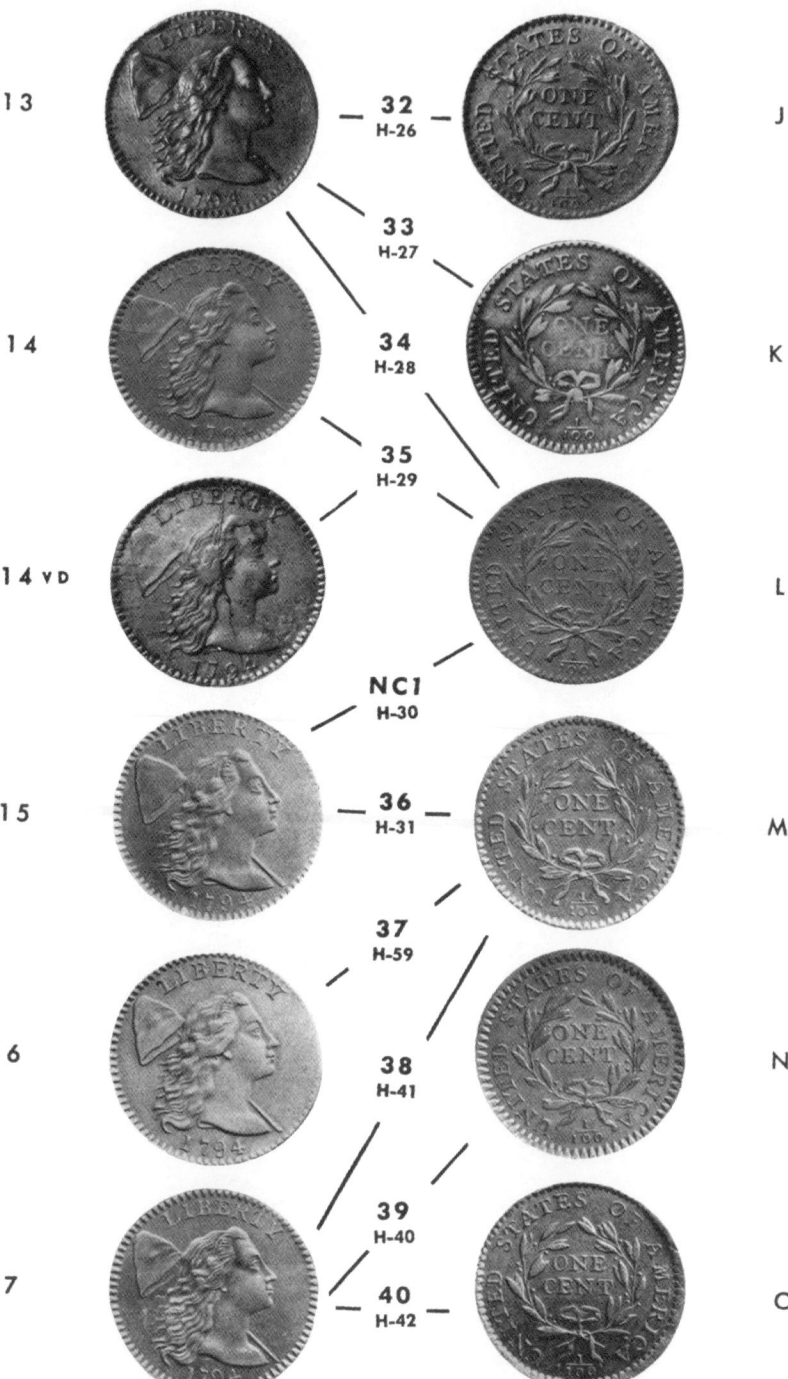

PLATE NO. 6

1 7 9 4

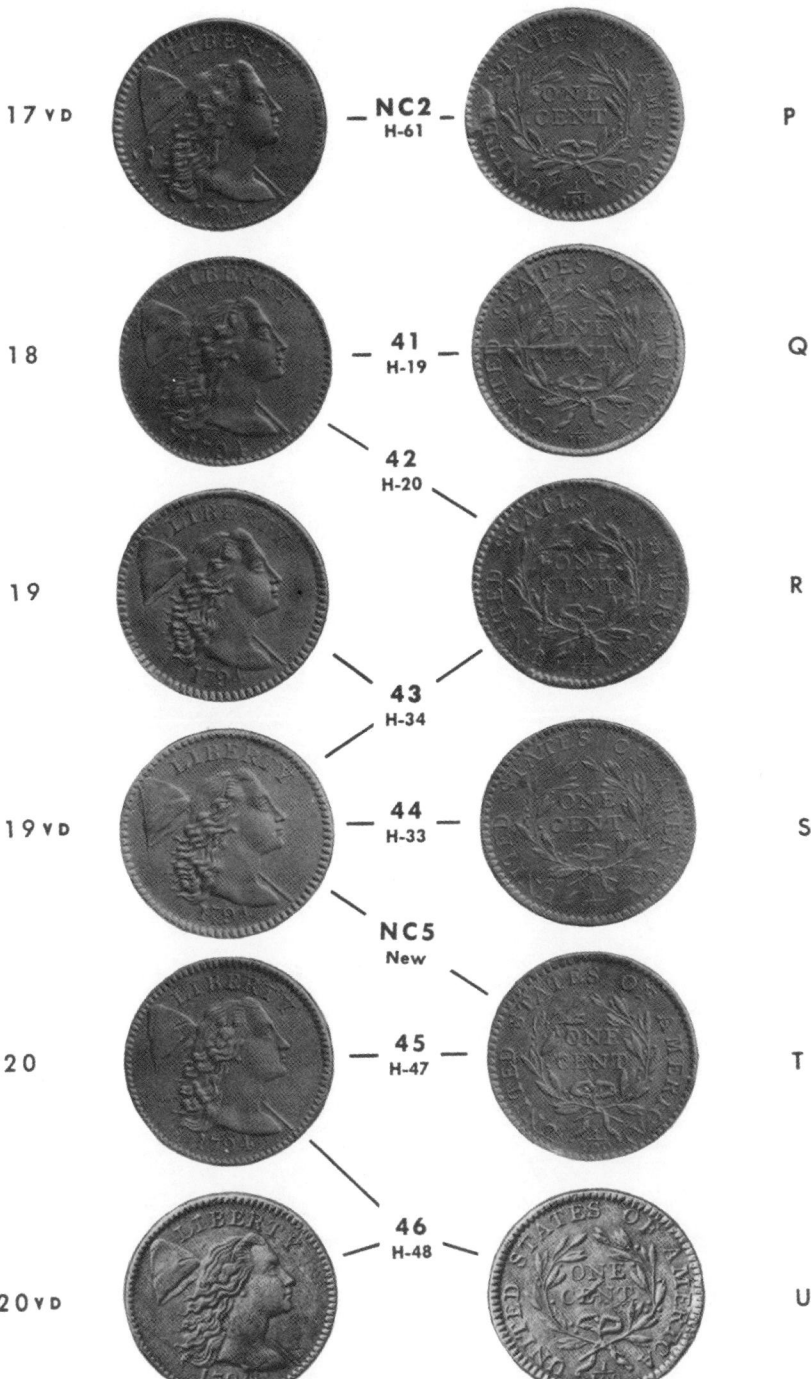

PLATE NO. 7

1 7 9 4

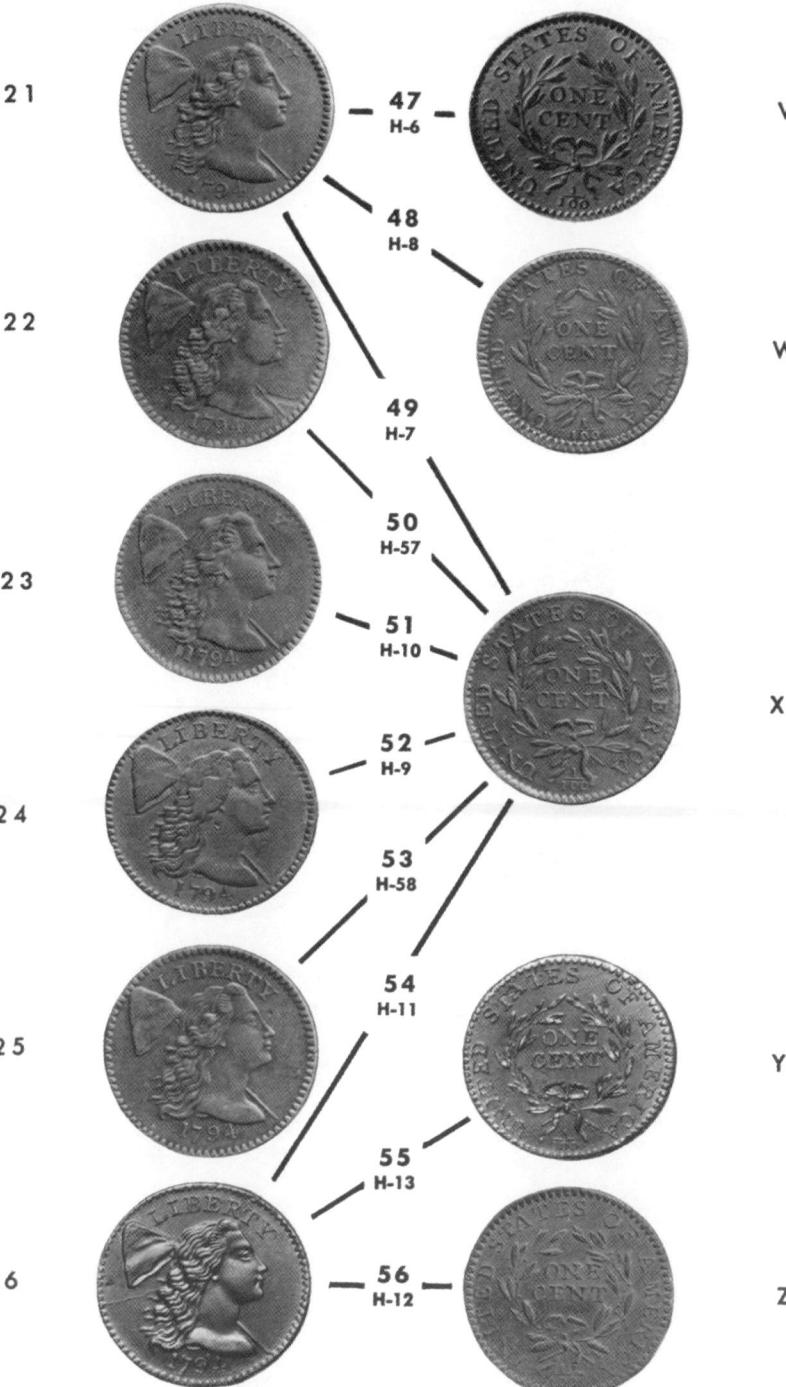

PLATE NO. 8

1 7 9 4

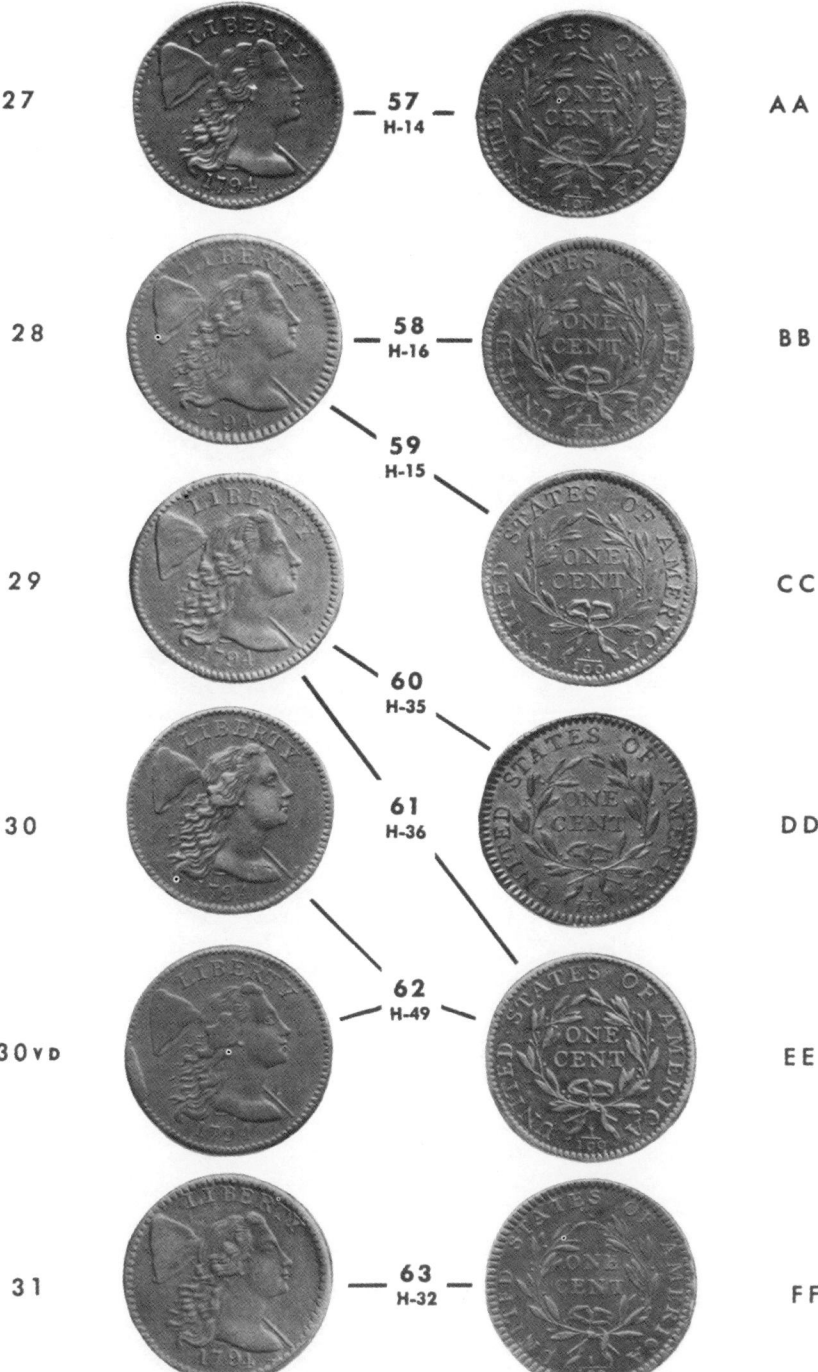

PLATE NO. 9

1 7 9 4

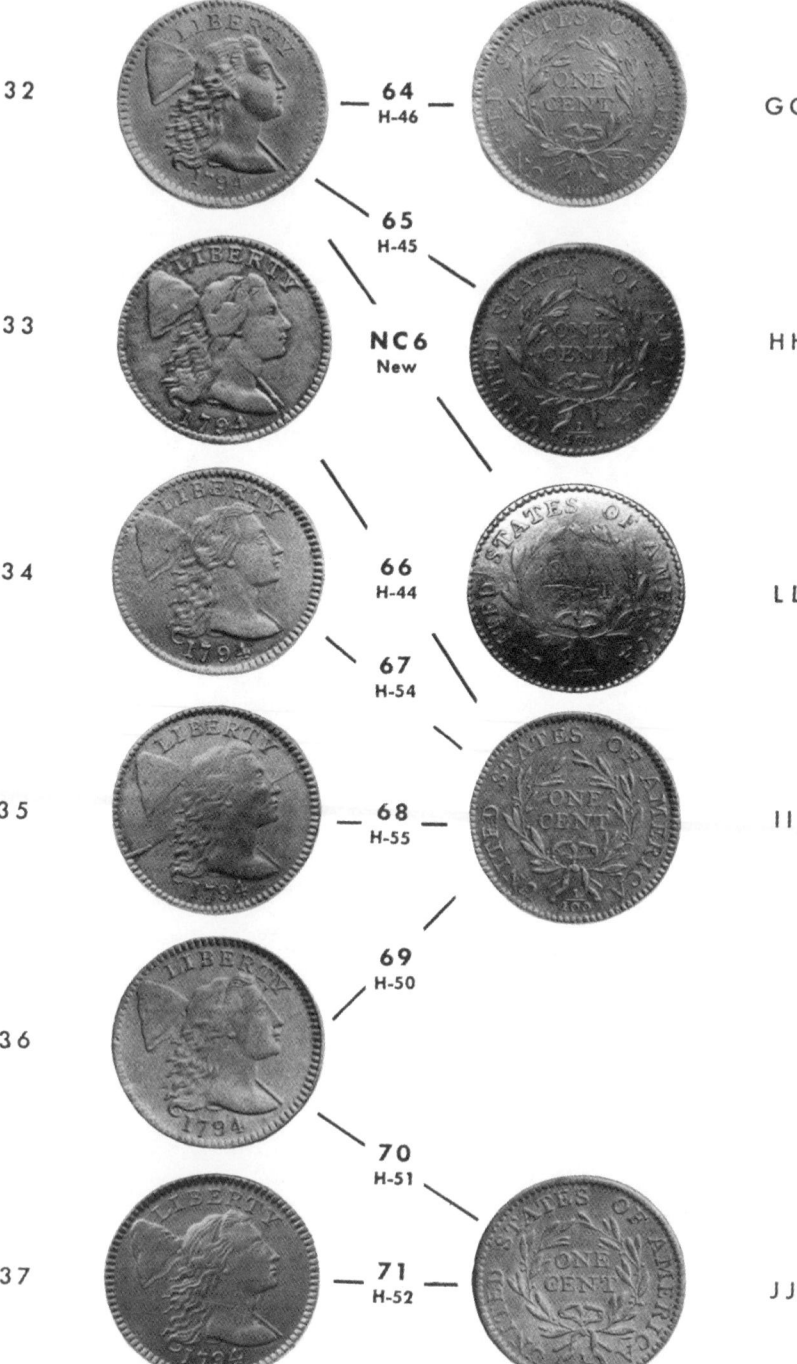

PLATE NO. 10

1 7 9 4 - 1 7 9 5

1 7 9 5

PLATE NO. 11

1 7 9 5

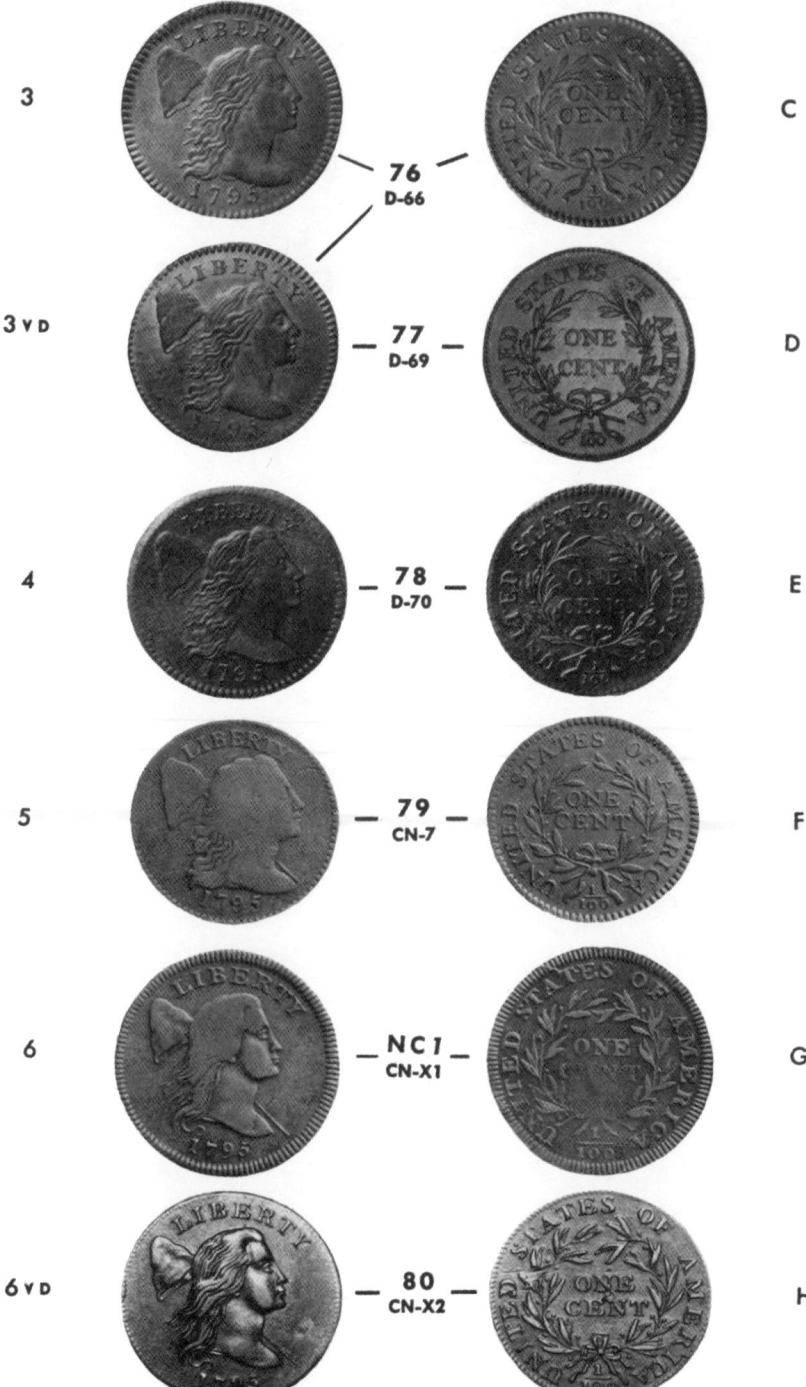

PLATE NO. 12

1 7 9 6

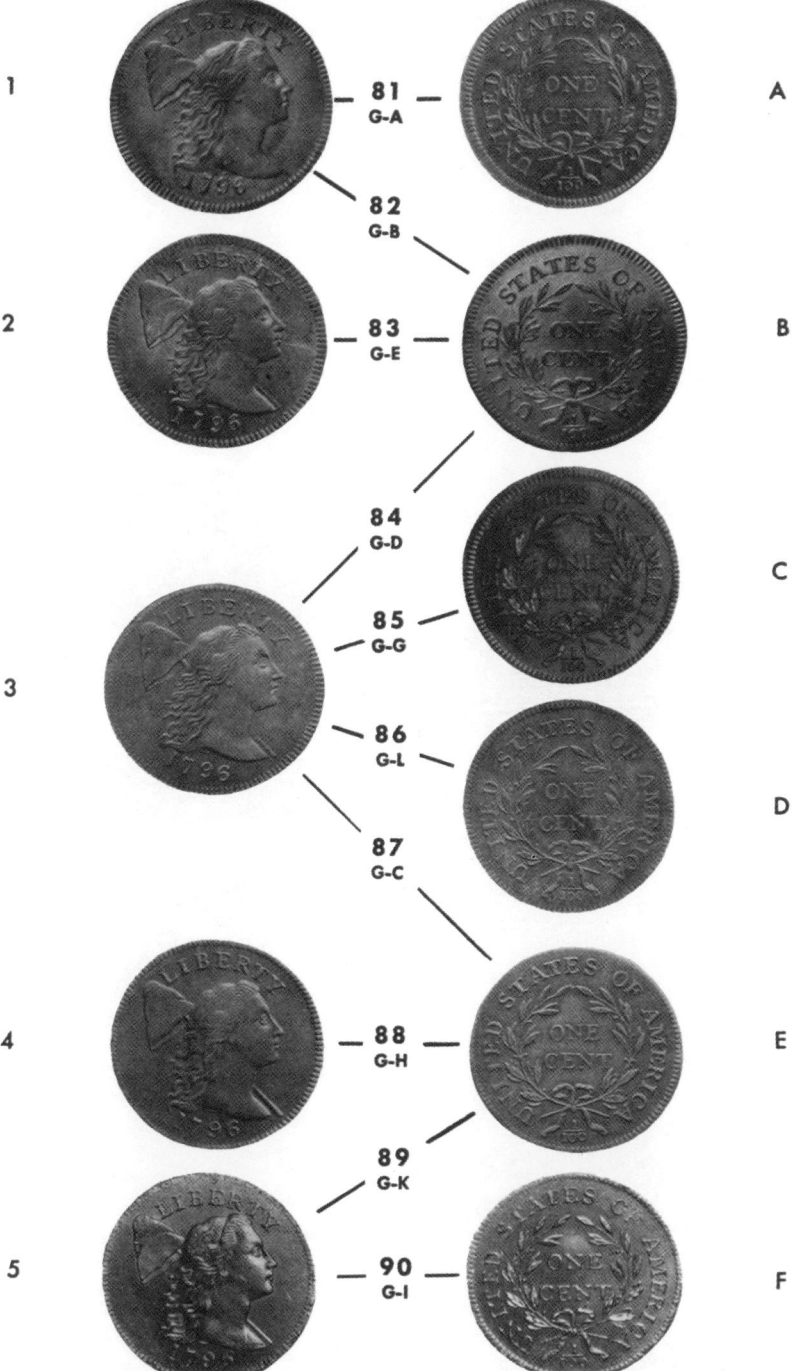

PLATE NO. 13

1 7 9 6

PLATE NO. 14

1 7 9 6

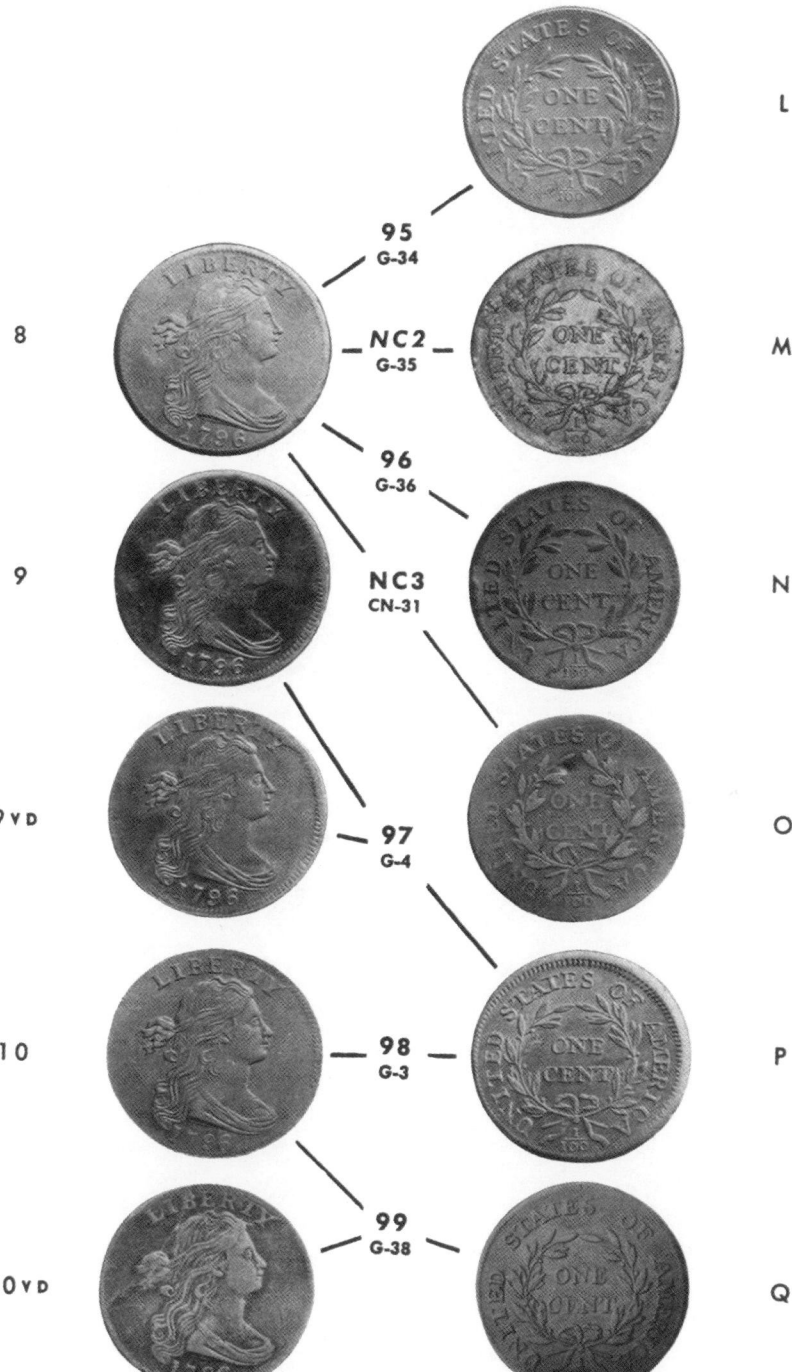

PLATE NO. 15

1 7 9 6

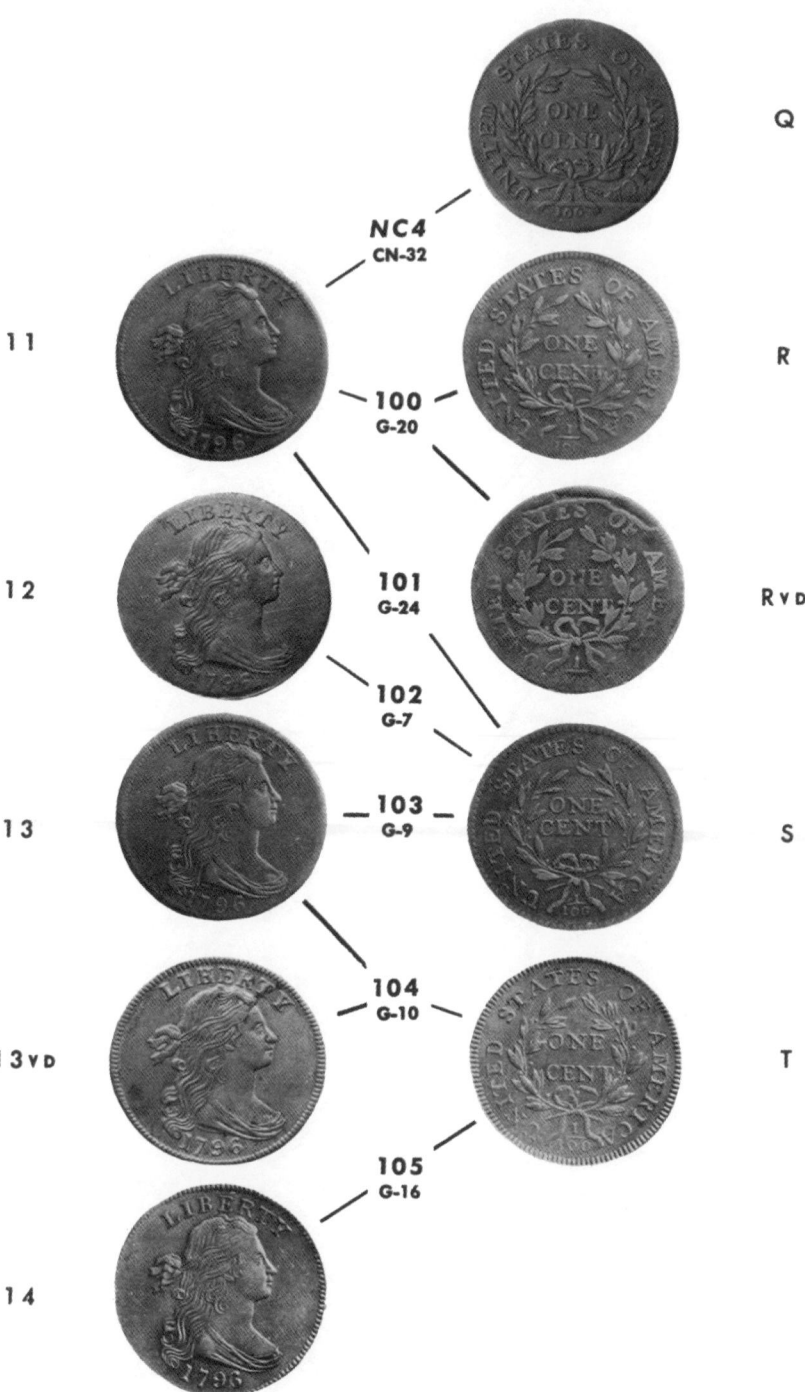

PLATE NO. 16

1 7 9 6

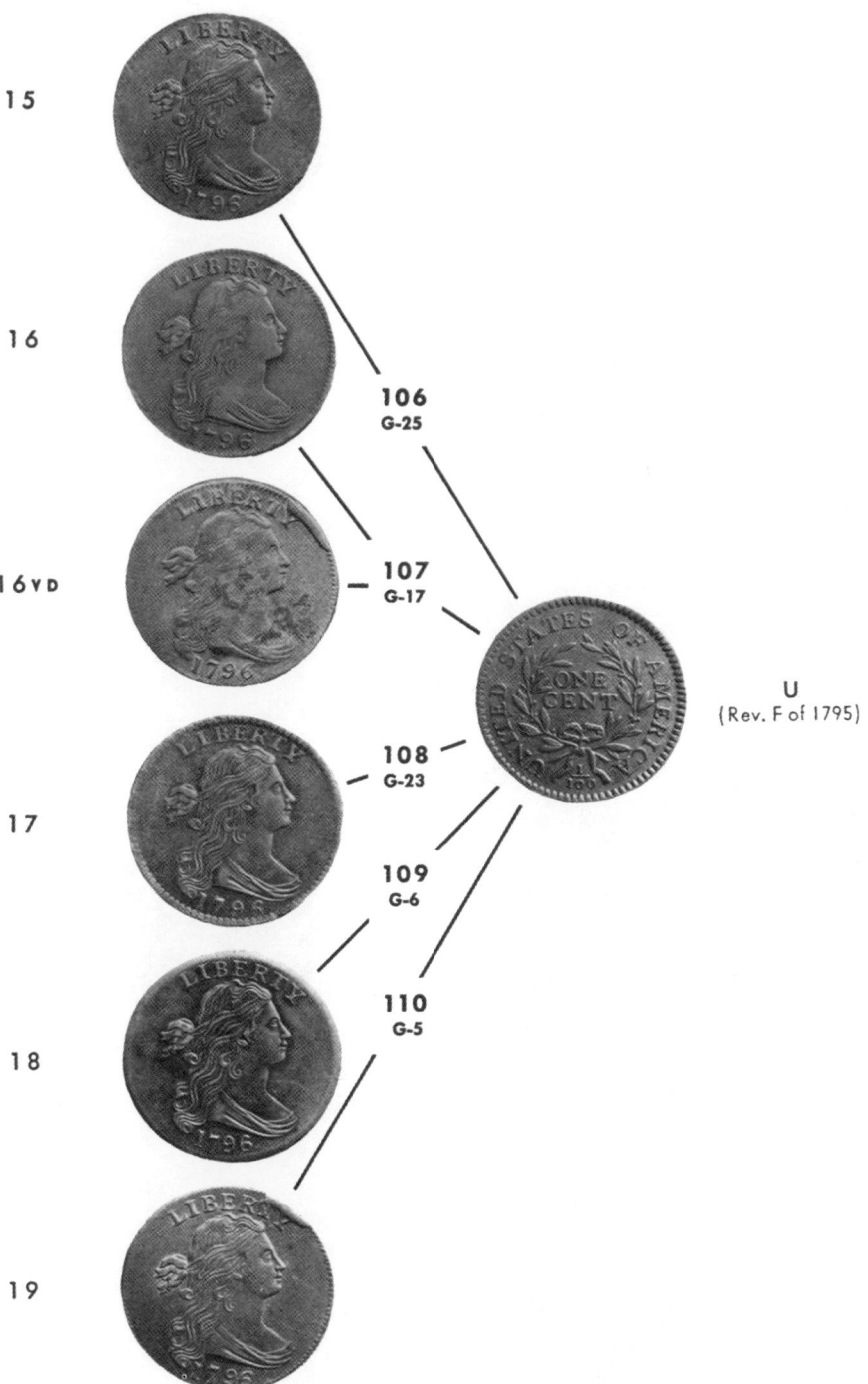

1 7 9 6

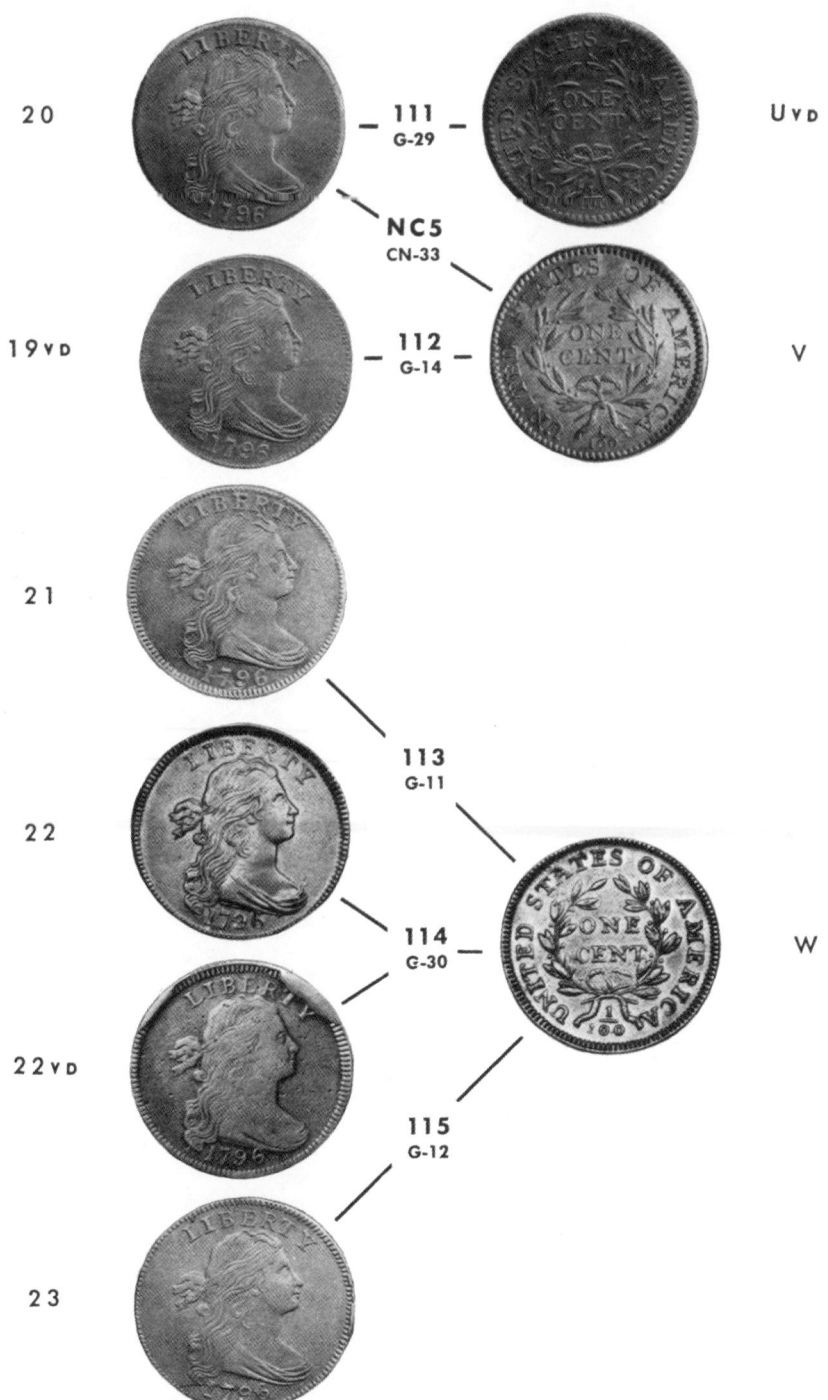

PLATE NO. 18

1796

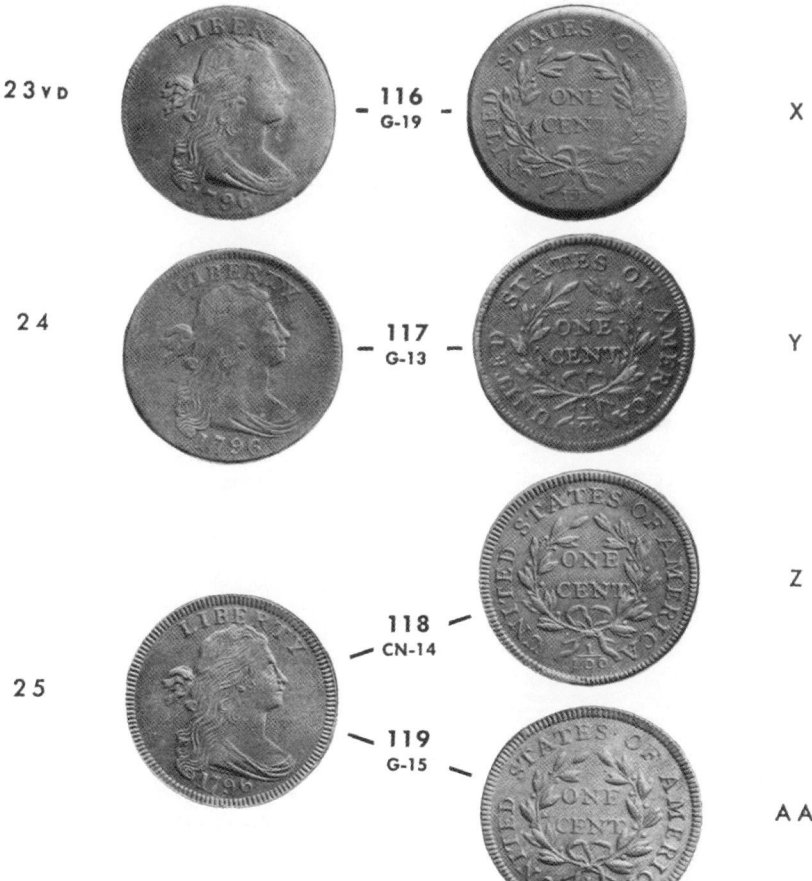

PLATE NO. 19

1 7 9 7

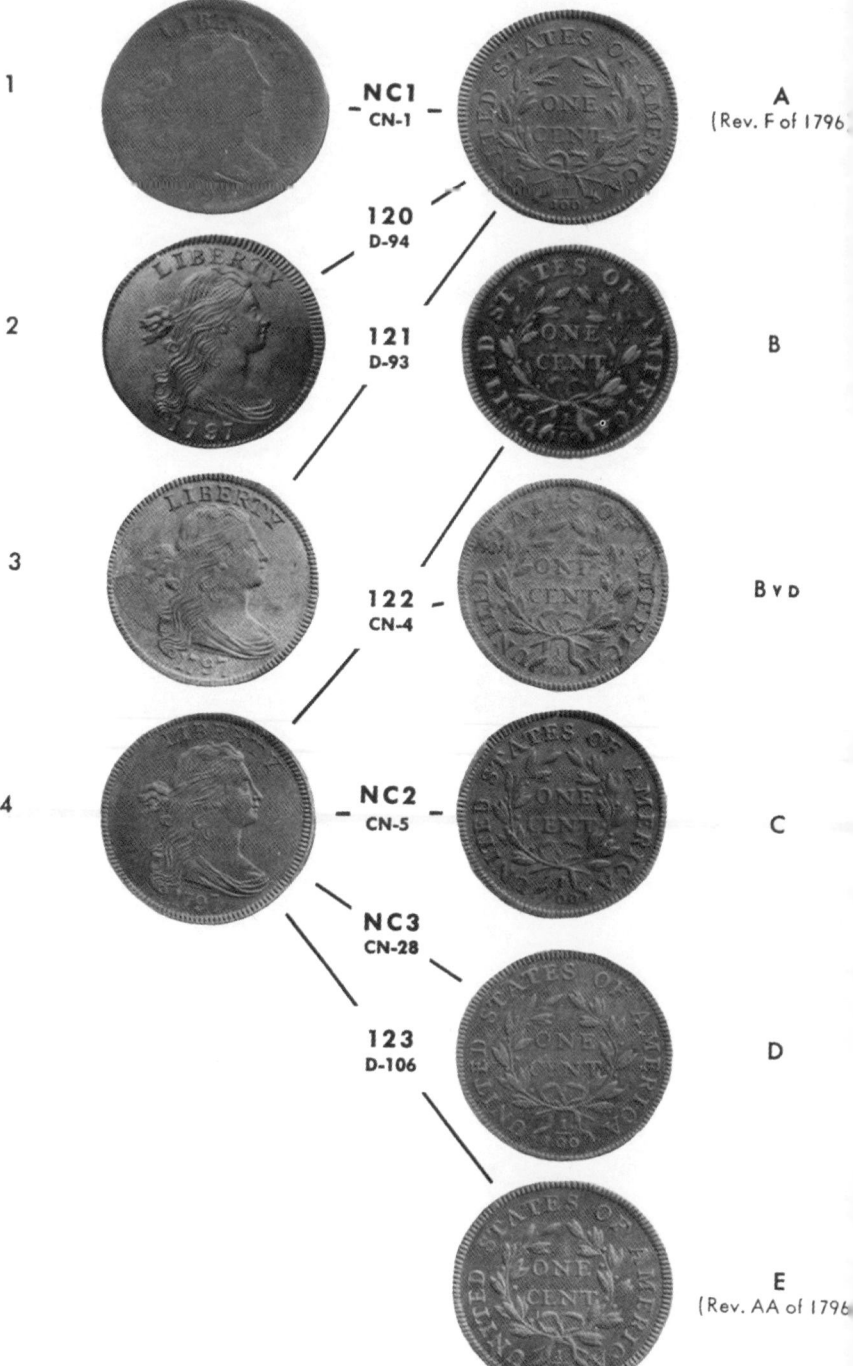

PLATE NO. 20

1 7 9 7

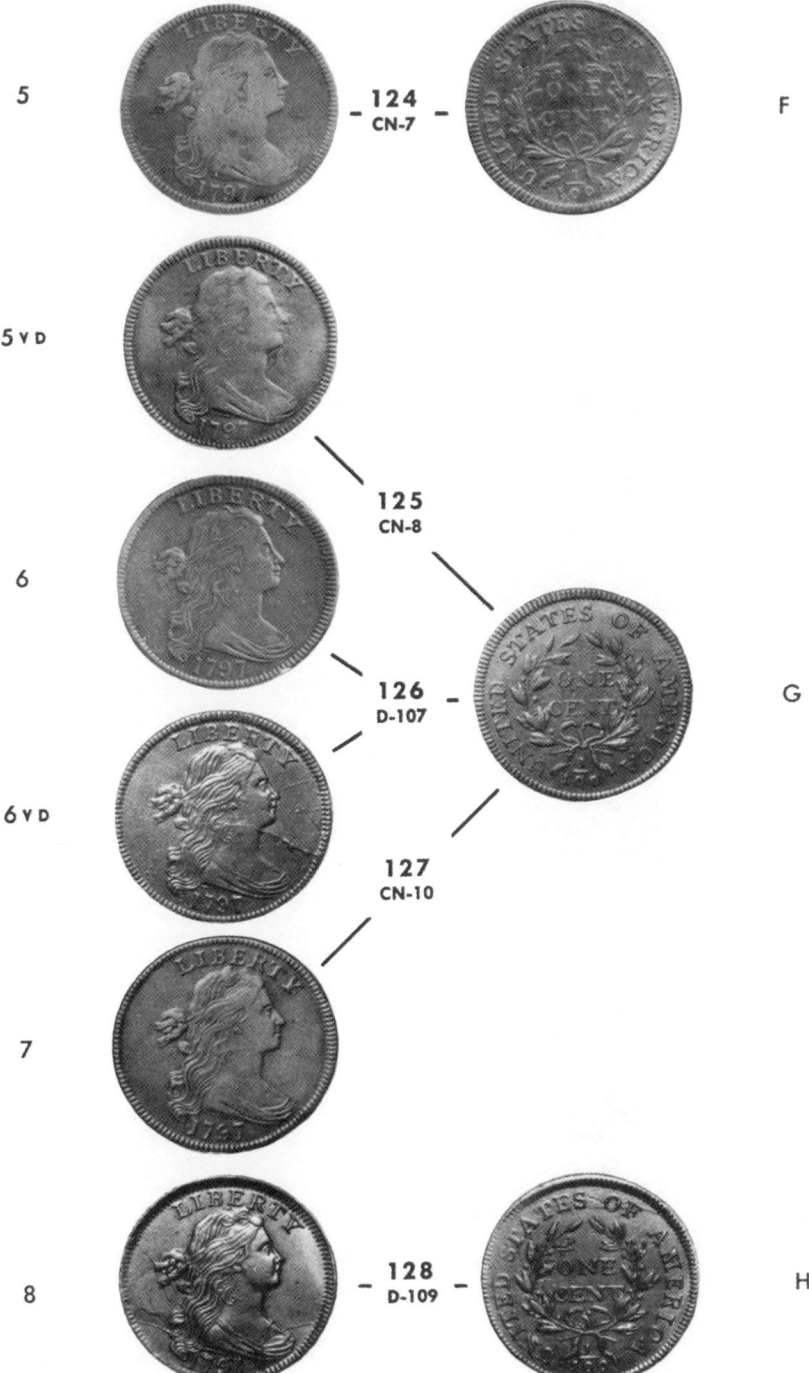

PLATE NO. 21

1 7 9 7

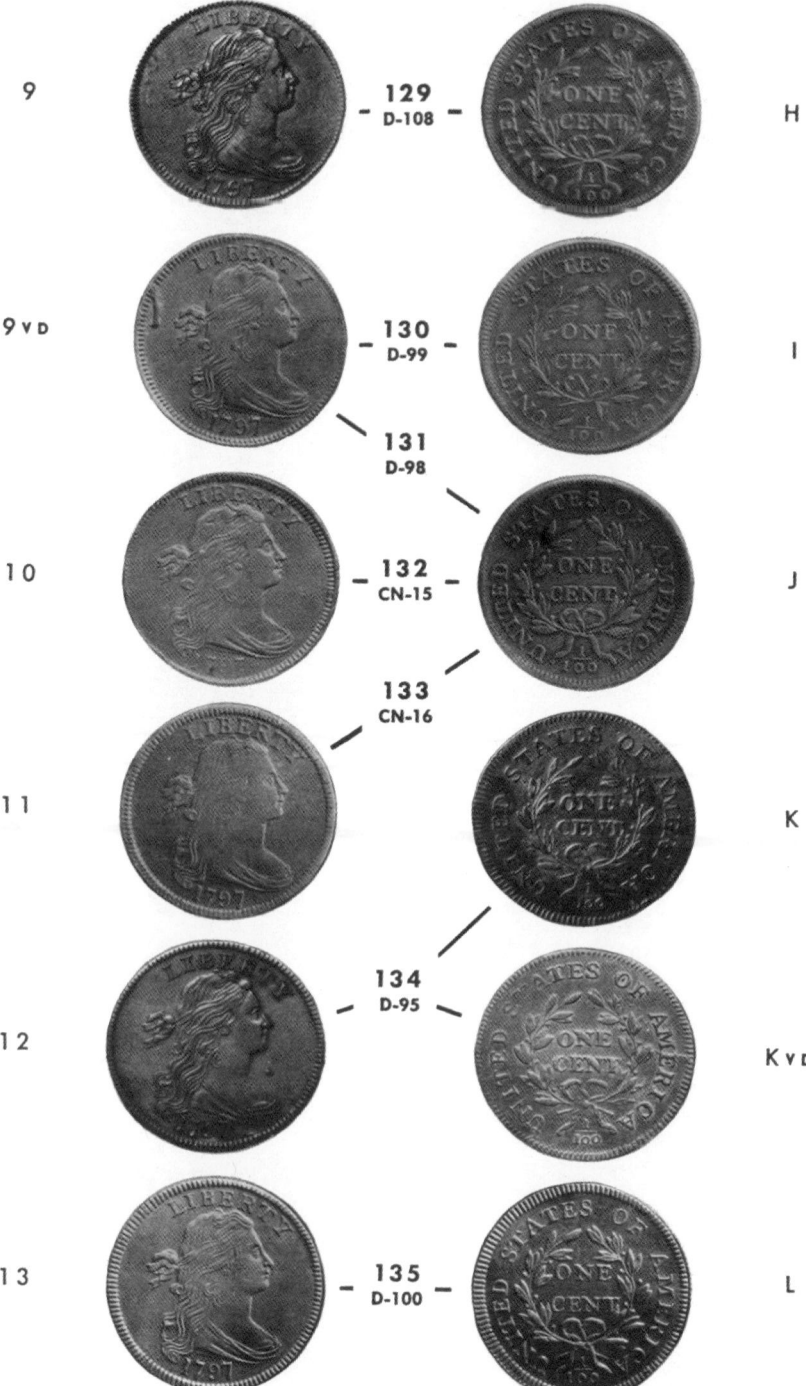

PLATE NO. 22

1 7 9 7

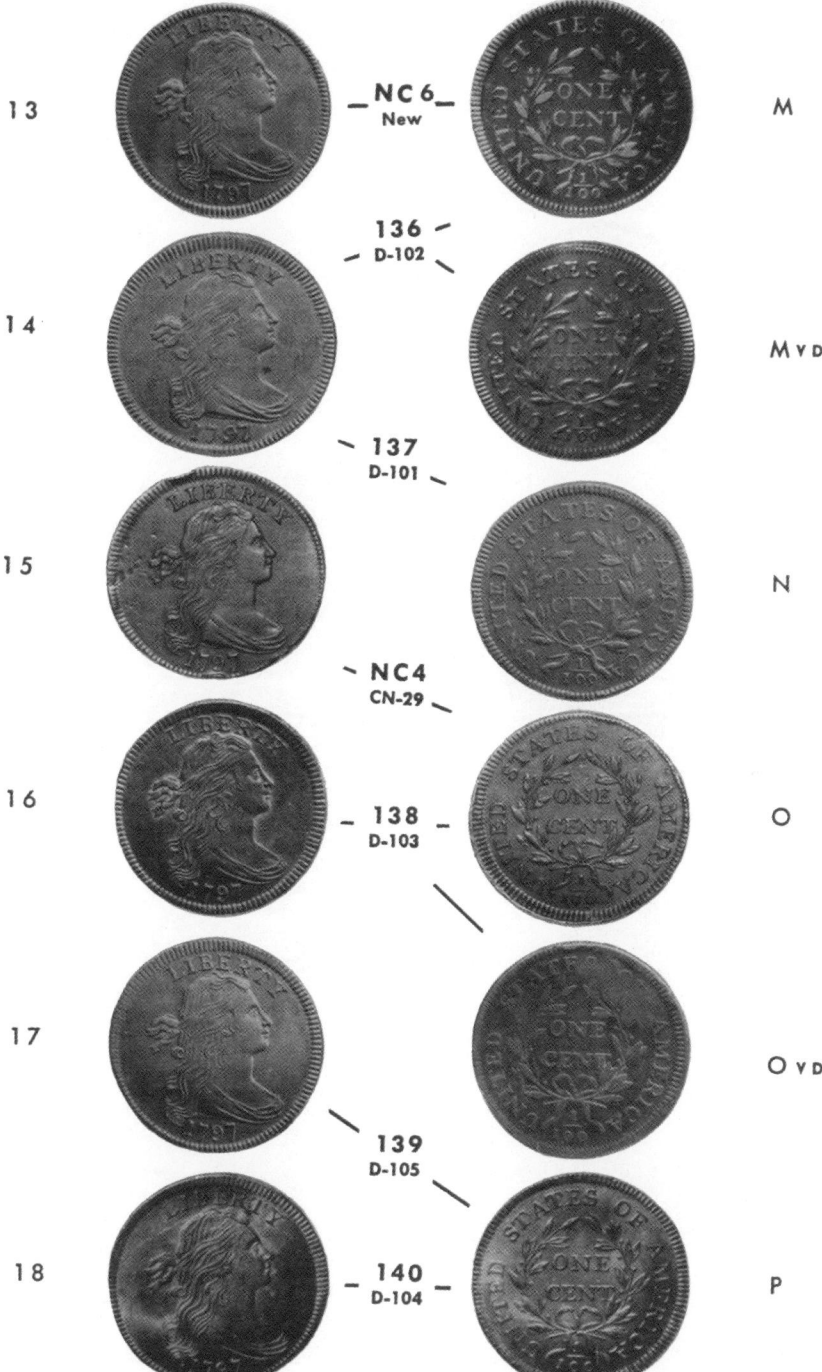

PLATE NO. 23

1 7 9 7

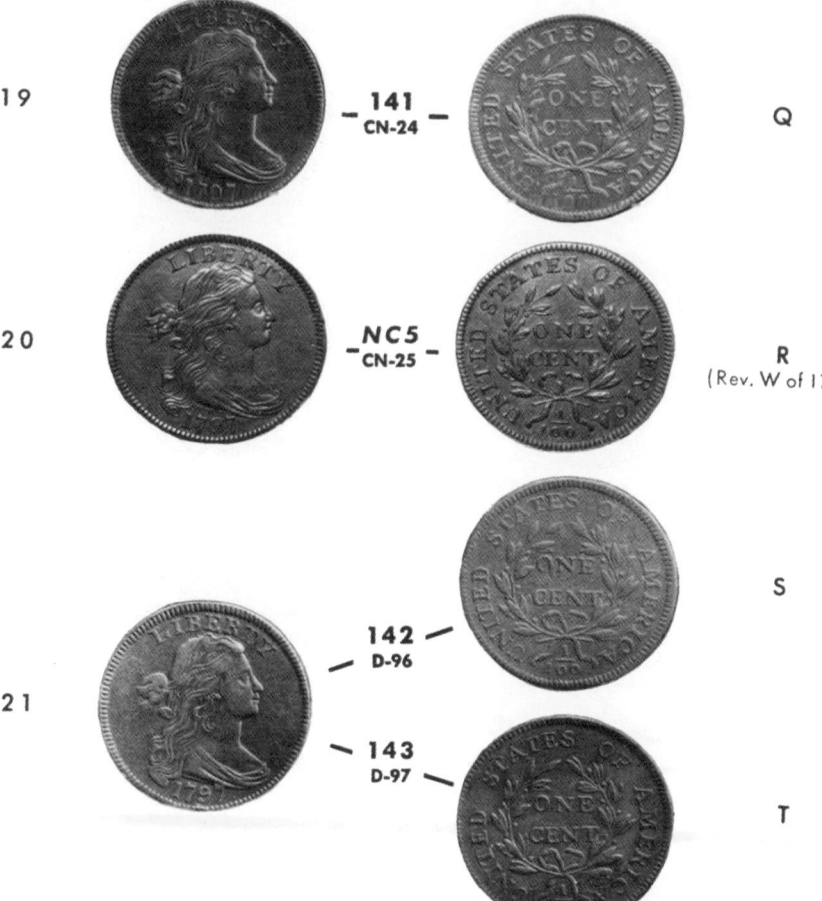

PLATE NO. 24

1 7 9 8

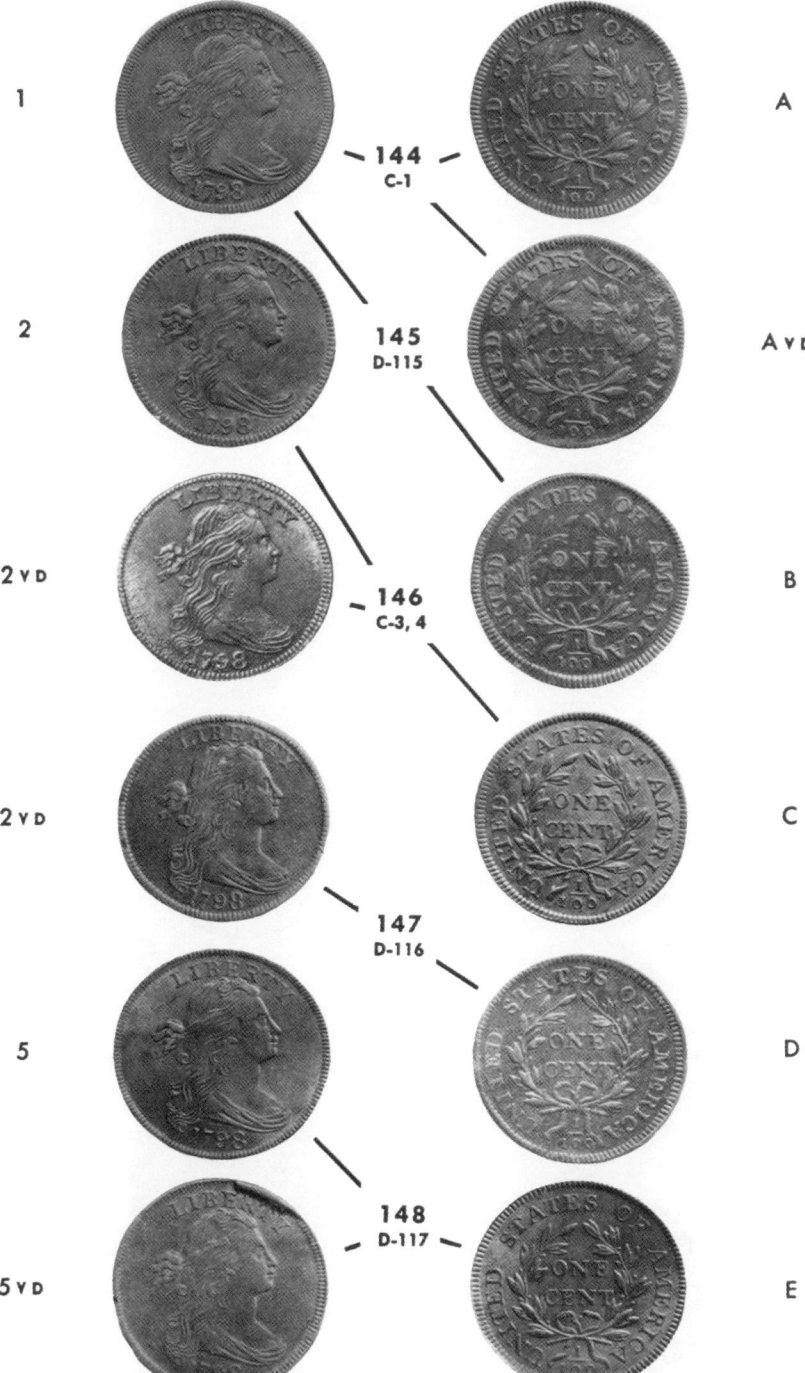

PLATE NO. 25

1 7 9 8

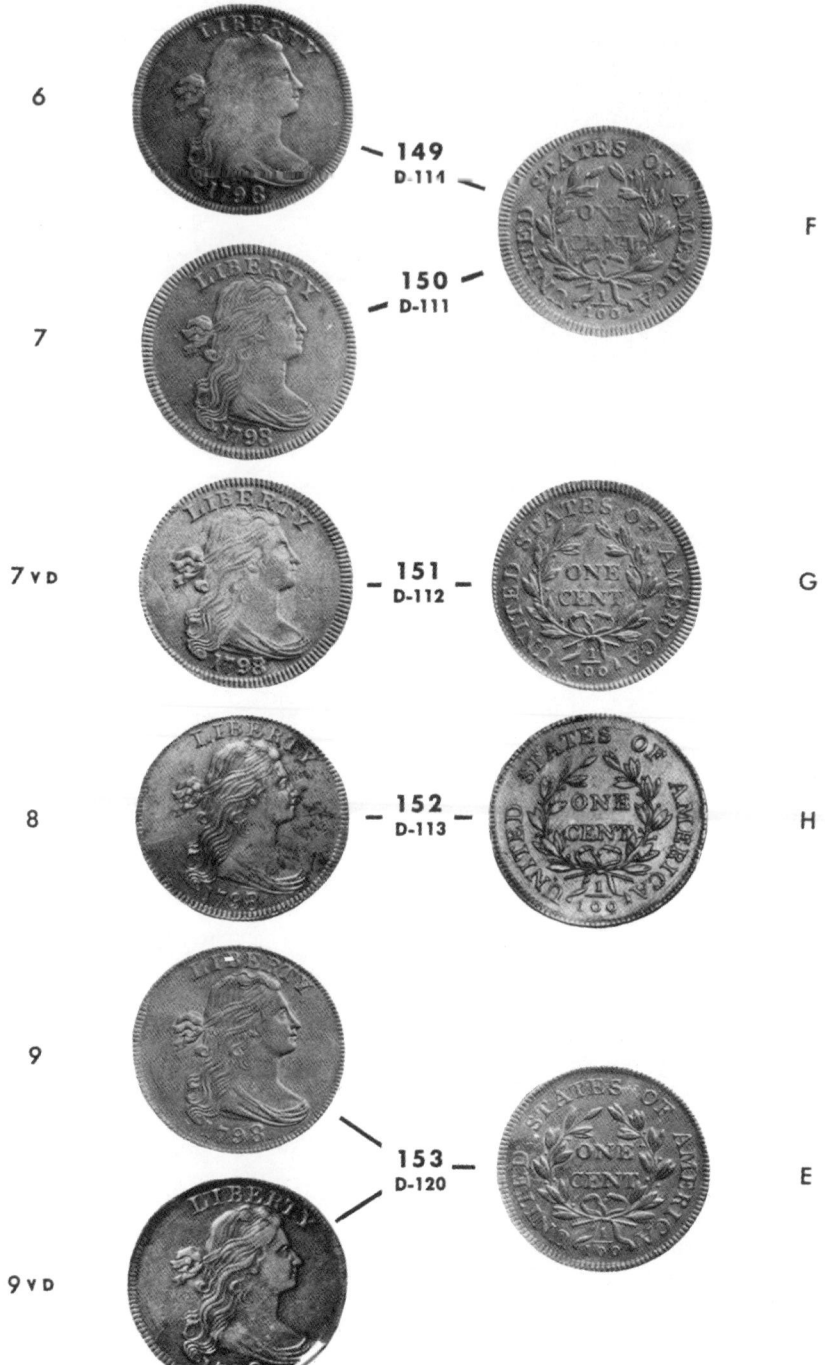

PLATE NO. 26

1 7 9 8

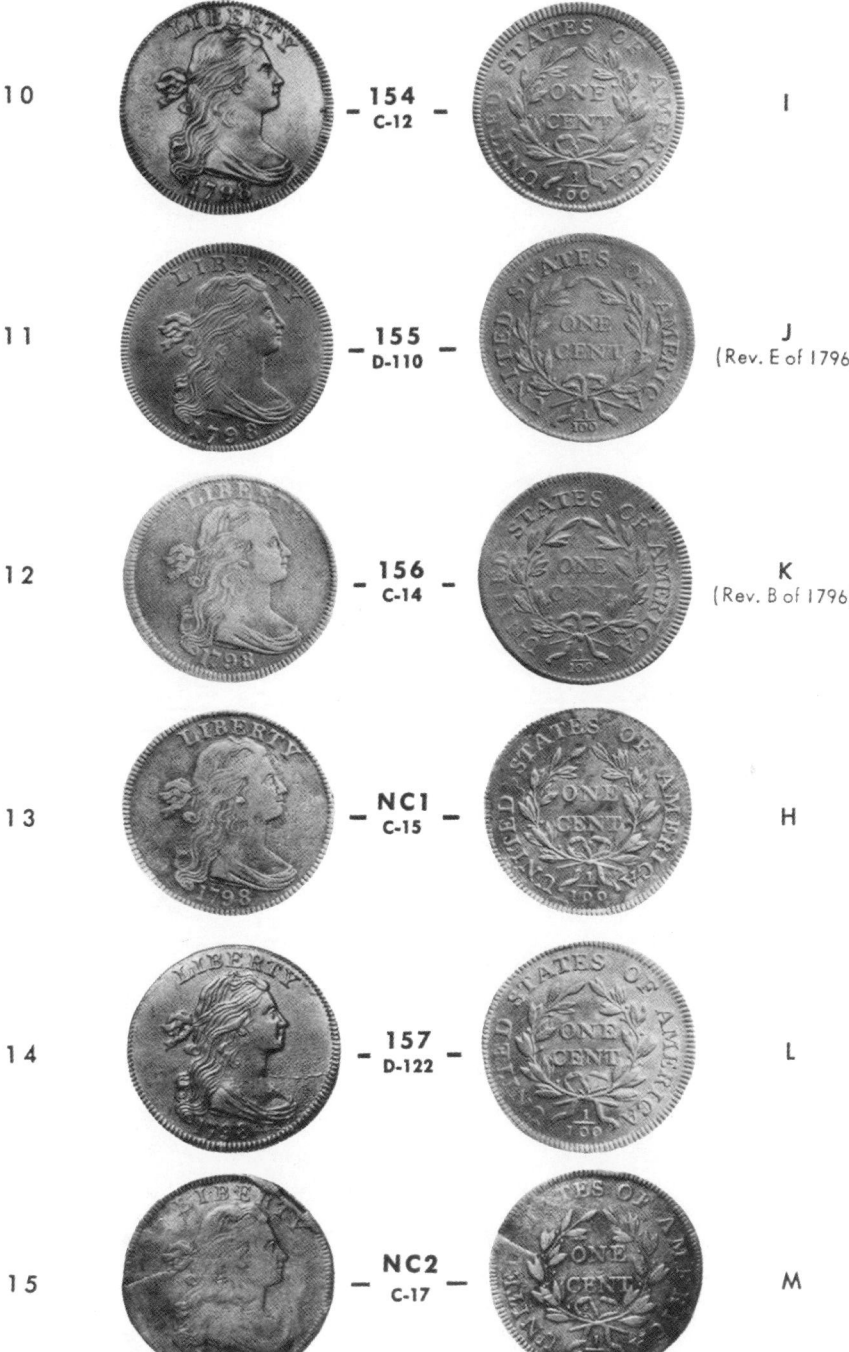

PLATE NO. 27

1 7 9 8

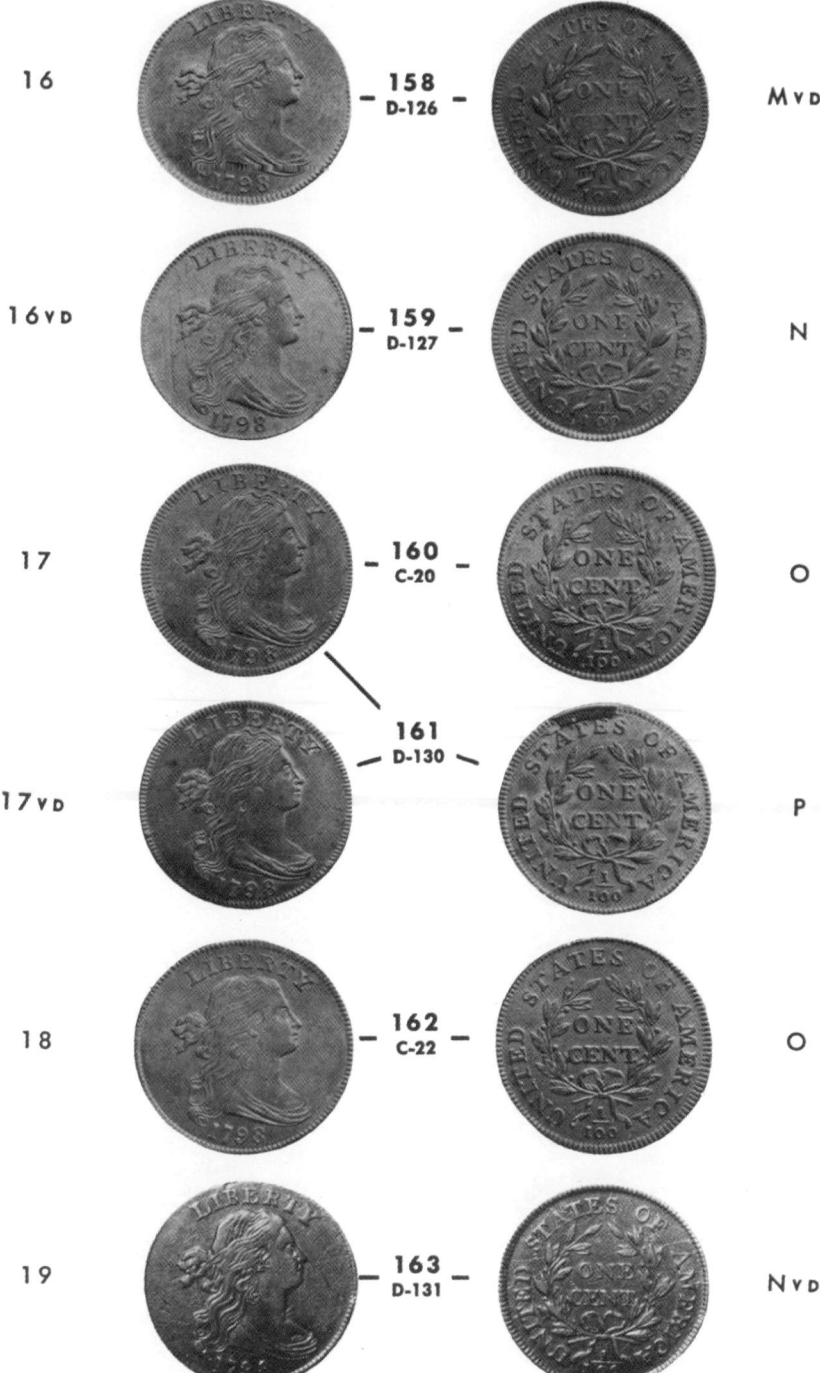

PLATE NO. 28

1 7 9 8

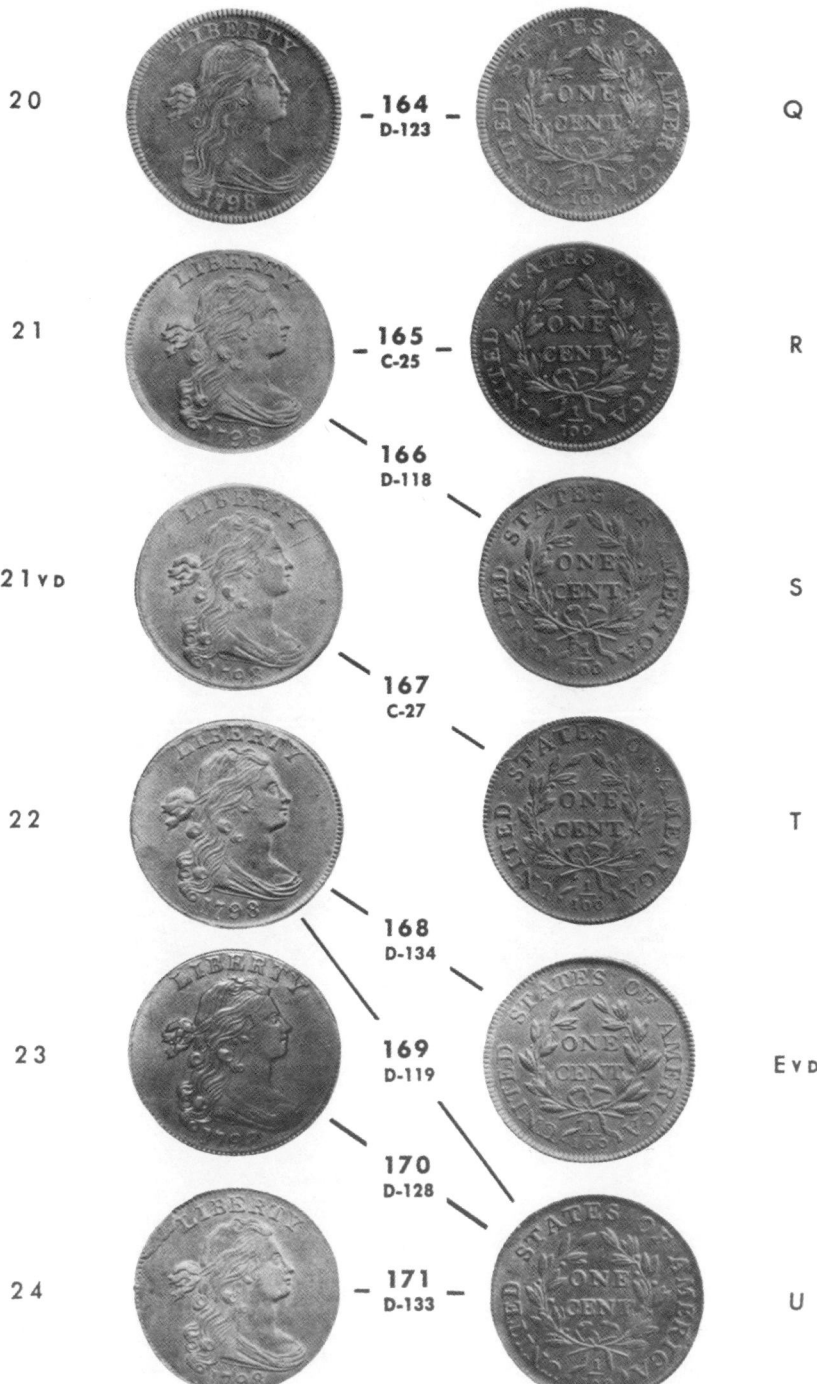

PLATE NO. 29

1 7 9 8

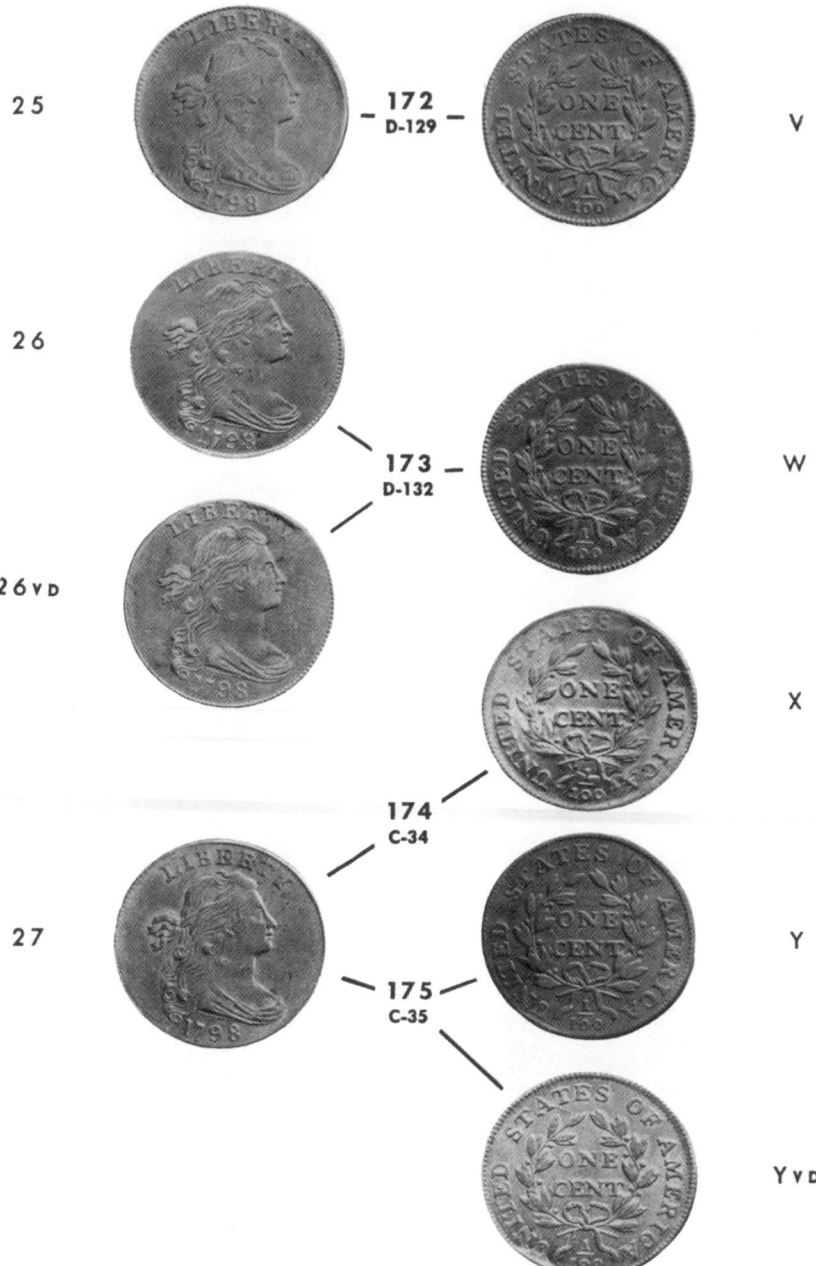

PLATE NO. 30

1 7 9 8

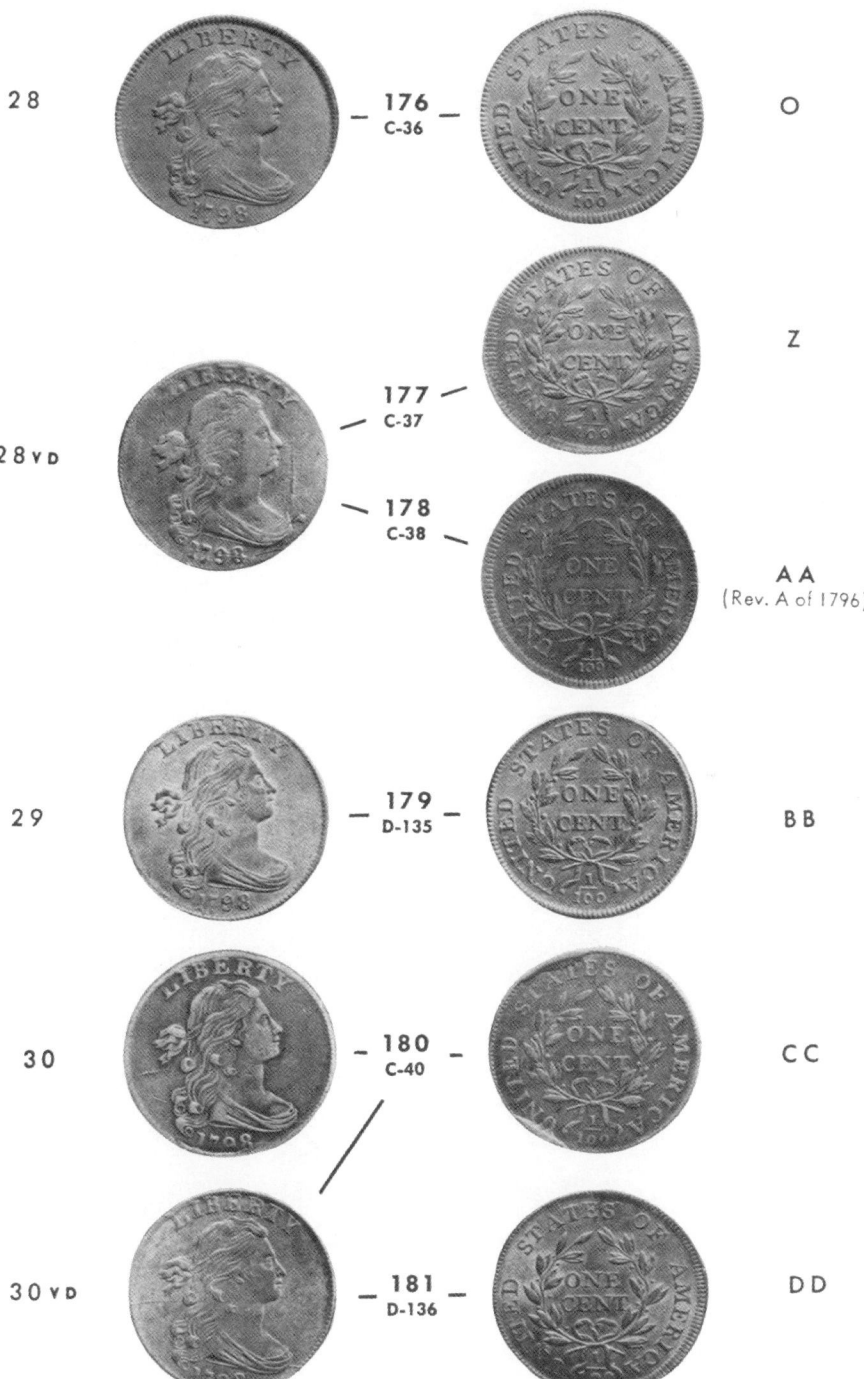

PLATE NO. 31

1 7 9 8

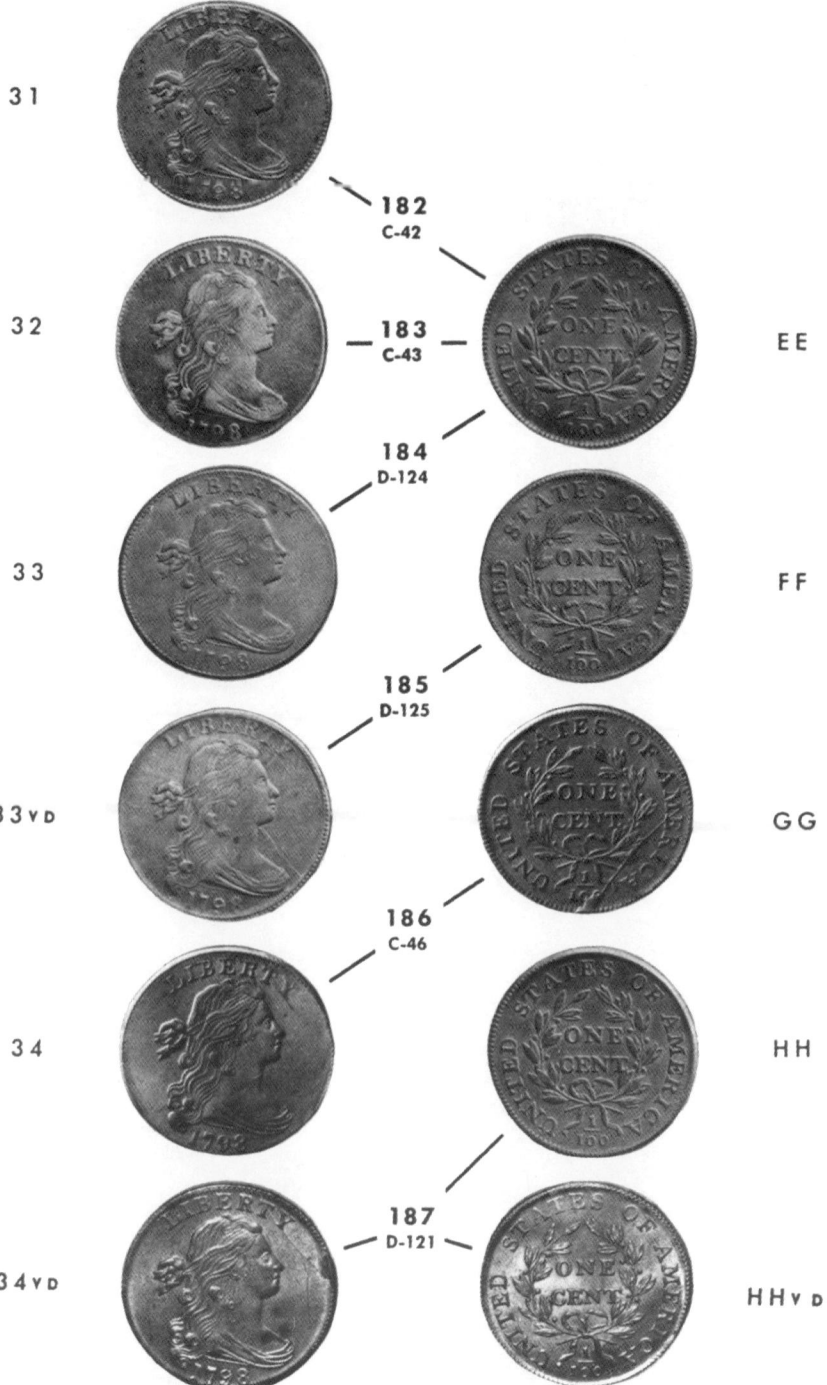

PLATE NO. 32

1 7 9 9

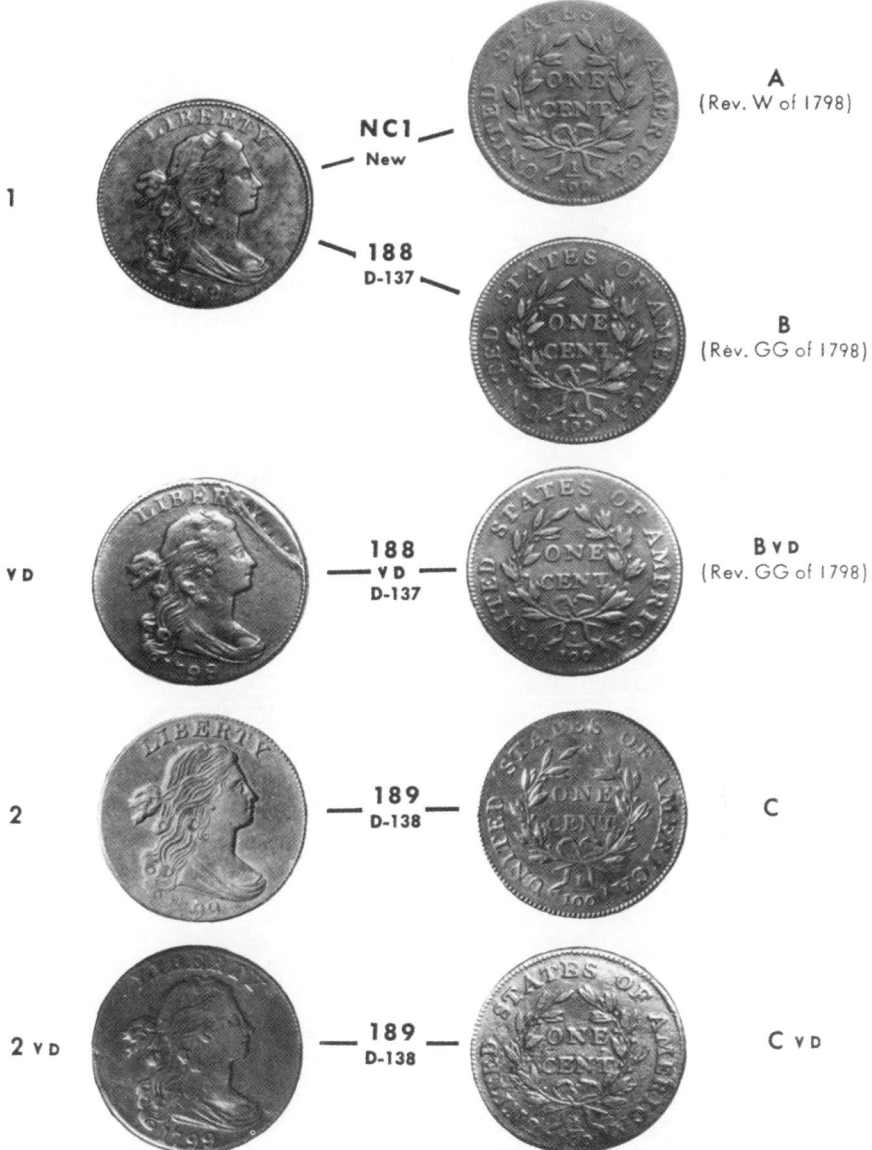

PLATE NO. 33

1 8 0 0

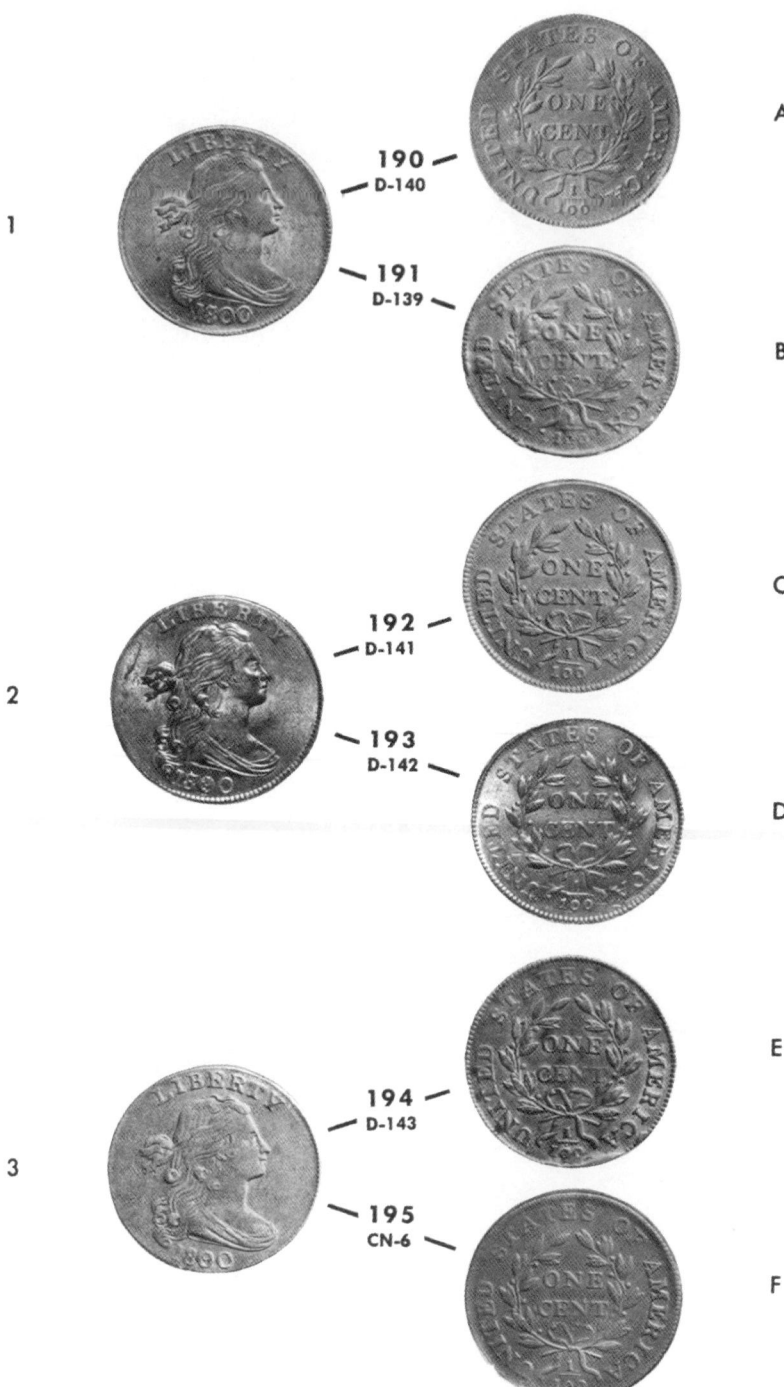

PLATE NO. 34

1 8 0 0

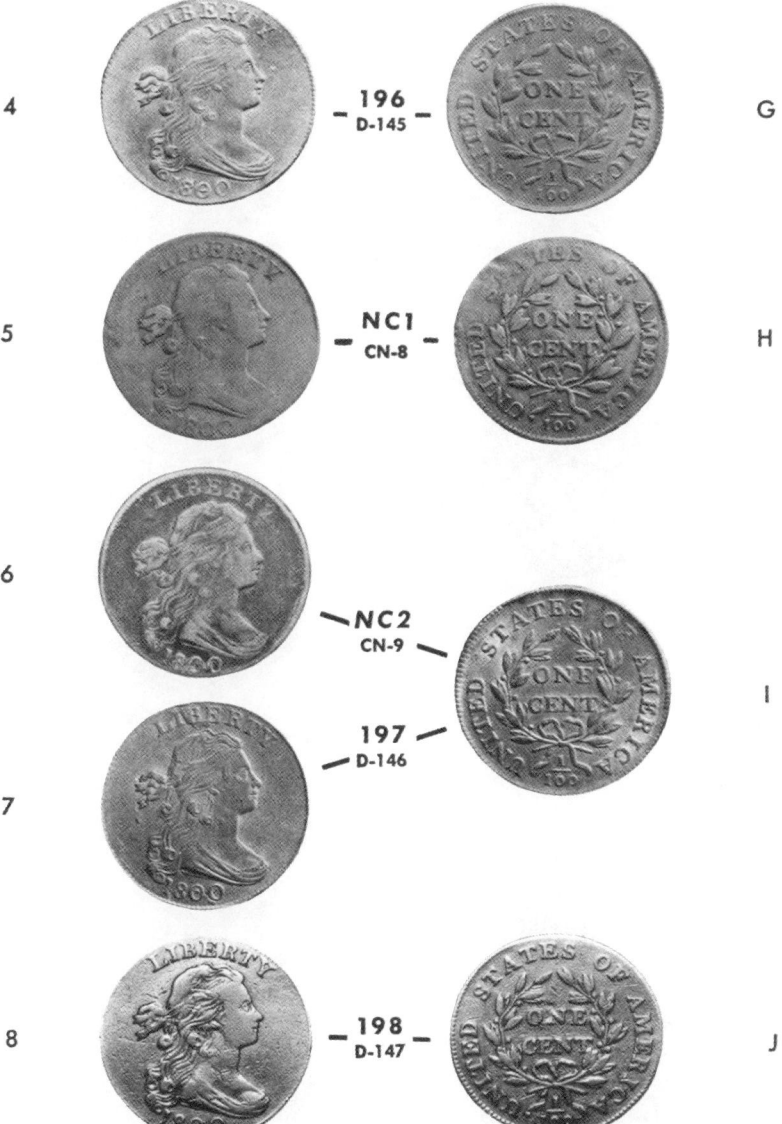

PLATE NO. 35

1 8 0 0

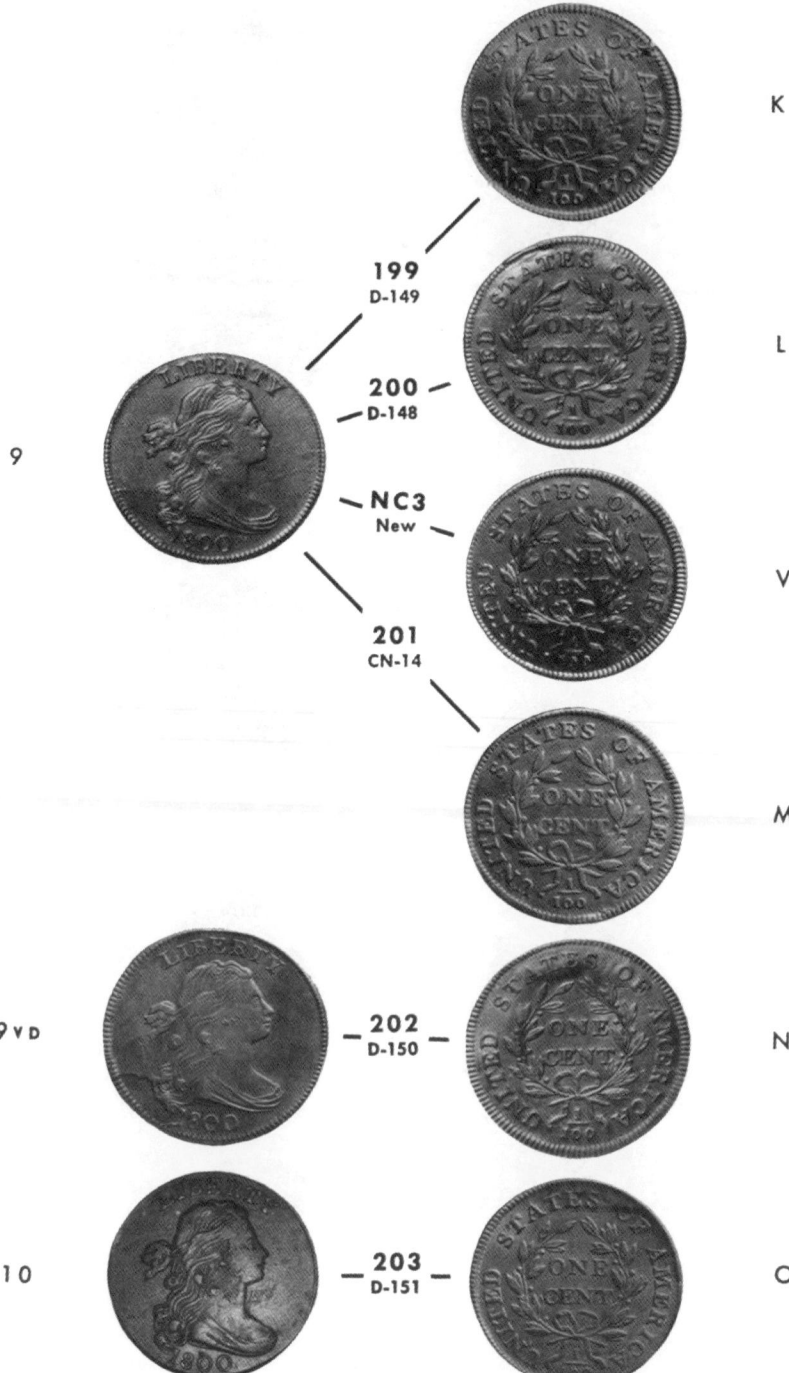

PLATE NO. 36

1 8 0 0

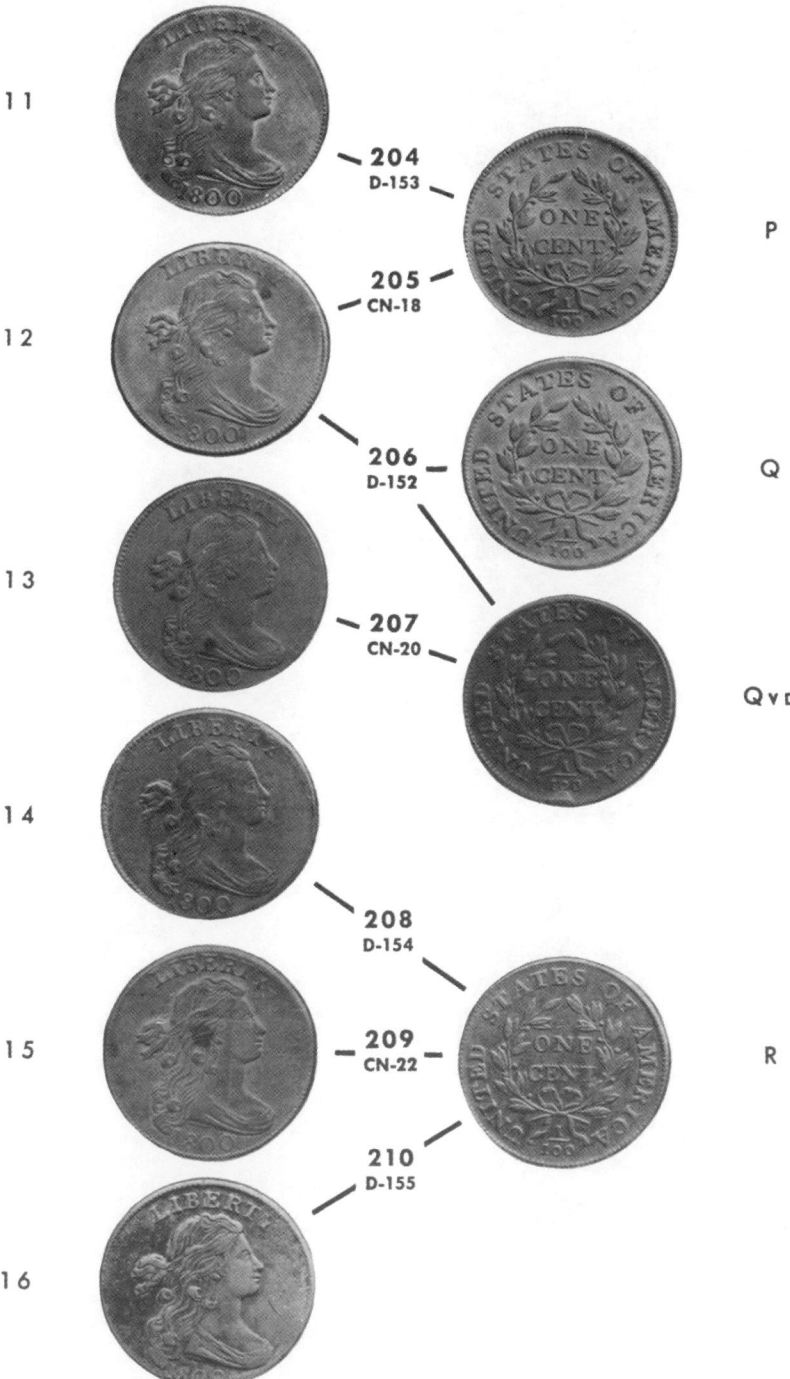

PLATE NO. 37

1 8 0 0

17   211   S
      CN-24

18   212   T
      CN-25

19   NC4   U
      CN-26

PLATE NO. 38

1 8 0 1

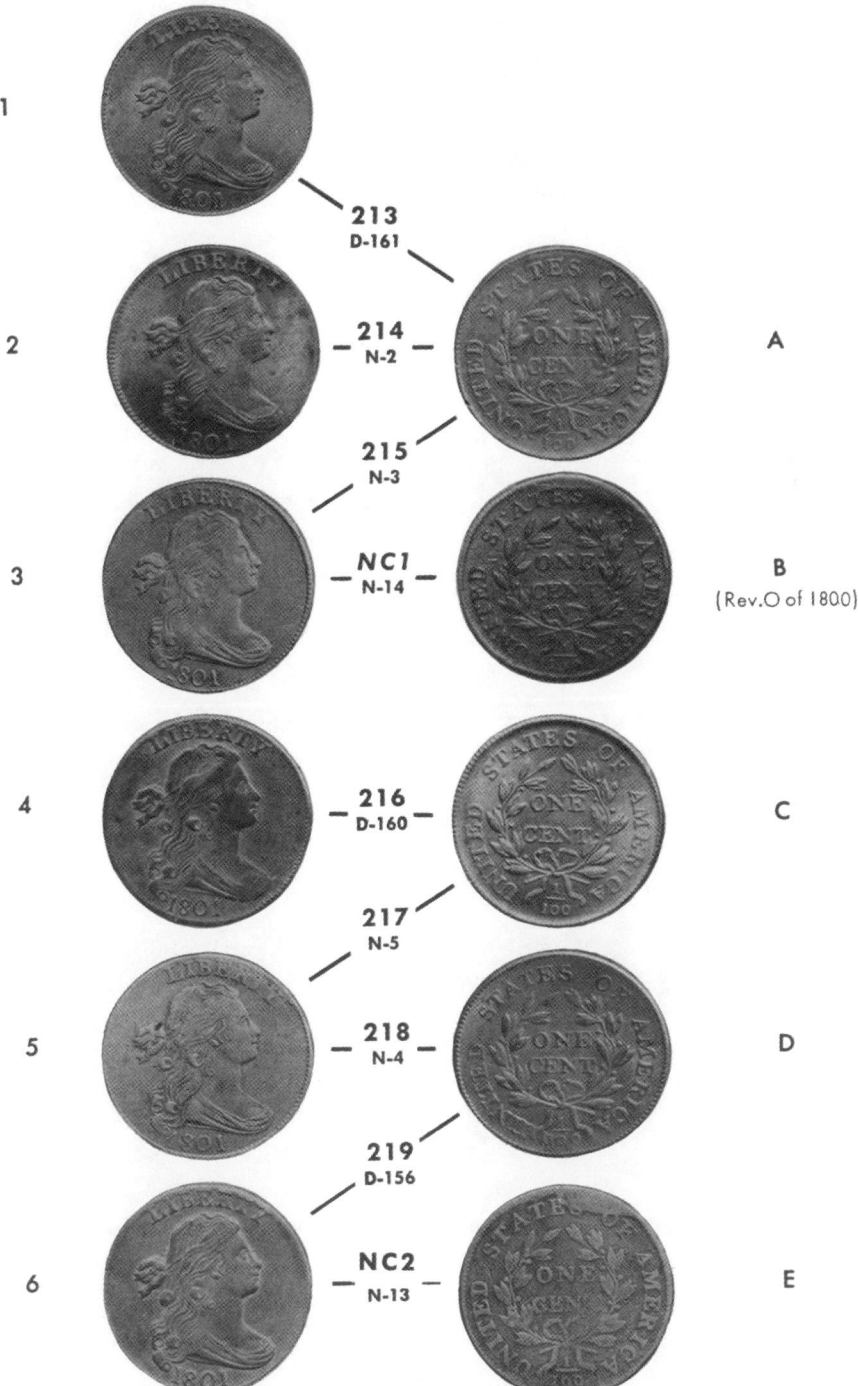

PLATE NO. 39

1 8 0 1

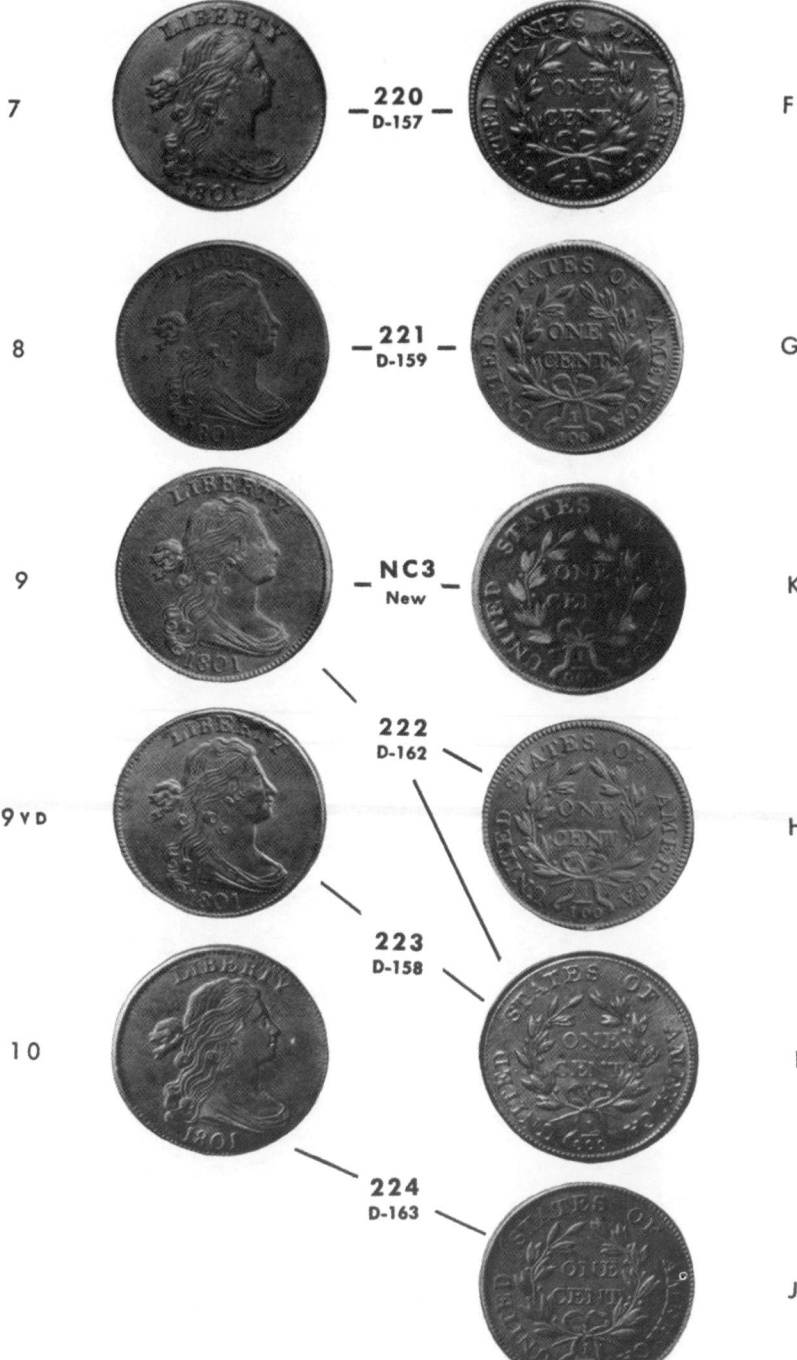

PLATE NO. 40

1 8 0 2

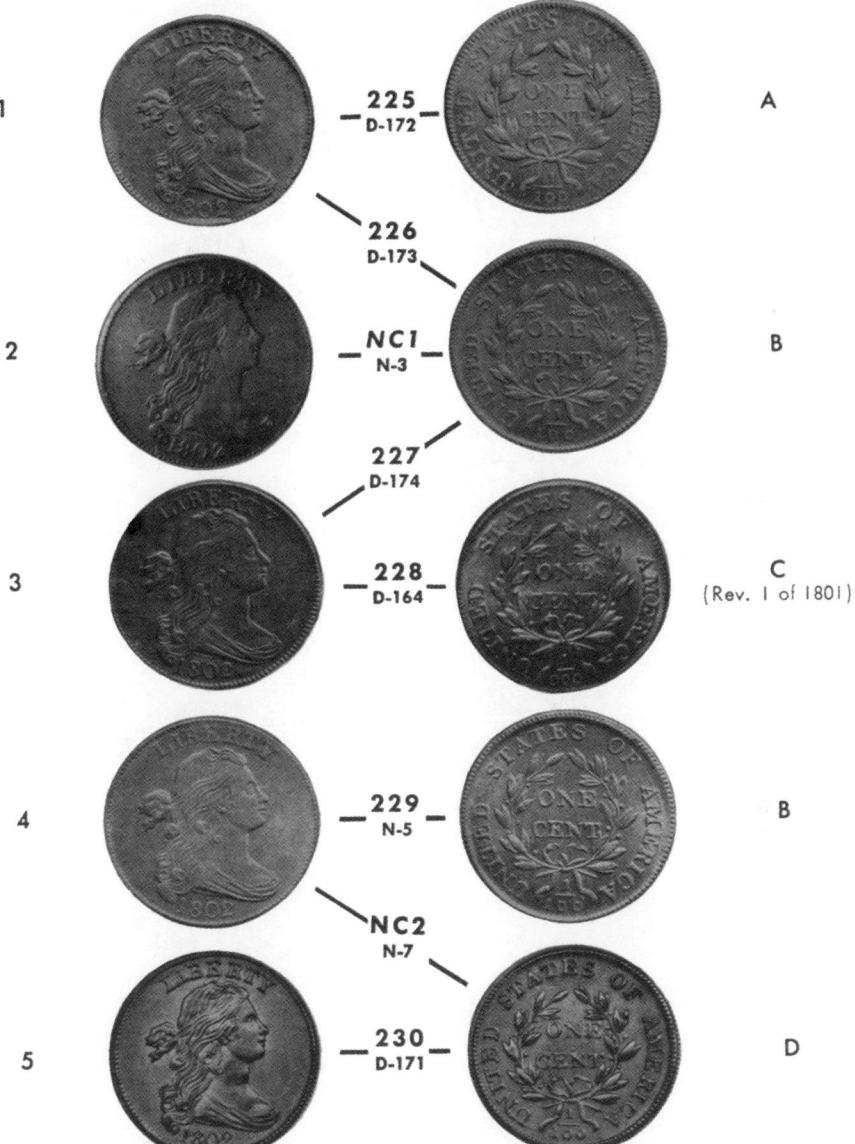

PLATE NO. 41

1 8 0 2

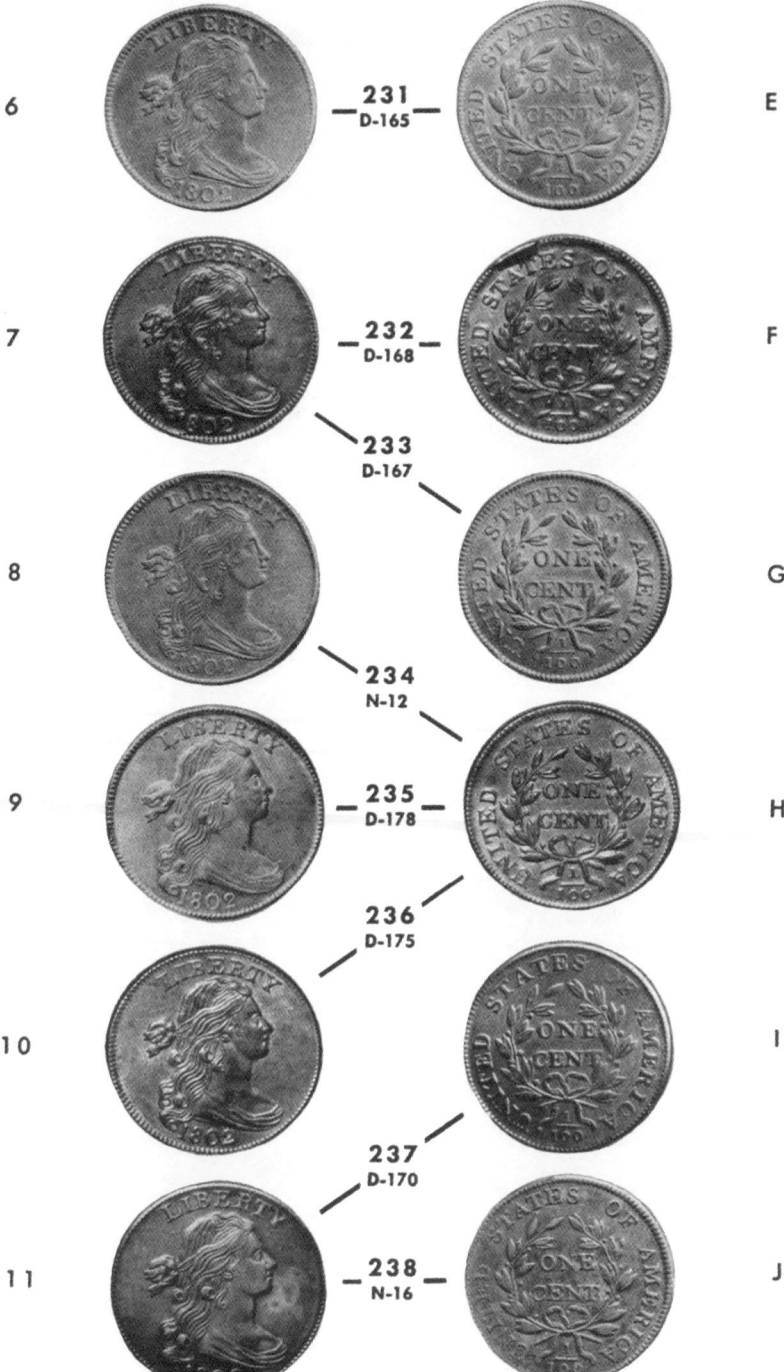

PLATE NO. 42

1 8 0 2 - 1 8 0 3

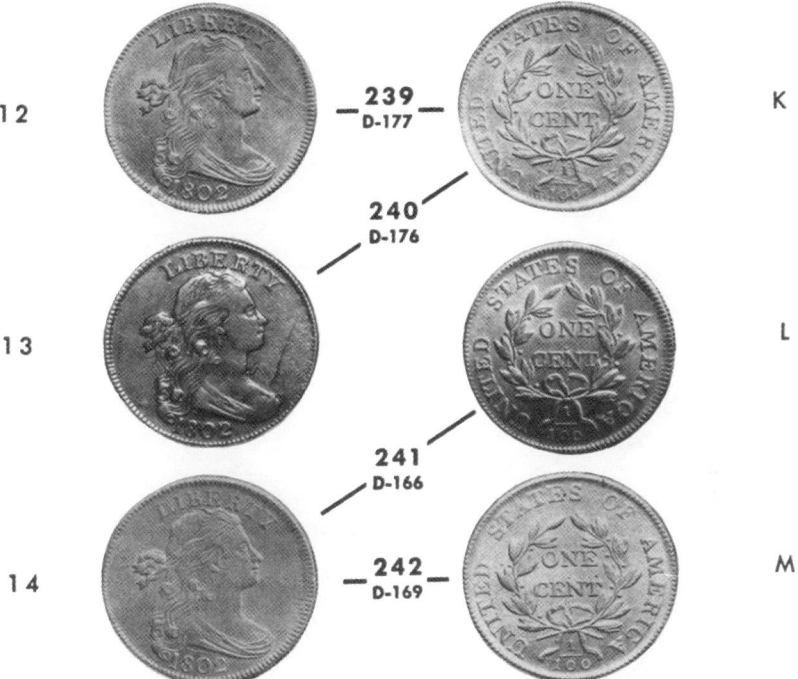

1 8 0 3

PLATE NO. 43

1 8 0 3

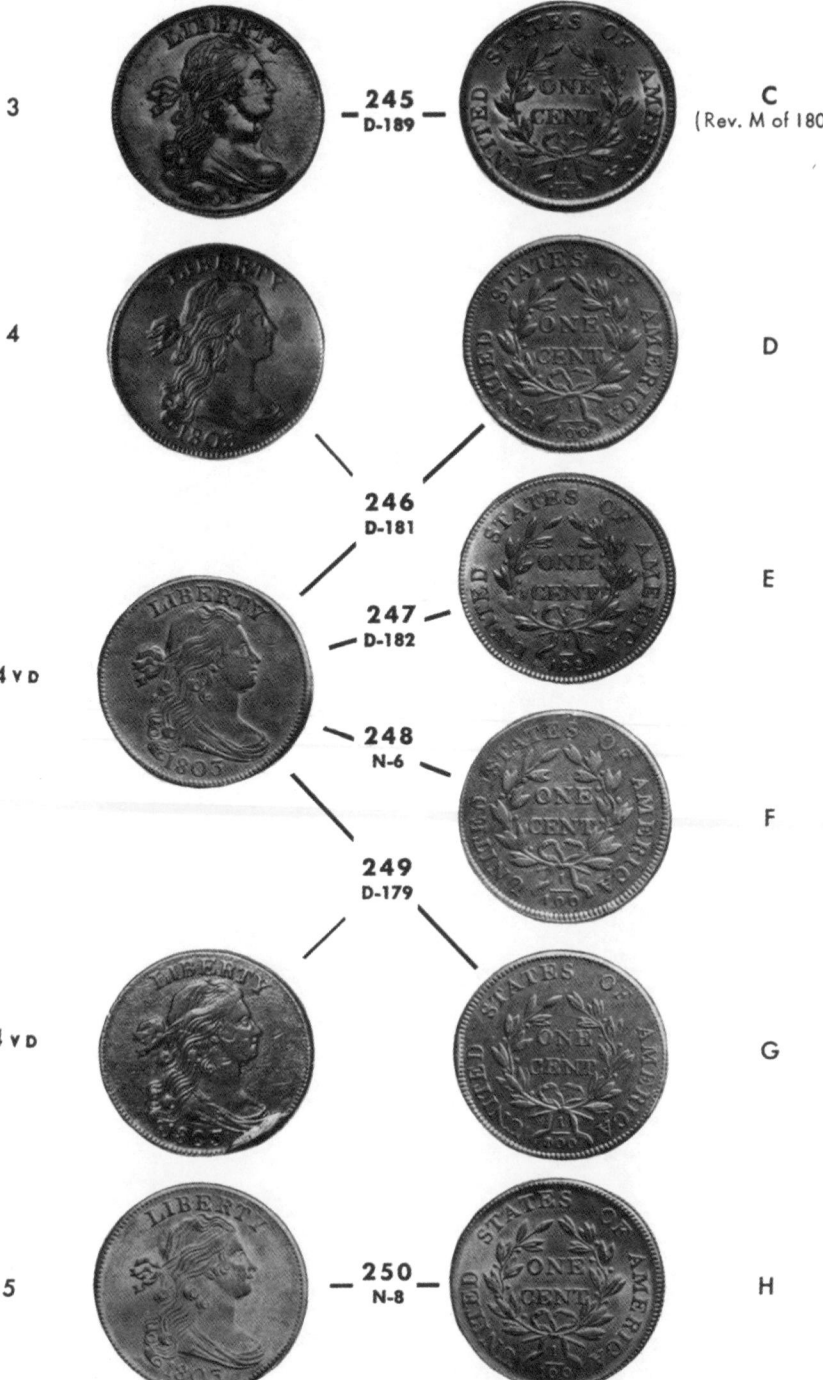

PLATE NO. 44

1 8 0 3

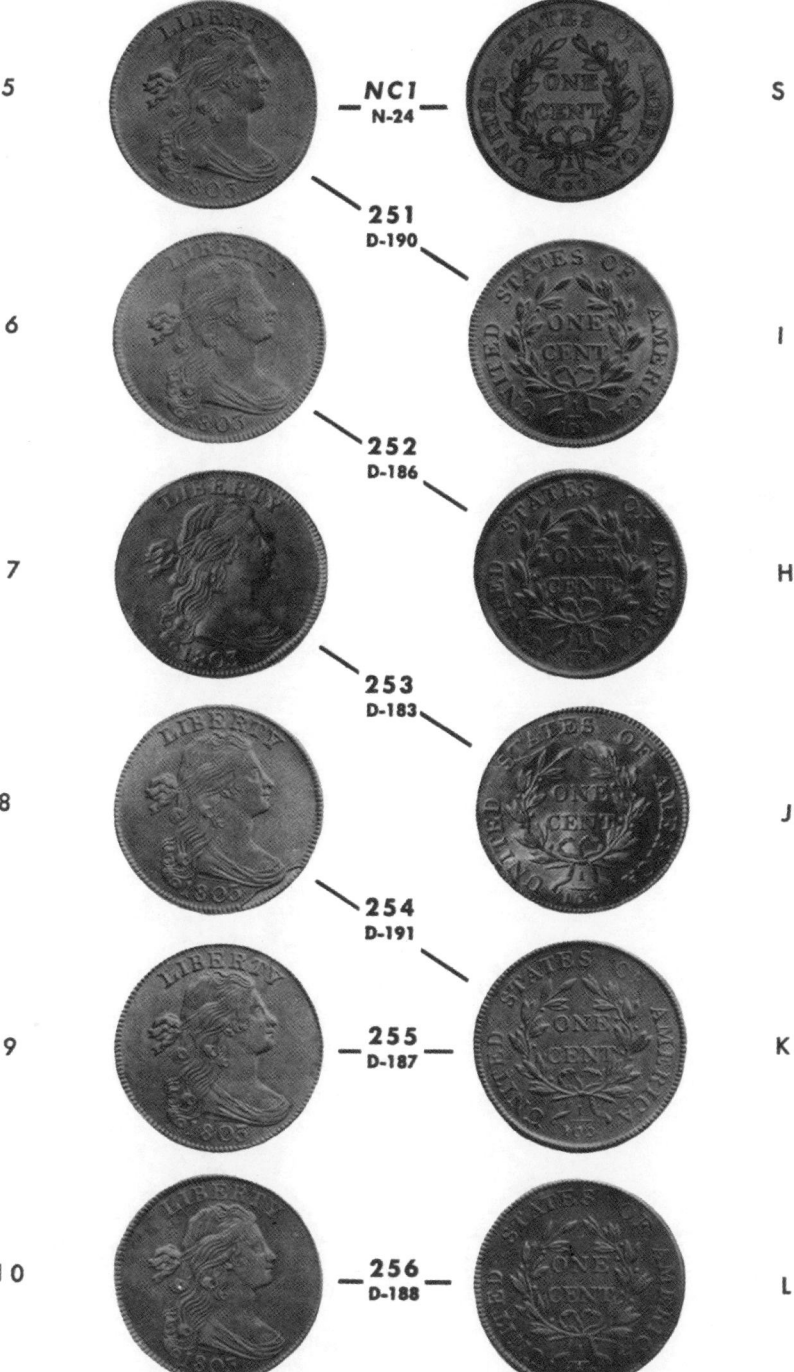

PLATE NO. 45

1 8 0 3

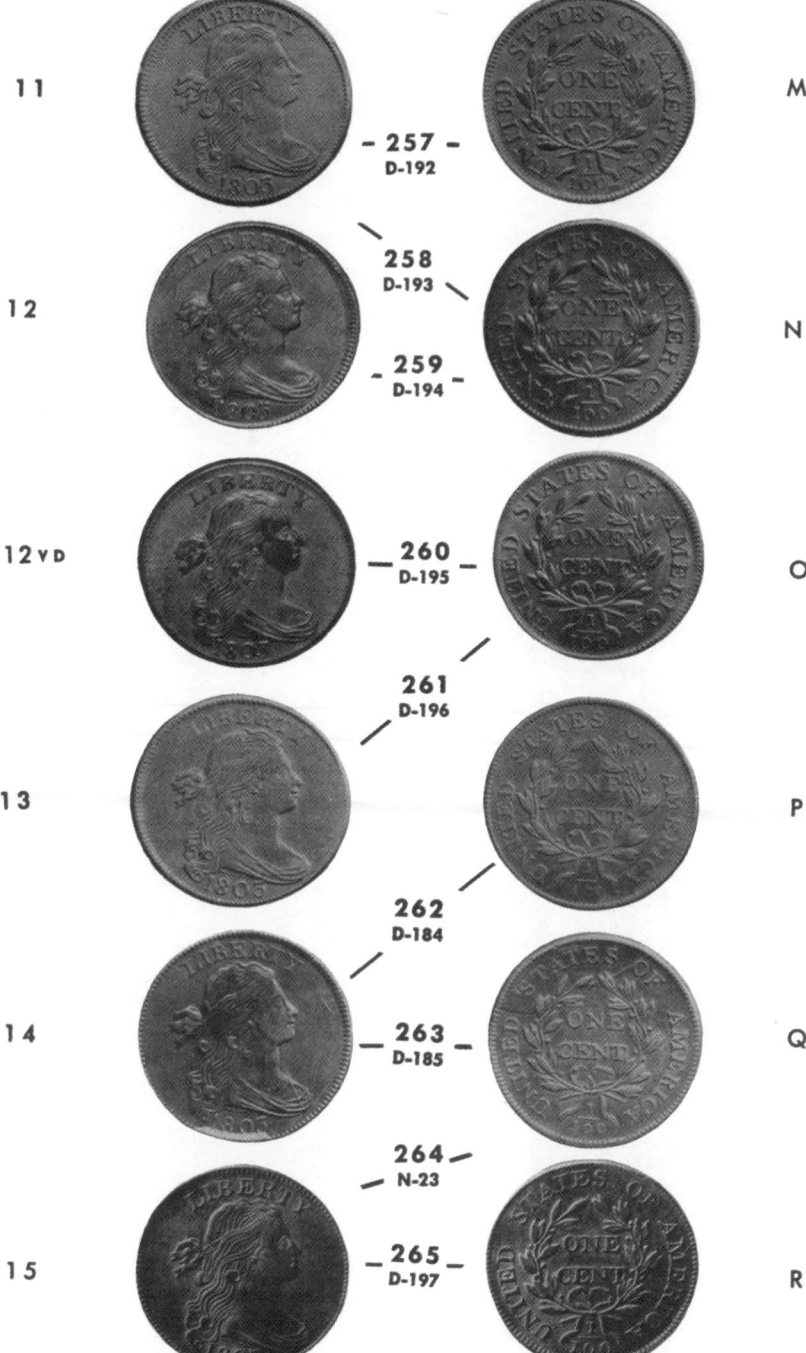

PLATE NO. 46

1804 - 1806

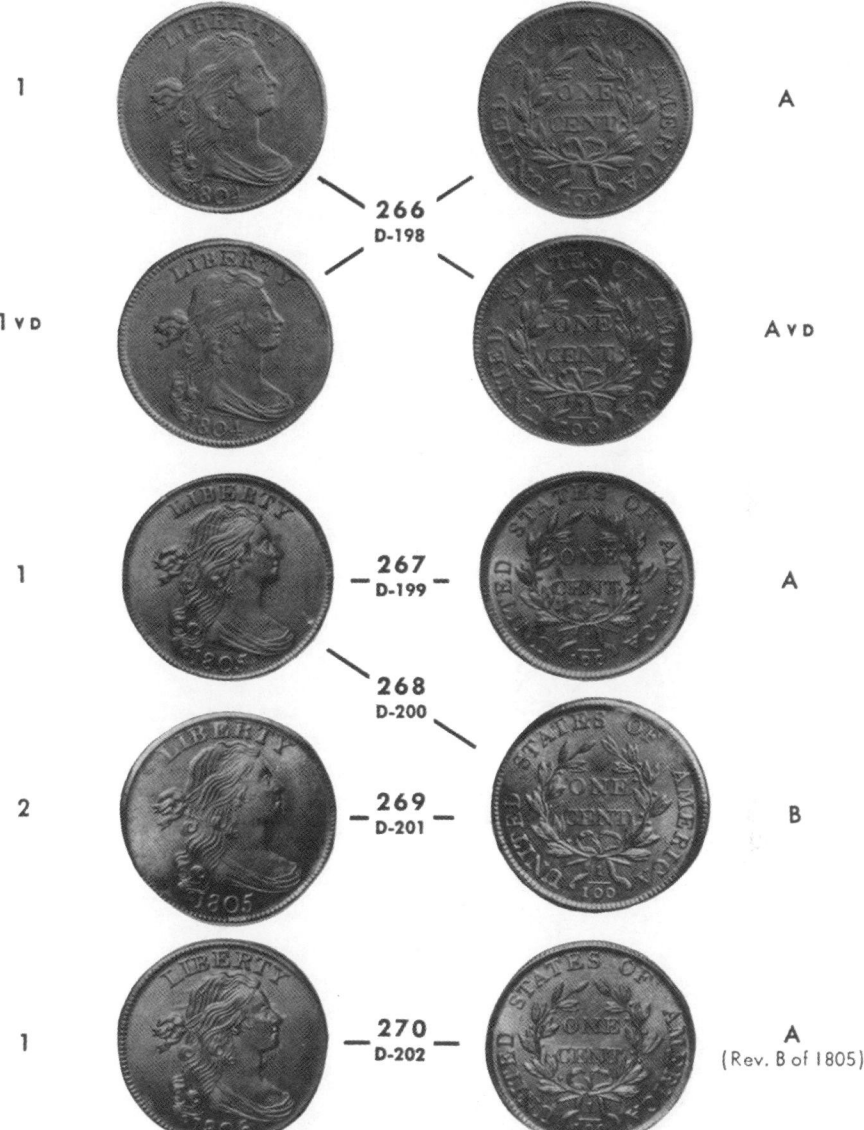

PLATE NO. 47

1 8 0 7 - 1 8 0 8

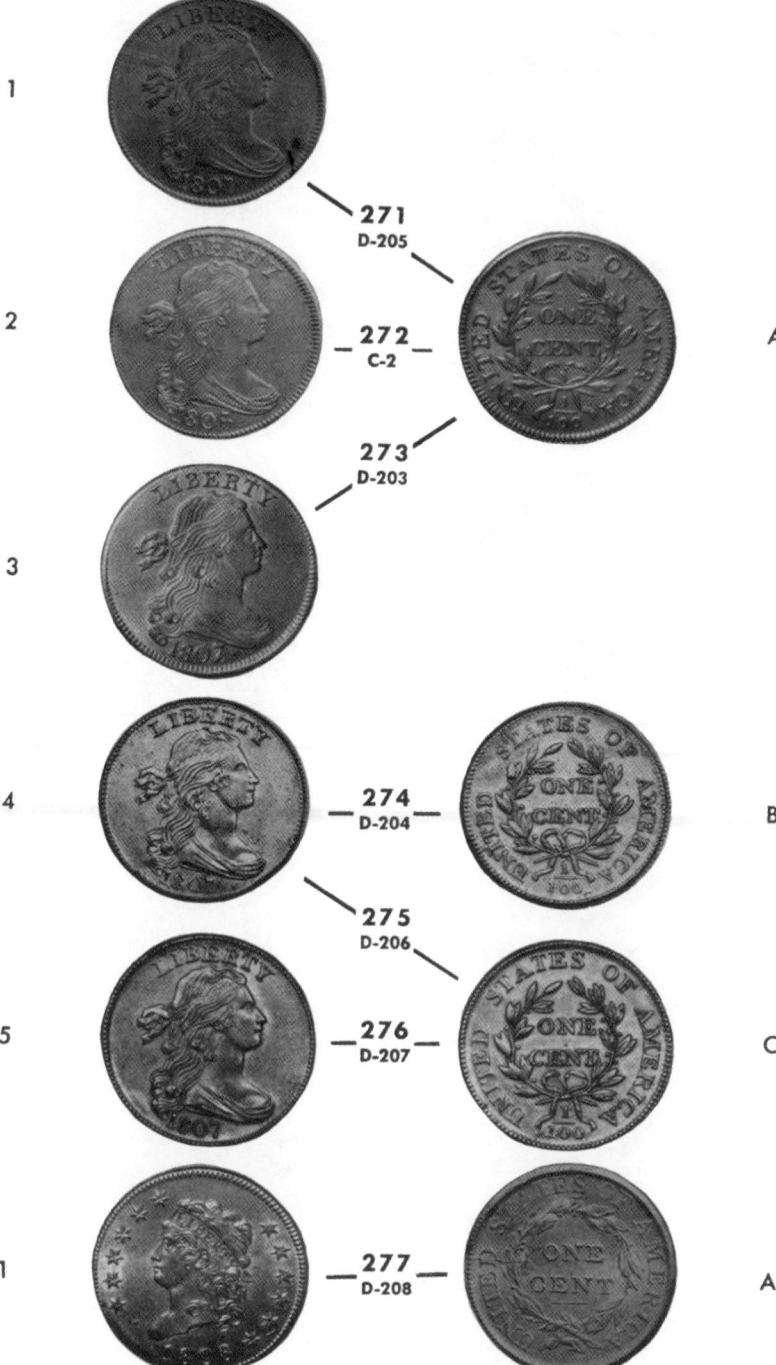

PLATE NO. 48

1 8 0 8 - 1 8 1 0

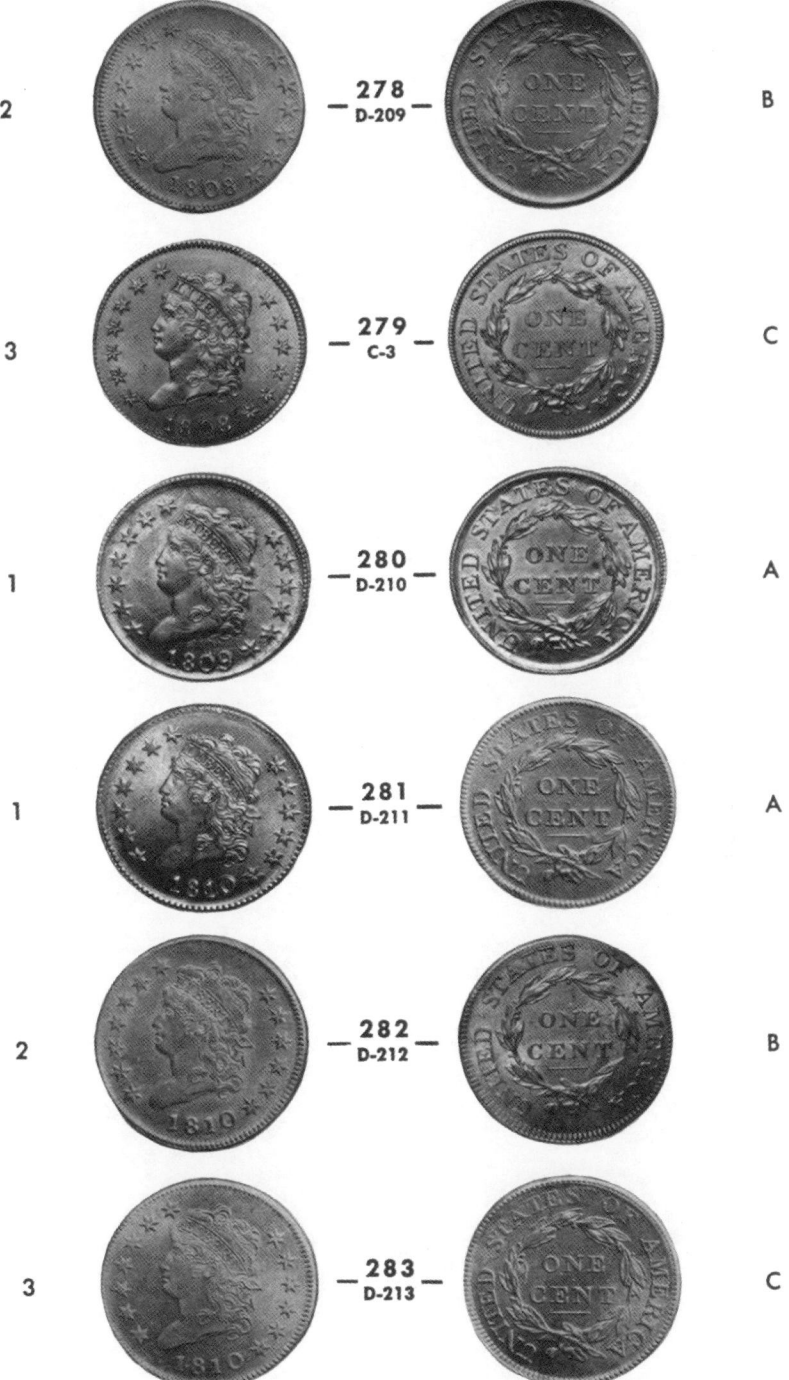

PLATE NO. 49

1810 - 1812

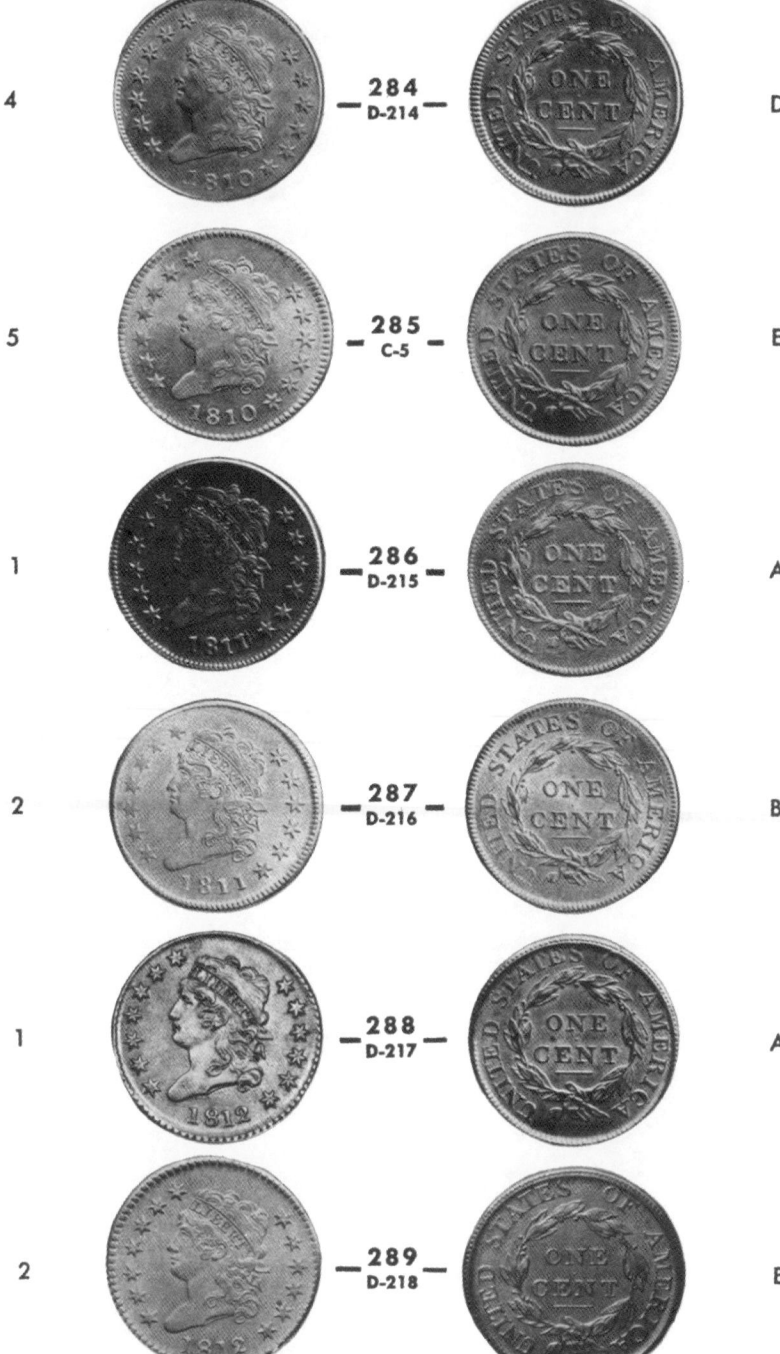

PLATE NO. 50

1812 - 1814

PLATE NO. 51

Appendix I
New Varieties

Twelve new varieties have been discovered since the 1965 edition of *Penny Whimsy*. Brief descriptions follow. In each Condition Census listing, the grade of the discovery coin is *underlined*.

1793 NC-6. New-L.

Obverse new. One bead centered above loop of R, another minutely left of center above I. Pole and 7 point directly to beads. 96 beads.

Reverse L; same as S-13, 14, 16.

Rarity 8. Two known. 8-4. Discovered by Ted Naftzger in 1978.

1794 NC-8. 8-New.

Obverse 8; same as S-25.

Reverse new. Leaves 13-18, berries 6-8. Four berries below R. Die break from rim between TA.

Rarity 8. Three known. 15-12-7. Discovered by W. C. Blaisdell in 1965.

1794 NC-9. 21-New.

Obverse 21; same as S-47, 48, 49.

Reverse new. Leaves 14-18, berries 5-6. Single berry below D S, single berry below AM. Die break from rim between zeros.

Rarity 8. Two known. 7-3. Discovered by Chuck Furjanic in 1974.

1795 NC-2. New-C.

Obverse new. Date spaced 1 79 5. Top of 5 buried in bust. Tops of RTY apart. Overstruck on a cut-down, rolled-out Talbot Allum & Lee token.

Reverse C; same as S-76.

Rarity 8. Unique. 4-0. Discovered by Walter Breen in 1968.

1795 NC-3. 3-New.

Obverse 3; same as S-76, 77.

Reverse new. Two leaves directly under (N)T, two leaves left of C(E) extending above center of C. Triple leaf at CA.

Rarity 8. Unique. 1-0. Discovered by Jack Beymer in 1979.

1796 NC-6. 25-Y.

Obverse 25; same as S-117, 118.
Reverse Y; same as S-117.
Rarity 8. Two known. 3-3. Discovered by Denis Loring in 1970.

NO PHOTO AVAILABLE

1797 NC-7. 11-S.
Obverse 11; same as S-133.
Reverse S; same as S-142.
Rarity 8. Unique 7-0. Discovered by Jules Reiver in 1968.

NO PHOTO AVAILABLE

1797 NC-8. 9-T.

Obverse 9; same as S-129, 130, 131.
Reverse T; same as S-143.
Rarity 8. Unique 25-0. Discovered by Ed Kucia in 1980.

1800 NC-5. 1-New.
Obverse 1; same as S-190, 191, NC-6.

Reverse new. Short, heavy fraction bar. Stem to third outer left leaf pair joined to adjacent berry. Leaf pair below (N)T stemless. Heavy rim break over AME.

Rarity 8. Unique. 10-0. Discovered by Stanley West in 1965.

1800 NC-6. 1-New.
Obverse 1; same as S-190, 191, NC-5.

Reverse new. F double punched except for top bar. First outer berry on left stemless. Lower inner right berry and top outer right berry nearly stemless.

Rarity 7. 25-7-6-5-5-4-4. First seen as lot 100 in Stack's Miles sale, 4/69.

1801 NC-4. New-H.

Obverse new. First 1 pointed. Date curved, 0 low. LIBERTY widely spaced.

Reverse H; same as S-222.

Rarity 7+. 10-4-4-3. First seen as lot 344 in Stack's Dupont sale, 9/54.

1801 NC-5. 6-New.

Obverse 6; same as S-219, NC-2.

Reverse new. Uppermost berry on left droops. Huge retained cud envelops STATES.

Rarity 8. Two known. 2-1. Discovered by Chris Victor-McCawley in 1987.

APPENDIX II

Additional Selected Reading

PENNY-WISE, the bimonthly journal of the Early American Coppers Club. Volume One, Number One was dated September 15, 1967. The current volume is XXIV.

COPPER QUOTES BY ROBINSON. The first edition was dated December 31, 1983. The current edition is the ninth.

Auction Catalogs:

    Kagin's, Philip Van Cleave Collection, 1/86

    New Netherlands, R.E. Naftzger, Jr. Collection, 11/13

    Stack's, Herman Halpern Collection, 3/88

    Superior Stamp and Coin:

        Dr. Charles L. Ruby Collection, part I, 2/74

        Robinson S. Brown, Jr. Collection, 9/86

        Jack H. Robinson Collection, 1/89

Bowers, David and Ruddy, James, **JOHN W. ADAMS COLLECTION of 1794 CENTS,** 1982 fixed price list.

Lapp, Warren A., and Silberman, Herbert A., **UNITED STATES LARGE CENTS 1793-1857** an anthology of readings from *The Numismatist*, Quarterman Publications, Inc., 1975.

Breen, Walter, **WALTER BREEN'S COMPLETE ENCYCLOPEDIA OF U.S. AND COLONIAL COINS,** Doubleday, 1988.